THE
ISRAEL
FACTOR

THE PICTURE ON THE FRONT COVER (RIGHT)

Oren Cohen, the gifted photographer of the IDF, captures its most moving moments. This picture show us the Israeli Defense Forces as both a natural and spiritual army. Soldiers carry the Torah to the battle very much like the Ancient Israelites carried the Ark of the Covenant that housed the Tablets of the Laws of God.

> "When you go out to battle against your enemies and see horse and chariot—a people more numerous than you—do not be afraid of them. For Adonai your God, the One who brought you up from the land of Egypt, is with you."
>
> —Deuteronomy 20:1

THE PICTURE ON THE BACK COVER (BELOW)

Dr. Dominiquae in Kfar Aza in 2023 after the massacre, with a delegation of the Ministry of Foreign Affairs.

THE ISRAEL FACTOR

DR. DOMINIQUAE BIERMAN

THE ISRAEL FACTOR
Copyright © 2024 by Dominiquae Bierman

All rights reserved. This book may not be copied or reprinted for commercial gain or profit. The use of short quotations or occasional page copying for personal or group study is permitted and encouraged. Permission will be granted upon request.

Unless otherwise identified, all articles are written by Dr. Dominiquae Bierman.

Unless otherwise identified, Scripture quotations are from the:
Tree of Life Bible
Used by permission. All rights reserved.

Cover photograph of IDF soldiers copyright © Oren Cohen.
All rights reserved. To contact Oren:
Oren26c. Instagram Oren3126@gmail.com
+972-52-263-6975

First Printing April 2024
Paperback ISBN: 978-1-953502-84-1
E-Book ISBN: 978-1-953502-85-8
Printed in the United States of America

Kad-Esh MAP Ministries
52 Tuscan Way, Ste 202-412, St Augustine, FL 32092, USA
www.Kad-Esh.org

Published by Zion's Gospel Press
shalom@zionsgospel.com
www.ZionsGospel.com

DEDICATION

This book is a compilation of articles spanning 15 years, written to the church and the nations worldwide.

In Memory

of all those Israelis murdered, kidnapped, raped, looted, displaced, burnt, wounded, and traumatized by Hamas and the citizens of Gaza in the Massacre of October 7, 2023.

> "For behold, ADONAI is coming out from His place to punish inhabitants of the earth for iniquity. The earth will disclose her bloodshed, no longer covering up her slain."
>
> —Isaiah 26:21

CONTENTS

Introduction 1
Chapter 1: A Visitation in Chile. 7

2024

Chapter 2: Ruth, The Restorer of Dead Dreams 21
Chapter 3: Misplaced Compassion 31
Chapter 4: Ishmael and Esau 37
Chapter 5: I Will Not Forget You 45
Chapter 6: We are More, and We are Here Now 51
Chapter 7: Why Did We Ring One Million Bells on January 14, 2024? . . . 59
Chapter 8: Let My People Go! 67
Chapter 9: The Case Against UN and for UNIFY 73
Chapter 10: The Kingdom at War 83
Chapter 11: Why Plant Fruit Trees in Israel?. 89
Chapter 12: The Separation has Begun. 95

2023

Chapter 13: The Israel Controversy 109
Chapter 14: Battle for Dedication 129
Chapter 15: Hanukkah in the War. 135
Chapter 16: The Houthis from Teman 139
Chapter 17: Why do Earthquakes Happen? 143
Chapter 18: Focus on Jerusalem 147
Chapter 19: Boots on the Ground: Israel War Report 155
Chapter 20: An Open-Hearted Letter from the Midst of the War 161

2022

Chapter 21: Do you know any Antisemites? 167
Chapter 22: Exposing Antisemitism in America 175
Chapter 23: Inheritance or Possession? 183

Chapter 24:	Dispelling the Palestinian Cause	189
Chapter 25:	The Distinction of the Covenant	195
Chapter 26:	The Battle of the Gods	203

2021

Chapter 27:	Israel—The Holy Triunity	209
Chapter 28:	The Israel Test	215

2020

Chapter 29:	Non-Negotiables—My Israel	223
Chapter 30:	Non-Negotiables—My Land	237

2019

Chapter 31:	Passover and Biblical Politics	251
Chapter 32:	Within Your Gates, O Jerusalem	259

2018

Chapter 33:	Reasoning with Scorpions	267
Chapter 34:	Seventy Years and Counting	277
Chapter 35:	Who Are the Heirs of the Land of Israel?	285

2017

Chapter 36:	Expel the Darkness	303
Chapter 37:	Stormy Weather—Hurricane Irma	315
Chapter 38:	The Overturning Has Begun	323
Chapter 39:	Time to UNEXIT	327
Chapter 40:	Blow The Trumpet, Sound the Alarm	335

2016

Chapter 41:	The Rule of Messiah on Earth	347

2015

Chapter 42:	A Ticking Bomb	359
Chapter 43:	Highway 60	367
Chapter 44:	Israel Red Alert	373
Chapter 45:	The Abomination of Desolation	381
Chapter 46:	Sheep and Goat Nations	389

2013

Chapter 47:	Watchmen on the Walls	397
Chapter 48:	Israel and the Nations—A Divine Alignment	403
Chapter 49:	Jerusalem, Such a Big Deal	417

2012

Chapter 50:	Breaking Through the Passivity Towards Israel	427
Chapter 51:	The Amalek Factor in the War with Hamas	435
Chapter 52:	The Rise and Fall of The Mosquito Killer	447
Chapter 53:	Tycoons of Righteousness	453
Chapter 54:	Spiders Over an Open Flame	463

2011

Chapter 55:	Can a Nation Be Born in One Day?	475
Chapter 56:	Time to Defeat Amalek	485
Chapter 57:	Under the Shadow of His Wings	493

2010

Chapter 58:	Prophetic Acceleration	501
Chapter 59:	Focus on Israel	509
Chapter 60:	The Raging Draconic Fires	517
Chapter 61:	Twenty-Four Hours Later	525
Chapter 62:	Why Remember the Shoah?	531

2009

Chapter 63:	A Call to True Unity	541
Chapter 64:	Restitution is Justice	549
Chapter 65:	Why Pray for Israel?	559

2024

Chapter 66:	Warning Signs in the Heavens	565
Closure		571
Appendix:	A Divine Call to Rally Around the Banner of Truth	575
Our Resources		581

INTRODUCTION

> Then He said, "Your name will no longer be Jacob, but rather Israel, for you have struggled with God and with men, and you have overcome."
>
> — GENESIS 32:29

THE SHOWDOWN OF THE ages is a battle between Jacob and Esau, as portrayed by Hamas, Hezbollah, Houthis, Fatah, and Iran. The whole Palestinian cause is born out of the Esau agenda. Jacob is now struggling with Elohim and men, and he must prevail in order to become fully Israel. Israel will have to withstand the inhumane pressure from all nations to give up its covenant right to its covenant land.

New and Old Prophetic Treasures

> Then He said to them, "Therefore every Torah scholar discipled for the kingdom of heaven is like the master of a household who brings out of his treasure both new things and old."
>
> —MATTHEW 13:52

This book is born of the heart of God. I have been writing "Shabbat Letters" and prophetic messages for over 30 years. Many of them are about the judgment that will be coming upon the UN and nations that have pushed for the Oslo Accords, the two-state Palestinian cause, and the division of Israel's covenant land. After the brutal attack by Hamas from Gaza on Simchat Torah, October 7, 2023, I received from the Almighty prophetic words with additional insight and sharpness. I have included both old and new messages in this book, and they all coincide. Some of the messages have been written by my disciples in different nations.

The judgment of the nations represented by the United Nations has begun because of "The Israel Factor".

It Starts with the Jews

There will be trouble and hardship for every human soul that does evil—to the Jew first and also to the Greek. But there will be glory, honor, and shalom to everyone who does good—to the Jew first and also to the Greek. For there is no partiality with God.

—**Romans 2:9-11**

The October 7, 2023 massacre by Hamas on Simchat Torah will not stop in Israel. It only started there because of the old concept of the two-state "solution." The deathly lie that was believed was that if we keep the Palestinians happy and rich, they would leave us alone, that Gaza would become the "Singapore of the Middle East" instead of the empire of terror that it became. The moral and financial support for the Palestinian cause from the UN and all the nations represented in it was the fertile ground for the massacre. We can expect that this old and harmful concept will be now judged in the nations as well, starting with the USA.

> "For behold, in those days and at that time, when I restore Judah and Jerusalem from exile, I will gather all nations and bring them down to the valley of Jehoshaphat. I will plead with them there on behalf of My people, even My inheritance, Israel, whom they scattered among the nations and they divided up My Land."
>
> —Joel 4:1-2

It is evil to push Israel to national suicide by giving up covenant land. The outcome of this is the brutal attack of Hamas on October 7, 2023, on 22 Israeli peace-loving communities. The God of Israel must judge all nations that oppose His eternal plan to bequeath the land, from the river in Egypt to the Euphrates River in the area of Syria-Iraq to the natural descendants of Abraham, Isaac, and Jacob, the Jewish people, the people of Israel.

> "He is Adonai our God. His judgments are in all the earth. He remembers His covenant forever—the word He commanded for a thousand generations—which He made with Abraham, and swore to Isaac, and confirmed to Jacob as a decree, to Israel as an everlasting covenant, saying, 'To you I give the land of Canaan, the portion of your inheritance.'"
>
> —Psalms 105:7-11

And what about large portions of the Church?

Over 140 global Christian leaders call for permanent ceasefire in Gaza

Jerusalem Post, March 27, 2024

Over 140 global Christian leaders called for a permanent ceasefire in Gaza and an end to foreign ministry support for Israel in a letter to US President Joe Biden and other US politicians on Tuesday. The letter was delivered the day after the United States did not veto a UN vote calling for an immediate ceasefire in Gaza during Ramadan. The resolution passed with 14 votes in favor.

Among the signatories are the presiding bishops of the Episcopal Church and the Evangelical Lutheran Church in America, as well as a Guatemalan Catholic cardinal.

The letter was organized by Churches for Middle East Peace, which plans to send it to other world leaders. The letter was released during the Holy Week, ahead of Easter, a time when Christians commemorate Jesus Christ's execution and resurrection.*

For the time has come for judgment to begin with the house of God. If judgment begins with us first, what will be the end for those who disobey the good news of God? Now, "if it is hard for the righteous to be saved, what shall become of the ungodly and the sinner?"

—1 Peter 4:17-18

---

* www.jpost.com/christianworld/article-793928

"And I will bless those who bless you, and the one who curses you I will curse. And in you all the families of the earth will be blessed."

—Genesis 12:3 NASB '95

CHAPTER 1

A VISITATION IN CHILE

All the nations will be gathered before Him, and He will separate them one from another, as a shepherd divides his sheep from his goats. And He will set the sheep on his right hand, but the goats on the left.

— MATTHEW 25:32

Argentina 2001

In late December 2001, Baruch and I personally witnessed the Argentinean Uprising. It seemed as though the whole nation had spilled over onto the streets, protesting the government and the banking system. Hard-working people had deposited their money in the banks, but when they needed to withdraw it, the banks had no money to give them. Much of the nation was left penniless, and their hearts were boiling. This was a nation in bankruptcy!

We had landed in Argentina only twenty-four hours before this fateful day. As is our custom whenever we arrive in any nation to which we are sent, we blow the shofar at the airport, "the gate" of the nation, or both. Argentina was no exception. Twenty-four hours later, this mass protest exploded. A sea of people of all ages: the young, old, babies, fathers, and mothers with their children, all flooded the main streets of Buenos Aires headed to the presidential palace—La Casa Rosada, or the Pink House. Our hotel was within walking distance from La Casa Rosada and we witnessed this event right before our eyes. We decided to take our video camera to act as "prophetic journalists" and ventured out into this wave of anger, frustration, and solidarity of the Argentinian people. Of course, the hotel staff warned us of the danger of getting ourselves killed in the midst of the mob, but we informed them that we had a special angelic escort. With that, we ventured out to an amazing experience.

Later on, the radio reported that several were injured and that most of the supermarkets were being looted by either hungry people, angry people, or both. We could also witness when the presidential helicopter took off from the roof of La Casa Rosada with the president fleeing Argentina. The people had managed to run the president off!

Meanwhile, we were literally trapped in our hotel. All our meetings for that day had to be canceled, including a pastor's meeting. One dear friend, a pastor and host, asked me half-jokingly in Spanish, my mother tongue, "Dominiquae, what on earth did you do when you arrived in Argentina?" I replied, "Nothing, I just blew the shofar at the airport of Eseiza." (This was not, nor would be, the only serious occurrence following my blowing the shofar, the silver trumpet, or both in a nation or a region.)

"Over a million intercessors have been praying for a change of government in Argentina," he added. It was then that I connected with the reason Yeshua told me to come to Argentina at this time.

A few weeks earlier, I had called a very good friend of mine, a great lover of Israel, Evangelist Alberto Mottessi, and told him that Yah was sending me to Argentina. He wanted to organize some big meetings there, but I said that my time was short and that I needed to be there in two weeks, which would not give him sufficient time to organize much. Nevertheless, many wonderful pastor friends such as Julio Donati received me well and blessed us. And, God had organized a greater meeting than anyone could have put together - a massive demonstration of all the people of Argentina in every major city and town. We got to blow the shofar before it began, be witnesses while it was going on, and walk the streets of the capital after it had subsided.

This is what we saw on the day after the uprising:

Walking on the street that leads to La Casa Rosada, we saw many buildings damaged by stones or bullet holes. There were burnt tires strewn here and there and nearly every building had walls or windows damaged. One particular building caught our attention because it had been damaged far more than any other. This building was riddled with bullet holes and all of its glass was completely smashed. It was an imposing building with very dark glass, and it seemed that the mob was particularly angry with this building. As we were observing the damage and pondering the "why" of this, I noticed police cars next to the building, and then I read the address. I remembered that address: This was none other than the Israeli Embassy of Buenos Aires!

Why would the mob take revenge against the Israeli Embassy for Argentina's financial distress? It immediately brought to mind Nazi Germany in 1933 when Hitler came into power and made the Jews the "scapegoat" for all of Germany's financial problems. After all the events from 1933 through 1945, as well as the occurrences of the terrible Second World War including the atrocious Holocaust which left us Jews bereaved of more than six million, it was clear to me that nothing had changed. The nations were still full of hatred towards the Jews. Given the "right" kind of circumstances, the Jews would be blamed and persecuted again. It did not surprise us when we received the report that The

Jewish Agency was organizing a massive aliyah, immigration to Israel, of Jews from Argentina, *one* day after the mass uprising took place in December of 2001. Since then, many, but not enough, Jews have come home to Israel from Argentina.

Chile 2001

Baruch and I arrived in my native land of Chile on December 24th, 2001, and nestled ourselves in a hotel in Santiago. We were to minister two days later in Valparaiso near the seaport, plus I was greatly anticipating a reunion with many of my relatives, especially my elderly maternal grandmother.

The 25th of December came, and I rose to pray quite early; however, I ventured out onto the balcony of my room to pray in privacy. What happened next completely caught me off guard. I have had many visitations from the LORD, both dreams and open visions, but I've never heard the LORD so clearly asking me such a serious question before. When ADONAI asks a question, it is not because He does not know the answer! So, I knew that He was trying to impart to me a message that I know now has become the major thrust of our ministry.

Preparing to pray, I settled comfortably in a chair looking out from the balcony. The Presence of Yah absorbed me, and I do not even remember the view from that balcony, uncharacteristic of me who never forgets a view! I only remember His question. It resonated into my entire being:

"Dominiquae, what would happen if I came back right now? How many nations would be sheep nations?"

"You see," He said, "I will judge the nations by these two standards:

1. My eternal, unchanging righteous Law
2. How the nations treat My Jewish people

A Visitation in Chile

He had my attention! Rapidly, passages of Scripture ran through my mind. One was Matthew 25:32: He will gather the nations and will separate them as the sheep from the goats. I considered many other verses. It did not take but a second for me to say, "None, LORD."

As He was talking, my spirit, mind, and heart were racing at the speed of light. It was like the whole Bible was opening before me with a new understanding and clarity about the condition of the world and of the nations, one like I had never had before! This was a visitation from Yah; the Almighty was manifesting His will to His soldier, and I was listening.

"I gave My disciples the commission to disciple the nations, all the ethnic groups of the earth, and to teach them My commandments. I said to make disciples of all nations and yet after 2000 years of My gospel being on earth, you cannot present to Me one sheep nation!"

I knew He was right. Not one nation had adopted YHVH's Commandments as their constitution. Neither was there any nation that I knew of that was guiltless concerning Israel. In 1938, a time when Hitler had already begun his plan to rid the world of its Jews, an international convention met in Evian, France to discuss the "Jewish problem." Not one nation was willing to give shelter to even some of the Jews from Germany and Europe in order to rescue them from Hitler's claws (except the Dominican Republic, which was willing to take a few of those who knew agriculture).

> **For I was hungry and you gave Me no food; I was thirsty and you gave Me no drink; I was a stranger and you did not take Me in, naked and you did not clothe Me, sick and in prison (in concentration camps and ghettos!) and you did not visit**

Me… Assuredly I say to you, inasmuch as you did not do it to the least of these you did not do it to Me.

—Matthew 25:42–45

All the nations knew what was happening. US bombers flew over Auschwitz countless times. They could have bombed the death camps of Birkenau but did not. England knew. The church knew, but not one denomination arose to oppose Hitler or the Holocaust.

We took a tour to Auschwitz in March 2003 and were shocked by a new exhibition on display. This exhibition consisted of documents and pictures detailing how the church of its time, both Catholic and Protestant, had given Hitler their blessing as he entered into government. Later on, not one church group or organization stood up to oppose him!

Here and there, individuals such as Corrie Ten Boom and Oscar Schindler stood bravely for what was right, but by far they were the minority. They were not part of any church or national effort; they were acting on their own.

I was beginning to get the picture. If Yeshua returned that day (Christmas Day 2001), *all* the nations, including the USA, Switzerland, Australia, Italy, Chile, Argentina, et cetera, would be judged as goat nations.

> Then He will say to those in the left hand, "Depart from Me you cursed ones, into the everlasting fire which has been prepared for the devil and his angels."
>
> —Matthew 25:41

In other words, all the nations of the earth are under a curse!

> I will bless those who bless you, and I will curse him who curses you; and in you all the families of the earth will be blessed (if they bless you).
>
> —**Genesis 12:3**

More Scriptures began to come to mind as the Holy Spirit, the Ruach HaKodesh, was leading me to the understanding of Yahveh's message. He took me to Isaiah 34:1–8.

> Draw near, O nations, to hear, and listen, O peoples! Let the earth hear, and all it contains, the world, and all its offspring!
>
> —**Isaiah 34:1**

I was 'earth', and I was listening!

> For ADONAI is enraged at all the nations, and furious at all their armies. He will utterly destroy them.
>
> —**Isaiah 34:2**

This is in the past tense, which means that YHVH has already done it in His mind. It is a 'done deal,' and ready to be manifested in the natural. There are no speculations here; the LORD has already decided to destroy all the nations because there is not one sheep nation in sight!

> So their slain will be thrown out, and the stench of their corpses will rise, and the hills will be drenched with their blood. Then all the host of heaven will dissolve...
> For ADONAI has a day of vengeance, a year of recompense for the hostility against Zion.
>
> —**Isaiah 34:3–4, 8**

YHVH has spoken and YHVH will do it.

I was trembling before the LORD as He kept on speaking to me, "Dominiquae, the devil has always wanted to destroy Israel, and also to cause Me to judge all the nations through Israel. Satan not only desires to annihilate Israel but also the whole human race. His plan has been to cause people to hate My Torah, My righteous laws, and My people, the Jews. I called the ecclesia, My called-out ones, to teach the nations to love My holy commandments and to love all peoples, especially the Jews, My chosen ones."

I broke before my Father, the judge of the universe who is love, and said, "Father, we the church have failed to teach the nations and to make disciples of all nations. After 2,000 years of 'gospel', we have miserably failed the great commission. We, the church, have not done the job."

"The church has done the job," the LORD said to me in a very stern tone, "but she has done the job wrongly. The church has used her authority to teach the nations to hate My Law and to hate My Jews."

My mind was spinning, and my heart was racing. Truly, historically speaking, every horrendous massacre of Jews from the second century and on has been carried out by the church, in the name of Christ, and due to antisemitic Christian doctrine. No one can refute, without making a fool of himself, that for the last 1,800 years, particularly the last 1,600 years since the infamous 'Council of Nicaea,' the Christian church has been the worst persecutor the Jewish people have ever known.

I have always felt surprised and distressed that Bible schools and seminaries do not teach this 'bloody history.' All the 'church history' books completely ignore the persecution of the Jews, which has been one of the most prevalent marks of the Christian religion since it was officially instituted by Emperor Constantine and the Gentile church fathers in AD 325. Christian events such as the Spanish Inquisition, the pogroms, the Crusades, and the Holocaust are not studied in any Christian Bible school. If they are mentioned at all, they are treated lightly and quickly.

But it was that day, Christmas day 2001, that the LORD visited me in Chile, one of the most antisemitic nations in the world; a country where "the Holy Office," the institution of the Spanish Inquisition, still exists; a country that has given shelter to many officers of the Nazi regime who are in hiding. It was there that the Almighty was visiting me and literally telling me that the whole world was going to hell and that the wrong teachings of the Christian church were sending them there!

He did not say, "Go to the nations and tell them that My laws are done away with and that they are free from My laws." He did not say, "Go into all the nations and tell them that the Jews killed Christ, so they deserve to be second-class citizens and live in hell forever as their Gentile church fathers such as John Chrysostom and St. Augustine had told them." And He did not say, "Go and tell the nations to get rid of the Jews because they are 'vermin' and 'plagues', such as their father Martin Luther had told them…"

No, no, no! The great commission was given to His Jewish apostles who were not Christian and knew nothing about Christianity. They were His disciples, His followers, and He had taught them the Torah. They had celebrated the biblical holy days with Him. They had eaten 'kosher' and clean food with Him. This is what He purposefully told His Jewish disciples:

> All authority has been given unto Me in heaven and on earth. Go therefore and make disciples of all nations, teaching them to observe (to do!) all things that I have commanded you; and lo, I am with you always and even to the end of the age.
>
> —MATTHEW 28:18–20

I wept before the God of Heaven, ELOHIM the Creator, and began to repent on behalf of the church. "LORD, forgive us! Please give us more time that we might teach the nations Your commandments and Your love for Israel."

I borrowed time from the God of Israel on that Christmas day of 2001 in my native land of Chile. And since then, my dear people, we have been running on borrowed time.

In my book, *The Healing Power of the Roots*, first printed in 1996, I said that the LORD had told me that teaching the Jewish roots to the church was a matter of life and death, as the church had been like a beautiful rose cut off from her garden (Israel, the Jews, and the Torah) and put in a vase for two days. But if it's not replanted back in the original garden, on the third day, it will die. Since I wrote that book, we have already entered into the third day, the third millennium...

And now YHVH has visited me about the nations. Preaching the good news of Yeshua, the Jewish Messiah, teaching YHVH's Torah, and teaching the nations to love Him and His Jewish people is a matter of life and death to *all* the nations of the earth!

> Moreover, in that day I will make Jerusalem a massive stone for all the people. All who try to lift it will be cut to pieces. Nevertheless, all the nations of the earth will be gathered together against her.

> It will happen in that day that I will seek to destroy all the nations that come against Jerusalem.
>
> —Zechariah 12:3, 9

"Close your eyes for a moment and feel the pulsating rhythm of the 'Hate-The-Jew' song as it captivates the nations of the world. The Muslims are dancing to its beat. Communist China is familiar with its tune. Europe often moves to its tempo. Some Americans are humming along. The 'church' has written the lyrics. And Satan is orchestrating it all!" (Brown*)

Disclaimer: We know that Israel has many Christian friends in the nations that stand by her. However, unfortunately, that is not the case for the majority of Christianity that is steeped in replacement theology.** To learn more about this, I highly recommend my book *The Identity Theft*.

---

* Dr. Michael Brown, as quoted in *Sheep Nations* by Dr. Dominiquae Bierman.
** Replacement Theology is a Christian doctrine established by Emperor Constantine and the gentile Bishops of the 4th century AD, replacing the original Gospel, Israel, Biblical feasts, and in general, all the Jewish roots of the faith. This doctrine caused antisemitism to flare up within Christianity until today, stating that the Jews are forever guilty of murdering Christ, although the Romans were the ones that executed him. For more information, read my book *The Identity Theft*; available at www.ZionsGospel.com

CHAPTER 2

RUTH, THE RESTORER OF DEAD DREAMS

> "Oy! For that day is monumental. There will be none like it—
> a time of trouble for Jacob! Yet out of it he will be saved."
>
> — JEREMIAH 30:7

Have you ever felt like all your dreams died, your cup of sorrow is full, and you have no future to hope for? I have, and Naomi, the wife of Elimelech from the House of Judah, did as well. She was thriving in exile in Moab, living the good life away from her land and family. She had a loving husband, but tragedy struck, and he died untimely.

However, she was left with her two sons, who got married to two lovely Moabite (Gentile) women. She was hoping to at least enjoy grandchildren, but her hopes were dashed onto the cold stone of tragic reality. Her two sons died as well, along with all her dreams and hopes for the future. All her men were dead, and she was left alone with her two daughters-in-law.

> **Then Naomi's husband, Elimelech, died, so she was left with her two sons. They married Moabite women—one was named Orpah and the second was named Ruth—and they dwelt there**

for about ten years. Then those two, Mahlon and Chilion, also died. So the woman was left without her children and her husband.

—Ruth 1:3-5

Many years before this heartbreaking story happened, another remarkable story took place. A young man named Yaakov (Jacob), at the beckoning of his mother, had to run away from his brother Esau, who, in his jealousy, wanted to murder him. Yaakov escaped the Land of Canaan, later renamed Israel, and headed towards Haran in Assyria. On his way out, exhausted, he laid his head on a cold, hard stone, as tough as his reality, and went to sleep. Then he dreamed.

He dreamed: All of a sudden, there was a stairway set up on the earth, its top reaching to the heavens—and behold, angels of God going up and down on it! Surprisingly, YHVH was standing on top of it, and He said, "I am YHVH, the God of your father Abraham and the God of Isaac. The land on which you lie, I will give it to you and to your seed. Your seed will be as the dust of the land, and you will burst forth to the west and to the east and to the north and to the south. And in you, all the families of the earth will be blessed—and in your seed. Behold, I am with you, and I will watch over you wherever you go, and I will bring you back to this land, for I will not forsake you until I have done what I promised you."

—**Genesis 28:12–15 stb**[*]

At the lowest point in his life, a refugee out of his homeland, banished by his own family to save his life, persecuted, and going to the unknown, Yah gave him this awesome dream. This dream of a land and

---

[*] Author's own version based on the Hebrew Bible

fruitful people would accompany Yaakov in his wanderings, struggles, and many hardships. This same dream is the one that caused Naomi, now bereaved of her husband and sons, to head out of exile in Moab to the Land of Judah. She was returning empty, and her cup of bitter sorrows was full. She had changed from Naomi to Mara, which means bitter in Hebrew.

> "Do not call me Naomi," she told them. "Call me Mara—since Shaddai (God) has made my life bitter."
>
> —Ruth 1:20

While heading out from Moab to Bethlehem of Judah (the same birthplace of the future Messiah), she tried her best to convince her bereaved and widowed daughters-in-law *not* to follow her.

> **Now Naomi said, "Go back, my daughters! Why should you go with me? Do I have more sons in my womb who could become your husbands?"**
>
> —Ruth 1:11

One of them, Orpah, meaning "the betrayer," was convinced, left her, and went back to her family and gods. The other one, named Ruth, meaning "the devout friend", stuck with her.

> **Ruth replied, "Do not plead with me to abandon you, to turn back from following you. For where you go, I will go, and where you stay, I will stay. Your people will be my people, and your God my God. Where you die, I will die, and there I will be buried. May Adonai deal with me, and worse, if anything but death comes between me and you!"** When she saw that

Ruth was determined to go with her, she no longer spoke to Ruth about it.

—Ruth 1:16-18

Naomi had lost all hope, dreams, inheritance, sons, and husband. She only had Ruth, who was not her flesh-and-blood daughter. Through Ruth, Mara would become Naomi again, and her hope and dreams for life would be resurrected; Yaakov's ladder dream would be restored in her. Ruth would marry Naomi's family member, Boaz, a man who had the legal power to restore to Naomi all the inheritance she had lost and the hope for continuity, for a future.

So Boaz took Ruth, and she became his wife, and he had relations with her. And the Lord enabled her to conceive, and she gave birth to a son. Then the women said to Naomi, "Blessed is the Lord who has not left you without a redeemer today, and may his name become famous in Israel.

—Ruth 4:13-14 NASB '95

Mara became Naomi again, meaning "the pleasant one," because of one Gentile woman from an enemy nation (Moab) who loved her unconditionally. This devout friend, this daughter-in-law and in love, became to her more than her flesh-and-blood sons that had died.

"Moreover, He will be to you a renewer of life and a sustainer of your old age, for your daughter-in-law, who loves you and is better to you than seven sons, has given birth to him." Naomi took the child and held it to her bosom, and took care of him. The neighboring women gave him a name saying "A son has been born to Naomi!" So they called him Obed. He was the father of Jesse, the father of David.

—Ruth 4:15-17

Ruth married Boaz from Naomi's family, and an accursed Moabite became a grafted-in Jew. She overturned the curse on her nation by loving a bereaved, destitute, and bitter Jew unconditionally and honoring her fully. She operated what we call the "Key of Abraham", but she did this unselfishly, with no ulterior motives whatsoever. This key of blessing those who blessed Israel, the natural seed, was promised through Abraham, Isaac, and Yaakov.

> "My desire is to bless those who bless you, but whoever curses you I will curse, and in you all the families of the earth will be blessed."
>
> —Genesis 12:3

Ruth was making restitution for what her people refused to do to help Israel in their time of need in the desert.

> "No Ammonite or Moabite is to enter the community of Adonai—even to the tenth generation, none belonging to them is to enter the community of Adonai forever—because they did not meet you with bread and water on the way when you came out of Egypt, and because they hired against you Balaam son of Beor from Petor of Aram-naharaim to curse you."
>
> —Deuteronomy 23:4-5

When she loved and blessed Jewish Naomi unconditionally and sacrificially, the curse of the Moabites was overturned in her life. She married the Jewish prince of Bethlehem, Boaz, and her widowhood and poverty were overturned!

> So Boaz took Ruth, and she became his wife, and he had relations with her. And the LORD enabled her to conceive, and she gave birth to a son.
>
> —RUTH 4:13 NASB '95

Obed was born to Ruth and Boaz, and with him, many generations later, King David, and many more later, King Messiah Yeshua from the House of David.

> Salmon fathered Boaz by Rahab, Boaz fathered Obed by Ruth, Obed fathered Jesse, and Jesse fathered David the king. David fathered Solomon by the wife of Uriah, and Jacob fathered Joseph, the husband of Miriam, from whom was born Yeshua, who is called the Messiah.
>
> —MATTHEW 1:5-6, 16

Out of Naomi, a woman as good as dead, with dead dreams and hopes, with no seed to her name, and with a bitter and full cup of sorrows, came forth the hope of Israel through all generations, Messiah Yeshua!

> "For this reason, therefore, I have requested to see you and to speak with you—since it is for the hope of Israel that I am bearing this chain."
>
> —ACTS 28:20

Naomi had made a disciple and daughter out of Ruth the Moabite the same way that gentiles are parented by the rich root of the olive tree, the Jewish Messiah, the Torah the Word made flesh.

"But if some of the branches were broken off and you—being a wild olive—were grafted in among them and became a partaker of the root of the olive tree with its richness, do not boast against the branches. But if you do boast, it is not you who support the root but the root supports you."

—Romans 11:17–18

The hope of Naomi and of all of Israel was restored through a Gentile, a Moabite from an accursed nation who became a devout friend and unconditional and sacrificial lover of her sorrowful mother-in-law and her people.

Ruth replied, "Do not plead with me to abandon you, to turn back from following you. For where you go, I will go, and where you stay, I will stay. Your people will be my people, and your God my God."

—Ruth 1:16

In the midst of this time of Jacob's Trouble, when tragedy hit Israel in an unprecedented way by the descendants of Esau, manifested through wicked Hamas, we are like Naomi/Mara again. Hamas brutally murdered our people, raped our women, beheaded our babies, burnt entire Jewish families alive in their bomb shelters, and kidnapped hundreds of our people to Gaza, among them young and old, women, children, babies, and even Shoah (Holocaust) survivors! Gaza civilians, including UNRWA and foreign journalists, broke into Israel, participated in the death orgy, and looted.

"In that day," declares Adonai, "will I not destroy the wise men from Edom and understanding from the hill country of Esau? Then your mighty men, O Teman, will be shattered, so everyone will be cut off from the hill country of Esau by slaughter. "Because of your violence towards your brother Jacob, shame will cover you, and you will be cut off forever. On the day that you stood aloof—on the day that strangers carried away his wealth while foreigners entered his gates and cast lots for Jerusalem—you were just like one of them."

—Obadiah 1:8-11

It will be grafted in Ruth, the bride of Messiah from the nations, who, along with her prayers, love, and sacrificial giving, will help restore our dead dreams of a promised land, abundant life, fruitfulness, and fulfillment.

"until the Ruach is poured out on us from on high, and the desert becomes a garden, and a garden seems like a forest."

—Isaiah 32:15

Will you answer the call to be that devout friend to Israel at this time of our sorrow? Will you make restitution for how your nation has treated the Jewish people in the many times of their need throughout all generations, when in exile and when in their promised land? Will you help us plant where Hamas rockets have destroyed agriculture and restore property where Hamas burnt and looted? Will you help us mend the hearts of the bereaved and wounded families and soldiers?

Your future and the future blessing of your nation depend on answering the call of Ruth.

For Macedonia and Achaia were pleased to make some contributions for the poor among the believers in Jerusalem. Yes, they were pleased to do so, and they are under obligation to them. For if the Gentiles have shared in their spiritual blessings, they also ought to serve them in material blessings.

—Romans 15:26-27

Will you cause bereaved Israel, the victim of the October 7, 2023, massacre by Hamas, to sing and rejoice because of your devout friendship in the time of our need? Will you help restore the dream of Jacob's ladder in her?

'Sing and rejoice, O daughter of Zion! For behold, I am coming, and I will live among you'—it is a declaration of Adonai. 'In that day many nations will join themselves to Adonai and they will be My people, and I will dwell among you.' Then you will know that Adonai-Tzva'ot has sent me to you. Adonai will inherit Judah as His portion in the holy land and will once again choose Jerusalem. Be silent before Adonai, all flesh, for He has aroused Himself from His holy dwelling.

—Zechariah 2:14–17

CHAPTER 3

MISPLACED COMPASSION

Prophetic Word for Purim 2024

"He has told you, humanity, what is good, and what ADONAI is seeking from you: Only to practice justice, to love mercy, and to walk humbly with your God."

— MICAH 6:8

I RECEIVED THIS WORD during my last retreat. The Holy Spirit whispered into my ears this phrase: "misplaced compassion".

The word compassion in Hebrew is *rachamim*, meaning *many wombs*, as in the Scripture below:

"Can a woman forget her nursing baby or lack compassion for a child of her womb? Even if these forget, I will not forget you."

—ISAIAH 49:15

Yah proceeded to expound on it, and He showed me an ectopic pregnancy. That is when the egg is fertilized outside of the uterus, usually inside the fallopian tube. This is dangerous for the mother, as she can start to bleed, and no ectopic pregnancy can survive. The fetus will die because it is misplaced; thus, it cannot live.

Misplaced compassion is like that terrible pregnancy; it is dangerous, and its fruit is death.

Since October 7, 2023, the UN and most of the world have misplaced compassion for the "Gaza civilians." They have reversed Israel to be the perpetrator rather than the victim. They have bashed Israel for fighting the most just war in its existence, which is, in fact, a war for its very existence! The UN did not condemn the massacre of Israeli civilians and the brutal rapes of Israeli women and has done nothing to release the hostages kidnapped, abused, and sexually abused by Hamas. UNRWA, a UN institution, participated in the massacre, facilitated it, and hosted Hamas shamelessly in their headquarters, schools, and hospitals.

The UN and the world have been chanting "ceasefire" to Israel because of the humanitarian crisis in Gaza but have not said one word about the terrible crisis in Israel due to Hamas's heinous crimes against her. Nothing, and no support for the hundreds of thousands of Israeli evacuees from the South (Hamas) and from the North (Hezbollah), refugees in their own land! Millions have been traumatized due to the thousands of rockets fired by Hamas and Hezbollah over Israel. Thousands have been wounded and bereaved, and there have been millions of dollars in property loss, job loss, agricultural loss, and school year loss. No! It is only about the "Gaza civilians", the ones who elected Hamas and encouraged and participated in the looting during the terrible massacre.

The Gaza civilians celebrated throughout the streets of Gaza when our women were being ruthlessly raped, our babies beheaded, our children, women, and men kidnapped, our people murdered, our families burnt inside bomb shelters, our fields and fruit trees destroyed, and 22 peace-loving communities vandalized and looted by the Gaza civilians that accompanied Hamas.

And the UN and the world that sides with her chants, "Compassion on the people of Gaza." They blame Israel for its misfortune and fail to blame Hamas, the real culprit of their misfortunes. Hamas used the Gazan women and children as human shields and hid in tunnels under schools, hospitals, and mosques, which were well-stocked with food and water, while the Gaza civilians on the top were starving.

Misplaced compassion is leading to death; it's causing bleeding. Its fruit is disastrous! When will the world have compassion for the true victim of this catastrophe? It is Israel, not Gaza civilians, who are the true victims. And it is Hamas that is to blame for the humanitarian crisis in Gaza, not Israel.

This letter starts with this Scripture that describes what Elohim requires of every human.

> He has told you, humanity, what is good, and what ADONAI is seeking from you: only to practice justice, to love mercy, and to walk humbly with your God.
>
> —MICAH 6:8

To practice justice, we cannot be biased and have misplaced compassion. The UN International Court of Justice did not practice justice when it tried Israel, the victim of the most horrendous massacre the world has ever seen since the Shoah (Nazi Holocaust). The UN and the world have misplaced compassion and mercy, accusing Israel, the victim, as if it were the perpetrator and not holding Hamas guilty and responsible for the humanitarian crisis in Gaza.

The UN and the world are not walking humbly with the God of Israel, the Creator of heaven and earth. It is rather defying Him and intending to dethrone Him by bashing on His chosen Jewish people, the people of Israel, to whom He gave the land of Canaan forever from the river in Egypt to the Euphrates.

> "and confirmed to Jacob as a decree, to Israel as an everlasting covenant, saying, "To you I give the land of Canaan, the portion of your inheritance."
>
> —Psalms 105:10–11

This "Palestinian baby" the UN is trying to birth through misplaced compassion is going to die; it cannot live, and neither can the UN continue. It is the mother of the Palestinian cause, the "Two State Deception," that birthed Hamas, Hezbollah, and the rest of the Palestinian terror groups, including UNRWA. The UN "Palestinian State" deception is an ectopic pregnancy, and it cannot live. UNRWA is the center of the womb of this misplaced Palestinian baby, and it is bleeding. Elohim is coming down like when they were building the Tower of Babel. The charade of the UN has gone long enough!

> "You conceive chaff; you will give birth to stubble. My breath is a fire that will consume you."
>
> — Isaiah 33:11

This is a prophetic word and a warning to all peoples and nations that are siding with the UN and joining in this misplaced compassion ruse. There are not many innocent civilians in Gaza. They have all been fed hatred for Israel and the Jews and genocide since birth, thanks to the Nazi-like educational system of UNRWA. My prayer is that the innocent will be spared, but know this:

The civilian people of Gaza are not receiving humanitarian relief: Hamas is. Biden is trying to stop Israel from completely eradicating Hamas and the Palestinian cause, saying that Israel will cross a red line by going into Rafah to finish Hamas. This is putting the USA in the valley of judgment. The UN was established in the USA, in San Francisco, California, and its headquarters are in New York City, NY.

In the context of this prophetic message, please pay attention to the signs in the heavens.

> "The sun will be turned into darkness and the moon into blood, before the great and awesome day of ADONAI comes."
>
> —JOEL 3: 4

This coming Rosh Chodesh Aviv (Nisan), April 8, a historical solar eclipse will occur throughout the USA, forming an X over the country. This is the ninth such eclipse in the history of the USA. The last one was the 1st of Tishri 2017, on the Feast of Trumpets/Shofars, after we registered the United Nations for Israel as a non-profit corporation in the State of Florida. This one on Aviv 1 will happen after the judgment over the UN in NYC has been released. Aviv/Nisan is the month of Passover. On the 1st of Aviv, the 9th plague fell on the Egyptians, the plague of darkness, which is what a solar eclipse does. The crossing point on the X that is being formed by the eclipse is a town called Little Egypt in southern Illinois.

> **For ADONAI is enraged at all the nations, and furious at all their armies. He will utterly destroy them. He will give them over to slaughter. So their slain will be thrown out, and the**

stench of their corpses will rise, and the hills will be drenched with their blood.
For My sword has drunk its fill in the heavens. See, it will come down upon Edom, upon the people I have devoted to judgment.
For ADONAI has a day of vengeance, a year of recompense for the hostility against Zion.

—Isaiah 34:2-3, 5, 8

Time is short, beloved; it is time to get right with Yah and to make *restitution* towards Israel.

CHAPTER 4

ISHMAEL AND ESAU

"As for Ishmael, I have heard you. See, I have blessed him and I will make him fruitful, and I will multiply him very very much. He will father twelve princes, and I will make him a great nation."

— GENESIS 17:20

It is time to make a distinction between Arab and Arab. We need to see the marks upon the two lineages, the one from Ishmael that will be great and fruitful and the one from Esau that will be completely destroyed. Obviously, Hamas, Hezbollah, and ISIS are following the pattern of Esau, while the Emirati Princes and part of Saudi Arabia and Egypt are following the pattern of Ishmael. The very word *Arab* means *mixture*. There is a mixture of those two lineages, but they have completely different futures. In the days to come, who is who among the Arabs will become clearer and clearer.

In Isaiah 60, we see a multiple of Arabs that come to honor Israel and YHVH in Jerusalem. They come bearing gifts.

"A multitude of camels will cover you, young camels of Midian and Ephah, all those from Sheba will come. They will bring gold and frankincense, and proclaim the praises of Adonai.

All Kedar's flocks will be gathered to you. Nebaioth's rams will minister to you. They will go up with favor on My altar, and I will beautify My glorious House."

—Isaiah 60:6-7

It is time to separate Edom from Ishmael among the Arabs. Edom must be destroyed, but the Ishmaelites who want to live in shalom with Israel will become part of the Isaiah 19 Highway. All these Saudi and Emirati princes may be Ishmael, but there is Edom among them.

"The house of Jacob will be a fire, and the house of Joseph flame, while the house of Esau will be straw—they will set them on fire and consume them. So there will be no survivors of the house of Esau." For Adonai has spoken.

—Obadiah 1:18

But why does the God of Israel want to exterminate Esau and especially the lineage of his grandson Amalek?

Adonai said to Moses, "Write this for a memorial in the book, and rehearse it in the hearing of Joshua, for I will utterly blot out the memory of the Amalekites from under heaven."

—Exodus 17:14

It is necessary because of the mixture with Fallen Angels and daughters of man that had been defiled by Fallen Angels. Eliphaz, Esau's son beget Amalek from a Canaanite woman named Timna.

Now Timna was a concubine to Esau's son Eliphaz, and she bore Amalek to Eliphaz. These are the sons of Esau's wife Adah.

—Genesis 36:12

The Canaanites had been devoted for destruction just like Noah's generation was devoted for destruction due to the sin of Genesis 5. Fallen Angels mating with the daughters of men (from Cain's line), bearing the Nephilim superhumans.

> The Nephilim were on the earth in those days, and also afterward, whenever the sons of God came to the daughters of men, and gave birth to them. Those were the mighty men of old, men of renown.
> So Adonai said, "I will wipe out humankind, whom I have created, from the face of the ground, from humankind to livestock, crawling things and the flying creatures of the sky, because I regret that I made them."

—Genesis 6:4, 7

In Canaan, there were many giants, a different race than normal humans.

> Once again there was a battle at Gath, where there was a man of great stature who had 24 fingers and toes, six on each hand and six on each foot. He too also descended from the giants.

—1 Chronicles 20:6

The sin of Genesis 6 kept on repeating itself throughout the ages, creating a hybrid race that has no conscience and no scruples like Hamas, ISIS, Hezbollah, the Houthis, and the race of the Ayatollahs in Iran, the Nazis in Germany. While not all of them are hybrids, many of them are, especially those without any kind of humanity like Hamas. Therefore, the battle against Amalek is from generation to generation, and it is Yah's battle.

> Then he said, "By the hand upon the throne of ADONAI, ADONAI will have war with Amalek from generation to generation."
>
> —Exodus 17:16

The battle of Israel against Hamas is Yah's battle, and He is fighting with Israel, especially as we lift up our hands in prayer like Moses did when Joshua fought Amalek in the valley.

> When Moses held up his hand, Israel prevailed. But when he let down his hand, the Amalekites prevailed.
>
> —Exodus 17:11

The End time battle is between the hybrids from Esau/Edom/Amalek's lineage and the Hebrews from Abraham, Isaac, and Jacob's lineage. The anti-Messiah manifests through Esau, the Messiah through His Jewish people and those truly grafted in from the nations. Revelation 12 describes it perfectly: The battle is against the Woman (Israel/the Jewish people) and against her offspring, both Jews and gentiles, in the same Jewish Messiah, that have the Torah and His name.

> So the dragon became enraged at the woman and went off to make war with the rest of her offspring—those who keep the commandments of God and hold to the testimony of Yeshua.
>
> —The Revelation 12:17

Ishmael indeed mocks Isaac when he is born and for that, he is disciplined by Yah.

> **Now Sarah saw the son of Hagar the Egyptian, whom she had borne to Abraham, mocking. Therefore she said to Abraham, "Drive out this maid and her son, for the son of this maid shall not be an heir with my son Isaac."**
>
> **—Genesis 21:9-10 nasb '95**

But Esau attempts to murder Yaakov; he wants all of Jacob's line dead. That is the same agenda as Hamas-Hezbollah-Houthis-Iran's Ayatollah regime.

> **So Esau bore a grudge against Jacob because of the blessing with which his father had blessed him, and Esau said in his heart, "Let the time for mourning my father draw near, so that I can kill my brother Jacob!"**
>
> **—Genesis 27:41**

Ishmael is different than Esau. He is promised greatness and fruitfulness. In the days to come, we will see the descendants of Ishmael aligning themselves more and more with Israel. However, some of them may need to be humbled. These are the ones that we call "moderate Muslims" or reasonable Muslims. They are very different from Hamas, ISIS, or Houthis, whose sole agenda is to annihilate Israel, the Jewish people, America, and all of the Western world. These will be destroyed; they have no scruples or conscience. You cannot talk with them or make peace with them.

> "For My sword has drunk its fill in the heavens. See, it will come down upon Edom (Esau, Amalek) upon the people I have devoted to judgment."
>
> —Isaiah 34:5

Anyone who aligns themselves with Hamas and the different descendants of Esau in the natural or in the Spirit will be devoted to destruction.

> "For ADONAI is enraged at all the nations, and furious at all their armies. He will utterly destroy them. He will give them over to slaughter.
> For ADONAI has a day of vengeance, a year of recompense for the hostility against Zion."
>
> —Isaiah 34:2, 8

However, in the end times, the descendants of Ishmael will learn to honor the descendants of Abraham, Isaac, and Jacob and will honor the God of Israel and the people of Israel. Ishmael in Egypt will be disciplined by Judah, and this will bear much fruit. Remember that his mother Hagar is an Egyptian; thus, we can find descendants of Ishmael in Egypt.

> "The land of Judah will terrify Egypt. Anyone who mentions it will be afraid, because of what ADONAI-Tzva'ot has surely purposed against it. In that day five cities in the land of Egypt will speak the language of Canaan, swearing allegiance to ADONAI-Tzva'ot. One used to be called the City of the Sun."
>
> —Isaiah 19:17-18

The outcome of Judah, the nation of Israel, fighting and defeating Egypt, will be repentance in Egypt, a turning from Allah to YHVH.

> "So ADONAI will strike Egypt—striking yet healing—so they will return to ADONAI, and He will respond to them and heal them."
>
> —ISAIAH 19:22

This will bring about the true Biblical peace plan for the Middle East.

> "In that day there will be a highway from Egypt to Assyria, and the Assyrians will come to Egypt, and the Egyptians to Assyria, and the Egyptians will worship with the Assyrians. In that day Israel will be the third, along with Egypt and Assyria—a blessing in the midst of the earth. For ADONAI-Tzva'ot has blessed, saying: "Blessed is Egypt My people, and Assyria My handiwork, and Israel My inheritance.""
>
> —ISAIAH 19:23-25

The Ishmaelites from all over will come in camels (ridden all over the Middle East) and dromedaries (typical of the deserts of Arabia) bearing gifts to the third temple in Jerusalem at the time Messiah sets up His kingdom in Israel.

> "Arise, shine, for your light has come! The glory of ADONAI has risen on you. For behold, darkness covers the earth, and deep darkness the peoples. But ADONAI will arise upon you, and His glory will appear over you. Nations will come to your light, kings to the brilliance of your rising.
> A multitude of camels will cover you, young camels of Midian and Ephah, all those from Sheba will come. They will bring

gold and frankincense, and proclaim the praises of ADONAI. All Kedar's flocks will be gathered to you. Nebaioth's rams will minister to you. They will go up with favor on My altar, and I will beautify My glorious House."

—ISAIAH 60:1-3, 6-7

CHAPTER 5

I WILL NOT FORGET YOU

By Pastor Perach Yang, Taiwan

"Can a woman forget her nursing baby or lack compassion for a child of her womb? Even if these forget, I will not forget you. Behold, I have engraved you on the palms of My hands. Your walls are continually before Me."

— ISAIAH 49:15-16

I HAVE SEEN AT least two recent news reports during the Israel-Hamas war where the IDF found an Arabic version of Hitler's autobiography "Mein Kampf" in Hamas territory. This reminded me of the vision I had last summer when I was praying about whether to go on the Sukkot Israel tour: I saw myself standing in the hallway of Yad Vashem (The Shoah Memorial Museum in Jerusalem). I knew then that it was the LORD's confirmation for me to go on this Sukkot tour to Israel. The tour started at the end of September, and Archbishop Dominiquae took us to different places in Israel to pray and blow the shofar. Unexpectedly, on the last Sabbath of the Sukkot Tour in Jerusalem, the air raid sirens sounded during the graduation ceremony of the GRM Bible School: it was October 7, the day of the Hamas massacre on the Gaza border.

In July of this year, our team participated in "10 Days of Prayer and Fasting" for mercy and comfort to Israel. On the first day of the month of Av, we made an offering to the Shavei Darom Children's Park. I had just watched Archbishop Dominiquae's message about the brutal disengagement of Gush Katif/Gaza, and we wanted to support those Jewish residents now relocated in the portal of the Negev. After we had sent the offering, I saw a vision of the buildings in the Auschwitz death camp. Then I understood that the purpose of our support was not only to comfort the Orthodox Jews who had lost their homes and moved to Shavei Darom but also to answer the lament of the Jewish blood poured on the ground.

"Comfort, O comfort My people," says your God.

—Isaiah 40:1

He said, "What have you done? The voice of your brother's blood is crying to Me from the ground."

—Genesis 4:10

On the ninth day of the ten days of fasting and prayer, I read Isaiah 49:15-16 and suddenly understood more of the meaning of the first vision I saw of myself standing in the hallway of Yad Vashem. Ruach (Holy Spirit) gave me the word "names".

What is the most important thing in Yad Vashem, apart from telling us the whole tragic history? The names. I remembered that there was a room filled with documents with the names of those who were slaughtered, and in the memorial for 1.5 million children, the names were read out loud one by one. I understood that Abba wanted us to know that He remembers all those names and many more whose names are not recorded in the museum. His Word says:

> "Can a woman forget her nursing baby or lack compassion for a child of her womb? Even if these forget, I will not forget you. Behold, I have engraved you on the palms of My hands. Your walls are continually before Me."
>
> —Isaiah 49:15-16

After returning from Israel, right after the Hamas massacre, many intercessors around the world prayed for the release of the Israeli hostages. They read their names aloud one by one, praying that they could return home. God has not forgotten any of the names of His people; He has not forgotten any of His children, and He has promised that He will avenge those people who were brutally killed. (Isaiah 34:8)

Archbishop Dominiquae's book *The Voice of These Ashes** was published just before Sukkot, and I wondered if this was a coincidence. Or is it that Yah wants to use His servant, whom He called on the ashes of Auschwitz to be the voice of the ashes of those who were exterminated, to also deliver this important message to the world at such a time as this—after this mass murder?

She writes in her book that when righteous acts of restitution are done, curses are broken, and prayers are answered. During King David's time, although it was not his fault, Israel still suffered the curse of three years of famine because of the injustice done to the Gibeonites. King David understood that the only way out of the curse his predecessor left him was through an act of restitution. The famine would never

---

* To order *The Voice of These Ashes*, visit www.ZionsGospel.com

break, and all of Israel could die unless the curse for the murder of the Gibeonites was broken. He turned to them to seek to appease them.

> Thus David said to the Gibeonites, "What should I do for you? And how can I make atonement that you may bless the inheritance of the LORD?" And he said, "I will do for you whatever you say." So they said to the king, "The man who consumed us and who planned to exterminate us from remaining within any border of Israel, let seven men from his sons be given to us, and we will hang them before the LORD in Gibeah of Saul, the chosen of the LORD." And the king said, "I will give them."
>
> —2 SAMUEL 21:3, 4B-6

What is most revealing is Heaven's response to this difficult act of righteous restitution. The curse broke, and YHVH's hand was moved to answer prayer on behalf of the land.

> "...Afterward, God was moved by prayer for the land."
>
> —2 SAMUEL 21:14B

The Voice of These Ashes is God's gift to our generation. Its cover may look painful, but its content is ultimately full of life and hope because it is a message from the LORD of life. He had the power to raise His Son from the dead, and He surely has the power to turn the painful cries of these ashes into life and blessing. Perhaps we were not alive during the Second World War, but if we were, how would we have responded to the Jews who were treated like lambs waiting to be slaughtered and sent to the death camps? Would we have dared to reach out to the Jews and speak out on their behalf? Or perhaps we would even have helped the Nazis to hate and kill the Jews? Our actions today, during this ongoing war following the Hamas massacre, will greatly impact us, our families, and the nation for which we stand.

Over the past two months, world news has allowed us to see global criticism and opinions about Israel's self-defense. But do we truly know that God does not forget His children? He said, "I will not forget you." Are the promises to Abraham in Genesis 12:3 just words?

> "And I will bless those who bless you, and the one who curses you I will curse. And in you all the families of the earth will be blessed."
>
> —Genesis 12:3 NASB '95

Now, in the middle of this war, let us open this book, *The Voice of These Ashes,* and listen carefully to the voice of God through His servant. Each of us has the opportunity to do what is right in the eyes of the Almighty and bring blessings rather than unbearable judgments and curses. This is the message of life and death at this time.

> "He who has ears, let him hear!"
>
> — Matthew 11:15

> "For I know the plans that I have in mind for you," declares Adonai, "plans for shalom and not calamity—to give you a future and a hope."
>
> —Jeremiah 29:11

CHAPTER 6

WE ARE MORE, AND WE ARE HERE NOW

By Rev. Hadassah Danielsbacka, Finland/USA

> "Fear not," he replied, "for those who are with us are more than those who are with them."
>
> — 2 KINGS 6:16

"I SAW YOU WERE reading the book of Joshua," the rabbi said once he had finished his prayers and wrapped up his tefillin. Meanwhile, I had prayed the anti-Amalek prayer and delved into the warfare with Joshua. "Yes, I love it! It's written for a time like this," I said. "He kept the faith to the very end, always encouraging others just to possess the land. This is what Israel is now doing; it's time to possess Gaza!" He agreed with a slightly puzzled look on his face.

We were on a plane on our way to the Israel March in Washington, DC, a rally that became the largest pro-Israel demonstration ever with almost 300,000 participants. The airplane was packed with Jews. "Do you ever miss New York?" I asked the rabbi, who had only been in Florida for a few months, having spent the rest of his life in a large Jewish community on Long Island. "No, I only miss Israel," he replied.

Joshua, too, must have missed Israel after seeing a glimpse of it and its abundant fruit, and then, because of his brethren's unbelief, he had to turn back to the desert. He was Moses's armor bearer, and after the 40 long desert years, when Moses died, he led the new generation to the promised land. Yah commissioned him:

> "Moses My servant is dead; now therefore arise, cross this Jordan, you and all this people, to the land which I am giving to them, to the sons of Israel. Every place on which the sole of your foot treads, I have given it to you, just as I spoke to Moses."
>
> — JOSHUA 1:2-3 NASB '95

Joshua had seen the rest of his generation die, one by one, year after year. Despite this, he had kept the faith and trust in God, along with his friend Caleb, and they were the only survivors of the "complaining generation." Now, it was the time for a great battle, and it would not be a short one but would demand persistence like never before. For 40 years, that persistence and faith had been developed in the character of Joshua, and it would be greatly needed.

YHVH defined the borders of the promised land to Joshua, just as he had defined them to Abraham, Isaac, and Jacob, and it was a much wider area than Israel of today:

> "From the wilderness and this Lebanon, even as far as the great river, the river Euphrates, all the land of the Hittites, and as far as the Great Sea toward the setting of the sun will be your territory."
>
> —JOSHUA 1:4 NASB '95

He also gave Joshua a promise, followed by instruction. Obedience to this instruction would define his walk and its outcome:

> "No one will be able to stand before you all the days of your life. Just as I was with Moses, so I will be with you. I will not fail you or forsake you. Chazak! Be strong! For you will lead these people to inherit the land I swore to their fathers to give them. Only be very strong, and resolute to observe diligently the Torah which Moses, My servant commanded you. Do not turn from it to the right or to the left, so you may be successful wherever you go. This book of the Torah should not depart from your mouth—you are to meditate on it day and night, so that you may be careful to do everything written in it. For then you will make your ways prosperous and then you will be successful. Have I not commanded you? Chazak! Be strong! Do not be terrified or dismayed, for ADONAI your God is with you wherever you go."
>
> —JOSHUA 1:5-9

He encountered many enemies, doubts, and sticky situations, even among his own army and people. He would need much persistence and faith to prevail over the long battle of possessing the land. Joshua was to conquer and destroy all the nations inhabiting the land of Canaan. God had given them plenty of time to repent—400 years! He foretold that already to Abraham:

> "Know for certain that your seed will be strangers in a land that is not theirs, and they will be enslaved and oppressed 400 years…
> Then in the fourth generation they will return here—for the iniquity of the Amorites is not yet complete.
>
> —GENESIS 15:13, 16

The habitants of Canaan committed sins of idolatry, temple prostitution, adultery, homosexuality, incest, murder, bestiality, gang rape, and child sacrifice. God told Israel clearly that it was for this wickedness that they were judged, and finally, their iniquity was complete.

> ...because of the wickedness of these nations, ADONAI your God is driving them out from before you, and in order to keep the word ADONAI swore to your fathers—to Abraham, to Isaac, and to Jacob.
>
> —DEUTERONOMY 9:5

Doesn't this remind us of today's Gaza, where children have been offered at the altar of Hamas and Islam - educated to hate, to kill, and to become martyrs, used as human shields to protect weapons, tunnels, and terror bases? Rockets and ammunition have been found under children's beds in daycares, UNRWA schools, and hospitals. Videos are testifying how small children dream of becoming martyrs and killing Jews. Indeed, many of them grow up into full-blown terrorists capable of committing a massacre, as happened on October 7.

Lebanese researcher Hussain Abdul-Hussain writes in the New York Post ("Don't speak for my people") on November 31, 2023:

> "I have been lucky to survive the Iraq-Iran War, the Lebanese Civil War, and many rounds of war between Israel and different Palestinian and Lebanese factions.
>
> I have lost my family in wars and assassinations. Each and every time one of the miseries my family, friends, and I faced was blamed on Israel. 'Once we eliminate Israel and liberate Palestine, life will become rosy'. This has been the excuse of the Arab World since I was born. I refuse to pass this excuse to my children."

This is what the children in Gaza learn: Once Israel is gone, we are well. In the time of Joshua, I am sure that the corrupt Canaanite nations that came together to fight Joshua and the Israelites thought the same: Once we destroy Israel, all will be "well" again—despite children being offered to Moloch and the land filled with immorality, horrendous violence, and abuse.

What if "Palestine will be free"? What would that freedom look like? Most probably much the same as the "freedom" of the Islamist caliphate of ISIS - Sharia law and terror would rule supreme, and they would pursue to take over the whole world as aggressively as Hitler did with his Third Reich.

By conquering the land, Joshua's mission was to cleanse and free the land from corruption that was about to destroy it altogether. The very earth was about to vomit out its inhabitants.

> **The land has become defiled, so I will punish its iniquity, and the land will vomit out its inhabitants.**
>
> **—Leviticus 18:25**

The land itself was crying to be cleansed, planted, cared for, restored, and brought to life. Joshua conquered Gaza, and it was given to the tribe of Judah. However, because they failed to drive out all of its corrupt inhabitants, the Philistines, the land did not come to rest. The strife continues until this very day when we witness Israel in the battle between light and darkness. This is a battle to finally possess the promised land at the seacoast:

> **The seacoast (referring to the area of Gaza) will become pastures, with meadows for shepherds and folds for flocks. The coast will belong to the remnant of the house of Judah, upon**

> which they will graze. In the houses of Ashkelon they will lie down in the evening.
>
> —ZEPHANIAH 2:6-7

When Israel gave Gush Katif in Gaza over to Hamas in 2005, uprooting its citizens, it was flourishing with organic greenhouses, fruits, vegetables, and farming. The land had been brought to life after hundreds of years of abuse and neglect. After the expulsion, Gush Katif quickly became a terror base of Hamas, with hundreds of rockets launched at surrounding regions.

Today, in the middle of the ongoing war, the Israeli flag is once again raised in the broken-down Gush Katif, and the IDF is proceeding in Gaza to cleanse the land of its corrupted terrorist invaders. Videos testify how the soldiers are raising Israeli flags in Gaza, celebrating Shabbat, and lifting prayers. They are worshipping the God of Israel, the possessor of all lands and nations upon the earth.

Joshua was to remember that Yah was with him, and that made him always a *majority*. When YHVH is on your side, you are always a majority. The Jewish prophet Elisha, when surrounded by enemy armies, told his servant: *"Do not fear, for those who are with us are more than those who are with them"* (2 Kings 6:16). He saw the heavenly armies and prayed Yah to open his servant's eyes to see them, too: *"O LORD, I pray, open his eyes that he may see." And the LORD opened the servant's eyes, and he saw; and behold, the mountain was full of horses and chariots of fire all around Elisha"* (2 Kings 6:17 NASB '95).

In the Washington DC rally, all our eyes were opened to see that there are *more of us*. And that nearly 300,000 was just a drop in the bucket; had we seen the angelic armies around us and Israel, we would not have been able to count them!

A Jewish woman wrote this after the rally: "At the rally, I met a Christian woman who was calling out her agreement, gospel-style, as we listened to the speeches. I started doing it, too - it was so good to resonate out loud, allowing my strongly felt feelings to pour out of me.

Later, I found myself sobbing for a long stretch. She reached out her hand and held mine in hers. Tight. For a good long while. I felt so held. I turned to her and asked: "Who are you? Where did you come from?" She said, "I came from Michigan today." "All the way, today?" I asked. "Yes," she said. And then, leaning close to me, she said, "Listen up. I wasn't here for the Holocaust, but I am here now."

We were not here at the time of the Shoah, but we were here at the time of this second Shoah on October 7, the massacre of Jewish people committed by Hamas and the so-called "Palestinian cause". And we are here now.

Let us be as persistent as Joshua was, never stopping to pray, give, and fight in the Spirit for Israel and the Jewish people. We will witness the full possession of the land!

> "For though it is a forest, you shall clear it, and to its farthest borders it shall be yours; for you shall drive out the Canaanites, even though they have chariots of iron and though they are strong."
>
> —JOSHUA 17:18 NASB '95

CHAPTER 7

WHY DID WE RING ONE MILLION BELLS ON JANUARY 14, 2024?

> "Rescue those being dragged off to death, hold back those stumbling to slaughter. If you say, "Look, we didn't know this." Won't He who weighs hearts perceive it? Won't He who guards your soul know it? Won't He repay each one according to his deeds?"
>
> — PROVERBS 24:11-12

We rang 1,000,000 bells on January 14, 100 days after the October 7 brutal massacre by Hamas from Gaza, inflicted on Israeli civilians plus people from 41 other nations. But why?

1. To remember the murdered, the wounded, and their families.
2. To return the kidnapped Israelis and others from Hamas in Gaza.
3. To reclaim a world without terror and antisemitism.

The word in Hebrew for *bell* is *paamon*. פעמון

The root word is *peima*, which means *beat*, also used in *heartbeat*; פעימת לב = heartbeat.

It is the heartbeat of the God of Israel and those aligned with Him that rang on January 14.

In the Bible, the High Priest had a robe hemmed by bells and pomegranates. When he walked in and out of the holy place, the bells would make a sound. If the sound of the bells was not heard, it meant he died in Yah's holy presence, and his sacrifice was not accepted.

> "On the hem of it, you are to make pomegranates of blue, purple and scarlet all around the hem, with golden bells between them: one golden bell and a pomegranate, then another golden bell and a pomegranate, on the hem of the robe all around. It must be worn by Aaron whenever he ministers. The sound will be heard when he goes into the holy place before ADONAI and when he comes out, so that he does not die."
>
> —Exodus 28:33-35

Archeologists have traced bells back to 3000 BCE, though they were developed extensively during the Bronze Age (c. 2000 BCE) in ancient China. During the Middle Ages, bell ringing took on a new significance. Bells were used to make announcements and mark significant events such as weddings and funerals. Bells were also used to signal the time of day and to warn of impending danger, such as fires and attacks by enemy forces. In older maritime days, ship bells would be struck to mark a successful passage or used to sound off as an emergency alarm. Farmers also historically used the cowbell to help identify their pastoral animals. They were placed around the animal's neck, and when it was time to herd them in the evenings, the sound made it easier for them to be found by their owners.

> "In that day "Holy to Adonai" will be inscribed on the bells of the horses and the pots in House of Adonai will be like the sacred bowls in front of the altar."
>
> —Zechariah 14:20

In England, bell ringing became highly developed during the 17th and 18th centuries. Towers were built with multiple bells that could be rung in complex patterns, creating a beautiful and intricate sound. As a result, bell-ringing became a popular pastime, with groups of people gathering to practice and perform together.

The Liberty Bell, previously called the State House Bell or Old State House Bell, is an iconic symbol of American independence located in Philadelphia. Originally placed on the steeple of the Pennsylvania State House (now renamed Independence Hall), the bell today is located across the street in the Liberty Bell Centre in Independence National Historical Park. The bell was commissioned in 1752 by the Pennsylvania Provincial Assembly from the London firm of Lester and Pack (known subsequently as the Whitechapel Bell Foundry) and was cast with the lettering "Proclaim LIBERTY Throughout all the Land unto all the Inhabitants Thereof," a Biblical reference from the Book of Leviticus (25:10). Though in the Bible, it is not a bell that must be sounded for the Jubilee but rather a shofar.

> Then on the tenth day of the seventh month, on Yom Kippur, you are to sound a shofar blast—you are to sound the shofar all throughout your land. You are to make the fiftieth year holy, and proclaim liberty throughout the land to all its inhabitants. It is to be a Jubilee to you, when each of you is to return to his own property and each of you is to return to his family.
>
> —Leviticus 25:9-10

Bell ringing also played a significant role in the history of the American Revolution. In 1775, Paul Revere famously rode through the streets of Boston, warning of the arrival of British troops. He used bells to signal his message, and the echoes of the bells were heard throughout the city. This event is now known as the "Midnight Ride of Paul Revere," an important moment in American history.

Bells were originally used for spiritual purposes, as they were believed to purify, ward off demons, and bring rain. Bells continue to be used in Eastern and Southern Asian religions, Russian Orthodox churches, Christian and Catholic services, and in Buddhist temples.

During the Middle Ages, bells were used to awaken people, announce important events, and communicate warnings.

Modernized Uses of the Bell

Throughout the 19th and 20th centuries, bell ringing continued to evolve and change. Different techniques were developed, and bells were used in new and innovative ways. For example, in the United States, bells were used to signal the arrival of trains and to announce the opening and closing of stock markets. Bells were also used to mark powerful events, such as the end of World War II. "For Whom the Bell Tolls" by Ernest Hemingway takes its title from a line in "Meditation" by John Donne about the tolling of bells for the dead.

Once the cash register was invented in the late 19th century, bells became commonplace whenever a sale was made. The register drawer would pop open, and a bell would make the now iconic "cha-ching" sound, thus becoming synonymous with making a sale. As a result, the National Cash Register Company created a film campaign during the 1950s titled "The Bell Heard Round the World" to promote their company across the United States. Also, the call to eat in many institutions and farms is announced by a bell ringing.

To summarize:

In many ways, the bell replaced the shofar in Christianity as a gathering, warning, announcement, freedom, and deliverance instrument. However, the use of bells in the Bible is obviously a priestly role that announces the coming of the High Priest. Most particularly, He is going to the Holy of Holies to obtain forgiveness and mercy for Israel for one more year on Yom Kippur. When the High Priest moved, the bells on the hem of his garment rang.

We gathered on January 14 to ring our bells on the 100th day since the brutal massacre by Hamas on the Jewish communities of the Gaza border in Israel. We also blew our shofars as the bells were ringing throughout the world,

- To remember the brutally murdered by Hamas, including civilians and fallen soldiers, the wounded, maimed, and lamed, the women monstrously raped, and their families.
- To return those kidnapped by Hamas into Gaza—women, babies, children, men, and the elderly, to urgently release them from cruel captivity without unnecessary delays.
- To reclaim a world without terror, hatred, antisemitism, and any form of racism.

Our High Priest, Yeshua, the Jewish Messiah, is on the move, ringing the bells on the hem of His robe on behalf of His nation, Israel, and His Jewish people.

> "Now here is the main point being said. We do have such a Kohen Gadol, (High Priest) who has taken His seat at the right hand of the throne of the Majesty in the heavens."
>
> —Hebrews 8:1

The blood of His Jewish people is crying from the ground.

> Then He said, "What have you done? The voice of your brother's blood is crying out to Me from the ground. So now, cursed are you from the ground which opened its mouth to receive your brother's blood from your hand."
>
> —Genesis 4:10-11

If the nations do not ring their bells to make a difference and to stop the wickedness of Islamic terror tied with the infamous Hamas-infused Palestinian cause, they will suffer the same fate as the Jewish communities on the Gaza border.

> For ADONAI is enraged at all the nations and furious at all their armies. He will utterly destroy them. He will give them over to slaughter. So their slain will be thrown out, and the stench of their corpses will rise, and the hills will be drenched with their blood.
> For ADONAI has a day of vengeance, a year of recompense for the hostility against Zion.
>
> —Isaiah 34:2-3, 8

Hamas-infused Palestinians have infiltrated America, Europe, and many nations in the world.

When we ring our bells and blow our shofars, we are magnifying the *Voice of these Ashes** from the communities and kibbutzim burnt by Hamas and other Gaza civilians in Israel. We are declaring together with the God of Israel, *no* to Hamas, *no* to Iran-induced terror, *no* to Hezbollah, *no* to the Houthis, *no* to all Islamic terror groups, *no* to the Two-State deception, *no* to the Hamas-infused Palestinian cause, and *no* to antisemitism.

We declare *yes* to the cause of Zion of restoring the nation of Israel to its own land from the river in Egypt to the Euphrates River in Iraq. (Gaza is included in the Biblical borders of the house of Judah.)

> **He remembers His covenant forever—the word He commanded for a thousand generations—which He made with Abraham, swore to Isaac, and confirmed to Jacob as a decree, to Israel as an everlasting covenant, saying, "To you I give the land of Canaan, the portion of your inheritance."**
>
> **—Psalms 105:8–11**

> **For Zion's sake, I will not keep silent, and for Jerusalem's sake, I will not rest, until her righteousness shines out brightly and her salvation as a blazing torch.**
>
> **—Isaiah 62:1**

> **I will bless those who bless you.**
>
> **—Genesis 12:3a nasb '95**

---

* To order my book *The Voice of These Ashes*, visit at www.ZionsGospel.com

CHAPTER 8

LET MY PEOPLE GO!

By Pastor Cesar Silva, Mexico

> Deliver those who are being taken away to death, and those who are staggering to slaughter, Oh hold them back. If you say, "See, we did not know this, "does He not consider it who weighs the hearts? And does He not know it who keeps your soul? And will He not render to man according to his work?
>
> — PROVERBS 24:11-12 NASB '95

THE ORDER OF THIS day:

"Deliver those who are being taken away to death;"

We remain firm in our position of constant support for Israel in her time of anguish. The massacre of October 7 continues to resonate when the images of that day are still vivid. The pain of the kidnapped and the anguish of their families who still have not received news of their loved ones, not knowing if they are dead or alive, is very present.

> Draw near, O nations, to hear, and listen, O peoples! Let the earth hear, and all it contains, the world, and all its offspring! For ADONAI is enraged at all the nations, and furious at all

their armies. He will utterly destroy them. He will give them over to slaughter.

—Isaiah 34:1-2

But why is He enraged? Because of hatred of the Jewish people (Zion), anti-Zionism and antisemitism.

For ADONAI has a day of vengeance, a year of recompense for the hostility against Zion.

—Isaiah 34:8

The massacre of October 7 will never be forgotten because everything will be not only in the minds of everyone, but it will one day be before the throne of judgment of the great I Am. No one escapes His presence; no one escapes His judgment. We could ask Pharaoh, Nebuchadnezzar, or Hitler if the judgment of the Eternal was stopped or overlooked in their days, and I think the answer will be very obvious: no, the punishment does not stop.

Yet all who devour you (Israel) will be devoured, and all your foes—all of them—will go into captivity. Those plundering you will be plundered, and all preying on you I give as prey.

—Jeremiah 30:16

Judgment and Revenge Will Come

Vengeance is Mine, and retribution; in due time their foot will slip. For the day of their disaster is near, and the impending things are hurrying to them.'

—Deuteronomy 32:35 NASB '95

But Yeshua said to turn the other cheek, right? "Where is the gospel of love that Yeshua taught us," you may ask. I want to remind you that while Yeshua was with them, such a massacre did not happen, but after His death, they would undergo persecution that would lead some of His disciples to death. That is why the Teacher told them:

> And He said to them, "But now, whoever has a money belt is to take it along, likewise also a bag, and whoever has no sword is to sell his cloak and buy one.
>
> —Luke 22:36 nasb '95

It is more than clear then that judgment and revenge will come and Israel has every right to defend itself as a nation.

> Thus says Adonai, "As for all My evil neighbors (in Gaza and all the Arab and Muslim nations) who strike at the inheritance that I bequeathed to My people Israel—I am about to uproot them from their land and pluck the house of Judah from them. Yet it will come to pass, after I have uprooted them, that I will again have compassion on them and I will bring them back, each one to his inheritance and each one to his land. So it will come to pass, if they will diligently learn the ways of My people—to swear by My Name, 'As Adonai lives,' just as they taught My people to swear by Baal—then they will be built up in the midst of My people. But if they will not obey, then I will uproot that nation, plucking it up and destroying it." It is a declaration of Adonai.
>
> —Jeremiah 12:14-17

Even so, the leaders of the nations and their people continue to grow hatred. What should we do to obey His command to free those who are in danger of death and to avert the punishment already prepared for the nations that attack Israel militarily, politically, or in the media? How should we respond to nations that do not help her in the time of her need and rather send financial support to those who want to annihilate Israel, chanting, "From the river to the sea, Palestine will be free?"

Pray and Give to Israel

I believe two things are necessary: Pray for Israel in this time of distress and support her financially to provide for urgent needs. Praying for Israel should be number one on our daily agenda. This will put the key of Abraham in the position of blessing. That ancient key is based on Genesis 12:3: "I will bless him who blesses you." When we put Israel first in our moments of prayer, we can receive answers to our personal requests, as well.

The second, and no less important, is our offerings to the people of Israel, which, as in the previous one, is also connected to the blessing of Genesis 12:3. Solomon tells us in Proverbs that an offering saves us from death.

> **Riches make no profit in the day of wrath, but righteousness* delivers from death.**
>
> **—Proverbs 11:4**

I invite you all to pray and give to actively support the people of Israel in this time of anguish and need.** When you give and bless Israel,

---

* In Hebrew, it refers to "righteous offering"
** Please visit www.UnitedNationsForIsrael.org to learn more on how you can support Israel at this time.

you will experience open heavens and revival upon you and your house, just as happened with Cornelius.

> **The angel said to him, "Your prayers and tzedakah (righteous offering) have gone up as a memorial offering before God.**
>
> —Acts 10:4

CHAPTER 9

THE CASE AGAINST UN AND FOR UNIFY

> "For nothing will be impossible with God."
>
> — LUKE 1:37

> Then ADONAI stretched out His hand and touched my mouth and ADONAI said to me, "Behold, I have put My words in your mouth. See, today I have appointed you (Dominiquae) over nations and over kingdoms: to uproot and to tear down, to destroy and to overthrow, to build and to plant." Moreover, the word of ADONAI came to me, saying, "What do you see, Jeremiah (Dominiquae)?" I answered, "I see an almond branch." Then ADONAI said to me, "You have seen correctly, for I am watching over My word to perform it."
>
> —JEREMIAH 1:9-12

THE UNITED NATIONS WAS established after World War II in an attempt to maintain international peace and security and to achieve cooperation among nations on economic, social, and humanitarian problems. Its forerunner was the League of Nations, an organization conceived under similar circumstances following World

War I. Established in 1919 under the Treaty of Versailles "to promote international cooperation and to achieve peace and security," the League of Nations ceased its activities after it failed to prevent global war.

UNIFY claims that the UN has failed to do the same, plus much more.

On June 26, 1945, in San Francisco, the United Nations was formally established with the signing of the UN Charter. Article 111 of this charter indicated that "The present Charter, of which the Chinese, French, Russian, English, and Spanish texts are equally authentic, shall remain deposited in the archives of the Government of the United States of America. Duly certified copies thereof shall be transmitted by that Government to the Governments of the other signatory states."

The name United Nations originated with President Franklin Delano Roosevelt in 1941, when he described the countries fighting against the Axis Powers (Germany, Italy, and Japan) in World War II. The name was first used officially on January 1, 1942 (when the Jews were burning in the Nazi ovens of Auschwitz and many more), when 26 states joined in the declaration by the United Nations pledging to continue their joint war effort and not to make peace separately.

As outlined in the charter, the two main bodies of the United Nations are the General Assembly, composed of all member nations, and the Security Council. Today, nearly 200 nations are members of the United Nations General Assembly. The UN Security Council consists of the five victors from World War II (known as "The Big Five") as permanent members—China, France, the United Kingdom, the USSR (now Russia), and the United States—and 10 other countries, elected by the General Assembly, that serve 2-year terms. The Security Council is the principal UN organ responsible for ensuring peace, and its decisions are binding on all member states. The five permanent members were given individual veto power over issues brought before the Council.

Other special agencies like the WHO (World Health Organization), UNICEF (UN International Children's Emergency Fund), UNESCO (UN Educational, Scientific, and Cultural Organization), and the World Bank and UNRWA (Palestinian Refugees Welfare) provide needed help across the world.

The UN has forfeited its charter for the following reasons:

1. The UN did not denounce the October 7 Massacre against 22 Israeli peace-loving communities and murdering 1200 civilians at the Gaza border.
2. The UN is biased: It does not defend Israeli civilians attacked, butchered, raped, burned, and kidnapped by Hamas, but it fights for the Gaza civilians that elected Hamas, and many participated with Hamas, murdering, kidnapping, and looting Israeli peace-loving communities, and many sympathized with Hamas and cooperated.
3. UNRWA's participation in the massacre.
4. At least 12% of UNRWA's officers are members of the terror organization Hamas, and many more are sympathizers.
5. UNRWA's headquarters in Hamas-ruled Gaza became terror base operations, housing weapons, Hamas terrorists, and launching pads for rockets against Israel.
6. Hospitals, schools, and mosques became terror base operations under the eyes of the UN and UNRWA, and the UN did not denounce it or stop it.

7. Hamas terror tunnels were built under hospitals, schools, and mosques with the full knowledge of UNRWA officials in Gaza, and the UN did not stop them.
8. Money sent via UNRWA to Gaza has been used to fund the building of terror tunnels, acquire weapons and rockets by Hamas, and support many of its activities that caused the massacre of October 7.
9. The UN has constantly bashed Israel, more than any other country, thus showing it is Antisemitic and Antizionist.
10. The UN crafted the Partition Plan in 1947 that eventually led to the Oslo Accords, the establishment of the PA, the rise of Hamas in Gaza, and countless terror attacks on Israelis culminating in the October 7 massacre.
11. The UN forfeited its charter to keep international peace and security for all nations by not denouncing or dismantling Hamas, thus preventing security for Israeli civilians and Gaza civilians who are used by Hamas as human shields.

Due to the reasons above, these consequences will follow:

1. This earthly and heavenly court of the United Nations for Israel accuses the UN of collaboration with at least one terror organization called Hamas and possibly many more.
2. Whereas the Creator of the nations is YHVH, the God of Israel, this court states that the UN has rebelled against the authority of the Creator of heaven and earth and has betrayed the trust placed on it by humanity and the nations entrusted to it.
3. Thus, the UN is not fit to provide peace and security to the nations it claims to represent.

4. The United Nations for Israel (UNIFY) demands the immediate dismantling of the UN charter, starting with UNRWA.
5. UNIFY demands the immediate investigation, arrest, and imprisonment of all UN/UNRWA officials who are collaborators of Hamas.
6. As the President of UNIFY and a prophet/messenger of the God of Israel, I now declare the Partition Plan of Palestine dead, the Oslo Accords canceled and burned to ashes, and the Two-State Solution Plan dissolved forever, whereas any nation that divides the covenant land of Israel from the River of Egypt to the Euphrates finds itself in the valley of judgment; thus, the UN is now judged guilty of attempting to divide YHVH's land given to the nation of Israel forever.
7. UNIFY demands the immediate dismantling of the PA that has collaborated with Hamas and has taught in its schools the hatred of Israel, removing the name of Israel from its maps, so that the name of Israel be remembered no more.
8. UNIFY demands the immediate indictment of the Biden/Obama administration for pushing Israel to national suicide during the time of war for its existence by demanding to reward the massacre of October 7 with the establishment of a Palestinian State.
9. Whereas the UN does not qualify as representing the sheep nations mentioned in Zechariah 2, UNIFY demands its complete dismantling, uprooting, and destruction as done to the Tower of Babel in Genesis 11.
10. We call on all member nations to exit the UN and rescue their lives.

Legal scriptural basis

1. Whereas the UN has tried to usurp the place of the Creator of the nations, the God of Israel, and His Word by discriminating against Israel constantly and by attempting to divide His land given to the nation of Israel forever.

"Then they said, "Come! Let's build ourselves a city, with a tower whose top reaches into heaven. So let's make a name for ourselves, or else we will be scattered over the face of the whole land." Then ADONAI came down to see the city and the tower that the sons of man had built. ADONAI said, "Look, the people are one and all of them have the same language. So this is what they have begun to do. Now, nothing they plan to do will be impossible. Come! Let Us go down and confuse their language there, so that they will not understand each other's language." So ADONAI scattered them from there over the face of the entire land, and they stopped building the city. This is why it is named Babel, because ADONAI confused the languages of the entire world there, and from there ADONAI scattered them over the face of the entire world."

—GENESIS 11:4-9

We ask you, Elohei Israel, to come down and dismantle the UN.

2. Whereas the UN crafted the Partition Plan leading to the Oslo Accords, the Two-State Solution, and the establishment of the PA, we demand the UN be put in the Valley of Judgment.

For behold, in those days and at that time, when I restore Judah and Jerusalem from exile, I will gather all nations and bring them down to the valley of Jehoshaphat. I will plead with them there on behalf of My people, even My inheritance, Israel, whom they scattered among the nations and they divided up My land.

—Joel 4:1-2

3. Whereas the UN-based UNRWA organization cooperated with Hamas in Gaza and the massacre against Israeli civilians (and of 41 other nations) on October 7, we demand Your judgment to fall upon UNRWA and the entire UN until it is completely void of authority and uprooted from the face of the earth.

"Because of your violence towards your brother Jacob, shame will cover you, and you will be cut off forever. On the day that you stood aloof—on the day that strangers carried away his wealth, while foreigners entered his gates and cast lots for Jerusalem—you were just like one of them. You should not look down on your brother on the day of his disaster, nor should you rejoice over the children of Judah on the day of their destruction. You should not speak proudly on the day of their distress. Do not enter the gate of My people on the day of their disaster. Yes, you. Do not gloat over their misery on the day of their disaster. Yes, you—do not loot their wealth on the day of their calamity. Do not stand at the crossroads to cut down his fugitives, and do not imprison his survivors in the day of distress." For the day of Adonai is near against all the nations. As you have done, it shall be done to you. Your dealings will return on your own head. For just as you have drunk on My holy mountain, so all the nations shall drink continually. Yes, they will drink, gulp down, and then be as though they had never existed. But on Mount Zion, there will be deliverance, and it will be holy. Then the house of Jacob will dispose of those who dispossessed them. The house of Jacob will be a fire, and the house of Joseph flame, while the house of Esau will be straw—they will set them on fire and consume them. So there will be no survivors of the house of Esau." for ADONAI has spoken."

—OBADIAH 1:10-18

4. Whereas the UN has gathered together to constantly attack, denounce, and bash the State of Israel, depriving it of any justice; whereas the PA has removed the name of Israel from its textbooks; whereas the textbooks used by UNRWA in Gaza teach hatred against the Jewish people and the State of Israel, and because Hitler's book *Mein Kampf* was found in the UNRWA run schools in Gaza.

God, do not keep silent. Do not hold Your peace, O God. Do not be still. For look, Your enemies make an uproar. Those who hate You lift up their head. They make a shrewd plot against Your people, conspiring against Your treasured ones. "Come," they say, "let's wipe them out as a nation! Let Israel's name be remembered no more!" For with one mind, they plot together. Against You, do they make a covenant. The tents of Edom and the Ishmaelites, Moab and the Hagrites, Gebal, Ammon, and Amalek, and Philistia with the inhabitants of Tyre—even Assyria—have joined them, becoming a strong arm for Lot's sons. Selah. Do to them as You did to Midian, to Sisera and Jabin at the Kishon River, who perished at En-dor—they became as dung for the ground. Make their nobles like Oreb and Zeeb—all their princes like Zebah and Zalmunna, who said, "Let us take possession of the pasturelands of God." My God, make them like tumbleweed, like chaff before the wind. As a fire burns a forest, and as a flame sets mountains ablaze, so pursue them with Your tempest, and terrify them with Your storm. Cover their faces with shame, so they may seek Your Name—ADONAI. Let them be ashamed and dismayed forever. Let them be humiliated and perish. Let them know that You alonewhose Name is ADONAI—are El Elyon over all the earth.

—PSALMS 83:2–19

5. And whereas You, El Shaddai, YHVH, ADONAI promised to Abraham, Isaac, and Yaakov that You will bless those who bless their descendants and utter a word of complete destruction and annihilation against those people and nations that take Israel lightly, we, UNIFY, demand that this key given to Abraham be put in the curse/ close position for the UN, all its charters, buildings, sub-organizations, finances, authority, and influence as You promised in Your Word.

6. We ask You, God of Israel, to spare the nations that have defunded UNRWA, that have stood by Israel in the UN, giving them time to exit this accursed and doomed organization before its full destruction.

7. We ask You, YHVH Tzva'ot, to raise up, favor, fund, anoint, and bless the United Nations for Israel for such a time and forever as this is the community of sheep nations, bringing blessing, justice, and shalom to the nations by standing with Your people Israel as Ruth with Naomi and upholding Your land covenant with them up to 1000 generations.

"Sing and rejoice, O daughter of Zion! For behold, I am coming, and I will live among you'—it is a declaration of ADONAI.

'In that day, many nations will join themselves to ADONAI, and they will be My people, and I will dwell among you.' Then you will know that ADONAI-Tzva'ot has sent me to you. ADONAI will inherit Judah as His portion in the holy land and will once again choose Jerusalem. Be silent before ADONAI, all flesh, for He has aroused Himself from His holy dwelling."

—ZECHARIAH 2:14–17

CHAPTER 10

THE KINGDOM AT WAR

By Apostle Dawid Yosef Lee, Malaysia

> "So then, anyone who knows the right thing to do and fails to do it is committing a sin."
>
> — JACOB 4:17 CJB

WE ARE IN THE end times, and Daniel was told that then many will "run back and forth, and knowledge will increase" (Dan. 12:4). Since the October 7 atrocities against Israel, we've witnessed through social media and local news numerous betrayals, acts of hatred, and false accusations. Some have even propagated lies in an attempt to deny the massacres suffered by Israel. The reprehensible nature of the Antimesitojuz principality* has been laid bare. As Yeshua foretold in Matthew 24:12, the love of many people has grown cold as a result of their distancing from the Torah—the righteous teachings of our Creator, Elohim, and His good news through the Jewish Messiah, Yeshua. Nevertheless, whoever holds on till the end will be saved. Those who possess discernment will shine like the brightness on heaven's

---

* Anti-Messiah, Anti-Israel, Anti-Torah, Anti-Jewish, Anti-Zionist

dome, and those who guide many towards righteousness will be like the stars forever and ever (Daniel 12:3).

The kingdom is now at war! But some might ask, "What kingdom?" My answer is the kingdom of God through Israel! Yeshua said, "If I drive out demons by the Spirit of God, then the kingdom of God has come upon you!" He said this 2000 years ago while preaching about the kingdom to the Jews in Israel. (Matthew 12:28)

Do you recognize the kingdom? Did you know that the kingdom of God on earth is manifested through the restoration of physical/natural Israel, both the land and the people? His holy prophets, all of them, spoke and prophesied about the restoration of Israel, both the land and the Jewish people.

> "So times of relief might come from the presence of ADONAI, and He might send Yeshua, the Messiah appointed for you. Heaven must receive Him until the time of the restoration of all the things that God spoke about long ago through the mouth of His holy prophets."
>
> —ACTS 3:20–21

Yeshua taught His disciples to pray to Abba for His kingdom to come on earth and His will to be done on earth as it is in Heaven. I believe in His Word, and for 2000 years, many have been praying for the kingdom to come. Then, on May 14, 1948, in one day, the nation of Israel was established. When Israel became a nation again after 2000 years of exile, many, especially Christians, couldn't believe it because many were taught that God had chosen the church to replace Israel, implying that Israel no longer held significance as the church had supposedly taken her place.

On that singular day of the reestablishment of the State of Israel, the God of Israel began the process of rebuilding and restoring the fallen sukkah of David (as prophesied in Amos 9:11–12; Acts 15:16–17), a promise made to King David that he would have a descendant sitting on the throne of Israel forever (Jer. 33:17). The God of Israel is preparing for the return of the Son of David—Yeshua—to take His rightful throne on earth in Yerushalayim (Jerusalem). HalleluYah!

Given that, why do many fail to recognize Israel as the kingdom of God manifesting on earth? The Son of Man, the Jewish Messiah Yeshua, who preached about the kingdom, holds the perfect answer.

> 'Now there was a man, a Pharisee named Nicodemus, a ruler of the Jewish people. He came to Yeshua at night and said, "Rabbi, we know that You, a teacher, have come from God. For no one can perform these signs that You do unless God is with Him!" Yeshua answered him, "Amen, amen, I tell you, unless one is born from above, he cannot see the kingdom of God."'
>
> —JOHN 3:1-3

Yeshua answered him, "I tell you that unless a person is born again from above, he cannot see the kingdom of God."

When the church of Constantine (325 AD) embraced replacement theology, teaching hatred towards the Jews or anything related to them, it became anti-Messiah/anti-anointing. People could not be born again because of their rejection of the anointing, which is the Holy Spirit, Ruach HaKodesh. Consequently, it fails to perceive the kingdom, blinded by a man-made religion that calls for separation from the Jewish Messiah, Yeshua, and His Spirit (the anointing).

We must understand that the root of this cancer in these religious teachings, which vehemently advocate for the rejection of all things

Jewish, is connected to the delay in the return of Yeshua as the sovereign King of the Universe. He will eventually reign on His throne in Israel. This is why it is important to act now and separate yourself from the teachings of replacement theology.

So now that we've understood what the kingdom is and why it's important, let us find out what we can do when the kingdom is at war. How can we stand with Israel during this time?

> **"For our struggle is not against flesh and blood, but against the rulers, against the authorities, against the powers of this dark world and against the spiritual forces of evil in the heavenly realms."**
>
> — EPHESIANS 6:12

Many in the Far East who receive the kingdom of God like a little child (Luke 18:17) have been actively standing with the kingdom of God in support of Israel. By the grace of Yah, after the annual Sukkot Tour ended, our group from the Far East could still stay in Israel for more than two weeks after October 7, becoming witnesses for Israel during this critical time. They were witnesses in an interview conducted in Moshav Yakhini, where a close Jewish friend had lost both his brother and cousin on the same morning. The team from the Far East also contributed by assisting in the Beit Hogla fruit orchard when their regular helpers had left for IDF reserve duty in Gaza.

After returning to our respective nations, the Far East continues to be 'the voice of these ashes', sharing the truth about what they witnessed firsthand regarding the brutality of Hamas toward the Israelis at the kibbutzim and moshavim in the Gaza Strip on the morning of October 7. We are active in social media, disseminating the truth about the kingdom of Israel and debunking numerous lies propagated by nations speaking against Israel. Our team keeps spreading the truth, one person at a time, to those who doubt or are confused by local media reports about Israel's war, becoming witnesses for Israel by speaking the truth.

One of our teams resides in a Muslim-majority country where displaying an Israeli flag could lead to a six-month jail sentence; they are fully aware that their battle is not against mere humans. The team has been echoing the sound of shofars across the land, proclaiming unity among nations in support of Israel, akin to a United Nations for Israel. They actively forbid and dismantle altars rooted in Sheol, knowing that such forces will not triumph against the kingdom of God through Israel.

The Act of Restitution

Archbishop Dominiquae writes in her book *The Voice of These Ashes*[*] that "Restitution means making reparations, repaying what was stolen or damaged with interest, and doing good in response to past evil committed by an individual or their ancestors against someone. This includes all nations that are represented by the United Nations and that have constantly bashed Israel unjustly. It includes every church that espouses replacement theology, pride, or a condescending attitude against the Jews or the State of Israel. It includes every government that opposes the restoration of the Jewish people back to every part of their covenant land, every mosque that spews venom and hatred against the Jews, and every family where Jews are made light of or mocked."

In 2 Samuel 21:4-6, we learn that when King David performed acts of restitution, curses were broken, and prayers were answered. The Far East teams have done acts of restitution by donating to planting fruit trees in areas where Hamas rockets have destroyed them, purchasing

---

[*] To order the *The Voice of These Ashes* book, visit at www.ZionsGospel.com

food vouchers for people displaced from the communities near the Gaza border, and more.

We invite you to join us and be part of this restoration act in making restitution! Your voice matters. Though you might think your actions are small, remember what Yeshua said:

> 'The Kingdom of Heaven is like a mustard seed that a man plants in his field. It is the smallest of all seeds, but when it grows, it becomes the largest of garden plants; it becomes a tree, and birds come and make nests in its branches.'
>
> —Matthew 13:31-32 nivuk

> 'Do not neglect doing good and sharing, for with such sacrifices God is well pleased.'
>
> —Hebrews 13:16

CHAPTER 11

WHY PLANT FRUIT TREES IN ISRAEL?

> Then ADONAI Elohim planted a garden in Eden in the east, and there He put the man whom He had formed.
>
> — GENESIS 2:8

During these days of the war of light vs. darkness, Israel against brutal Hamas, we are engaging more than ever to bring life and comfort to the suffering Jewish people.

"Comfort, comfort My people," says your God.

—ISAIAH 40:1

One of our main projects is planting 1200 fruit trees as a living memorial for those murdered by Hamas during the October 7 massacre on the 7th Day in Shmini Atseret/ Simcha Torah.

"Remember what Amalek did to you along the way as you came out of Egypt—how he happened upon you along the way and attacked those among you in the rear, all the stragglers behind you, when you were tired and weary—he did not fear God."

— Deuteronomy 25:17-18

Why is this so important? What is the big deal about trees, especially fruit trees? Why is it that Hamas has been launching thousands of rockets for many years since 2005 to destroy the fields of the farmers near the Gaza border?

Why was it a big trophy for the Palestinian cause, Hamas terrorists, and their sympathizers to destroy the hot houses and fruitful fields of Gush Katif in Gaza? Why did they turn this booming, blooming, exquisite agriculture into terror fields of death to launch Qassam rockets on innocent Israeli civilians and their farms and fields? Why is it that the Gazan Arabs did not continue to work the fields of Gush Katif and use the state-of-the-art agricultural infrastructure and hot houses left by the expelled Israelis to produce more fruits and vegetables? Why is it that Jews plant trees and farms and Palestinian Arabs in Gaza, led by Hamas, plant terror bases?

This is the difference between a culture of life and a culture of death. We are warned in the Torah not to destroy fruit trees!

> "When you lay siege to a city for a long time, making war against it to capture it, you are not to destroy its trees by swinging an axe at them. For from them you may eat, so you shall not chop them down. For is the tree of the field human, that it should be besieged by you?
>
> —Deuteronomy 20:19 stb

When Elohim created the earth, the first thing He did after creating Adam was plant a garden. He forever established the relationship between humans and trees. Humans are called to work in the gardens, to create farms that in turn produce wonderful food for humans. It is healthy agriculture that sustains life on earth, and it is the first job given to man.

> "Then ADONAI Elohim took the man and gave him rest in the Garden of Eden in order to cultivate and watch over it."
>
> — GENESIS 2:15

When the Jews started returning to Israel from their exiles, they bought swamps, desert fields, and rockeries from the Turks. They envisioned conquering the land through agriculture, not bullets. This, in turn, would bring prosperity to the Arabs in the land and to the entire Middle East. Israel's neighbors have chosen bullets again and again, attacking the Jewish nation again and again, leaving us no choice but to fight and defend ourselves.

> "I am for shalom, and thus I speak, but they are for war!"
>
> —PSALMS 120:7

Israel is known for its agriculture, as the land flows with milk and honey. Islam ruled Israel through the Ottoman Empire for 400 years, from the 16th to the 20th centuries. Turkish law forced a tax on every tree people had. The Arab inhabitants of the land deemed money to be more important than trees, and they chopped down their trees, effectively creating a desolate desert land. Look all over the Middle East; wherever Islam rules, it creates a desert. Only Israel is the exception! Here, the Jews rule, and the desert has been and is being conquered by agriculture and the planting of trees. Israel's agricultural innovations and drip irrigation technology have brought *life* and prosperity to many nations.

> "Then you will live in the land that I gave to your fathers. You will be My people and I will be your God.
> I will multiply the fruit of the tree and the produce of the field, so that you will no longer bear the disgrace of famine among the nations."
>
> —Ezekiel 36:28, 30

The enemy would like to see Israel's agriculture fail in order to bring death and famine. It has done its best for years to burn and destroy our fields, and now, after the brutal Hamas massacre of October 7 and the ensuing war with thousands of rockets falling on our fields, it has paralyzed much of our agriculture in the South through Hamas and in the North through Hezbollah.

> "Then the nations that are left all around you will know that I, Adonai, have rebuilt the ruined places, and replanted what was desolate. I, Adonai, have spoken it. So I will do it."
>
> — Ezekiel 36:36

5 Important Reasons to Plant Fruit Trees in Israel Right Now

Planting fruit trees in Israel is an act of spiritual warfare, self-defense, solidarity, restitution, and thanksgiving.

Spiritual warfare

We fight the death brought by Hamas with *life* by planting trees.

Self-defense
We help Israel defend itself against food shortage and famine.

Solidarity
We identify with Israel's agricultural trouble imposed by Hamas's destruction and link arms with her to bring *life* and rebuild.

Restitution
We make restitution for all the antisemitism in the nations against the Jewish people and their nation, Israel.

Thanksgiving
We give thanks to God and to Israel for such glorious agriculture that has brought prosperity to the world, and now the nations help Israel by bringing prosperity back to her through planting fruit trees.

> "Behold, days are soon coming"—it is a declaration of ADONAI—"when the plowman will overtake the reaper and the one treading grapes, the one sowing seed. The mountains will drip sweet wine and all the hills will melt over. Yes, I will restore the captivity of My people Israel. They will rebuild desolated cities and dwell in them. They will plant vineyards and drink their wine. They will also make gardens and eat their fruit. Yes, I will plant them on their land, and they will never again be plucked up out of their land that I have given to them." ADONAI, your God, has said it.
>
> —Amos 9:13-15

We invite you to take part in the rebuilding and restoration of Israel by planting fruit trees and helping the farmers of the Gaza border restore their glorious agriculture ruined by Hamas. Undoubtedly, the

God of Israel will be watching and blessing every tree and every one of you in the nations that donate to plant them.*

I will bless those who bless you.

—Genesis 12:3a NIV

---

* To plant trees in Israel, visit www.UnitedNationsForIsrael.org

CHAPTER 12

THE SEPARATION HAS BEGUN

> "...then the sons of God saw that the daughters of men were good and they took for themselves wives, any they chose. Then ADONAI said, "My Spirit will not remain with humankind forever, since they are flesh. So their days will be 120 years. The Nephilim were on the earth in those days, and also afterward, whenever the sons of God came to the daughters of men, and gave birth to them. Those were the mighty men of old, men of renown."
>
> — GENESIS 6:2-4 STB

THE HAPPENINGS OF GENESIS 6, creating a hybrid race between fallen humans and fallen angels, and repeated themselves even after the flood. That is why there were giants in the Land of Canaan. That is also why the people of Israel were commanded to stay separate from the Canaanites and even kill them all. The land was full of *hamas*, violence, and wickedness. The seed of man was now mixed with the perverted seed of fallen angels.

Nowadays, we see that, since the establishment of the State of Israel, Israel's enemies are mostly Arabs. The Arab nations around Israel have tried to annihilate her again and again. The Arab Palestinian cause, through Fatah, Hamas, Hezbollah, and so on, has committed acts of terror that are so despicable and beastly that it is impossible to describe. The Hamas Massacre of October 7, 2023, was so brutal that it will be remembered as another Shoah (Holocaust) Memorial Day. But who are these beasts that are able to rape mothers in front of their husbands and children, behead babies, rip pregnant women's wombs open, then urinate into their wombs, burn entire families alive (while they broadcast live and boast about it), kidnap children, babies, the elderly, and so much more. Who are these beasts without a conscience? Could it be that they are a hybrid race, and that is why they show no sign of scruples or humanity? That they are demon-possessed, it's obvious, but how about hybrids?

The meaning of the word *Arab* is very revealing; it means *mixture* or *hybrid*.

Could it be that this word contains the answer to the brutality that some (not all) Arabs show when they murder Jews? This would explain the complete absence of any conscience. Being a criminal is one thing, but being a brutal beast like Hamas, ISIS, or the Nazis is another thing. Hybrids are not salvable; they are not redeemable. They have perverted the seed of man and beast; and they can only be destroyed, like at the time of Noah, for they have filled the earth with hamas.

> "Now the earth was ruined before God, and the earth was filled with (hamas in Hebrew) violence."
>
> —GENESIS 6:11

Hamas means *violence.*

If so, we need to pray that Yah will separate those among the Arabs who are not mixed breeds (with fallen angels) from the hybrids (with fallen angels and beasts included). Not all Arabs are mixed breeds or demon-possessed by the evil spirit of Islam, but many are. I pray they will wake up before it's too late for them. A good example is Hassan Yusef, the son of a Hamas leader, who is now very vocal about destroying Hamas. He knows what he is talking about.

> "So it will come to pass if they will diligently learn the ways of My people—to swear by My name, 'As ADONAI lives,' just as they taught My people to swear by Baal—then they will be built up in the midst of My people. But if they will not obey, then I will uproot that nation, plucking it up and destroying it." It is a declaration of ADONAI.
>
> —JEREMIAH 12:16–17

The Palestinian cause that I term "Hitler's Child" is a hybrid cause between East and West: East through the Mufti Haj Amin al-Husseini and West through Adolf Hitler. This mufti was the most honored personality by the Arabs of the pre-State of Israel. He was a brutal butcher and performed serious massacres against the Jews in the land in 1929 and 1936. He was a close relative of the infamous terrorist and PLO leader, Yasser Arafat. The mufti met with Hitler in Berlin in 1941, and they agreed to birth the Palestinian cause. The purpose was the extermination of the Jews, executing Hitler's Final Solution from within the land of Israel. Neither the PLO nor the Fatah, all the way to brutal Hamas-ISIS and all other terror factions, have ever hidden their agenda. They broadcast it in Arabic on all their TV channels, loud and clear. Whether they fight politically or through brutal terror, it is always the same agenda of Hitler's Child: the annihilation of Israel and every Jew from the face of the earth.

"Thus says ADONAI, "As for all My evil neighbors who strike at the inheritance that I bequeathed to My people Israel—I am about to uproot them from their land and pluck the house of Judah from them. Yet it will come to pass, after I have uprooted them, that I will again have compassion for them, and I will bring them back, each one to his inheritance and each one to his land." So it will come to pass if they will diligently learn the ways of My people—to swear by My name, 'As ADONAI lives,' just as they taught My people to swear by Baal—then they will be built up in the midst of My people. But if they will not obey, then I will uproot that nation, plucking it up and destroying it." It is a declaration of ADONAI.

—JEREMIAH 12:14–17

The Palestinian cause, all the way to Hamas, is a fallen-angel-cause that originated from fallen angels and humans that mated physically, spiritually, and politically. All the hybrids are doomed to destruction. They have no salvation, like during the time of Noah. The sooner, the better.

"Then ADONAI saw that the wickedness of humankind was great on earth and that every inclination of the thoughts of their hearts was only evil all the time. So ADONAI regretted that He made humankind on earth, and His heart was deeply pained. So ADONAI said, "I will wipe out humankind, whom I have created, from the face of the ground, from humankind to livestock, crawling things, and the flying creatures of the sky, because I regret that I made them."

—GENESIS 6:5-7

The acts of brutality perpetrated by Hamas on October 7, 2023, on innocent Jewish families living peacefully near Gaza are only possible when there is absolutely no conscience at all. This is typical of the beastly mixed breed.

Both Ishmael and Esau's seeds (many Arabs come from them) were mixed with some of the mixed breeds among the giants in the land. Thus, Abraham told Eliezer to get Isaac a bride of pure seed from his family in Haran.

> "...so that I may make you take an oath by ADONAI, the God of heaven and the God of earth, that you will not take a wife for my son from among the daughters of the Canaanites, among whom I am dwelling."
>
> —GENESIS 24:3

Rebecca also asked Isaac to send Jacob to get a bride from her family, not from the daughters of Canaan like Esau.

> "Then Esau saw that the daughters of Canaan were contemptible in his father Isaac's eyes."
>
> — GENESIS 28:8

The daughters of Canaan did the same as the daughters of Cain in Genesis 6 and mated with fallen angels. Their offspring became the giants in the land. Islam is fallen angel worship; it has taken root among the Arabs and whatever ethnicity has mixed with fallen angels or their offspring. Nazism is also a fallen angel activity, creating a "pure" Aryan race of mixed breeds doomed for destruction.

The Jewish people who have not intermarried for generations bother the mixed breed. As long as there are true Jews, the aspiration of the fallen angels, the beast, the anti-Messiah, and ultimately Lucifer to rule the earth will be doomed to failure. Thus, YHVH said to blot out the memory of Amalek from under heaven. Amalek was a grandson of Esau who had mixed himself with the daughters of Canaan, ones who were "contemptible." They had lent themselves to procreate with fallen angels and had borne giants and Nephilim. Amalek was a mixed breed, and like all mixed breeds, they hate the true seed of Abraham, Isaac, and Jacob and try to destroy the Jews in every generation.

> "ADONAI said to Moses, "Write this for a memorial in the book, and rehearse it in the hearing of Joshua, for I will utterly blot out the memory of the Amalekites from under heaven." Then Moses built an altar and called it ADONAI-Nissi. Then he said, "By the hand upon the throne of ADONAI, ADONAI will have war with Amalek from generation to generation."
>
> —Exodus 17:14–16

Remember Haman the Agagite in Persia? He was an Amalekite who, sure enough, did his best to exterminate the Jewish people in order to rule supreme. But for Mordechai and Queen Esther! Still, this Amalek remains present in Persia, modern-day Iran, through Islam.

The Torah does not allow mixed marriage in order to prevent marriage with hybrids. The *brit chadasha* (new covenant) forbids marriage between believers and unbelievers, thus always preventing the mixture between God-Elohim the Creator and *Beli-al*, meaning "non-submitted to the One above." The *Beli-al* are Lucifer and the fallen angels in charge of powers, principalities, and their *hybrid* offspring.

The Separation has Begun

"What harmony does Messiah have with Belial? Or what part does a believer have in common with an unbeliever?"

—2 Corinthians 6:15

Warning: Though many Jews have not yet recognized Yeshua as the Messiah, that does not make them "unbelievers." In fact, many of them have faith in YHVH, which will put the faith of many so-called "believers" to shame. It will be these Jews who will encounter Yeshua in a miraculous way as they stand up to the whole world who comes against them! These are the religious Zionist Jews, the Torah-observant ones.

"Then I will pour out on the house of David and the inhabitants of Jerusalem a spirit of grace and supplication, when they will look towards Me whom they pierced. They will mourn for him as one mourns for an only son and grieve bitterly for him as one grieves for a firstborn. On that day, there will be great mourning in Jerusalem, mourning like Hadad-rimmon in the valley of Megiddo. The land will mourn clan by clan. The clan of the house of David by itself and their wives by themselves, the clan of the house of Nathan by itself and their wives by themselves,"

— Zechariah 12:10-12

The Hamas brutal massacre and all the Palestinian cause supported by Arabs and most Muslims are clearly a battle for world rulership. The only ones that stand in their way are the true seed of Abraham, Isaac, and Jacob, the Jewish people—especially the Torah-keeping ones, who have true faith and have remained Jewish for generations. However, all the Jews are this wicked beast's target.

> And from out of his mouth, the serpent spewed water like a river after the woman in order to sweep her away with a flood.
>
> —THE REVELATION 12:15

And this is especially true of the Messianic Jews that are Torah observant (keep His commandments) and are filled with His Spirit (the Spirit of prophecy is the testimony of Yeshua—Rev. 19:10a).

> **So the dragon became enraged at the woman and went off to make war with the rest of her offspring—those who keep the commandments of God and hold to the testimony of Yeshua.**
>
> —THE REVELATION 12:17

Satan thought that by crucifying the King of the Jews, Yeshua, he accomplished his goal. However, He rose from the dead, glorified. His people, the Jewish people, who carry that Spirit of the Resurrection of the Messiah even when they do not know Him. What many during this war against the beast of Hamas call "the Spirit of Israel" that is upon the IDF and the civilians is none other than the Spirit of Messiah that is upon Israel as a nation. Thus, Israel will prevail against all odds and will defeat the beast, the false prophet, and the anti-Messiah.

It will not be easy, but it is happening even right now. The Spirit of Israel will prevail because the Spirit of the Messiah upon Israel will prevail.

> But Judah will be inhabited forever—Jerusalem from generation to generation.
>
> —JOEL 4:20

Warning: Try not to figure out the God of Israel. Just stand with His Jewish people against all odds; the separation has begun between:

1. Wheat (pure human seed, physical and spiritual)
2. Tares (hybrid seed of humans with fallen angels, physical and spiritual)
3. Sheep Nations (that stood with Israel at the time of her need) (see Matthew 25:32)
4. Goat Nations (that were neutral or opposed Israel, pro-Palestinian, antisemitic, anti-Zionist)

"So the slaves of the landowner came and said to him, 'Master, didn't you sow good seed in your field? Then where did the weeds come from?' But he replied, 'An enemy did this.' Now the slaves say to him, 'Do you want us, then, to go out and gather them up?' But he says, 'No, for while you are gathering up the weeds, you may uproot the wheat with them. Let both grow together until the harvest. At harvest time, I will tell the reapers, "First, gather up the weeds and tie them in bundles to burn them up; but gather the wheat into my barn."'"

—Matthew 13:27–30

It is now harvest time, and the separation has begun: wheat and tares, sheep and goat nations will all be revealed. Those who stand with Israel, the Jewish people, the God of Israel, and the land of Israel will be separated from those who oppose His eternal covenant with the people of Israel. This includes all the Arabs in the world that are being tested by this.

And confirmed to Jacob as a decree, to Israel as an everlasting covenant, saying, "To you I give the land of Canaan, the portion of your inheritance."

—Psalms 105:10–11

Those who oppose this eternal covenant will be completely destroyed.

"Draw near, O nations, to hear, and listen, O peoples! Let the earth hear, and all it contains is the world and all its offspring! For Adonai is enraged at all the nations and furious at all their armies. He will utterly destroy them. He will give them over to slaughter. So their slain will be thrown out, the stench of their corpses will rise, and the hills will be drenched with their blood. Then all the hosts of heaven will dissolve, and the skies will be rolled up like a scroll, so all their array will wither away, like a leaf drooping from a vine, like a fig shriveling from a fig tree.
For Adonai has a day of vengeance, a year of recompense for the hostility against Zion."

—Isaiah 34:1-4, 8

Are you *actively* standing with Israel against all odds? Neutrality is the same as complicity with the brutal Hamas Massacre, the Shoah (Holocaust) of October 7, 2023. Babies were «cooked» in ovens, mothers were repeatedly raped, babies were beheaded, entire families were burnt alive inside their bomb shelters, and hundreds were kidnapped. Gaza civilians were no better; they came out in the thousands, mostly young and Arab children, full of hatred for the Jews, to loot, to cheer, to gloat, and to spoil. Yes! Gaza's *civil* population. Gaza is

Hamas; Hamas is Gaza and Hezbollah and Iran and Fatah and ISIS and Nazism and more!

Neutrality is *not* an option! Siding with the UN, which did not condemn these hyenas' crimes, is not an option. The God of Israel is watching, recording, and separating.

> "Now this is the writing that was inscribed: MENE, MENE, TEKEL UPHARSIN."
>
> —Daniel 5:25

The handwriting is on the wall of the UN, any nation, church, or individual that sides with the fallen angel, mixed breed cause, called the Palestinian cause in its entirety. It is either Israel and the Jewish people or them. They have made this abundantly clear, and there are no excuses for ignorance, neutrality, or any other antisemitic, anti-Zionist attitude.

> "For the day of Adonai is near against all the nations. As you have done, it shall be done to you. Your dealings will return on your own head. For just as you have drunk on My holy mountain, so all the nations shall drink continually. Yes, they will drink, gulp down, and then be as though they had never existed. But on Mount Zion, there will be deliverance, and it will be holy. Then the house of Jacob will dispossess those who dispossessed them."
>
> —Obadiah 1:15-17

CHAPTER 13

THE ISRAEL CONTROVERSY

Israel's 75th Anniversary Special Edition

> "'Nevertheless, I will bring health and healing to it; I will heal my people and will let them enjoy abundant peace and security. I will bring Judah and Israel back from captivity and will rebuild them as they were before. I will cleanse them from all the sin they have committed against me and will forgive all their sins of rebellion against me. Then this city will bring me renown, joy, praise and honor before all nations on earth that hear of all the good things I do for it; and they will be in awe and will tremble at the abundant prosperity and peace I provide for it.'"
>
> — JEREMIAH 33:6-9 NIV

Conflicting opinions

Why are the nations in uproar and the peoples devising a vain thing?

—Psalm 2:1 nasb '95

The Israel Factor

AFTER 75 YEARS OF the miraculous establishment of the modern-day State of Israel, the controversy against it and its people seems to be raging more than ever. Many people groups are claiming the Land of Israel as "theirs." Others have gone as far as to contest the fact that the Jewish people in the land today are not the real, natural seed of Abraham, not real Jews but rather the sons of a certain Khezar ethnic group in Turkey. Even within Israel, there are different controversies.

The "right-wing," for the most part, is against the dividing of the land for "peace" with the Palestinians; the "left-wing" is for peace at all costs, and the majority is hanging between the two. Among the Orthodox Jews, the pendulum fluctuates between the extreme "right" that is calling for the deportation of all the so-called "Palestinians" to Jordan and the extreme "left" that says that we have no rights to the land until the Messiah comes, so we are in sin having a secular Israel State.

Among Christians, there are lots of controversies about Israel's right to the land. Among the extreme "right," we have the Christian Zionists who are standing with Israel at all costs, even if they have to fight themselves for the land. They are rallying themselves with the Likud and PM Benjamin Netanyahu. Then there are those of us who are rallied with the fullness of the land covenant and the settlement movement represented by Nahala, the Religious Zionists, and Itamar Ben Gvir. We are very aware that any treaties like the Abraham Accords that stop the settlement of Judea and Samaria manifest in the judgment of the nations and great suffering for Israel.

> "For behold, in those days and at that time, When I restore the fortunes of Judah and Jerusalem, I will gather all the nations and bring them down to the valley of Jehoshaphat. Then I will enter into judgment with them there on behalf of My people

and My inheritance, Israel, whom they have scattered among the nations; and they have divided up My land."

—Joel 3:1-2 NASB '95

And then there are millions of Christians that side with the Palestinian cause, which is nothing but Hitler's child. This was concocted between the mufti of Jerusalem, Haj Amin Al Husseini, and Adolf Hitler in 1942 in Berlin. Their purpose was to implement the Nazi Final Solution within the borders of the covenant land and use the Palestinian cause as the "Trojan Horse" to bring about the annihilation of the Jews in their land.

Israel is the only country in the Middle East where the common Arab man and woman are allowed to prosper. The Palestinian cause is a deathly, murderous, antisemitic fabrication. Their own Arab people suffer from this as the babies and little children are intoxicated with hatred against the Jews. Just like Hitler used the children and the youth to become haters and murderers of Jews, so is the Palestinian cause following Hitler's style and pattern. Their military training marches to the goose step just like the Nazi army did. The sad part is that millions of dollars and euros are funneled through Christian NGOs to usurp land and actually fund terror against Israel.

Much of the antisemitism we see today in universities and on the streets is fueled by the supporters of the Palestinian fabrication. This happens in Israel, America, France, and everywhere else in the world. Supporting the Trojan Horse of Hitler is the same as Nazi antisemitism!

The Arabs will only prosper in Israel once they honor Israel; other than that, they will be destroyed by the God of Israel.

> "Thus says YHVH concerning all My wicked neighbors who strike at the inheritance with which I have endowed My people Israel, "Behold I am about to uproot them from their land and will uproot the house of Judah from among them. And it will come about that after I have uprooted them, I will again have compassion on them; and I will bring them back, each one to his inheritance and each one to his land. Then if they will really learn the ways of My people, to swear by My name, 'As YHVH lives,' even as they taught My people to swear by Baal, they will be built up in the midst of My people. But if they will not listen, then I will uproot that nation, uproot and destroy it," declares YHVH."
>
> —Jeremiah 12:14-17 stb

And there is no such thing as Palestinians; these are all Arabs with roots in other Arab nations. Please watch my video Hitler's Child,* and be enlightened with information faithful to historical truth. Christians that support the Palestinian cause with their money and activism have forgotten that the Messiah is Jewish and that He has given His people the land and brought them back. These Christians are putting themselves and their nations under a terrible curse.

> "For Adonai has a day of vengeance, a year of recompense for the hostility against Zion."
>
> —Isaiah 34:8

Please read and gift my book *The Identity Theft*** to reeducate the entire Church in this urgent matter.

---

* Watch at www.youtube.com/watch?v=lJCQuQm3Pnw
** To order, visit www.ZionsGospel.com

Let us Hear His Words

For Zion's sake I will not keep silent, for Jerusalem's sake I will not rest, until her righteousness shines out brightly, and her salvation as a blazing torch. Nations will see your righteousness, and all kings your glory. You will be called by a new name, which Adonai's mouth will bestow.
On your walls, Jerusalem, I have set watchmen. All day and all night, they will never hold their peace. "You who remind Adonai, take no rest for yourselves, and give Him no rest until He establishes and makes Jerusalem a praise in the earth.

—Isaiah 62:1-2, 6-7

Thus says Adonai Elohim: "Look, I will lift My hand to the nations, and raise My banner to the peoples! They will bring your sons on their chest, and carry your daughters on their shoulders. Kings will be your guardians, their princesses your nurses. They will bow down to you with their face to the ground, and lick the dust of your feet. Then you will know that I am Adonai—those hoping in Me will not be ashamed." Can plunder be taken from the mighty, or captives of the righteous freed? For thus says Adonai: Yes, captives of the mighty will be taken and the prey of the tyrant will be freed. For I will oppose your adversary. I will save your children. I will feed your oppressors their flesh. They will be drunk with their blood as with sweet wine. Then all flesh will know that I, Adonai, am your Savior and your Redeemer, the Mighty One of Jacob."

—Isaiah 49:22-26

> Hear the word of ADONAI, O nations, and declare it in the distant islands, and say: 'He who scattered Israel will gather and watch over him, as a shepherd does his flock.' For ADONAI has ransomed Jacob. He redeemed him from the hand of one stronger than he. They will come and sing on Zion's height, radiant over the bounty of ADONAI—over the grain, the wine, the oil, and the young of the flock. Their life will be like a watered garden, and they will never languish again. Then will the virgin rejoice in the dance, both young men and old men together. For I will turn their mourning into joy, and I will comfort them, and make them rejoice out of their sorrow. I will fill the soul of the kohanim with fatness and My people will be satisfied with My goodness." It is a declaration of ADONAI.
>
> —JEREMIAH 31:10-14

The Land of Israel is called the glory of all the lands!

> On that day I swore to them, to bring them out from the land of Egypt into a land that I had selected for them, flowing with milk and honey, which is the glory of all lands.
>
> —EZEKIEL 20:6 NASB '95

Thriving in the Midst of Controversy

In the midst of all this controversy and against all odds, a thriving Jewish nation has arisen out of the ashes of the Nazi Shoah (Holocaust) and of 2000 years of mainly Christian and Muslim persecution. This is a mosaic of people that has one thing in common: they have preserved their Jewish identity as descendants of Abraham, Isaac, and Jacob and have declared on every Passover for 2000 years: "next year in Jerusalem." They come from all over the world and in all colors, but they have paid with their blood for their identity, as the only common denominator has been that they have all suffered persecution and discrimination for being Jewish and holding to their Jewish faith or desire for the Land of Israel. Unfortunately, better than all the DNA tests as to "who is a Jew" were those who persecuted and massacred the Jews for being "Jewish" and holding to the Torah and to the traditions. The best "DNA test" was Hitler himself, who found Jewish blood all the way to the third and fourth generations of those who converted to other religions and deported them to death camps!

The survivors of these have established modern-day Israel and have purchased the land with their blood, have fought all the numerous wars, intifadas, terror attempts, and "world opinion," and are still here fighting to this day.

In that sense, I would agree with our first prime minister after 2000 years of painful exile, Mr. David Ben Gurion, who stated that whoever wanted to join their destiny with Israel and invest their blood, sweat, and tears in making this land bloom was welcome! Where were all those who claim today ownership of the land when he made the statement? Where were the "Ephraimite Christians" when he called people from the nations to help us conquer the vast and unbearably hot Negev-Desert of Israel? Where were the people of Gaza when the first Israeli settlers nearly 40 years ago came to make the "accursed sands" bloom and were received with bread and salt by the local Arab Sheikh?

Where were all the peoples of the earth that covet the Land of Israel today, when in the last 2000 years prior to the return of the Jews, the land languished in disrepair to the point that Mark Twain, the famous Christian writer, said while visiting it in the 19th century that it looked so desolate as if "forgotten by God" and that he saw goats eating gravel as there was nothing else to eat!

...A desolate country whose soil is rich enough, but is given over wholly to weeds... a silent mournful expanse... a desolation... we never saw a human being on the whole route... hardly a tree or shrub anywhere. Even the olive tree and the cactus, those fast friends of a worthless soil, had almost deserted the country."*

A land full of rocks, sand, and swamps has been turned into a Garden of Eden, a modern-day, high-tech, vibrant country by a bunch of "Holocaust survivors" and other Jewish survivors from many nations that their only common denominator was that they suffered for being Jews and it is only under their hand that the Holy Land has bloomed in 2000 years!

> **In that day I will raise up the fallen booth of David, and wall up its breaches; I will also raise up its ruins and rebuild it as in the days of old; that they may possess the remnant of Edom and all the nations who are called by My name," declares the LORD who does this.**
>
> **—AMOS 9:11-12 NASB '95**

Is the modern-day nation of Israel perfect? By no means! The Prophet Ezekiel expressed the condition of the people who were going to return in no uncertain terms:

> For I will take you out of the nations; I will gather you from all the countries and bring you back into your own land. I will sprinkle clean water on you, and you will be clean; I will cleanse you from all your impurities and from all your idols. I will give you a new heart and put a new spirit in you; I will remove from you your heart of stone and give you a heart of flesh. And I will put my Spirit in you and move you to follow

---

* *Innocents Abroad* by Mark Twain

my decrees and be careful to keep my laws. Then you will live in the land I gave your ancestors; you will be my people, and I will be your God.

—Ezekiel 36:24-28 niv

But he also stated that YHVH was going to restore His people for the sake of His holy name so that the nations may fear His name.

> May God be gracious to us and bless us. May He cause His face to shine upon us—Selah
> so that Your way may be known on earth, and Your salvation among all nations.

—Psalm 67:2-3

The Key Issue

This writer believes that as Christians in the nations join in and cooperate in practical and spiritual ways with the restoration of Israel, the covenant promise given to Abraham will come into effect, and they will be mightily blessed!

> And I will bless those who bless you, and the one who curses you I will curse. And in you all the families of the earth will be blessed.

—Genesis 12:3 nasb '95

YHVH is defining His enemies or His friends according to their stand and behavior towards His plan to restore the Jewish people to His land and to save all of Israel. On which side you are will determine the blessing or the curse on this earth and forever for you, your family, and your nations.

> The King (Yeshua the Jewish Messiah) will answer and say to them, 'Truly I say to you, to the extent that you did it to one of these brothers of Mine (Jewish people), even the least of them, you did it to Me.'
>
> —Matthew 25:40 nasb '95

Who is the Owner of the Land of Israel?

First of all, as we celebrate Israel's 75th anniversary, let us remember that the land belongs to YHVH.

> The land, moreover, shall not be sold permanently, for the land is Mine; for you are but aliens and sojourners with Me.
>
> —Leviticus 25:23 nasb '95

He has given it to the people of Israel forever!*

> All the land that you see I will give to you and your offspring forever.
>
> —Genesis 13:15 niv

Remember your servants Abraham, Isaac and Israel, to whom you swore by your own self: 'I will make your descendants as numerous as the stars in the sky and I will give your descen-

---

* Genesis 12:7, Genesis 13:15, 15:18, 17:18, 24:7, 26:3, 28:4, 13, 35:12, 48:4, Exodus 32:13, 33:1, Deuteronomy 1:8, 11:9, 34:4, 2 Chronicles 20:7, Nehemiah 1:8, Jeremiah 23:8, Jeremiah 30:10,11, 46:27-28, 1 Chronicles 16:13-18

dants all this land I promised them, and it will be their inheritance forever.'

—Exodus 32:13 NIV

He has remembered His covenant forever, the word which He commanded to a thousand generations, the covenant which He made with Abraham, and His oath to Isaac. Then He confirmed it to Jacob for a statute, to Israel as an everlasting covenant, saying, "To you I will give the land of Canaan as the portion of your inheritance.

—Psalm 105:8-11 NASB '95

The descendants of Abraham, Isaac, and Jacob in the flesh are the Jewish people of today.*

From the Babylonian Exile and Until This Day, the History of Israel is the History of the Jewish People.

Judah has preeminence over all the other tribes, which is why the people of Israel today are called Jews, though other nations may join them!**

Judah, your brothers shall praise you; your hand shall be on the neck of your enemies; your father's sons shall bow down to you.

—Genesis 49:8 NIV

YHVH said Judah and Jerusalem are established forever.***

---
* See Hosea 1:6, 7, the Book of Esther, Ezra and Nehemiah
** Genesis 49:8, Numbers 2:9, 10:14, Judges 20:18, 2 Samuel 19:43
*** Jeremiah 33:7, 12-26, Joel 3:1, 20-21, Zechariah 2:9-13

> But Judah will be inhabited forever—Jerusalem from generation to generation. I will acquit their bloodguilt that I had not acquitted, for ADONAI dwells in Zion.
>
> —JOEL 4:20-21

Yeshua the Messiah is Jewish, born in the Tribe of Judah.*

> So all the generations from Abraham to David are fourteen generations, from David until the Babylonian exile are fourteen generations, and from the Babylonian exile until the Messiah are fourteen generations.
>
> —MATTHEW 1:17

Gentiles are grafted into the "Jewish olive tree" whose root is the Torah and the Jewish Messiah Yeshua!**

> Thus says ADONAI-Tzva'ot, "In those days it will come to pass that ten men from every language of the nations will grasp the corner of the garment of a Jew saying, 'Let us go with you, for we have heard that God is with you.'"
>
> —ZECHARIAH 8:23

There is a representation of all 12 tribes among the Jewish people of today. They joined with Judah when the House of Israel, Northern Kingdom (10 "lost" tribes) was divorced by YHVH. These did not lose their Israelite identity, and Paul recognized them as Israel, and so did Yaakov (Jacob). They are part of Israel as Jews to this day.***

---

* Matthew 1, Micah 5:2, and Revelation 5:5)
** Romans 11:17, Isaiah 56, Zechariah 2: 9-13, Zechariah 8:23
*** Acts 26:7, Yaakov 1:1 (James)

> Jacob, a slave of God and of the LORD Yeshua the Messiah, to the twelve tribes in the Diaspora: Shalom!
>
> —YAAKOV (JAMES) 1:1

Notice that he was not addressing the "Ephraimites" or grafted-in Gentiles but rather the natural descendants of the 12 tribes that were dispersed abroad after the Assyrians conquered the Northern Kingdom. A remnant of them was still connected to Judah and was not lost among the Gentiles like most of the 10 tribes. They are among the Jewish people to this day.

Commonwealth of Israel

The Gentiles grafted into the covenant through the blood of Yeshua, the Jewish Messiah, become part of the Commonwealth of Israel, not as partakers of the land but of the covenant and the same Elohim Gospel and Torah.

> Therefore, keep in mind that once you—Gentiles in the flesh—were called "uncircumcision" by those called "circumcision" (which is performed on flesh by hand). At that time you were separate from Messiah, excluded from the commonwealth of Israel and strangers to the covenants of promise, having no hope and without God in the world. But now in Messiah Yeshua, you who once were far off have been brought near by the blood of the Messiah. For He is our shalom, the One who made the two into one and broke down the middle wall of separation.
>
> —EPHESIANS 2:11-14

It is the same way that India is part of the Commonwealth of Great Britain yet cannot claim ownership of its land.

A very important thing to consider is that most commonwealth citizens are not qualified to hold 'right of abode.' Basically, you cannot settle in the UK unless you go through immigration controls. If you have direct relatives who were born in the UK, you may qualify for the right to abode. If granted entry, you can settle and after five years apply for British Naturalization.*

YHVH never divorced Judah and, together with those who escaped the judgment from the Northern Kingdom, comprises the Jewish people and the Land of Israel of today.

> Then she conceived again, and bore a daughter. And He said to him: "Name her Lo-ruhamah—for no longer will I have compassion on the house of Israel that I should ever pardon them. But on the house of Judah I will have compassion and deliver them by ADONAI, their God, yet not by bow, sword or battle, nor by horses and horsemen."
>
> —HOSEA 1:6-7

Many non-ethnic Jews became as Jews during history such as Rahab, Ruth, Tamar and many during the time of Queen Esther during the Persian Empire.**

> In each and every province and in each and every city, wherever the king's commandment and his decree arrived, there was gladness and joy for the Jews, a feast and a holiday. And many

---

* www.worldimmigrationguide.net
** Esther 8:17, Matthew 1

among the peoples of the land became Jews, for the dread of the Jews had fallen on them.

—Esther 8:17 nasb '95

Mostly, those Jews that survived terrible persecutions and humiliations and remained faithful to their identity have made it to live in the Land of Israel.

A Remnant Like Ruth

Many millions in the world may have Israelite blood but forsook their identity due to persecution or idolatry, and they cannot claim rights to the land, though a remnant will return eventually.

Ephraim became the fullness of the Gentiles, or a multitude of nations, for redemptive purposes[*]. As uncircumcised Gentiles (Christians), they can come into the covenant but cannot claim "Israelite identity" or rights to the land. This very subject is distracting many from participating as grafted in from the Gentiles in the restoration of Israel (Jewish people today) and is bringing unnecessary tension, confusion, and contention.

A remnant of Christians like Ruth has been settling in the Land because of their sacrificial love towards the Jewish people. YHVH is choosing those particular individuals. They don't come with "claims" or to "compete" for the rights to the Land but to serve the Jewish people.**

> **Boaz replied and said to her, "All that you have done for your mother-in-law since your husband's death has been fully reported to me—how you left your father and mother and the land of your birth, and came to a people you did not know**

---
* Genesis 48:13-19
** Ruth 1:16, 17, 2:11, 12, Isaiah 49:22, Isaiah 60:22, Genesis 12:3

before. May Adonai repay you for what you have done, and may you be fully rewarded by Adonai, God of Israel, under whose wings you have come to take refuge."

—Ruth 2:11-12

Foreigners will build up your walls, and their kings will minister to you. For in My fury I struck you, but in My favor I will show you mercy.

—Isaiah 60:10

Thus says Adonai Elohim: "Look, I will lift My hand to the nations, and raise My banner to the peoples! They will bring your sons on their chest, and carry your daughters on their shoulders. Kings will be your guardians, their princesses your nurses. They will bow down to you with their face to the ground, and lick the dust of your feet. Then you will know that I am Adonai—those hoping in Me will not be ashamed."

—Isaiah 49:22-23

The Palestinian Claim to the Land

God, do not keep silent. Do not hold Your peace, O God. Do not be still. For look, Your enemies make an uproar. Those who hate You lift up their head. They make a shrewd plot against Your people, conspiring against Your treasured ones. "Come," they say, "let's wipe them out as a nation! Let Israel's name be remembered no more!"

—Psalm 83:2-5

The Palestinians are Arabs that lived in the land under the rule of the Turks; most of them were immigrants from Turkey and from other Arab States. The "Palestinians" became a people under Haj Amin al-Husseini for the sole purpose of annihilating the Jewish people in the land. They have been used as a weapon by the Arab nations as a Trojan horse against the State of Israel.

The Word says that the enemies of Elohim have a controversy against Israel, and they will *remove* the name. Today, the Palestinian Authorities have removed the names of Israel and Jerusalem from all their maps in all their schools!

The Word says that the only hope for Israel's wicked neighbors who want to usurp her inheritance is that they forsake Islam and become as Jews, believers in the God of Israel. If not, they will be utterly destroyed.

> **Thus says ADONAI, "As for all My evil neighbors who strike at the inheritance that I bequeathed to My people Israel—I am about to uproot them from their land and pluck the house of Judah from them. Yet it will come to pass, after I have uprooted them, that I will again have compassion on them and I will bring them back, each one to his inheritance and each one to his land. "So it will come to pass, if they will diligently learn the ways of My people—to swear by My Name, 'As ADONAI lives,' just as they taught My people to swear by Baal—then they will be built up in the midst of My people. But if they will not obey, then I will uproot that nation, plucking it up and destroying it." It is a declaration of ADONAI.**
>
> **—JEREMIAH 12:14-17**

---

* Psalm 83:4

Since YHVH is the owner of the Land and He has given it to the descendants of Abraham, Isaac and Jacob forever, He calls all those nations that contend with Israel for the Land: My wicked neighbors.

Any nation that comes against the Jewish people, the people of Israel will be seriously judged.*

> For ADONAI is enraged at all the nations, and furious at all their armies. He will utterly destroy them. He will give them over to slaughter.
> For ADONAI has a day of vengeance, a year of recompense for the hostility against Zion.
>
> —ISAIAH 34:2, 8

Those who seek to divide the Land of Israel will be seriously judged.

> Behold, in those days and at that time, when I restore the fortunes of Judah and Jerusalem (in effect since 14th of May 1948), I will gather all the nations and bring them down to the valley of Jehoshaphat then I will enter into judgment with them there on behalf of My people and My inheritance, Israel, whom they have scattered among the nations; and they have divided up My land.
>
> —JOEL 3:1-2 NASB '95

All of Israel (Jewish people today) will be saved!**

> For I do not want you, brethren, to be uninformed of this mystery—so that you will not be wise in your own estimation—that a partial hardening has happened to Israel until the fullness of the Gentiles has come in; and so all Israel will

---

* Genesis 12:3, Exodus 23:22, 27, Zechariah 2, Zechariah 12, Isaiah 34, Joel 3, Obadiah
** Romans 11:25, Jeremiah 31:31-34, Isaiah 61:4,7, Zechariah 12, Jeremiah 31:27-34

be saved; just as it is written, "The Deliverer will come from Zion, He will remove ungodliness from Jacob." "This is My covenant with them, when I take away their sins."

—Romans 11:25-27 nasb '95

Again, we see that Paul makes a distinction between the salvation of *all* of Israel (the Jewish people today) and the salvation of the fullness of the Gentiles (or Ephraim and House of Joseph according to Genesis 48:19). All of Israel, as a Jewish nation, has a day of national salvation after the fullness of the Gentiles has come in (into salvation).

The Key Issue

This writer believes that as Christians in the nations join in and cooperate in practical and spiritual ways with the restoration of Israel, the covenant promise given to Abraham will come into effect, and they will be mightily blessed!

> And I will bless those who bless you, and the one who curses you I will curse. And in you all the families of the earth will be blessed.
>
> —Genesis 12:3 nasb '95

YHVH is defining His enemies or His friends according to their stand and behavior towards His plan to restore the Jewish people to His land and to save all of Israel. On which side you are will determine the blessing or the curse on this earth and forever for you, your family, and your nations.

The King (Yeshua the Jewish Messiah) will answer and say to them, 'Truly I say to you, to the extent that you did it to one of these brothers of Mine (Jewish people), even the least of them, you did it to Me.'

—Matthew 25:40 nasb '95

CHAPTER 14

BATTLE FOR DEDICATION

Hanukkah 5784/2023
By Rev. Debra Barnes, USA

For I consider the sufferings of this present time not worthy to be compared with the coming glory to be revealed to us. For the creation eagerly awaits the revelation of the sons of God.

— ROMANS 8:18-19

As we enter the season of recognizing the Feast of Dedication, known as Hanukkah, it reminds us of the Maccabees' battles and subsequent victory over Greek oppression and their idolatry in 164 BC. This time, living under the Greek kings of Damascus forced the Jewish people to abandon their worship of God, their holy customs, and their reading of the Torah. It was an extremely challenging time, involving much persecution and battles, after which we know that cleansing and then rededicating the holy Temple in Jerusalem was necessary.

Israel is once again engaged in fierce battles, forcing changes to their lifestyle by causing major upheaval in nearly every area of society in the

Holy Land. Is our day similar to the time of the Maccabees? And how can we effectively stand with His chosen people at this time?

We know that history repeats itself, especially when it comes to biblical accounts recorded. They were written to serve as examples for us to learn from and gain wisdom from for our lives today. And we know that all battles involving Yah's people have a common thread: Who will receive worship? Will it be the One True and Living God of Abraham, Isaac, and Jacob, or another god? Thus, the battleground is defined as Islam (in any form, led by various leaders) desires to see Allah worshipped throughout all of Israel and actually throughout the entire world. They firmly believe anyone who refuses to bow must be annihilated.

So our battle is similar to the Maccabees in that we see our very lives and freedom to worship in jeopardy. Any totalitarian regime throughout history has always meddled into the very depths of the souls of men by dictating how worship will be regulated. Ultimately, this is always the end game. So what does the Feast of Dedication mean to us today, as there is no physical Temple in Jerusalem right now to be the center of worship? Or is there?

> **Don't you know that you are God's temple and that the Ruach Elohim dwells among you? If anyone destroys God's temple, God will destroy him, for God's temple is holy, and you are that temple.**
>
> **—1 Corinthians 3:16-17**

We are the Temple that He desires to inhabit. Trauma can defile a temple, often setting up the idol known as fear, which requires us to bow down repeatedly whenever we sense danger (real or imagined). War is famous for bringing this abomination front and center into our lives, sidetracking us from joyful worship and fruitful lives, which are meant to bring honor and glory to Him. He wants our temple cleansed from all fear through understanding His perfect love.

> **In this way, love is made perfect among us, so that we should have boldness on the Day of Judgment. For just as He is, so also are we in this world. There is no fear in love, but perfect love drives out fear. For fear has to do with punishment, and the one who fears has not been made perfect in love.**
>
> **—1 John 4:17-18**

So, how do we stand with Israel at this time when the very soul of the nation is so challenged by fear? Show them His perfect love. Yes, by bringing humanitarian aid and comforting those who mourn in Zion. Yes, by being available to serve however He directs, even if called to the front lines, as in the case of our leadership team of Archbishop Dominiquae and Rabbi Baruch, Jan, and Robert. And by offering fervent prayer to set the captives free—especially for those hostages brutally abducted and abused.

We can stand with His brethren within each nation as well, as most are in turmoil and searching for light and hope amidst growing darkness. This is being done by broadcasting and lifting our Heavenly Father via GRM in our current thriving prison ministry. The efforts towards those incarcerated in the U.S. may not seem as important as having an open rally with flags waving and signs declaring solidarity with our ally Israel. But such efforts, which lift up the One True God of the Universe, actually boldly declare our solidarity with those who worship the same God we do. By making disciples, we are thereby challenging the "evangelists" of Islam who continually seek to defile the temples of those held behind bars and beyond. Remember, ultimately, it is a war to build altars within the hearts of mankind to establish who receives worship.

So, our battlefields are varied at this time, and every effort we make is critical when directed by the Ruach. Petitions to our Congressmen in the U.S. are producing positive governmental policies as well as providing financial aid to Israel. Signing the petition against antisemitism (created by Archbishop Dominiquae) and sharing it widely brings this monster out from the shadows, where it can be defeated. Letter-writing campaigns, some even initiated by children in America, have received worldwide attention and brought great encouragement right onto the IDF battlefields.* Organizing gatherings, the largest being in Washington, DC recently, which brought in excess of 290,000 Jewish and non-Jewish attendees into view, also encourages those in the Holy Land to know they are not alone.

The issue of who will be worshipped in Israel and America is still at the center of this war. It is a battle of the ages recorded in Exodus 17:16, stating that the LORD will have war with Amalek "from generation to generation", until He will "utterly put out the remembrance of Amalek from under heaven" (Ex. 17:14).

I believe that through all of our efforts, UNIFY is covering this battle well on all fronts. Many captives of all false religious systems are finally being set free with the true gospel made in Zion,** thoroughly cleansing human temples and dedicating them to our Heavenly Father. All others who refuse to bow their knee will become Yeshua's footstool, like those Greek rulers of old who now cease to exist, thanks to the valor of a remnant led by the passionate Maccabees.

---

* See www.israeltoday.co.il/read/connect-with-israeli-soldiers-send-us-your-letters-and-well-deliver-them if you wish to participate.

** To learn the original Gospel, we invite you to study our GRM Israel Bible School at www.GRMBibleInstitute.com

We are all part of today's faithful remnant. Remain steadfast to continue supporting the war effort. Be brave, be strong!

CHAPTER 15

HANUKKAH IN THE WAR

THIRTY YEARS AFTER THE signing of the Oslo Accords, which was witnessed by the UN (and signed by Israel, the PLO, the USA, and the European Union), Israel was at a death and life crossroads on October 6 this year. A civil war and unceasing Palestinian terror were threatening to tear her up from within; there was an all-out war with world opinion, and the UN was crushing her from without. The crossroads of self-destruction brought about by the Oslo Accords turned into a dead-end street on October 7. Hamas defined forever the outcome of the Oslo Accords dream of peace through a two-state solution or, rather, a two-state deception. The bloodbath of Palestinian terror that ensued following the Oslo Accords is deemed pale compared with the Palestinian Hamas Massacre of Shabbat, Simcha Torah of October 7, the *black Shabbat.*

Thousands of terrorists from Gaza infiltrated the south of Israel, and peaceful kibbutzim and moshavim were raided, burnt, and looted by Hamas terrorists and Gaza civilians. One thousand four hundred people, mostly civilians, including men, women, and children, were murdered. Babies were beheaded, pregnant women's wombs were ripped open, countless women were brutally raped and gang-raped multiple times, men's genitals were castrated, entire families were burnt to a crisp inside their bomb shelters, and hundreds were kidnapped, injured, and abused in Gaza. The horrors are impossible to stomach.

This was a pogrom, a Shoah, and these were the modern Nazis, a result of the Palestinian cause fueled by the Oslo Accords and the heartfelt support of the UN, US, EU, and the entire world that was chanting "peace, peace", but there was no peace. For how can you make peace with a snake, with Hitler, with Amalek?

> **Remember what Amalek did to you along the way as you came out from Egypt—how he happened upon you along the way and attacked those among you in the rear, all the stragglers behind you, when you were tired and weary—he did not fear God.**
>
> —**Deuteronomy 25:17-18**

The October 7 massacre thrust Israel into a righteous war of light vs. darkness, a fight for the survival of the Jewish nation vs. the Palestinian Hamas reign of terror, not only in Israel but in the entire Middle East and, in fact, in the entire world.

This is Hanukkah in the midst of the war named *Iron Swords*, which was renamed the *War of Spiritual Restoration* by the patriotic media. Through these heartbreaking happenings, the spirit of David has been restored to the IDF. Israel has united in its purpose to destroy Hamas and all the false peace narratives and to restore sanity and shalom to the land. Everyone has now been recruited to help: all the reservists, men and women, and all civilians. We are all part of one unified nation with a spirit like the ancient Maccabees. Heroes are being made in Israel every day of this righteous war.

We want to thank all those heroes in the nations, Maccabee-like lovers of the Jewish Messiah, who are standing with us unconditionally with your prayers, your money, and your participation in pro-Israel rallies. Your stand and support for Israel is invaluable; please do not stop as Israel needs you now more than ever.

> **In the same way, let your light shine before men so they may see your good works and glorify your Father in heaven.**
>
> —**Matthew 5:16 nasb '95**

For Yah will bless those who bless Israel, especially at this time.

> **But Judah will be inhabited forever—Jerusalem from generation to generation.**
>
> —**Joel 4:20**

AM YISRAEL CHAI

CHAPTER 16

THE HOUTHIS FROM TEMAN

> "The sons of Eliphaz: Teman, Omar, Zephi, Gatam, Kenaz, Timna and Amalek."
>
> — 1 CHRONICLES 1:36

THE WARS THAT ISRAEL is forced to fight these days are on all fronts. They include Hamas in Gaza, Fatah and Hamas in Judea and Samaria, Hezbollah at the border with Lebanon, and the Houthis at the Red Sea and Eilat border.

You must have heard before about all of those hateful, brutal Islamic Palestinian terror groups that chant constantly: From the river to the sea, Palestine will be free... from Jews. This chant calls for the annihilation of Israel. But who are the Houthis from Teman (Yemen) in Africa that are threatening Israel and intercepting and attacking ships in the Red Sea, sending lethal missiles to the city of Eilat?

This war, like all wars that Israel has been pushed to fight, is rooted in Biblical happenings, ancient hatreds fueled by fallen angels, demonic powers and principalities, and Lucifer himself. He wants to see Israel annihilated as proof that he is the true god and messiah. His tools are the descendants of Esau, especially through Amalek and Teman. These are the sons of Eliphaz, the son of Esau.

> So Esau bore a grudge against Jacob because of the blessing with which his father had blessed him, and Esau said in his heart, "Let the time for mourning my father draw near, so that I can kill my brother Jacob!
>
> —GENESIS 27:41

Esau, also called Edom, never forgave Jacob, who was chosen to be the firstborn, as Esau sold his inheritance to him. The inheritance is the entire land of Canaan and preeminence over the other brethren. This ancient hatred is the spiritual force behind the Houthis of Teman (Yemen). It is in their bloodline and the familiar evil spirits they carry.

> "Because you have a long-standing hatred and have delivered Bnei-Yisrael to the power of the sword in the time of their calamity, in the time of their final punishment, therefore, as I live'—it is a declaration of ADONAI—'I will destine you for blood, and bloodshed will pursue you. Since you did not hate bloodshed, therefore bloodshed will pursue you. I will make Mount Seir (Esau-Edom, near Eilat on the Red Sea) an utter desolation. I will cut off from it all who come and go."
>
> —EZEKIEL 35:5-7

This ancient hatred is portrayed by the manifesto of the Houthis in their emblem:

Allah is great, Death to America, Death to Israel, Damnation to the Jews, Victory to Islam.

The descendants of Esau spread all over the East and the South to the tip of Africa, where Yemen is today. Though the Houthis are rebels within Yemen/Teman and not the ruling party, they are controlling the whole area through terror, even as far away as Saudi Arabia and the United Arab Emirates.

What is the fate of the Houthis?

> About Edom, thus says ADONAI-Tzva'ot: "Is there no longer wisdom in Teman? Is counsel lost to the prudent? Has their wisdom vanished? Flee! Turn back! Stay low, inhabitants of Dedan, for I will bring Esau's calamity on him at the time that I punish him."
>
> —JEREMIAH 49:7-8

The sooner, the better, we pray.

CHAPTER 17

WHY DO EARTHQUAKES HAPPEN?

When He arises to make the earth tremble.
— ISAIAH 2:19B NASB '95

The World Health Organization describes the earthquakes in Turkey as the worst natural disaster in a century in what it characterizes as its Europe region.[*]

In the aftermath of the terrible earthquake and series of earthquakes in Turkey and Syria, in February 2023, the Spirit of the Most High gave me this message during my monthly time of retreat unto Him:

"Why would you be surprised, oh human, that the earth is trembling under your feet? It is I who created the heavens and the earth, and all its elements respond to Me," says the High and Exalted One. "The earth merely expresses my anger at the idolatry, injustice, and rebellion of humanity against My plan and Me."

---

[*] www.aljazeera.com/amp/news/liveblog/2023/2/14/turkey-syria-earthquake-live-news-death-toll-tops-36000

> "For the Lord of hosts will have a day of reckoning against everyone who is proud and lofty and against everyone who is lifted up, that he may be abased."
>
> — Isaiah 2:12 nasb '95

Beloveds, Turkey, and Syria have demonstrated terrible idolatry to a fallen god named Allah, terrible injustice to its inhabitants, and blatant and arrogant rebellion against the God of Israel's master plan to restore the Jewish people to their own promised land. Their rulers have blasphemed the God of the covenant, the land of the covenant, and the people of the covenant. YHVH is very patient, but there is a tipping point, and we are at the time of this tipping point. A terrible earthquake or another catastrophe could be on its way to any nation that is poking the Almighty in the eye by opposing His divine plan to restore Israel, and no one will be spared, not even Israel's long-standing ally, the USA and not even Israelis themselves that oppose His plan.

> "And it will be against all the cedars of Lebanon that are lofty and lifted up, against all the oaks of Bashan, against all the lofty mountains, against all the hills that are lifted up, against every high tower, against every fortified wall, against all the ships of Tarshish and against all the beautiful craft. The pride of man will be humbled and the loftiness of men will be abased; and the YHVH alone will be exalted in that day,"
>
> —Isaiah 2:13-17 stb

YHVH is judging all the idols and gods of this world, starting with those who oppose His master plan to restore His Jewish people to their God-bequeathed Land.

> "But the idols will completely vanish."
>
> —Isaiah 2:18 NASB '95

No manner of logic, humanism, or "deals of the century" will help in this day. The pride of man will be abased. Earthquakes are calling humankind to repentance, to the fear of YHVH. Turkey and Syria, together with Iran, have been sponsors of terror against Israel. They have Jewish blood on their hands, among many other sins.

> "Men will go into caves of the rocks and into holes of the ground Before the terror of YHVH and the splendor of His majesty, when He arises to make the earth tremble."
>
> —Isaiah 2:19 STB

And while many nations and individuals are in idolatry, in immorality, espouse injustice, and are prideful against YHVH and against His people Israel, they are in danger of being visited by His judgment. We are experiencing the happenings of the end of times. His patience has almost run out.

> "In that day men will cast away to the moles and the bats their idols of silver and their idols of gold, which they made for themselves to worship, in order to go into the caverns of the rocks and the clefts of the cliffs Before the terror of YHVH and the splendor of His majesty, when He arises to make the earth tremble."
>
> —Isaiah 2:20-21 STB

And to those who put their trust in a human government to save them or in a global solution to the world's problems, He says:

> "Stop regarding man, whose breath of life is in his nostrils; for why should he be esteemed?"
>
> —Isaiah 2:22 NASB '95

The God of Israel, YHVH, the Creator of Heaven and Earth, the Lord of the Armies, has arisen to judge the earth for all its idolatry, immorality, greed, injustice, and especially for the hostility of the nations towards Zion, Israel, His Jewish people.

For YHVH has a Day of Vengeance for they have quarreled against Zion.

> —Isaiah 34:8 STB

CHAPTER 18

FOCUS ON JERUSALEM

> It will come about in that day that I will make Jerusalem a heavy stone for all the peoples; all who lift it will be severely injured. And all the nations of the earth will be gathered against it.
>
> — ZECHARIAH 12:3 NASB '95

Why is Jerusalem such a Big Deal? So many people with so many opinions; so many nations have coveted her; so many passions are provoked by this *one city*! What makes Jerusalem the Center of the World? Yerushalayim is the city of the great King, the throne of YHVH, the headquarters of the kingdom of YHVH on earth, and the eternal capital of Israel!

> At that time they will call Jerusalem the throne of ADONAI and all the nations will gather into it, to Jerusalem, in the Name of ADONAI. No longer will they walk according to the stubbornness of their evil heart.
>
> —JEREMIAH 3:17

All nations that attempt to divide the Holy City will be seriously judged and destroyed! (Joel 3)

But Why Do They Want to Divide the Holy City?

This division is to appease the so-called "Palestinians" or the "Palestinian people" who have a claim to the land of Israel (the city of Jerusalem included), on behalf of their "rights" to the land. Please stay with me to the end of this letter so you can understand the magnitude of this lie that has been fed through the media to all the gullible millions of people on the planet!

There is No Such Thing as a Palestinian People

Until 1948, many different people lived in the land of Israel under British Mandate rule. There were a variety of Arabs coming from different Arab countries all around; there were Turks left from the time of the Turkish Empire that ruled the land of Israel, then called Palestine, for 400 years prior to the Brits, and there were British people, French people and an assorted variety of Jews from different nations. There were Christians, Muslims, Jews, and everything in between! There was no such thing as "Palestinian people," but everyone who lived in the land of Israel, named Palestine (since the Roman Conquest of the First Century AD), were citizens of Palestina and carried a Palestinian ID. Christians had that ID, and Muslims and Jews had it as long as they lived in Palestina.

This was no homogenous "nation" at all. A Palestinian was one who lived in the land renamed Palestina under whatever rule was available. If the Turks ruled, they were Turkish in Palestine; if the Brits ruled, they were under Britain in Palestine. None of the Arab citizens of Palestine then tried to form for themselves a "national identity" since there was an array of different people groups. These groups had no common vision; rather, they just wanted to live in the land of Israel under whatever conqueror would be ruling at the time. There was no national assembly, no centralized rule, no national identity, no common cause, and absolutely *nothing* to define them as Palestinian people! Jews living at that time carried a "Palestinian ID," and so did Christians or Muslims!

So Where Do These Palestinian People Come From?

The entity "Palestinian people" is a rebellious term in every way! It only means Arabs who were living in the land prior to the establishment of the miracle-born State of Israel. Arabs who refused to submit to Israeli rule, although they had no problem submitting under Turkish or British rule prior to this. Remember that we are not talking about a "nation" but about individual decentralized Arab villages throughout the land of Israel, then called Palestina. They refused to come to terms with the reality that YHVH had restored Israel to her land.

Later on, when Israel won the 1967 miracle Six-Day War against all odds, more covenant land became Israel's, and all the citizens living there were told by the Arab nations not to submit to Israeli rule and not to allow the refugee camps to be dismantled so they could live in more humane conditions. These Jordanian citizens were also called "Palestinians," as Jordan is in the confines of the land of Israel as well!

Great Britain established the country of Jordan in the land that had been promised to the Jewish people, thus breaking the contract made in 1917 through the Balfour Declaration to establish a Jewish homeland in *all* of Palestine! (70% of that land was given to the Hashemite family to build a *new country* called Jordan that never existed before). The Brits broke the promise to Israel and lost the British Empire!

> And I will bless those who bless you, and the one who curses you I will curse. And in you all the families of the earth will be blessed.
>
> —Genesis 12:3 NASB '95

I repeat: the Arab nations forbade these war refugees from receiving any help from Israel in order to keep them poor so that world opinion would favor the "Palestinian cause." As a point of comparison, those Arabs who have become Israeli citizens are the most prosperous in all the Middle East, and their quality of life in Israel is *much* better than in any Arab nation!

Hitler's Baby

The Palestinian people of today are an array of non-related Arab villages united under one cause only, namely the annihilation of Israel, which is Hitler's baby! In 1938, the biggest Muslim entity and authority, Haj Amin al-Husseini, the Grand Mufti of Jerusalem, visited Hitler and asked him to build him an Arab army. The purpose of al-Husseini was to implement Hitler's "Final Solution" (of extermination of Jews) from within the land of Palestine. Hitler gladly complied, and the PLO (Palestinian Liberation Organization) was born. Through Hitler's strategy, Haj Amin centralized most of the Arabs living in Palestine under one central organization that had only one common purpose: "Liberate" or rid the land of Israel of any Jews and take over Palestine for the sake of the Muslim world! The most well-known leader of the PLO was the late Yasser Arafat, the terrorist who received a Nobel Prize and shook hands with Prime Minister Yitzchak Rabin, who was assassinated in Tel Aviv!

Hitler's and Haj Amin's plan then and now was the extermination of all Jews in the land of Israel, and that plan has never changed and is being implemented through Hamas, Hezbollah, and the "milder" Fatah. All these groups have only one thing in common: Annihilate Israel and let Muslim rule be implemented in the Holy Land!

That is the reason why Mr. Abu Mazen, who is supposedly sitting at the negotiation table with Israel in order to make a "peace treaty" based on the "Two-State Solution," has refused to this day to recognize Israel as the Jewish state. He does not recognize Israel's right to exist because this would be contrary to the original and only agenda of the Palestinian Authority established by its founder, Haj Amin al-Husseini: Hitler's "Final Solution".

> "In those days and at that time, when I restore the fortunes of Judah and Jerusalem, I will gather all nations and bring them down to the Valley of Jehoshaphat there I will put them on trial for what they did to my inheritance, my people Israel, because they scattered my people among the nations and divided up my land.
>
> —Joel 3:1-2 NIV

Why the Name Palestinian?

The name Palestine was given to the vanquished land of Israel by conquering Rome during the first century AD. Rome changed all of the Biblical names for defilement names: Israel was changed to Palestine, and Yerushalayim to *Aelia Capitolina*. Until today, the Arabs call Israel "Palestine" and Yerushalayim they call *Al Kuds* or "The Holy." They would not mention the covenant names of Yisrael and Yerushalayim, and in their maps and school studies, the name of Yisrael is forbidden.

The name Yisrael is mentioned over 2000 times in the Holy Scriptures, and the name Yerushalayim is mentioned over 800 times in the Holy Scriptures!

> **See how your enemies growl, how your foes rear their heads. With cunning they conspire against your people; they plot against those you cherish. "Come," they say, "let us destroy them as a nation, so that Israel's name is remembered no more."**
>
> **—Psalm 83:2-4**

The etymology of the name Palestinian is Philistines. Those were the ancient archenemies of Israel, whose Goliath David defeated and whose temple of idolatry Samson brought down. These principalities are still trying to annihilate Israel through the local "Palestinians," not because all of them are evil but because they are ruled by a demonic principality called Islam! Islam, meaning "submission," is submitted indeed to a demon called Allah from the demonic pantheon of Muhammed's family.

Muhammed, the prophet of Islam, is buried in Mecca, and all Muslims are commanded to make a pilgrimage to the Black Stone (Kaba) of Mecca once in a lifetime. The spirit of the Philistines lives through Islam and the fake "Palestinian cause," that is, the Arab cause to rule Israel and to have a completely Muslim Middle East and world! Yerushalayim, and especially Mount Zion, Mount Moriah, or the Temple Mount, is the center of the world, and whoever rules from there rules the nations.

That is why when the Greeks defiled the Jewish Holy Temple and replaced holy worship with pagan worship, they ruled the world; then the Romans also ruled the world after conquering Yerushalayim, and Islam has been ruling ever since a Muslim Ummayad Calif by the name of Abdul Malek built the Golden Dome of the Rock on the Temple Mount in 691 AD, establishing Jerusalem as a Muslim place of worship. Islam is a world-conquering religion! Establishing a Palestinian state is bringing Islam into high gear for world conquest. The rule of the Anti-Messiah (Anti-Christ) is being established via the Palestinian "solution!"

Why Do the Palestinians Want Yerushalayim?

In fact, the Holy City of Yerushalayim is not mentioned in the Koran, not even one time, and it is not "holy" to the Muslim religion! The only cities mentioned as holy in the Koran are Mecca and Medina, mainly Mecca. When the Muslim Arabs pray on the Temple Mount in the Mosque of Al Aqsa, they pray with their rear ends to the original location of the Holy of Holies where the Ark of the Covenant was.

The Muslim shrines on the Temple Mount are the anti-Messiah system and the abomination that causes desolation.

> So, when you see standing in the holy place 'the abomination that causes desolation,' spoken of through the prophet Daniel—let the reader understand.
>
> —MATTHEW 24:15

It is time to raise up our prayers over Jerusalem like never before, taking our post as watchmen over the Holy City.

> On your walls, Jerusalem, I have set watchmen. All day and all night, they will never hold their peace. "You who remind ADONAI, take no rest for yourselves, and give Him no rest until He establishes and makes Jerusalem a praise in the earth.
>
> —ISAIAH 62:6-7

Yerushalayim ACHAT! (Is One Undivided City)

CHAPTER 19

BOOTS ON THE GROUND: ISRAEL WAR REPORT

This report is a first-hand account of what is happening two and a half weeks into the war. The details given will be sharper than what you may be hearing in the news. Archbishop Dominiquae and Rabbi Baruch Bierman have been "boots on the ground" in Israel since the Sukkot Tour ended, helping to convey the following insights in order to be more effective intercessors at this critical time in history:

> Whoever rewards evil for good will never leave his house.
> —Proverbs 17:13

> Acquitting the wicked and condemning the righteous—both are an abomination to Adonai.
> —Proverbs 17:15

This is what we are seeing even now, including in the media, as we fight this war on multiple fronts. Liberal Israelis were deeply deceived about the nature of the enemy until now. It is truly a wake-up call for Israel and the world.

Many interviews have been conducted and stories have been told in the aftermath of the initial attack. The two hostages released recently were 80 and 85 years old, and it is interesting that one of them extended such a hand of mercy that she even helped take sick Gazans to the hospital. Some kibbutz communities close to the border were on the left side of politics, so compassionate and yet naive enough to state that terrorists' actions in the past were Israel's fault. They were not shown mercy by the terrorists on October 7.

We now know that those at the music festival being held at the border with Gaza were there to show their love, releasing an atmosphere of peace for our Arab neighbors. This gathering had roots in the new age and involved much drug use. As you now know, it was the biggest slaughter, with many taken hostage.

An Israeli interviewed from the community that previously "welcomed the Arab Gazans home" during the Jewish disengagement in 2005 at Gush Katif said, "We were shocked and did not know the wickedness of this enemy." There were deceived Israelis who would even pass money through the fence for those poor Gazans.

Liberal Judaism in America has been awakened as well. We heard about the female president of a synagogue in Detroit, Michigan, who was brutally stabbed and murdered outside her home, despite the fact that she had founded a society based on coexistence and worked tirelessly for peace.

What is all this showing us? The depth of deception in Israel ran deep, and had this not happened now, something worse would have occurred. We see this because the northern border violence escalated immediately, and Arabs in the Samaria region became even bolder in their attacks. Our personal experience with them happened during our visit to the synagogue at Jericho in the Jordan Valley. And now we know even Eilat was in danger from an attack out of Yemen.

This wicked demon spirit, espousing a fallen angel named Allah, is the root. When I asked Yah why this happened, He answered directly: "It's because Israel was so divided."

Unity is a key element to success, for good or for evil to prevail. Genesis 11: Unity at the Tower of Babel tells us that nothing is impossible when people are united. The unity of a husband and wife, a congregation, or an entire country causes them to achieve their goals, whether righteous or evil.

What happened, beginning with the Gush Katif disengagement, ended with this massacre on October 7. We see now that our image in the media is wickedly twisted by the U.N. (Babel unity against Israel), and they are united to bring Israel to the brink of extinction. We must pray for the division of this wicked agenda; then the U.N. will come down. And we *must* pray for more unity in Israel, which had its worst division in history this year as religious Jews and woke Jews clashed. They are truly awake now, not asleep. But we must remain so to the end, as our memories tend to be short whenever conflicts become extended. It is then that we are tempted to compromise.

Remember, Israel has bent over backward to be nice to the enemy that hates us. We are told by Yeshua to "turn the other cheek" when someone slaps our face. We have done this multiple times and have no more cheek to give now. The mentality of "treat them well, and they will love us" does not work, even though it has been repeatedly tried throughout the land, even in our prison system.

We are seeing the Final Solution executed from within Israel, just as the Mufti and Hitler came to an agreement to accomplish it. It is imperative that we pray for the world/UN global Palestinian cause agreement to be broken! The U.S. must also not prevail to pressure for a ceasefire, standing firmly as an ally and not being a voice for the wicked Freemasonic-driven globalist agenda.

UNIFY is being called to remain alert to what is planned at the northern border as well as around Gaza, acknowledging that the Judea and Samaria region is also a hotbed for wicked terrorists. We learned that there was a plot to even attack the children playing in our orchard in Oriad, yet thankfully, Yah kept them safe.

This existential threat from all sides is real, even as we recently learned of terrorists attempting to attack by sea. Unless Yah shows up, it will be a bloodbath in Israel. Our cry must be, "With the help of Yah, together we will win!" This is like in Jeremiah 30 describing the time of Jacob's trouble, but out of it we shall be saved. We believed for years that Jews would again return to Gaza and rebuild. Let it be known, as we heard prophetic words on Channel 14 calling this the "resurrection region."

Our greatest threat is for our leaders and decision-makers to compromise because the hostage situation puts us between a rock and a hard place. It will be worse if we compromise now, regardless. Pray for NO compromise!

In the midst of all this, a rabbi reported that a light had come to the Ultraorthodox Jewish community. As you know, they do not serve in the IDF,[*] which has often caused extreme friction among secular Jews. And some even side with Arabs to give land to them. Approximately 3,000 Ultra-Orthodox are now volunteering to serve (though not in combat)—Praise Yah for this show of unity! And we believe this will open up aliyah to their counterparts from America as well!

Prime Minister Netanyahu said in his recent speech:

---

[*] A very small sect, Neturei Karta

"Quoting the wife of a fallen officer of Golani who died on October 7, while burying her husband:

From the pains of this war, we will be born again as a nation.

We will establish yearly dates of national mourning.

We will all give answers after the war about what happened on this black Shabbat of the 7th of October, but for now, we need to be *united* to win this war until we gain full victory for the very existence of our nation.

We will restore all the settlements.

Our war with Hamas is the war of the whole world with evil.

My job is to lead us to a smashing victory.

I quote from the Prophet Isaiah:

"No more will violence be heard in your land, devastation nor destruction within your borders. But you will call your walls salvation and your gates Praise."

—Isaiah 60:18

Together, we will fight. Together, we will win."

For that, our prayers are more important now than ever. Every one of us is required to engage in prayer according to the Word and by revelation of Ruach. This is no time for anyone to be sleeping; wake up and become seriously anointed, full of the sharp sword of the Word. Pray with understanding and with authority. The righteous are to be bold as a lion!*

Pray that Yah comes down and disrupts unity in the camps of the enemy of Israel (including the U.N., Iran, PLO, Hamas, Hezbollah, Taliban, and Fatah), and confuses their language! Pray for the war

---

* Proverbs 28:1

being fought in the media. Pray to deepen the unity within Israel so that Yah puts His strategies within the minds of our government, military leaders, and citizens.

This is the platform from which we will be united and see victory! May Yah bless each and every one joined together by His Ruach in this time of Jacob's trouble.*

---

* Transcribed from an audio recording by Rev. Debra Barnes, Alabama, USA.

CHAPTER 20

AN OPEN-HEARTED LETTER FROM THE MIDST OF THE WAR

We are Present and We are Here to Stay
At the Dead Sea Hotel with the evacuees from Sderot,
October 30, 2023.

I CAME TO REST after about two intense months following the organizing and leading of our annual Sukkot Tour until the Hamas massacre of October 7, Shabbat, on Simcha Torah, and then the ensuing war against an indescribable evil, with all its demands for help. We departed the USA on my 64th birthday, September 5, the very day the PNG Embassy opened in Jerusalem. What a joy that was!

I may be the only one paying full price at the Dead Sea Hotel. It is a miracle that I even found a room. Many citizens of Sderot are here; people are here recovering from the shaking events of October 7 and the week following—the present-day Shoah. Most of the hotels in Israel are full of evacuees from the south and the north, about 200,000 of them!

I came to rest so I can continue helping in Yah's anointing and wisdom. However, my heart breaks with every conversation I initiate with the people. So many children! What horrors have they seen? Some even tell me their story. Yes, and even the story of their miraculous survival from the shocking, brutal massacre. Most are eagerly hoping for the IDF to do its job in Gaza thoroughly, eradicating all traces of Hamas so Sderot and all the Negev can live in shalom. Amen.

Security forces dressed in bright orange and yellow vests and soldiers in army fatigues are everywhere in the hotel. So are volunteers, educators, and psychologists. School activities are organized for the children. Their mayor, Alon David, is taking good care of them. It helps. They are enveloped with care, at least here in this hotel. The serene surroundings of the Dead Sea shores and its healing waters are a blessing to their shaken, bereaved, and traumatized souls.

There is no tourism in Israel; the skies are shut to flights due to the constant Hamas rockets falling all over Israel. I am glad that our flights have been canceled again and again so we can be here to pray, to give, to comfort, and to broadcast the truth. We are shoulder to shoulder; we are part of the spiritual Air Force and boots on the ground.

Every smile I give, every prayer I say, every hug and listening ear I lend helps someone. Every effort of my husband to drive me all over Israel and cater to me in this holy mission is a great help. Every prayer our UNIFY members and partners send, every offering they give, helps someone and often even hundreds and thousands of "someones." Every shopping voucher to the evacuees, every shekel provided to help the soldiers, every $$$ sent to outfit emergency squads in hostile areas—it all helps.

It also brings hope and a smile to the face of the receivers. "Someone in the nations cares for us. We are not alone". I can hear your voices in my spiritual ears saying: "No, Israel, you are not alone! We, the sons and daughters of the God of Israel, through the Jewish Messiah, are with you!"

An Open-Hearted Letter from the Midst of the War

As we look back on history to this day, we will be able to say to our children, grandchildren, families, and congregations, yes, and even to the nations:

We, the United Nations for Israel, were there, boots on the ground, all the way from our Sukkot Tour to the Hamas massacre of October 7, the present Shoah—the devastation, and later throughout the lengthy war. We were *present*. We will also be present at the time of resurrection in our May 2024 tour, which was prophetically named "From Devastation to Resurrection" much before this War of Independence of 2023. Yes, we, the representatives of our future sheep nations, the UNIFY members, are here to *stay*.

> "Ruth replied, "Do not plead with me to abandon you, to turn back from following you. For where you go, I will go, and where you stay, I will stay. Your people will be my people, and your God my God. Where you die, I will die, and there I will be buried. May ADONAI deal with me, and worse, if anything but death comes between me and you!"
>
> — RUTH 1:16-17

Your faithful stand and unconditional love comfort my heart. In the heat of battle, I did not notice that I was in mourning, too. All 1,400 murdered, the 239 kidnapped (including babies, children, and elderly), the nearly 6,000 wounded, the millions traumatized, the destroyed houses, the over 200,000 evacuees, the constant rockets sending us to the nearest shelter, the 300,000 IDF troops drafted, including my own close family members and friends: they are all part of our national family. We are Israel.

> "'In that day many nations will join themselves to Adonai and they will be My people and I will dwell among you.' Then you will know that Adonai-Tzva'ot has sent me to you. Adonai will inherit Judah as His portion in the holy land and will once again choose Jerusalem. Be silent before Adonai, all flesh, for He has aroused Himself from His holy dwelling."
>
> —Zechariah 2:15-17

Thank you for staying with us for the duration until He comes.

X 2022

CHAPTER 21

DO YOU KNOW ANY ANTISEMITES?

> ...delivering you from your people and from the Gentiles—to whom I am sending you to open their eyes, so that they may turn from darkness to light and from the power of Satan to God, that they may receive forgiveness of sins and a place among those who are sanctified by faith in me.
>
> — ACTS 26:17-18 ESV

On April 9th, 1990—on Passover eve—my husband and I were sent by the Holy Spirit from Jerusalem to the nations, first to Hawaii in the USA, then from there to Dallas to study at Christ for the Nations (CFNI). We continued from Dallas to Santa Rosa Beach, Florida, from Florida to Hong Kong and China, and then on to 50-plus nations and hundreds of cities.

We have ministered to many thousands of people and have been privileged to be used as vessels of truth and revival. We have been received by ordinary people and by government officials, as well. We have also been persecuted by religious authorities, very much like Shaul-Paul the Apostle, except it was not so much from religious Jews, but rather from Gentiles. We discovered that not everyone loves truth and that many prefer darkness to light, as long as it is convenient. We noticed that most people are religious, but not many are covenant believers. Many people attended church or some religious congregation, but most did not walk with Yeshua in their daily lives.

> "holding to an outward form of godliness but denying its power. Avoid these people!"
>
> —2 Timothy 3:5

During our studies at CFNI in Dallas, we discovered that most of the students were hungry for a Move of God. Prominent and anointed speakers frequented the pulpit and inspired us to expand our faith and to reach out to the lost with signs, wonders, and miracles following. One day, we were in the main auditorium watching a movie about the powerful revival that had been going on in China since the 1980's. My spirit was tremendously stirred up, and I ran to the prayer room off the stage, where I sobbed and wept uncontrollably. Waves of the Holy Spirit's grief were washing through my intense intercession.

Meanwhile, many students in the auditorium began to cry out for revival, being stirred in their hearts by what they were seeing. As cries were going throughout the auditorium, the spirit of prophecy came intensely upon me, and I shouted, "Revival is *here*, but you do not want it!"

Then, I quickly ran back and kept interceding and sobbing in the prayer room.

Little did I know then what my prophetic statement and cry really meant. It took me years to understand that the end-time awakening and revival are all about the Jews, about Israel, and the Jewish roots of the faith. It is about Yeshua as a Jewish Messiah and the restoration of

His Jewish identity, together with the original *besora* (gospel) that was brought to the nations by the Jewish Apostle Paul.

> "You worship what you do not know; we worship what we know, for salvation is from the Jews."
>
> —JOHN 4:22

One day I had an open vision and I saw Shaul-Paul jumping up and down with great joy telling me, "Go, and recover my gospel!" Little did I know that, since Paul brought the gospel from Jerusalem to the nations, wicked wolves had come among the flock and had deceived many into believing deceptive doctrinal lies. These lies would cause the murder of millions of Jews because of violent antisemitism and cause death to many more millions of Christians because of deception. These doctrines also espoused the supremacy of Christians over Jews and the church over the synagogue.

> "True enough. They were broken off because of unbelief, and you stand by faith. Do not be arrogant, but fear—for if God did not spare the natural branches, neither will He spare you."
>
> —ROMANS 11:20-21

Statues of two women were then placed in many of the ancient church buildings: Church Triumphant versus Vanquished Synagogues. Preachers encouraged the people to be hostile and hateful of all Jews and everything Jewish. The blood libel of "the Jews killed Christ" and "the Jews killed God" was repeated again and again from many pulpits. This unleashed an untold evil! Jews were persecuted, humiliated, spoiled, massacred, and expelled from almost every country in Europe.

Despising the Jews and everything Jewish was not only acceptable but often encouraged by the clergy.

> "Notice then the kindness and severity of God: severity toward those who fell; but God's kindness toward you, if you continue in His kindness; otherwise you too will be cut off!"
>
> —ROMANS 11:22

It is easy to debunk the myth that has caused the extermination of millions of Jews, culminating with Hitler and the Nazi Shoah (Holocaust). Consider the facts: the Jews at the time of Yeshua were under the Roman Empire and had no authority to crucify or execute anyone. Though there was a Jewish mob incited and bribed by the apostate high priest, Caiphas, to call for Yeshua's execution, thousands of Jews were following and believing in Him. The Roman soldiers crucified Him, plucked His beard, mocked Him, spat upon Him, and put a crown of painful thorns on His head. Unfortunately, no preacher has ever told their flock this: the Romans killed Christ, and *they* deserve to die. Ultimately, Yeshua said no one can take His life. He died willingly for both Jews and gentiles to conquer Satan, sin, and death, for all who would put their trust in Him.

> "For this reason the Father loves Me, because I lay down My life, so that I may take it up again. No one takes it away from Me, but I lay it down on My own. I have the authority to lay it down, and I have the authority to take it up again. This command I received from My Father."
>
> —JOHN 10:17-18

This is the nature of a lie. Hitler was heard saying, "Tell a lie and make it big enough, then repeat it again and again, and everyone will believe it."*

> "You are of your father the devil, and you want to do the desires of your father. He was a murderer from the beginning and does not stand in the truth, because there is no truth in him. Whenever he speaks lies he is just being himself—for he is a liar and the father of lies."
>
> —JOHN 8:44

Antisemitism as a term was coined in the 19th century. This is when hating the Jews began to be recognized as a social ill for the first time since the birth of Christianity as a state religion (in the 4th century in Eastern Rome).

Here is the definition of antisemitism in the Merriam-Webster Dictionary:

hostility toward or discrimination against Jews as a religious, ethnic, or racial group

Today, antisemitism has taken the twist of anti-Zionism, opposing politically the prophesied return of the Jewish people back to their Land. Deceptive and lying statements such as "baby killers," "Zionism = racism," and "Zionism = Nazism" are all too prevalent in today's American society, as well as in many other countries around the world!

Religious persecution and hostility against the Jews came out of the Christian church (from the 4th century until the 20th century), culminating in the Nazi Shoah. This was when Hitler expelled the Jews of Germany, saying, "Jews get out, you Christ-killers," spoken while lifting a cross on the streets of Berlin, much like the Spanish Inquisition had

---

* Recommended reading: *The Identity Theft* book; available at www.ZionsGospel.com

done 500 years earlier. But since the establishment of the State of Israel, another variant of this same deathly, social "virus" has been spread; this is bringing false allegations and false political rhetoric in the name of "the Palestinian cause."

> "God, do not keep silent. Do not hold Your peace, O God. Do not be still. For look, Your enemies make an uproar. Those who hate You lift up their head. They make a shrewd plot against Your people, conspiring against Your treasured ones. "Come," they say, "let's wipe them out as a nation! Let Israel's name be remembered no more!""
>
> —Psalms 83:2-5

In my TV program titled Hitler's Child,* I prove that the alleged "Palestinian cause" is Hitler's Child. It is a monstrous plan concocted by the Muslim Grand Mufti of Jerusalem, who visited Hitler in Berlin in 1941. This wicked and cruel Muslim leader asked this monster of a man, Hitler, to help him train an army that would annihilate the Jews in the Land of their ancestors - thus implementing the Final Solution from within. Hitler complied gladly, and the PLO was born. The Palestinian Liberation Organization (PLO) would now fight politically, socially, and with acts of terror to wipe Israel off the map, or so they thought. Out of the PLO came the Fatah, Hezbollah, Hamas, Al Qaida, The Muslim Brotherhood, and all the different terror factions.

Their common purpose is to get rid of the Jews and of the State of Israel altogether. To that effect, they train babies and children of preschool age to hate Jews, to handle guns, and to murder Jews, thus becoming a "shaheed" or martyr when they grow up. They use children to throw stones and handle knives to smash the skulls of Israelis and to

---

* Watch Hitler's Child at www.youtube.com/watch?v=lJCQuQm3Pnw

murder them. They ram cars and heavy machines against unsuspected civilians at bus stops. They send up colorful balloons full of explosives so Jewish children will grab them, and they will explode, causing terrible physical destruction.

All this is being done in the name of "Free Palestine". Then they call the Jews "baby killers"! Those Arabs who espouse the Palestinian cause and all of their followers (from among America, Europe, South America, Africa, Asia, and all nations) are actually siding with Hitler's plan for the Final Solution and extermination of the Jews.

They are working with the same principle as Hitler: "Tell a big lie, repeat it, and everyone will believe it!" Whether you are a Jew, a Muslim, a Christian, an atheist, a Buddhist, a Hindu, young or old, male or female, if you are supporting the Palestinian Cause, you are siding with Hitler and the Grand Mufti of Jerusalem. Being anti-Zionist and against the State of Israel makes *you* an official antisemite.

This is an urgent call of repentance to billions of deceived people on this planet!

Come out of this lie, as the plague from the Almighty will come out to judge and destroy all of those who hate His Jewish people and His Jewish Messiah, Yeshua.

> **For ADONAI is enraged at all the nations, and furious at all their armies. He will utterly destroy them.**
> **For ADONAI has a day of vengeance, a year of recompense for the hostility against Zion.**
>
> **—ISAIAH 34:2, 8**

"My desire is to bless those who bless you, but whoever curses you I will curse, and in you all the families of the earth will be blessed."

—Genesis 12:3

CHAPTER 22

EXPOSING ANTISEMITISM IN AMERICA

An Urgent Prophetic Watchman Warning

> "Then whoever hears the sound of the shofar but ignores the warning, if the sword comes and takes him away, his blood will be on his own head."
>
> — EZEKIEL 33:4

THE PLAGUE OF ANTISEMITISM is a real threat and is prevalent on both sides of the pendulum. On the left side of politics, it manifests through organizations like BLM and Antifa. On the right side of politics, it manifests through Neo-Nazism, its sympathizers, and various white supremacy groups. America has been so polarized in its views and ideologies that most of its citizens judge everyone and everything according to the political glasses of their ideology, whether it be Republican or Democrat, right or left-wing.

However, there is an illness in society, a cancer threatening to kill us from within, to kill the very heart of our nation. This has been destroying us from within and bringing us to the edge of societal collapse like many empires in the past. This latent and violent ill is violating an ancient promise that could make it or break it for America's future. It contains a *key* that makes the world go around. This ancient key confirms the worst fears of all those who espouse the infamous *Chronicles of the Elders of Zion*. It is true: The Jews, indeed, control the world!

But not in the way all Jew-haters have been taught or indoctrinated. The Jews control the world through this ancient promise repeated numerous times in the most important book ever written, the Holy Bible.

Whether you are a Jew, a Christian, white or black, this book contains eternal truths easily provable by history as well as personal testimonials. The ancient Holy Scriptures indeed confirm that the key to the well-being of all nations is connected with the people of Israel, the Jewish people of today. This key factor will cause entire societies to either thrive or collapse.

In the present-day USA, members of both sides of the political spectrum have been groping in the darkness, trying to find the culprit for the terrible condition of our nation. Their list includes: the destructive divide, the anger, the hatred, the faith, moral breakdown, the all-encompassing fraud and corruption, the threats of more pandemics and recessions, the destruction of the decent Biblical family, the murder of the innocents, the terrible injustice, the bursting to the seams of the prison system, posthumanism AI takeover, transhumanism on the horizon, the floods, the fires, the storms, the increase in homelessness, the lack of national security, the fall of the almighty dollar—threatening to be replaced by cryptocurrency, and the list goes on and on. Truly, unless a miracle happens in America, this Titanic will sink, and many will die.

In the midst of all these terrible challenges, there is one trend that could make it or break it for America. This I will call "the straw that breaks the camel's back" - the very thing that pokes the God of Israel, the Creator of heaven and earth, in the eye: an alarming and steady growth in antisemitism (which I will call anti-Jewish), including hatred and persecution of the Jews for being Jewish or for supporting the State of Israel. While all the other challenges mentioned look more important and more evil and poignant, we have missed the *ancient key* that makes the world go around. We have given this issue *very little* importance, thinking it to be marginal and secondary at best. In our ignorance of God and His Word, we have been blinded to notice what He considers to be of utmost importance for the wellbeing and national security of any nation or empire, including the United States of America.

This *key* that we have missed, I call it
The Key of Abraham.

The wellbeing and safety of the entire world depend on this all-encompassing key.

El Shaddai[*] said to Abram about him and his natural descendants, the people of Israel, the Jewish people of today,

> "I will bless those who bless you, and him who dishonors you I will curse, and in you all the families of the earth shall be blessed."
>
> — Genesis 12:3 esv

Whenever dishonoring, discrediting, persecuting, and harming the Jews becomes tolerated and ignored, that society, that nation, will go down and will be destroyed. This includes antisemitism and anti-Zionism. This world is on the verge of a catastrophic judgment because of the cause of Zion, the violation of the principles of the Key of Abraham.[**]

---

[*] The Most High in Hebrew
[**] Order my book *The Key of Abraham* at www.ZionsGospel.com

> "Draw near, O nations, to hear, and give attention, O peoples! Let the earth hear, and all that fills it; the world, and all that comes from it. For the LORD is enraged against all the nations, and furious against all their host; he has devoted them to destruction, has given them over for slaughter.
> For the LORD has a day of vengeance, a year of recompense for the cause of Zion."
>
> —Isaiah 34:1-2, 8 ESV

The first thing all of America needs to repent for, above any other issue, is tolerating, ignoring, or minimizing anti-Jewish feelings in all forms. Entire churches and denominations are called to repent for replacement theology that encompasses nearly every Christian doctrine with jealousy, pride, and ultimately hatred against "the murderers of Christ"– the Jews of 2000 years ago and the supposed "murderers of Palestinian children," the Israelis of today.

The disinformation campaign about the Jews and Israel is running deep, both in religious circles as well as humanistic non-religious circles - among Christians, agnostics, atheists, and Muslims. It is a plague that encompasses all sectors of society, from the Black Hebrews to the White Supremacists, from the Democrats to the Republicans, and from the BLM and Antifa groups to the Neo-Nazi groups.

Turning away from antisemitism is a call for all of America and, in fact, for all of the world. This includes denouncing it, rejecting it, and removing it from our faith doctrines and anti-Zionist political ideology. We are all called to expose this evil and oppose it everywhere—at home, church, and school, in the media, social media, universities, government halls, and the courts. We are being called to *outlaw* any group that is based on antisemitic Nazi rhetoric, like the Neo-Nazis that are allowed to parade with their swastikas, writing, publishing, and chanting "death to the Jews." Lest we outlaw this evil in the USA, the curse of God Almighty is upon our nation, and the American dream will be a dream of the past.

> "Death and life are in the power of the tongue, and those who love it will eat its fruits."
>
> —Proverbs 18:21 ESV

This is a wake-up call to repent in prayer and action before the God we have offended by hating, tolerating hatred, and by not protecting His Jewish people, the natural heirs of Abraham, Isaac, and Jacob. He will keep His covenant with them forever, whether we like it or not, even in their total imperfection and sin.

> **He remembers his covenant forever, the word that he commanded, for a thousand generations, the covenant that he made with Abraham, his sworn promise to Isaac, which he confirmed to Jacob as a statute, to Israel as an everlasting covenant, saying, "To you I will give the land of Canaan as your portion for an inheritance."**
>
> —Psalm 105:8-11 ESV

Unless we repent of this great evil and make restitution for our actions, the next pandemic, hurricane, unquenchable fire, recession, or mass shooting is on its way. We must stop pointing fingers to the right or the left. We must all, as a nation indivisible before God, repent in dust and ashes for offending Him by touching the pupil (apple) of His eye (His Jewish people) and by failing to defend them by just legislations that outlaws all forms of Jewish hatred, including anti-Zionism both in written, digital, and spoken form or in action.

> "For thus said the LORD of hosts, after his glory sent me to the nations who plundered you, for he who touches you touches the apple of his eye:"
>
> —Zechariah 2:8 ESV

There is no reason why the Jews in New York would be afraid to go to synagogue or to wear a *yarmulke** in public. There is no reason why the Jews of Orlando or Tampa, Florida, would have to suffer outrageous Neo-Nazi parades and displays of hatred allowed by the city under the guise of a misinterpreted First Amendment. There is no reason why most Jewish students in most of the colleges and universities of the country would have to hide their Jewishness and their natural love and sympathy for the State of Israel. Countless Jewish students in the country suffer mental anguish and terror daily by the great evil of antisemitism and anti-Zionism fueled by faculty and pro-Palestinian students alike. Paid professors have been methodically impregnating America's best learning institutes with hatred against the Jews and Israel.

This distressful state of affairs is well known and tolerated by all governments and legislators from both sides of politics and by a sleeping, accommodating society. We can no longer plead ignorance of this! The statistics are known; these are established facts of the present situation, albeit ignored by most or dismissed as unimportant vs. "other important matters." But this is not so in God's eyes,

---

* A skullcap, called also as a *kippah*, worn by Jewish men during prayer.

"Rescue those who are being taken away to death; hold back those who are stumbling to the slaughter. If you say, "Behold, we did not know this," does not he who weighs the heart perceive it? Does not he who keeps watch over your soul know it, and will he not repay man according to his work?"

—Proverbs 24:11-12 ESV

Neo-Nazism is connected to many, if not most, of the mass shootings in America, with Buffalo, NY, being only one of them. When we ignore hatred against the Jews, hatred and death curses permeate our society. And no matter how much we fight to uproot immorality and murder of innocents, we will fail, for America is under the curse of this *ancient key* that makes the world go around.

The Key of Abraham

"I will bless those who bless you, and him who dishonors you I will curse, and in you all the families of the earth shall be blessed."

— Genesis 12:3 ESV

The remedy? Repentance and restitution started from churches, Christian groups, and home groups all over America, branching into *both* political parties with state officials and legislators.*

1. Humility, prayer, and repentance.
2. Turning from the evil ways of Jew dishonor and hatred.

---

* 2 Chronicles 7:13-14

3. Outlawing Jew-hating groups that have antisemitism and any racial bias in their ideology, like the Neo-Nazis, BLM*, and Antifa.
4. Global reeducation of our society from nursery to nursing home, from kindergarten to university, from church to church, through media and social media.**

Taking these steps will ensure the continuity of America and any nation as a wholesome, blessed society and a future sheep nation founded on Biblical Judeo-Christian Messianic values.

> When I shut up the heavens so that there is no rain, or command the locust to devour the land, or send pestilence among my people, if my people who are called by my name humble themselves, and pray and seek my face and turn from their wicked ways (of Jewish hatred, antisemitism, anti-Zionism, ignoring or tolerating it), then I will hear from heaven and will forgive their sin and heal their land.
>
> —2 Chronicles 7:13-14 ESV

---

* Black Lives Matter movement
** Recommended: *The Identity Theft* book and GRI (Global Reeducation Initiative) online course against antisemitism; available at www.against-antisemitism.com

CHAPTER 23

INHERITANCE OR POSSESSION?

> "...saying: "To you I give the land of Canaan as your allotted inheritance."
>
> — 1 CHRONICLES 16:18

A VERY INTERESTING INHERITANCE battle in my family has presented a special case to study the Torah about the matter. One of my second cousins took advantage of his proximity to a property left by my late paternal grandfather from Chile. Most of us heirs were not aware of the existence of this property or at least had forgotten about it.

> "You will take possession of the land, so you will settle in it, because I have given it to you to possess."
>
> —NUMBERS 33:53

My cousin, whom I will call Ted, lives in Chile, whereas most of the other heirs do not. He took advantage of his proximity to the property and effectively took possession of it. Since he works in an office that deals with abandoned properties, he also knew the laws in Chile that stipulate that anyone who lives for five years on a property that has been abandoned by its owners can become the official owner of the property.

Ted also proceeded to repair, remodel, and make it nice for him to live in. I would like to bring light to the difference between *inheritance* and *possession*. This subject sheds light on the struggle of the Jewish people as the rightful heirs of the land of Canaan for up to 1000 generations.

> "He remembers His covenant forever—the word He commanded for a thousand generations—which He made with Abraham, and swore to Isaac, and confirmed to Jacob as a decree, to Israel as an everlasting covenant, saying, "To you I give the land of Canaan, the portion of your inheritance.""
>
> —Psalms 105:8-11

The Holy Scriptures talk about two words for what is commonly called *inheritance*. One is *nahala*, and the other one is *Yerusha*, from which also derives the word *Yerushalayim*, the real name of the Holy City of Jerusalem.

> "But Judah will be inhabited forever—Jerusalem from generation to generation."
>
> —Joel 4:20

Nahala means inheritance by legal right.

Yerusha means inheritance by effectual possession.

Nahala is a passive term, while Yerusha requires *action*. In the case of Ted, he is one of the heirs of this nahala, like all my cousins and their descendants, but he took effective possession of a property we had all abandoned, forgotten, or were ignorant of its existence. He took advantage of the situation and took possession legally, whether we like it or not. Because the property had been abandoned, anyone who is not a legal heir could have taken effective possession legally, and the family would have lost it altogether.

> "Thus says ADONAI: "In a time of favor I will answer you. In a day of salvation I will help you. I will keep You and give You as a covenant to the people, to restore the land, to make them possess its desolate inheritances,"
>
> —ISAIAH 49:8

If the Jewish people, the legal heirs of the Land of Israel, do not take possession of all empty and abandoned lands, we can lose them. Furthermore, if they do not remove illegal squatters and illegal settlers who have a warrant of eviction, they set a precedent to lose more land in the future.

> So Joshua said to Bnei-Yisrael, "How long will you be slack about going in to possess the land which ADONAI, the God of your fathers, has given you? Appoint for yourselves three men from each tribe, and I will send them, and they will arise and walk through the land, and describe it according to their inheritance, and then return to me."
>
> —JOSHUA 18:3-4

It is very important to have the Jewish people move to Israel to possess the land of their God-given inheritance effectively.

> "For your waste and desolate places and your destroyed land will now be surely too small for the inhabitants, and those who swallowed you up will be far away. The children of your be-

reavement will yet say in your ears, "The place is too cramped for me! Make room for me to settle in.""

—Isaiah 49:19-20

The Land of Israel belongs to the people of Israel forever, but it is not until we take effective possession that we can live in it and enjoy our inheritance. An action needs to take place, which often involves a monetary price, a battle, and considerable effort to take effective possession and turn it into a *Yerusha*.

When the first aliyahs of Jews came back to the land to effectively possess their inheritance after 2000 years of exile, they found it abandoned and neglected. All those Arabs and Turks that had used the land for their own benefit never cared for it.

There was no central government, meaningful infrastructure, life-giving agriculture, import, export, or anything. Various villagers had small farms that produced the food their families needed. The land was barren. They had not forested it, and to avoid taxes under the 400 years of the Ottoman empire, they cut down most of the trees, turning the land into a desert. Many areas in Northern Israel, especially in Galilee, were left swampy and infested with malaria. Then the Jews, the legal heirs, began to return and take effective possession, at great expense of finances and life, and made it bloom!

> "The land that was desolate will be tilled instead of being a wasteland in the sight of all that passed by."
>
> —Ezekiel 36:34

The Jewish *Olim**, or new immigrants forested it and established agricultural community farms called *kibbutzim*. At the risk of death by malaria, they drained the swamps. Then, infrastructure, roads, and highways were built. The legal heirs took effective possession of their land. However, because of unbiblical politics and Arab propaganda, many areas of the land were still left abandoned. Arab nations fought the newly established State of Israel and, though outnumbered, won every battle. Later, the Arab States and the world weaponized the Arab inhabitants of the land and created, together with Hitler and the Nazi regime, the Palestinian cause based mostly on lies, for the purpose of eradicating the Jewish people from their rightful *nahala* and *yerusha*.

As long as the Jews keep taking effective possession of all parts of the Land of Promise, they will win every war. Taking possession is a bloody thing; it is both a legal and a physical battle. Taking possession often involves paying a bitter price for the land, including finances, personal safety, and life. Most of the land that Israel has today was purchased either with money by the Jews, obtained as war spoils after being unjustly attacked by Arab armies and defending herself, and/or received legally from the United Nations that voted on the partition between a Jewish and an Arab State.

We can expect that, as this battle continues and as long as the Jewish people keep paying the high price for possessing their land, they will expand more and more. The nations may rage, but the God of Israel left the nahala, the inheritance of the Land of Canaan, to the natural descendants of Abraham, Isaac, and Yaakov from the River of Egypt to the Euphrates. As long as the heirs keep paying the price to take possession legally, they will succeed.

---

* Ascenders to the Holy Land

Legally, it means taking possession by:

1. Purchase from Arab owners.
2. Settling abandoned lands that no one has cared for.
3. Defending themselves from war or terror and getting it as spoils of war—like the Golan Heights, East Jerusalem, Judea, Samaria, and the Jordan Valley after the Miracle Six-Day War.

Nowadays, the Land that the first Jewish returnees found barren and neglected at the end of the 19th century has become a vibrant country. Effective possession, Yerusha, has happened in various areas, but there is much more to do to fulfill Yah's promise.

> "They will say, 'This land that was a wasteland has become like the garden of Eden. The waste, desolate and ruined cities are fortified and inhabited.'"
>
> —Ezekiel 36:35

Inheritance without taking effective possession is a wasted and lost inheritance. Have you received a promise from YHVH? Then, pay the price to possess it. This requires faith, knowledge of the Torah of God, His promises, then the laws of your country, and endurance.

> "Then the nations that are left all around you will know that I, YHVH, have rebuilt the ruined places, and replanted what was desolate. I, YHVH have spoken it. So I will do it."
>
> —Ezekiel 36:36 STB

CHAPTER 24

DISPELLING THE PALESTINIAN CAUSE

"He remembers His covenant forever the word He commanded for a thousand generations which He made with Abraham, and swore to Isaac, and confirmed to Jacob as a decree, to Israel as an everlasting covenant, saying, "To you I give the land of Canaan, the portion of your inheritance."

— PSALMS 105:8-11

We want to share with you an article called *Israeli versus Arab Land Claims* by Alan Futerman and Walter Bloc. It dispels the Palestinian cause as a concocted lie with no historical and logical basis. This should be taught in all schools and universities!

Israeli versus Arab Land claims

Alan Futerman & Walter Block, Dec 11, 2023,*

> If neither Jews nor Arabs owned most of the land, did they have a right to establish a state there? The present conflagration is not, ultimately, about land titles. It is about the rejection of a Jewish state.

---

* Alan Futerman & Walter Block, Dec 11, 2023, 7:48 AM (GMT+2) (www.israelnationalnews.com/news/381754?utm_source=telegram&utm_medium=social&utm_campaign=share)

We can date, pretty accurately, how long Christianity has existed. Given that we are now in December 2023, we can say without much fear of contradiction that this religion has existed for roughly 2023 years.

What about Judaism? This is a bit rougher to estimate. As a high, the claim is "almost 4,000 years." A low is "more than 3,000." We will adopt the shorter estimate to be conservative.

How does Islam register? Estimates vary here, too, but not as widely. According to one source, it was the year 610, "following the first revelation to the prophet Muhammad at the age of 40." In the view of another, it was 622, "the year of the hijra, or 'emigration,' which marks the beginning of the Muslim calendar." A third authority claims this religion began "at the start of the 7th century CE," which is compatible with the other two dates. For round numbers, we will posit that the Muslim religion has been around for 2023 − 600 = 1423 years.

What does this historical record have to do with Israeli versus Arab land claims? According to John Locke, whom we regard as definitive in matters of this sort, the first person to homestead land is its rightful owner. That is, he who "mixes his labor" with virgin territory is deemed the proper owner of the land in question. Most, though not all Israelis are Jewish, while the same consideration applies to the other side: most, but not all Arabs are Muslims, adherents of the Islamic religion. We also rely upon Robert Nozick's insight about "legitimate title transfer" of land: we assume, other things equal, that it passes from parents to children.

Therefore, in any dispute between Arabs and Jews over land titles, the presumption lies with the latter. They were "around" for a longer period of time, and thus had more opportunities to come to be the legitimate owners of property. The Jews were busily occupying the contested land for more than double the time the Muslims were so doing.

To be sure, it is only a presumption that this determines proper ownership titles. It would not apply to land in much of sub-Saharan Africa, or northern Canada, nor much of South America or Australia or Siberia: neither group was known to have occupied any of these areas, historically. However, it certainly does apply to the Middle East, where the two groups contend as to rightful ownership over disputed territory. Which property, specifically? Take, for instance, the Temple Mount in Jerusalem, the most sacred site for Judaism. The Muslim constructions there came much later, centuries later. The Jews were there first.

But sites as the Temple Mount are small compared to the entire area, so what do we make of that? Jewish presence in the land was almost uninterrupted for 2,000 years. Yes, in small numbers, but still this occurred. The situation began to change at the end of the nineteenth century. By 1890, there were roughly 43 thousand Jews and some 432 thousand Muslims in the area. That, of course, began to change as time passed. The only reason there was no Jewish majority by 1948 is because the British severely restricted Jewish immigration in the 30's and 40's, thereby condemning millions to be slaughtered in Europe. In any case, only a few years later, population in Israel tripled. Jerusalem had a Jewish majority as early as the 1850s, though. Remember, this was west of the Jordan River, comprising an area that now holds about 9.4 million people in Israel, 3 million in Judea and Samaria, and 2 million in the Gaza Strip. And yet, it still is mostly empty (with about two-thirds of the territory consisting of desert, the Negev). If that is the case today, imagine what was the case 150 years ago. There was very little evidence of homesteading in most of the land by any group at the beginning of the twentieth century.

As the Jews returned in large numbers, they homesteaded much of their land once again. Their economy, agricultural development, and industrial investment were stronger than that which prevailed in the neighboring countries; this attracted Arabs to immigrate as well. Moreover, by 1948, roughly 9% of the land was owned by Jews and 20% nominally by Arabs (including about 3% by those who later became Israeli Arabs). But observe that the latter "Arab lands" were mostly regarded as uncultivable, hence, really unhomesteaded. Thus, it was not legitimately owned. In reality, these were titles based mostly on government concessions to absentee (that is non-) landowners. Actually, most of the land was government-owned (the Ottomans before WWI, and then the British).

So, if neither Jews nor Arabs owned most of the land, did they have a right to establish a state there? Well, yes, as long as it was a country that intended to build a society that respects and protects individual rights. In this sense, the UN Partition Plan of 1947 proposed two states mainly on the basis of demographic considerations. The Arabs rejected it (although by accepting they would have been in fact creating a second Arab state in the area after Jordan), and the Jews accepted. The rest is history. Now the Israel population contains 20% Arab citizens with equal rights, while Arab countries (including Palestinian Arab areas) are quite literally judenrein.

But what if there was an Arab state in Palestine before 1948? After all, it could be argued that there is no single country (with the exception of micro-states such as Lichtenstein or Monaco, or even these) that is based on fully homesteaded territories. So, if neither Arabs nor Jews owned most of the land, that is irrelevant. The relevant point is that there wasn't an Arab state; it was controlled by the British. Moreover, the charge against Israel is that it stole Palestine. In reality, Jews purchased much of it, and homesteaded much more of it later. And won even more of it in self-defense wars.

The Romans definitely conquered the Jews in Judea between 66 and 135 CE. This demonstrates that members of the Jewish faith were there at that time. The same cannot be said for the Arabs. They came later.

As for the Palestinian Arabs, they were Johnny-come-latelies as a group. And even in the twentieth century, both Jews and Arabs of Palestine were known as Palestinians. Several Jewish organizations, from *The Jerusalem Post* to the Israel Philharmonic Orchestra, were then *The Palestine Post* and The Palestine Philharmonic Orchestra, respectively. Once Israel was created, Jews were then known as Israelis. The term "Palestinian" was left for the Arabs by default. Does that mean that there were no Arabs in the area? Not at all. But Palestine was paradoxically not a Palestinian Arab entity, only a historical area (in fact, named by the Romans as such in order to denigrate the expelled Judean Jews).

The present conflagration is not, ultimately, about land titles. It is about the rejection of a Jewish state, even if it consists of a single synagogue in Tel Aviv whose property is deemed as kosher by John Locke himself. But who is the rightful owner of the contested territories? Israel's critics claim that the Jews were land-stealing "colonizers." As we have seen, this is not at all the case.

For more information on this covenant subject, please read my book *The Identity Theft*[*] to get equipped to stand for Israel against all antisemitism and lies spreading from the Palestinian cause. Your stand with Israel defines not just your destiny as an individual but the destiny of your family, community, and nation!

> "And I will bless those who bless you, and the one who curses you I will curse. And in you all the families of the earth will be blessed."
>
> —GENESIS 12:3

Join the United Nations for Israel for such a time as this![**]

---

[*] To order *The Identity Theft* book, visit at www.ZionsGospel.com
[**] Join the United Nations for Israel at www.UnitedNationsForIsrael.org

CHAPTER 25

THE DISTINCTION OF THE COVENANT

> But against any of the sons of Israel a dog will not even bark, whether against man or beast, that you may understand how the LORD makes a distinction between Egypt and Israel.
>
> — EXODUS 11:7 NASB '95

IT IS TO YHVH's honor to make a distinction, a marked difference between those who are His people and those who are not His people. That is the only way He can show the world who He is. He is glorified through His people, and He does that by keeping the terms of His covenant. Regarding Israel, He says that He has an eternal covenant or, in Hebrew, *brit olam*.

> I will establish My covenant between Me and you and your descendants after you throughout their generations for an everlasting covenant, to be God to you and to your descendants after you.
>
> —GENESIS 17:7 NASB '95

As a nation, YHVH has an irrevocable, everlasting covenant with Israel.

> From the standpoint of the gospel they are enemies for your sake, but from the standpoint of God's choice they are beloved for the sake of the fathers; for the gifts and the calling of God are irrevocable.
>
> —ROMANS 11:28-29

Notice that they are enemies of the Gospel for the sake of the Gentiles, but there is a time when that enmity ends, and YHVH keeps the covenant with Abraham, Isaac, and Jacob in its totality. The totality of the covenant includes the promise of the entire Land of Israel and an intimate walk with the LORD of the land and their God (the God of Israel) through the new covenant.

> "Behold, days are coming," declares YHVH, "when I will make a new covenant with the house of Israel and with the house of Judah...
> "But this is the covenant which I will make with the house of Israel after those days," declares YHVH, "I will put My law within them and on their heart I will write it; and I will be their God, and they shall be My people."
>
> —JEREMIAH 31:31, 33 STB

The "I will's" of Elohim make the distinction of the covenant very clear. In other words, He will keep His side of the covenant regardless of the condition of the people.

> For I will take you from the nations, gather you from all the lands and bring you into your own land. "Then I will sprinkle clean water on you, and you will be clean; I will cleanse you from all your filthiness and from all your idols.
>
> —EZEKIEL 36:24-25

Notice that He returns Israel to the land in a very sinful condition and full of idolatry. Nevertheless, He keeps His side of the covenant, regardless of their condition; and then, in the land, He cleanses them from their filth. This reminds me of the terms of the Gospel. He brings us into His arms just as we are and cleanses us within His embrace. He does that because He is faithful to His promises and makes a distinction between those in the covenant and those outside of the covenant. What makes the difference is the blood of the covenant! He made the distinction in Israel when they put the blood of the Lamb on the doorposts of their homes.

> "I will sanctify My great Name, which has been profaned among the nations—which you have profaned among them. The nations will know that I am ADONAI"—it is a declaration of ADONAI—"when I am sanctified in you before their eyes."
>
> —EZEKIEL 36:23

> 'The blood shall be a sign for you on the houses where you live; and when I see the blood I will pass over you, and no plague will befall you to destroy you when I strike the land of Egypt.'
>
> —EXODUS 12:13

Making a distinction does not mean that He winks at the sin of His people, neither Jew nor grafted-in Gentile. It just means that He is committed to us by blood and will fulfill His commitment regardless of what we do. Nevertheless, He seriously deals with His people who do not line up with His will and commandments. In other words, "Don't push grace to the limits!"

The privileges of the covenant also "call us to task" and to be humble to walk in His ways.

> 'For I am with you,' declares YHVH, 'to save you; for I will destroy completely all the nations where I have scattered you, only I will not destroy you completely. But I will chasten you justly and will by no means leave you unpunished.'
>
> —Jeremiah 30:11 stb

The distinction of the covenant promises special benefits and privileges such as favor, provision, and protection because Yah is a good Father! But just like any good father (Him being the best), He does not leave His children unpunished when they "misbehave." However, His chastisement is not for the purpose of breaking His covenant, but is done because He is just. However, even when He is executing His justice on the earth, you can clearly see the distinction between Israel and the nations. He does bring an end to the nations, but *never* will He bring an end to Israel, even if their sins are very serious! You could say He has a «soft spot» for His own kids, and He is pretty upset when someone else "touches" them.

> For YHVH'S indignation is against all the nations, and His wrath against all their armies; He has utterly destroyed them, He has given them over to slaughter.
> For YHVH has a day of vengeance, a year of recompense for the cause of Zion.
>
> —Isaiah 34:2, 8 stb

When we talk about Israel and the Gentile portion of the church, we also talk about the distinction of the covenant. In other words, this distinction towards Israel continues, and it also affects those who are Gentiles in the new covenant.

> But if some of the branches were broken off, and you, being a wild olive, were grafted in among them and became partaker with them of the rich root of the olive tree, do not be arrogant toward the branches; but if you are arrogant, remember that it is not you who supports the root, but the root supports you.
>
> —ROMANS 11:17-18

Notice that the Apostle Paul is speaking here to the Gentiles, and He basically tells them that the Father is very jealous of His Jewish people. He is ensuring that His newly adopted children from the Gentiles know that they cannot usurp their place or treat them badly without it carrying serious consequences. In other words, He is still making a distinction between Israel and the nations, even if they are grafted into the olive tree. The ingrafting of s through the Gospel does not nullify His everlasting covenant with Israel, and He is calling His children to attention on this life and death matter.

> Behold then the kindness and severity of God; to those who fell, severity, but to you, God's kindness, if you continue in His kindness; otherwise you also will be cut off.
>
> —ROMANS 11:22

You can see that He is making sure that His in-grafted children are very careful in their attitude toward His Jewish people—especially when His Jewish people are being chastised. Unfortunately, this serious warning was not heeded, and in many Christian circles, it is still not heeded. In fact, some people get offended, and they then try to shut off the entire subject of repentance towards Israel because of the past and present sins of the church and many of those who profess Christianity in one way or another.

I would love to stop preaching on this subject and "move on," but the Holy Spirit is literally "on me" to keep repeating it again and again—because this is a matter of life and death. At present, He is judging both the church and the nations for this serious sin of "arrogance against the Jews." Some call it antisemitism; I call it anti-MESITOJUZ. It means anti-Messiah, anti-Israel, anti-Torah, anti-Jewish, and anti-Zionist.

He is judging His church first and then the nations!

For it is time for judgment to begin with the household of God; and if it begins with us first, what will be the outcome for those who do not obey the gospel of God?

—1 Peter 4:17

As we cry out for revival, let us remember the "Key of Abraham",* which makes the clear distinction between those who bless Israel in action and those who curse her. This is the factor that will determine the end-time revival.

And I will bless those who bless you, and the one who curses you I will curse. And in you all the families of the earth will be blessed.

—Genesis 12:3 NASB '95

If you have read my book *Sheep Nations*,** you know that the word *curse*, in this case, means to "take Israel lightly" or ignore her altogether. Many people have not done any personal evil against Israel, but they

---

* Order the book *The Key pf Abraham* at www.ZionsGospel.com
** Order the book *Sheep Nations* at www.ZionsGospel.com

have ignored her altogether. Millions of Christians treat Israel as if it were "any other nation." They have forgotten to honor the distinction of the covenant that YHVH Himself made and that He Himself honors. That is actually cursing Israel by treating her "lightly" and YHVH's will on this lightly. This is a plague in many churches, among many Christians, and within many nations.

The key to the end-time revival is thorough repentance on this issue and the ensuing restitution. Then YHVH will hear from heaven and answer our cries for revival.

If My people who are called by My name humble themselves and pray and seek My face and turn from their wicked ways, then I will hear from heaven, will forgive their sin and will heal their land.

—2 Chronicles 7:14

May Yah make a distinction between all those who love Israel in action, especially as you partner with us to continue preaching this message for the salvation of the nations and the restoration of Israel. At these times of great shakings and fearsome occurrences, those of you who have chosen to join us in this urgent message will have special favor and protection as He promised.

Stay faithful to Yeshua and His everlasting covenant with Israel, and you will enjoy the fullness of the distinction of the covenant!

CHAPTER 26

THE BATTLE OF THE GODS

> He who sits in heaven laughs! YHVH mocks them. So He will speak to them in His anger, and terrify them in His fury: "I have set up My king upon Zion, My holy mountain."
>
> — PSALMS 2:4-6 ST

THE GODS ARE FIGHTING over Jerusalem. Nations directed by these gods are taking sides, and the God of Israel—the only God that counts—is sitting in the heavens and laughing. We should be laughing with Him, though, as humans, it is painful to witness this epic battle - the showdown of the ages.

I woke up this morning in the Holy City to this Word, and then I saw headlines that read as follows:

Australia reverses recognition of West Jerusalem as Israel's capital.

On Tuesday, Oct. 18, Australia reversed the previous government's recognition of West Jerusalem as the capital of Israel and said the issue should be resolved as part of peace talks between Israel and Palestine.[*]

---

[*] www.fb.com/TheStarOnline

Hahaha! Who are you, "mighty Australia," that you think your opinion matters to the God of Israel? The pride and conceit of the gods ruling the nations have come to the brim. The judgment is inevitable. All the kingdoms of these gods will be shaken until they bow down before only one God. It will not be easy to be on this earth for the next seven years, but if we are privileged to be alive at this time, it is to serve YHVH Tzevaot! And, yes, to execute the judgment that is written.

> **For it is written, "I will destroy the wisdom of the wise and bring to nothing the understanding of the intelligent."**
>
> —1 Corinthians 1:19

These are exciting times, terrible times, shaking times, and transitioning times from one age to another. It is all about Jerusalem.

> "Moreover, in that day I will make Jerusalem a massive stone for all the people. All who try to lift it will be cut to pieces. Nevertheless, all the nations of the earth will be gathered together against her."
>
> —Zechariah 12:3

These are times of distinction, definition, and separation.

> Then those who feared YHVH spoke with one another. YHVH paid attention and heard them, and a book of remembrance was written before him of those who feared YHVH and esteemed his name. "They shall be mine, says YHVH Tzevaot, in the day when I make up my treasured possession, and I will spare them as a man spares his son who serves him. Then once more you shall see the distinction between the righteous and

the wicked, between one who serves God and one who does not serve him."

—Malachi 3:16-18 stb

The "but" in the story of the coming shakings is, "But for those who fear My name,"

"But for you who fear my name, the sun of righteousness shall rise with healing in its wings. You shall go out leaping like calves from the stall. And you shall tread down the wicked, for they will be ashes under the soles of your feet, on the day when I act, says YHVH Tzevaot."

—Malachi 4:2-3 stb

We are called to be watchmen over this awesome yet terrible process of the restoration of the kingdom to Israel.

"For Zion's sake I will not keep silent, for Jerusalem's sake I will not rest, until her righteousness shines out brightly, and her salvation as a blazing torch. Nations will see your righteousness, and all kings your glory. You will be called by a new name, which YHVH's mouth will bestow."

—Isaiah 62:1-2 stb

This is the time to take sides, to choose whom you will serve, the God of Israel or the gods of the nations.

"If I forget you, O Jerusalem, let my right hand wither. May my tongue cling to the roof of my mouth if I cease to remember you, if I do not set Jerusalem above my chief joy."

—Psalms 137:5-6

CHAPTER 27

ISRAEL—THE HOLY TRIUNITY

> He remembers His covenant forever—the word He commanded for a thousand generationswhich He made with Abraham, and swore to Isaac, and confirmed to Jacob as a decree, to Israel as an everlasting covenant, saying, "To you I give the land of Canaan, the portion of your inheritance."
>
> — PSALMS 105:8-11

There is no other name that provokes more emotion than the name of Israel: in some, it's love, and in some, irrational hatred. But why is this? What is it about Israel that makes it the center of world attention, both positive and negative?

Israel, The Holy Triunity:
1. The God of Israel
2. The People of Israel
3. The Land of Israel

One obedient man by the name of Abram was made into a nation by the God who created the heavens and the earth. This God has many names. Among others, He is called the God of Abraham, Isaac, and Jacob, and also the God of Israel.

The grandson of Abraham was named Yaakov (Jacob), and after an intense struggle with the angel of God, he was renamed Israel, which means the prince of God. It was to Abraham and his descendants (his son Isaac and grandson Jacob) that God promised a land called Canaan, which was later renamed Israel. Because of this historical promise, the land was named The Land of Israel or the Land Belonging to Israel (Jacob), the grandson of Abraham. Jacob-Israel fathered 12 sons, who were termed the 12 tribes of Israel, with one of the tribes called to bring salvation and redemption to the whole world. This is the tribe of Judah, from which the term Jew or Jewish derives.

The King of the Jews would be born into the royal house of the tribe of Judah, the house of David. This King, though born of the womb of a Jewish young woman named Miriam, was born in a miraculous way of her virgin womb. And, though being the second Adam, he was called the Son of God as prophesied by the Israelite prophets of old. Whoever would accept this Jewish King and surrender to Him would receive forgiveness of sins and salvation - and whoever would reject Him would die in their sins and be lost for all eternity. This Israelite Jewish King, termed Messiah or the Anointed One, was named by His Father, the God of Israel.

YESHUA
Meaning SALVATION

Thus, the Holy Triunity was born.

The God who created Heaven and Earth—Elohim, El Shaddai, YHVH, the Great I Am—became the God of Israel. The people that He created to be a blessing and a light to all the nations was now called the people of Israel. The land granted by the Almighty to His people was now called the Land of Israel.

Any separation between these three prophetic components would impact the world adversely.

This holy triunity will be the prophetic wheel that will make the world go round.

The God of Israel made a key promise to Abraham. This key of Abraham serves as a protection to His people, Israel, as well as being a rudder for the right relationship of the nations with Israel, extending all the way to the Jewish people of today.

> **And I will bless those who bless you, and the one who curses you I will curse. And in you all the families of the earth will be blessed.**
>
> —**Genesis 12:3 nasb '95**

Light to the Nations

Israel was to be a light unto the nations by instructing them on the holy principles of morality and worship, given to her as a marriage covenant. This is called the Torah or instruction. The foundation of this Torah would be *ten Words* that became like a Heavenly constitution for any moral, Godly, and successful society.

Also, divinely appointed feasts were given as a frame of holy worship, starting with Shabbat Day (the day of rest), which has been established since creation. These feasts would be holy convocations, sweet dates with the Creator, and would be celebrated forever—even by non-Jews who adhere to the worship of the God of Israel and His Jewish Son, Yeshua, the Savior of the world.

> **Also the foreigners who join themselves to Adonai, to minister to Him, and to love the Name of Adonai, and to be His**

servants—all who keep from profaning Shabbat, and hold fast to My covenant—these I will bring to My holy mountain, and let them rejoice in My House of Prayer. Their burnt offerings and sacrifices will be acceptable on My altar. For My House will be called a House of Prayer for all nations.

—Isaiah 56:6-7

Then all the survivors from all the nations that attacked Jerusalem will go up from year to year to worship the King, Adonai-Tzva'ot, and to celebrate Sukkot.

—Zechariah 14:16

Grafted In

When Yeshua, the Jewish Messiah, was sent to give His life on the altar for the salvation and redemption of both Jews and Gentiles, He also became the Torah in human form or the living Torah. All the Word of His Father, as previously given to the people of Israel, became flesh and dwelt among us. Gentiles are invited to partake of the new covenant as given to the people of Israel. There is no new covenant made with any Gentile nation, as the God of Israel chose His people to bring forth salvation and redemption to the world.

> "But this is the covenant I will make with the house of Israel after those days"—it is a declaration of Adonai—"I will put My Torah within them. Yes, I will write it on their heart. I will be their God and they will be My people. No longer will each teach his neighbor or each his brother, saying: 'Know Adonai,' for they will all know Me, from the least of them to

the greatest." It is a declaration of ADONAI. "For I will forgive their iniquity, their sin I will remember no more."

—JEREMIAH 31:33-34

They are invited to partake of the rich root of the olive tree (Romans 11), which represents the nation of Israel, with all the righteous instructions of holy lifestyle, morality, and holy worship.

However, they were warned not to become arrogant by usurping the place of God's chosen people –or by disdaining them for lingering to recognize their own Messiah.

> But if some of the branches were broken off and you—being a wild olive—were grafted in among them and became a partaker of the root of the olive tree with its richness, do not boast against the branches. But if you do boast, it is not you who support the root but the root supports you.

—ROMANS 11:17-18

Blindness came upon them in part (not in full) so that salvation, Yeshua, could go to the nations. The ultimate purpose was to make them *jealous* to have their Messiah back. However, history tells us that Gentiles did become arrogant by establishing a religious system that humiliated and persecuted Jews - all the way to extermination in the Romanized name of their Messiah, Jesus Christ. This is a religious system divorced from the Jewish Messiah, His Torah instructions, His Holy convocations, and feasts, attempting to usurp the place of His chosen people, Israel.

This has caused untold woes and destruction to the Jewish people throughout 1600 years. It has also brought endless curses to individuals, churches, families, and nations who have lifted their hands against

His people. This has not provoked Israel to jealousy, so then the heart desire of the Apostle Paul has gone largely unfulfilled.

> "For thus says ADONAI-Tzva'ot, He has sent me after glory to the nations that plundered you—because whoever touches you touches the apple of His eye—"
>
> —ZECHARIAH 2:12

Am Israel Chai!
The people of Israel are alive!

CHAPTER 28

THE ISRAEL TEST

> "For thus says Adonai-Tzva'ot, He has sent me after glory to the nations that plundered you—because whoever touches you touches the apple of His eye—"
>
> — ZECHARIAH 2:12

WILL THE CHURCH PASS the test this time when Israel is at its lowest? Or will history try to repeat itself, like during the time of the Shoah (Holocaust) when churches just "sang a little louder" when the Jews were burning?

> "Rescue those being dragged off to death, hold back those stumbling to slaughter. If you say, "Look, we didn't know this." Won't He who weighs hearts perceive it? Won't He who guards your soul know it? Won't He repay each one according to his deeds?"
>
> —PROVERBS 24:11-12

Christians had been conditioned through replacement theology to hate Jews. They believed hideous things about them. After all, many of the revered church fathers called them "children of Satan", murderers of our LORD, pigs, donkeys, vermin, and the like. Hitler only took a ride on existing Christian theologies and beliefs, and it was easy; they were ripe.

You will be appalled by what circulates in Christian circles nowadays. You would think we are again in the Dark Ages. The following is from a Christian and very patriotic group chat in the US:

"Ashkenazi Jews…descendants of Cain. They call themselves Jews because they kept being run out of countries for their Luciferian practices. People accept Jews… people do not accept Satanists! This goes back to the beginning… it's why they are so concerned with bloodline."

You would think that people in this chat group would rebuke them or shut them down, but no! Actually, some gave their emphatic "amen" to this blood libel of sorts, except one Christian lady who is married to a Jew and thus tried to defend them, but her voice was drowned. This is what she said:

"That is the most ridiculous thing I have ever read. I married into an Ashkenazi Jewish family, and they are nothing of the sort. And neither are any of their relatives. This is how antisemitism is fed."

I reported the post and other posts to the admin of Telegram as violent and serious antisemitism. I hope they will pay attention. We must denounce this; we cannot stay silent!

Yes, Epstein was a Jew, Soros is a Jew, and there are "bad apples" among the Jews. Still, there are also many such bad people among Americans, Norwegians, Ecuadorians, and of every nationality and ethnic group. But only the Jews are vilified as the "culprit" for all evil. This is beyond ignorance; this is plain wicked and deathly dangerous! It must be exposed, denounced, and pulverized! Wasn't the Nazi Shoah (Holocaust) enough to immunize the world against this wickedness?

Apparently not! The Bible calls this "hostility against Zion," and He is fixing to judge all the nations because of this.

> "For ADONAI is enraged at all the nations, and furious at all their armies. He will utterly destroy them. He will give them over to slaughter.
> For ADONAI has a day of vengeance, a year of recompense for the hostility against Zion."
>
> —ISAIAH 34:2, 8

Another very prevalent lie is about all Jews being the synagogue of Satan, as mentioned in the book of Revelation. This lie seems prevalent among the Black Hebrews as well as many white Americans.

> "I know your tribulation and your poverty (yet you are rich), as well as the slander of those who say they are Jewish and are not, but are a synagogue of satan."
>
> —THE REVELATION 2:9

Internet searches of "synagogue of Satan" produce quite a few links to sites that claim the "synagogue of Satan" refers to the Jewish people today and that promote all kinds of conspiracy theories about how the Jews run the world. Quite frankly, this is a misinterpretation and misapplication of the verses in Revelation. The synagogue of Satan refers to specific Jewish communities in Smyrna and Philadelphia who were persecuting the Messianic believers of the first century, not to any modern situation. Likewise, no modern situation should be used as an interpretive tool to explain a passage firmly rooted in the first-century Roman world.

As our team was walking through downtown Georgia, I saw a booth of the Black Hebrews Church. They had all kinds of slogans and signs about them being the true Israel. I passed and asked them, "If you are the true Israel, what is the nation of Israel in the Land of Israel?" These belligerent young men began to quote in unison with beat and rhythm from the book of Revelation about Israel being the synagogue of Satan and not true Jews. Only those of the Black Hebrews Church are the true Jews. They were vocal, committed, and aggressive. The whole street could hear them.

In Hanukkah of 2019, some members of this kind of church group murdered a rabbi and Jewish worshippers celebrating Hanukkah in the private home of the rabbi. You could not have a public booth with megaphones speaking against homosexuals and drag queens in America. They would probably arrest you for a hate crime. But calling Israel and all Jews in loudspeakers "the synagogue of Satan" is OK. Black Lives Matter, but Jewish lives do not matter. Wake up, America!

I wish I could say that these are only marginal groups, except they cover various segments of the population, including blacks, whites, Latinos, you name it! Even spirit-filled evangelicals have asked me questions that make me wonder how deep antisemitism runs even inside the veins of those who would be considered "good Christians." And it is especially in times of crisis, uncertainty, financial shakings, and civil unrest that this latent hatred against the Jewish people, God's eternally chosen people, erupts.

We are now living in such times, and we must wake up before it is too late!

Hitler said: tell a lie big enough and repeat it often until the whole world will believe it.

In 2001, when all of Argentina spilled onto the streets to overthrow their wicked government that had confiscated all savings accounts and pensions, we were there—sent by the Holy Spirit from Jerusalem to blow the shofar at the Ezeiza airport right before it erupted. We documented everything; we went on the streets and saw that in the aftermath, many buildings had been perforated with bullets. But one stood out among them—a building that suffered the most damage. It was none other than the Israeli Embassy.

We turned to interview people, cameras on hand, and asked them why this revolution. The first answer was, "Because of the Jews!" They are to blame for all the woes of Argentina! Strange answer in a country that gave shelter to escaped Nazi officers more than any other country besides America, maybe, where the largest pro-Nazi rally outside of Berlin was held (in New York). But it's not really strange. Satan hates the Jews; he hates Israel. We are the only reason he cannot rule supremely! Our mere existence proves the God of the Bible true. When England's Queen Victoria asked Prime Minister Benjamin Disraeli,* a British Jew, "What proof is there that God exists?" His answer was: The Jews, my lady, the Jews.

> "So now, do not fear, Jacob My servant," says ADONAI, "nor be dismayed, O Israel, for behold, I will save you from afar, your seed from the land of their exile. Jacob will again be quiet and at ease, and no one will make him afraid. For I am with you," declares ADONAI, "to save you, for I will make a full end of all the nations where I scatter you. but I will not make a full end of you. For I will discipline you justly, but will not leave you unpunished."
>
> —JEREMIAH 30:10-11

---

* In office from 1874 to 1880.

We must reeducate the whole world, especially Christendom. It is a matter of life and death. The misinformation, bias, and ignorance seem to be almost as deep as during Hitler's time, albeit much more dangerous and all-encompassing because of social media. The handwriting is on the wall. Will the world, especially the church in America and in every nation, pass the Israel test this time?

> "For the day of ADONAI is near against all the nations. As you have done, it shall be done to you. Your dealing will return on your own head. For just as you have drunk on My holy mountain, so all the nations shall drink continually. Yes, they will drink and gulp down, and then be as though they had never existed. But on Mount Zion there will be deliverance, and it will be holy. Then house of Jacob will dispossess those who dispossessed them."
>
> —OBADIAH 1:15-17

CHAPTER 29

NON-NEGOTIABLES—MY ISRAEL

> Be silent before ADONAI, all flesh, for He has aroused Himself from His holy dwelling."
>
> — ZECHARIAH 2:17

> I say then, they did not stumble so as to fall, did they? May it never be! But by their false step salvation has come to the Gentiles, to provoke Israel to jealousy.
>
> —ROMANS 11:11

ONE OF THE MAJOR tenets of replacement theology and "The Identity Theft" of the Messiah* is the lie that the church superseded or replaced Israel. In many old churches, statues of two women were placed in prominent locations in the church building. One statue was of a queenly woman standing erect with a crown on her head, and the other statue was of a poor, broken, humiliated, bowed-down woman. The queenly woman represented the "Church Triumphant" over the "Vanquished Synagogue," or the Christians triumphing over the broken and humiliated Jews.

---

* To learn more, order *The Identity Theft* book at www.ZionsGospel.com

The understanding of Christianity since the divorce from the Jewish roots during the fourth century—because of the codification of the decrees in the Council of Nicaea—was that Israel is under a curse forever. The preachers constantly declared to the masses that the church had inherited all the blessings given by God to the people of Israel, and the Jews had inherited all the curses. Antisemitism was and still is a founding doctrine in many denominations and churches. "We are Israel," many Christians say arrogantly; "We are the Israel of God. The old Israel missed the time of their visitation when Jesus Christ came, so now we, the Gentile Christians, have inherited the covenant and all its blessings." And yet God is very clear in the Scriptures that He will never break His covenant with Israel. He may discipline her, but He will never destroy her, forsake her, or stop being the God of Israel.

> "So now, do not fear, Jacob My servant," says ADONAI, "nor be dismayed, O Israel, for behold, I will save you from afar, your seed from the land of their exile. Jacob will again be quiet and at ease, and no one will make him afraid. For I am with you," declares ADONAI, "to save you, for I will make a full end of all the nations where I scatter you. But I will not make a full end of you. For I will discipline you justly but will not leave you unpunished."
>
> —JEREMIAH 30:10–11

Nations will come, and nations will go, and any nation that rises against Israel will end, but Israel will remain forever.

> "Yet all who devour you will be devoured, and all your foes—all of them—will go into captivity. Those plundering you will be plundered, and all preying on you I give as prey. For I will restore health to you and will heal you of your wounds." It is

a declaration of ADONAI. "For they called you an outcast: 'Zion—no one cares about her.'" Thus says ADONAI, "Indeed, I will return Jacob's tents from exile, and have compassion on his dwellings. The city will be rebuilt on her mound. The citadel will stand in its rightful place. Out of them will come thanksgiving and the sound of celebration. I will multiply them, so they will not decrease. I will also honor them, so they will not be insignificant. His children also will be as formerly—his community set up before Me—and I will punish all his oppressors."

—JEREMIAH 30:16–20

It was an enormous shocker to most of Christendom when Israel was reborn in its own land on May 14, 1948, after the Nazi Shoah (Holocaust) had decimated the Jewish population by annihilating over six million people. Yet despite the destruction of most of Europe's Jewish communities and synagogues (entire villages were wiped off the face of the earth), this "Vanquished Synagogue" rose like a phoenix from the ashes of Auschwitz, Birkenau, Treblinka, Sobibor, and many more death camps and concentration camps. These were true survivors; these Jewish skeletons had lost everything to a hate-filled regime that was the culmination of all that Christianity had taught throughout the years since Constantine and the Council of Nicaea. Hitler said, "I am doing the will of God," and he also called Martin Luther a "genius" for writing how to deal harshly with the Jews in his book *On the Jews and their Lies*.*

Both Catholic and Protestant churches have been indoctrinated throughout generations about the Jews. Replacement theology taught most of them to mock and hate us. This has continued until today in

---

* Süss and Luther

many circles. I wish I could tell you that this is over, but it is not over. There are constant posts on the internet with antisemitic events related to those that profess some Christianity or another.

Recently, a group from New Jersey called the "Black Hebrews" murdered Jews in cold blood who were celebrating the Jewish holiday of Hanukkah in the private house of their rabbi. This group claimed that they were the true Hebrews and not these Jews, and because they supposedly murdered Christ, they deserved to die. It shocked many people that this happened in the 21st century USA. Still, I am not surprised, as this demonic principality is hiding in the doctrine of many churches and denominations. And yet the God of Israel said in his Holy Word many times that Israel is His chosen nation forever—and He did not mean the church or any Christian nation.

Lately, during the coronavirus, or COVID-19 pandemic, a white Baptist pastor in Florida posted terrible accusations against Israel, saying that the Israelis caused the coronavirus. We call this a blood libel. This is when Jews and, in this case, the whole State of Israel are accused of crimes they did not commit, thus inciting the masses to hate them. Another antisemitic pastor and broadcaster in the USA said that the coronavirus is a punishment from God to the Jews for not following Jesus.

> **Thus says the LORD, who gives the sun for light by day and the fixed order of the moon and the stars for light by night, who stirs up the sea so that its waves roar; The LORD of hosts is His name: "If this fixed order departs from before Me," declares the LORD, "Then the offspring of Israel also will cease from being a nation before Me forever." Thus says the LORD, "If the heavens above can be measured and the foundations of the**

earth searched out below, then I will also cast off all the offspring of Israel for all that they have done," declares the LORD.

—JEREMIAH 31:35–37 NASB '95

We must restore the Jewish identity of the Messiah to have a holy division in the Church: between those who will accept Him as a Jew and will bless and make restitution towards natural Israel and between those who will continue claiming that they are the true Israel, and that Israel in the Middle East is a counterfeit country with a people that deserve to die. The lives of many deceived Christians are hanging in the balance. The restoration of the church's stolen identity—from a Romanized usurper of Israel to a grafted-in Ruth-like church (one that joins Israel through the blood of the Jewish Messiah Yeshua)—is the key to the salvation of the nations and for the end-time revival.

YHVH-Elohim, the God of Israel, promised His covenant with Israel will be forever. He never said that He would replace Israel with the church. In fact, He said that the church needs to be grafted in or join Israel, not replace Israel.

> But if some of the branches were broken off and you—being a wild olive—were grafted in among them and became a partaker of the root of the olive tree with its richness, do not boast against the branches. But if you do boast, it is not you who support the root but the root supports you. You will say then, "Branches were broken off so that I might be grafted in." True enough. They were broken off because of unbelief, and you stand by faith. Do not be arrogant, but fearfor if God did not spare the natural branches, neither will He spare you.
>
> —ROMANS 11:17–21

The Jewish apostle to the Gentiles is a rabbi named Shaul, also known by his Roman name Paul, who warned the Gentile believers never to be arrogant against the Jews or think they could usurp their place. In fact, his warning is so serious he stated that if Gentiles become arrogant against the Israelite-Jewish branches, their arrogance could cost them their eternal salvation. How many people has God broken off the olive tree by worshipping a Romanized Christ who hates the people of Israel? How many were broken off and are being removed from the olive tree of salvation for hating the Jews, being arrogant against them, and preaching that the church is now Israel, replacing the nation of Israel altogether?

Paul also warned about building on any other foundation but the one he declared, which is Yeshua the Messiah, the anointed Jewish King and Savior promised to Israel alone. But replacement theology, with its five-headed monster, has been intertwined in Church doctrine until this day, constantly building on a Roman-pagan foundation that breeds antisemitism.

> **For no one can lay any other foundation than what is already laid—which is Yeshua the Messiah. Now if anyone builds on the foundation with gold, silver, precious stones, wood, hay, straw, each one's work will become clear. For the Day will show it, because it is to be revealed by fire; and the fire itself will test each one's work—what sort it is. If anyone's work built on the foundation survives, he will receive a reward. If anyone's work is burned up, he will suffer loss—he himself will be saved, but as through fire.**
>
> —1 Corinthians 3:11–15

How many pastors are in danger of having all their hard labor burnt in the fire of YHVH's judgment because of replacement theology and overt or covert antisemitism? Espousing the deceptive theology that the Church replaced Israel is dangerous, and they root it in jealousy that breeds murder.

> **Then He said, "What have you done? The voice of your brother's blood is crying out to Me from the ground. So now, cursed are you from the ground which opened its mouth to receive your brother's blood from your hand. As often as you work the ground, it will not yield its crops to you again. You will be a restless wanderer on the earth."**
>
> **—Genesis 4:10–12**

Cain was jealous of Abel and rose to murder him rather than repent for his jealousy. If you are looking down on Israel and the Jews, harboring spiritual arrogance and thinking to yourself that the Church is better than Israel or has superseded Israel, think twice, lest the Almighty dismantles church after church, denomination after denomination—for He said that He has a day of vengeance to vindicate Israel. On that day, you cannot show him your denominational credentials to rescue yourself from His judgment.

> **For Adonai has a day of vengeance, a year of recompense for the hostility against Zion.**
>
> **—Isaiah 34:8**

Please remember that judgment always starts first in the house of God.

For the time has come for judgment to begin with the house of God. If judgment begins with us first, what will be the end for those who disobey the good news of God?

—1 Peter 4:17

Here is the good news: A Jew died for you, and His name is Yeshua. However, if people insist on downplaying His natural family, the known people of Israel with whom He has an eternal covenant, He might turn to become an enemy.

"For thus says Adonai-Tzva'ot (The Lord of the Armies), He has sent me after glory to the nations that plundered you (Israel My people)—because whoever touches you touches the apple of His eye—"

—Zechariah 2:12

The Key of Abraham

I will bless those who bless you, but whoever curses you I will curse, and in you all the families of the earth will be blessed.

—Genesis 12:3 nasb '95

Israel is not "the elder brother" but the mother of the nations. Our relationship with a mother differs from our relationship with a brother.

I will introduce you to the key of Abraham: the divine key that can open or close the gate of blessing and salvation for individuals, families, and entire nations. This key, given to Abraham, Isaac, and Jacob, repeats throughout the Scriptures.

Israel is the only nation with which the God of the Universe has a covenant, and until now, it is still so. All the blessings to the Gentiles come through the people of Israel, the original descendants of Abraham, Isaac, and Jacob, with whom God made the covenant. God's only covenant is with Abraham, his descendants, and all of those who:

- Join in with Israel through a Jewish Messiah
- Bless Israel

"Behold, days are coming"—it is a declaration of ADONAI—"when I will make a new covenant with the house of Israel and with the house of Judah—"
"But this is the covenant I will make with the house of Israel after those days"it is a declaration of ADONAI"I will put My Torah within them. Yes, I will write it on their heart. I will be their God and they will be My people."

—JEREMIAH 31:30, 32

This scripture refers to the new covenant. Gentiles join this covenant through the blood of Yeshua, the Jewish Messiah. God is not obligated to bless any nation unless that nation is grafted in with Israel and blesses Israel. Those are the only stipulations for the blessing of the nations. Are they good to Israel, or are they not? Are they walking in the ways of the God of Israel as given to Israel, or are they not?

This is the key to the salvation and blessing of the nations. It has been lost for nearly 1,700 years but is now being restored. When it is fully restored, the salvation of the nations will follow, and only then will we offer the Father many sheep nations!

> "I will bless those that bless you, and I will curse him who curses you and in you (Abram) all the families of the earth will be blessed,"
>
> —Genesis 12:3

Now let us study this verse from the Hebrew:

The word for blessing here is *bracha*. *Lebarech*, from the word *bracha*, means "to decree a word of life, goodness, favor, health, success, and prosperity over someone." This blessing has many wonderful and positive events and opportunities that will bring great joy, happiness, wholeness, prosperity, greatness, abundance, fruitfulness, and fulfillment (Deut. 28:1-14)! However, this word comes from the word *breech*, which means the "knee" in Hebrew. So let me paraphrase this verse for you:

> "I (the God of Israel) will bow down My royal knee to lift up and favor those who bow down their knees, and humble themselves to honor, speak well of, defend and do good to My people Israel"
>
> —Genesis 12:3a

YHVH Tzva'ot, the Lord of the armies, the God of the universe, the Creator of heaven and earth, has committed Himself by His unfailing and unchanging Word to bow down His royal knee to bless, favor and exalt those who humble themselves and bow down their knees to exalt and honor Israel! However, if they do not, He equally commits Himself to curse them.

> "I will curse those who curse you,"
>
> —Genesis 12:3b

Two Hebrew words are used in this verse for the word curse; one is *klala*, and the other is *meera*. *Klala* comes from the word *kal*, which means "light" (opposite of heavy). This curse refers to those who take Israel and the Jews lightly and do not honor or respect them as His chosen ones. God uses the same word for those who curse their father or mother:

> **And he that curses his father or his mother shall surely be put to death.**
>
> **—Exodus 21:17**

Those who disrespect their parents will die! Taking parents lightly, mocking them, not listening to their instructions, or disrespecting them brings evil to one's life. God likens Israel to a parent, a mother, the mother of the nations. He calls the nations to honor her as a mother. God commands us to honor our parents despite their imperfections: our lives depend on it!

> **Honor your father and your mother just as ADONAI your God commanded you, so that your days may be long and it may go well with you in the land ADONAI your God is giving you.**
>
> **—Deuteronomy 5:16**

If we do not humble ourselves to honor our parents even in their imperfection, it will not go well with us. When we take them lightly (*kal-klala*), the curse or destruction comes to us, which is *meera*. Israel is regarded by the Almighty as the mother of the nations. She is the one who brought mankind the Bible, the Messiah, and the gospel. Without Israel, there would be no salvation for any nation, in the same way that without your natural birth mother, you could not have been born. This alone is enough to cause you to honor and be thankful for your mother, even in her imperfection. She gave life to you! Israel gave life to all the nations. The Messiah is Jewish, and salvation is of the Jews.

> You worship what you do not know; we worship what we know, for salvation is from the Jews.
>
> —JOHN 4:22

Meera means to "declare a word decree for the destruction of someone." It is followed by many evil occurrences that will bring anguish, distress, grief, sickness, confusion, loss, lack, bankruptcy, loneliness, strife, rejection, futility, fear, failure, terror, self-destruction, and total annihilation.* Notice that in both cases (the blessing and the curse), God connects them with issuing a decree or speaking a word. From the beginning, everything is created by Elohim issuing a decree and speaking His Word:

> In the beginning Elohim created the heavens and the earth. The earth was without form, and void; and darkness was on the face of the deep. And the Spirit of Elohim was hovering over the face of the waters. Then Elohim said: "Let there be light;" and there was light.
>
> —GENESIS 1:1–3
> (FREE TRANSLATION FROM THE HEBREW)

Israel, beloved ones, is forever the chosen people of God, and no church can replace it or supersede the mother of the nations. From Israel comes the Bible, the Messiah, the gospel, and the Jewish apostles to the nations. She may fall sometimes and be in unbelief for a while,

---

* Deut. 28:14-68

but the God of Israel is restoring her to become the chief sheep nation that all other nations will follow.

> Hear the Word of ADONAI, O nations, and declare it in the distant islands, and say: "He who scattered Israel will gather and watch over him, as a shepherd does his flock."
>
> —JEREMIAH 31:10

> "'Sing and rejoice, O daughter of Zion! For behold, I am coming and I will live among you'—it is a declaration of ADONAI. 'In that day many nations will join themselves to ADONAI and they will be My people and I will dwell among you.' Then you will know that ADONAI-Tzva'ot has sent me to you. ADONAI will inherit Judah as His portion in the holy land and will once again choose Jerusalem. Be silent before ADONAI, all flesh, for He has aroused Himself from His holy dwelling."
>
> —ZECHARIAH 2:10–13

The lie that the Church replaced Israel has prevented Christian nations from becoming sheep nations that will join with the God of Israel, honoring Israel as the mother of the nations, not replacing her. His judgment is now at the gates of every nation that has its foundation in Christianity—both personal and national repentance is mandatory if we are to see revival and global salvation.

A genuine believer in Messiah will love and honor Israel, the chosen people, and the brethren of Yeshua Himself, who is a Jew. When we restore His Jewish identity, antisemitism will be a thing of the past, and the bride of Messiah will arise in all her glory. For those Christians who will not receive this urgent message, the only thing to look for is the judgment.

> Draw near, O nations, to hear, and listen, O peoples! Let the earth hear, and all it contains, the world, and all its offspring! For ADONAI is enraged at all the nations, and furious at all their armies. He will utterly destroy them. He will give them over to slaughter.
> For ADONAI has a day of vengeance, a year of recompense for the hostility against Zion.
>
> —Isaiah 34:1-2, 8

My prayer is that many will repent and become defenders of Israel in these very perilous end times.

A Prayer of Repentance for Hostility Against Israel

Father in Heaven, I ask your forgiveness for harboring the lie that the Church replaced or superseded Israel. I now realize that I was wrong and that this lie is dangerously rooted in deception and jealousy. I totally reject replacement theology and the doctrine that the Church replaces Israel. Thank you for delivering me from all the curses that fall upon those who take Israel lightly, are arrogant against her, or harm her or her reputation. Please teach me how to honor Israel as the mother of the nations and how to make restitution for the sins committed against her by Christians because of the terrible deception of replacement theology. In Yeshua's name. Amen.

CHAPTER 30

NON-NEGOTIABLES—MY LAND

Moreover, the land is not to be sold permanently, because the land is Mine. For you are sojourners with Me.

— LEVITICUS 25:23

The coronavirus follows the same pattern that White House Correspondent William Koenig describes in his book *Eye to Eye*, where he shows 127 events of anti-Biblical politics against Israel by espousing the division of the land, the two-state solution, and the defining of borders by US Presidents. In every one of those cases, within 24 hours, a terrible catastrophe or a storm would happen in the USA that would cost billions of dollars in damage and damage to life as well. Some of these are well-known events such as 9/11 and Hurricane Katrina, both after the US committed itself to supporting the Palestinian cause by dividing Israel or uprooting Israeli settlements (like in the case of Gush Katif in Gaza). Within 24 hours, disasters would hit the USA.

In a talk show hosted by Pastor Sam Rohrer from *Stand in the Gap Today*, Bill Koenig was the guest speaker on Passover Eve, April 8, 2020. He mentioned the following:

On January 28, 2020, President Donald Trump presented the Middle East Plan that he called the "Deal of the Century". He also presented a MAP, defining the borders of Israel under his plan. In this map, 70% of the Biblical Land of Judea and Samaria would be under a Palestinian State.

Within hours of him presenting his peace plan to divide Israel, Miami was hit with a 7.7 earthquake on the Richter scale.

Jan. 28, 2020, 4:04 PM EST / Updated Jan. 28, 2020, 8:15 PM EST

By Janelle Griffith nbcnews.com

A powerful magnitude 7.7 earthquake struck south of Cuba and northwest of Jamaica on Tuesday, the U.S. Geological Survey said. The quake was felt in Miami, and police said some buildings were being evacuated in the city.

Within 24 hours, the US administration was discussing what to do concerning the coronavirus pandemic that had been developing since it was discovered in Wuhan on December 31, 2019. On January 30, the outbreak was declared a public health emergency of international concern by the World Health Organization; this was only two days after the peace plan to divide Israel was submitted on January 28, 2020, and accepted by PM Benjamin Netanyahu.

At the same time, the EU and the international community reiterated their allegiance to the division of the Land of Israel. They insisted on Israel returning to the pre-1967 borders prior to the Six-Day War. The international community insisted on defining the borders of the Promised Land that the God of Israel had already defined thousands of years ago.

The COVID-19 pandemic became a judgment on the whole world, quarantining most of the world population and affecting the economy of all - especially of the USA and Israel, as PM Netanyahu agreed to a plan that is not God's plan for Israel.

Bill Koenig believes (and so do I) that the coronavirus is a judgment on the whole world for two reasons:

1. For attempting to divide the Land of Israel into two states by defining anti-Biblical borders and drawing maps that are an affront to the living God.
2. By disobeying God's moral laws and commandments

It is very likely that any further attempt to bring any kind of peace plan, dividing Israel and establishing a Palestinian State contrary to the covenant, will catapult the world into what the Bible calls the wrath of God. COVID-19 will look like a pussy cat then.

Yah's Name Dwells in the Land of Israel

But if you return to Me and obey My mitzvot, and do them, then even if your dispersed people are at the ends of the heavens, I will gather them from there, and bring them back to the place where I have chosen for My Name to dwell.'

—NEHEMIAH 1:9

But I have chosen Jerusalem that My Name would abide there and I have chosen David to be over My people Israel.'

—2 CHRONICLES 6:6

For now I have chosen and consecrated this House so that My Name may be there forever. My eyes and My heart shall be there perpetually.

—2 Chronicles 7:16

Israel is a Covenant Promised Land to Abraham, Isaac, and Jacob and Their Natural Descendants

When the sun set and it became dark, behold, there was a smoking oven and a fiery torch that passed between these pieces. On that day ADONAI cut a covenant with Abram, saying, "I give this land to your seed, from the river of Egypt to the great river, the Euphrates River: the Kenite, the Kenizzites, the Kadmonites,"

—Genesis 15:17-19

Live as an outsider in this land and I will be with you and bless you—for to you and to your seed I give all these lands—and I will confirm my pledge that I swore to Abraham your father.

—Genesis 26:3

I also established My covenant with them, to give them the land of Canaan, the land of their pilgrimage where they journeyed.

—Exodus 6:4

The Borders of the Land are Between the River of Egypt and the Euphrates River in Syria

"I will set your border from the Sea of Reeds to the sea of the Philistines, and from the wilderness to the Euphrates River. For I will deliver the inhabitants of the land into your hand, and you are to drive them out before you.

—Exodus 23:31

From the wilderness and this Lebanon to the great river, the Euphrates River—all the land of the Hittites—to the Great Sea toward the setting of the sun will be your territory.

—Joshua 1:4

Now Solomon ruled over all the kingdoms from the River to the land of the Philistines up to the border of Egypt. They brought tribute and served Solomon all the days of his life.

—1 Kings 5:1

And he ruled over all the kings from the Euphrates River to the land of the Philistines, and as far as the border of Egypt.

—2 Chronicles 9:26

The Land of Israel or Jerusalem is not mentioned one time in the Quran, and certainly not as a land of promise to the Arab people. The people of Israel have a history of over 4000 years with the land of Yah, while the Arabs have a history from the 7th century on and off, which is a maximum of 1300 years. But it was always through conquest and abuse of the land. They never worked it, tilled it, or made it bloom; this only happens when the Jews return to establish the land after 2000 years of exile following numerous Biblical promises.

Israel Would Return to Their Promised Land Against All Odds

"You, son of man, prophesy to the mountains of Israel and say: 'Mountains of Israel, hear the word of ADONAI. Thus says ADONAI Elohim: "The enemy has said against you, 'Aha! Even the ancient high places have become our possession!' Therefore prophesy and say, thus says ADONAI Elohim: 'Because they ravaged and crushed you from every side, so that you became the possession of the rest of the nations and you became the talk and evil gossip of people,' therefore, mountains of Israel, hear the word of ADONAI, thus says ADONAI Elohim to the mountains, the hills, the streams and the valleys, the desolate wastes and the cities that are forsaken, which have become prey and derision to the rest of the surrounding nations.
Therefore thus says ADONAI Elohim: 'Surely in the fire of My wrath I have spoken against the rest of the nations, and against all Edom, that have taken My land for themselves as a possession with the joy of all their heart and contempt in their souls, in order to seize it as plunder.'
Therefore, prophesy to the land of Israel and say to the mountains and the hills, the streams and the valleys, thus says ADONAI Elohim: 'Behold, I have spoken in My wrath and in My fury, because you have suffered the scorn of the nations.' Therefore thus says ADONAI Elohim: 'I have lifted My hand.

Surely the nations that surround you will themselves suffer scorn.

"'But you, mountains of Israel, you will shoot forth your branches and yield your fruit for My people Israel; for their return is near. For behold, I am for you. I will turn to you. You will be tilled and sown. I will settle a large population upon you—the whole house of Israel, all of it. The cities will be inhabited. The desolate places will be built up. I will multiply man and beast upon you. They will increase and be fruitful. I will cause you to be inhabited as you were before. I will do better for you than at your beginnings. You will know that I am ADONAI. I will cause people, my people Israel, to walk upon you. They will possess you, and you will be their inheritance. You will no longer deprive them of children.'"

—EZEKIEL 36:1-12

Judgment and Destruction Falls on Every Nation that Opposes His Land Covenant with the Jewish People

All enemies of Israel will be destroyed unless they desist from the two-state solution. It is not biblical; it is a man's invention, and it will never succeed. The only hope for the so-called Palestinians is to forsake their evil agenda of destroying the people and the Land of Israel and humble their hearts to honor and bless Israel and to worship the God of Israel. Palestine does not exist in the Bible, however the Philistines exist.

Thus says ADONAI, "As for all My evil neighbors who strike at the inheritance that I bequeathed to My people Israel—I am about to uproot them from their land and pluck the house of Judah from them. Yet it will come to pass, after I have uprooted them, that I will again have compassion on them and I will bring them back, each one to his inheritance and each one to his land. "So it will come to pass, if they will diligently learn the ways of My people—to swear by My Name, 'As ADONAI lives,' just as they taught My people to swear by Baal—then they will be built up in the midst of My people. But if they will not obey, then I will uproot that nation, plucking it up and destroying it." It is a declaration of ADONAI.

—JEREMIAH 12:14-17

He is ADONAI our Elohim. His judgments are in all the earth. He remembers His covenant foreverthe word He commanded for a thousand generationswhich He made with Abraham, and swore to Isaac, and confirmed to Jacob as a decree, to Israel as an everlasting covenant, saying, "To you I give the land of Canaan, the portion of your inheritance." When they were but few in number, few indeed, and foreigners in it, wandering from nation to nation, from one kingdom to another people, He allowed no one to oppress them—for their sake He rebuked kings: "Touch not My anointed ones, and do My prophets no harm."

—PSALM 105:7-15

For, behold, in those days, and in that time, when I restore the fortunes of Judah and Jerusalem, I will gather all nations and will bring them down into the valley of Jehoshaphat; and I will execute judgment on them there for my people, and for my heritage, Israel, whom they have scattered among the nations. They have divided my land, and have cast lots for my people, and have given a boy for a prostitute, and sold a girl for wine, that they may drink.

—Joel 3:1-3

Draw near, O nations, to hear, and listen, O peoples! Let the earth hear, and all it contains, the world, and all its offspring! For ADONAI is enraged at all the nations, and furious at all their armies. He will utterly destroy them. He will give them over to slaughter. So their slain will be thrown out, and the stench of their corpses will rise, and the hills will be drenched with their blood. Then all the host of heaven will dissolve, and the skies will be rolled up like a scroll—so all their array will wither away, like a leaf drooping from a vine, like a fig shriveling from a fig tree.

For My sword has drunk its fill in the heavens. See, it will come down upon Edom, upon the people I have devoted to judgment. The sword of ADONAI is filled with blood, gorged with fatthe blood of lambs and goats, the fat of kidneys of rams. For ADONAI has a sacrifice in Bozrah, a great slaughter in the land of Edom. Wild oxen will go down with them, bull calves with mighty steers. So their land will be soaked with blood and their dust greasy with fat. For ADONAI has a day of vengeance, a year of recompense for the hostility against Zion.

—Isaiah 34:1-8

ADONAI will roar from Zion and give His voice from Jerusalem. Heaven and earth will shudder, but ADONAI will be a refuge for His people, and a safe place for the children of Israel. So you will know that I am ADONAI, your God, dwelling in Zion, My holy mountain. Then will Jerusalem be holy, and foreigners will cross through her no more. It will be in that day, the mountains will drip sweet wine, the hills will flow with milk, and all the wadis of Judah will flow with water. A spring will flow out from the House of ADONAI and water the valley of Shittim.

Egypt will become a desolation and Edom a desert wasteland, because of the violence against the children of Judah, because they shed innocent blood in their land. But Judah will be inhabited forever Jerusalem from generation to generation. I will acquit their bloodguilt that I had not acquitted, for ADONAI dwells in Zion.

—JOEL 4:16-21

"For thus says ADONAI-Tzva'ot, He has sent me after glory to the nations that plundered you—because whoever touches you touches the apple of His eye—'For behold, I will shake My hand against them and they will be plunder to their servants.' Then you will know that ADONAI-Tzva'ot has sent me. "'Sing and rejoice, O daughter of Zion! For behold, I am coming and I will live among you'—it is a declaration of ADONAI. 'In that day many nations will join themselves to ADONAI and they will be My people and I will dwell among you.' Then you will know that ADONAI-Tzva'ot has sent me to you. ADONAI will inherit Judah as His portion in the holy land and will once again choose Jerusalem. Be silent before ADONAI, all flesh, for He has aroused Himself from His holy dwelling."

—ZECHARIAH 2:12-17

The wrath of YHVH is already beginning with an all-encompassing judgment through globalism and pandemics of plagues. The only nations that will be rescued from it are the nations that join Him in

His quest to restore all of Israel to all of the land He has promised from the River of Egypt to the Euphrates. Nothing else will do, and no deals can be made with His land. Any deal that includes a Palestinian state or relinquishing of lands or financial support to the Palestinian cause will end up in judgment, just like the Deal of the Century is at present.

His land is non-negotiable!

For He will bless those who bless Israel and those who curse her and take her lightly or covet her land will be cursed and completely annihilated; the mouth of YHVH has spoken. (Genesis 12:3)

2019

CHAPTER 31

PASSOVER AND BIBLICAL POLITICS

> Now behold, the cry of Bnei-Yisrael has come to Me.
> Moreover I have seen the oppression that the
> Egyptians have inflicted on them.
>
> — EXODUS 3:9

WHEN WE THINK ABOUT the Biblical Feast of Passover (or in Hebrew Pesach), we connect it with freedom from slavery, the exodus from Egypt into the Promised Land, and salvation by the blood of the lamb. But how often do we relate it to an act of what I would call "Biblical politics?" After all, in this first Passover, YHVH, the God of Israel, intervened in the politics and rulings of Pharaoh, the king of Egypt. It concerned an issue of social justice, especially the Egyptian monarch's behavior towards His covenant people, the children of Israel. They were being used and abused without pay for nearly 430 years, and their cry reached the ears of the Almighty! He then proceeded to call a divinely-appointed deliverer by the name of Moshe (or Moses) from the tribe of Levi, who would become the priestly tribe after their deliverance from Egypt.

> "Come now, I will send you to Pharaoh, so that you may bring My people Bnei-Yisrael out from Egypt."
>
> —Exodus 3:10

I heard the term *Biblical politics* from the Holy Spirit in the year 2000, and it was connected with the politics of the president of the USA. It includes two issues:

1. The moral and internal affairs of the nation (including social justice)
2. The foreign policy of the USA concerning Israel

At that time, Yah (God) made me understand that if a nation followed Biblical politics on both of the above issues, it could become a sheep nation and enjoy the eternal blessings of the Most High, but if not, then judgment would follow. In the case above, during the time of President George W. Bush, Biblical politics were not implemented, and judgment followed in America: the terrible 9/11 Twin Tower terror attack in NYC, the devastation of New Orleans and surrounding areas by Hurricane Katrina, numerous other storms and fires, a terrible financial recession, and destructive oil spills in the Gulf of Mexico. Afterward, there followed two terms of office of a political administration that were antagonistic to Israel, to the believers in Messiah in the land, and to its inhabitants in general.

> For behold, in those days and at that time, when I restore Judah and Jerusalem from exile, I will gather all nations and bring them down to the valley of Jehoshaphat. I will plead with them there on behalf of My people, even My inheritance,

Israel, whom they scattered among the nations and they divided up My land.

—Joel 4:1-2

We can praise Yah (God) for the change of spirit in the present-day politics of the USA since 2017, as it has been implementing more and more Biblical politics in both internal policies and foreign affairs concerning Israel. It is also worth mentioning the relocating of the US Embassy to the Holy City of Jerusalem—the eternal, Biblical capital of Israel—and President Donald Trump's acceptance of the Golan Heights as Israeli territory.

Biblical politics is a term that the God of Israel downloaded on me, just like He did the message of sheep nations on December 25, 2001, while in my native land of Chile. However, the principle of Biblical politics has existed since time immemorial.

All the nations will be gathered before Him, and He will separate them from one another, just as the shepherd separates the sheep from the goats.

—Matthew 25:32

The Almighty God of Israel, YHVH, who created the heavens and the earth, always intervenes in the affairs of men and in the affairs of kings, rulers, and governments. This is His response to the heart cry of His covenant people, whether it is the people of Israel, the Jewish people, or those believers from among the nations that are grafted into the Israeli olive tree (Romans 11) and worship the Jewish Messiah Yeshua. Our heartcry in prayer and worship and from the depth of our being is very important—it moves the outstretched hand of Yah on our behalf, to intervene in the government and politics of our nations! He was moved to act in Egypt, and His Israelite people were set free after 430 years of slavery. The demonic, idolatrous system of the time that enslaved them was devastated by ten terrible plagues and, last but not least, was drowned in the waters of the famous Red Sea together with all of its might!

> **As in the days of your coming out from the land of Egypt I will show him wonders. Nations will see and be put to shame despite all their might.**
>
> —Mɪᴄᴀʜ 7:15-16

Biblical politics in action causes deliverance and miraculous breakthroughs to His covenant peoples—while the antagonistic governments of the earth that oppose YHVH'S kingdom, Word, and covenant suffer serious judgment. We can see this in numerous scriptures.

> **For Aᴅᴏɴᴀɪ has a day of vengeance, a year of recompense for the hostility against Zion.**
>
> —Iꜱᴀɪᴀʜ 34:8

This is why He has downloaded on me the vessel of glory, the United Nations for Israel (known by the acronym UNIFY), to carry His Biblical political agenda to all the nations of the earth! The UNIFY historical and prophetic embassy is now located at the gates of Jerusalem in the Jerusalem mountains.* A holy United Nations has been prophesied over 2500 years ago by the Prophet Zechariah:

> **'In that day many nations will join themselves to Aᴅᴏɴᴀɪ and they will be My people and I will dwell among you.' Then you**

---

* We no longer have the embassy at the Mountains of Jerusalem, but are located in other strategic areas in Israel and Jerusalem.

will know that ADONAI-Tzva'ot has sent me to you. ADONAI will inherit Judah as His portion in the holy land and will once again choose Jerusalem. Be silent before ADONAI, all flesh, for He has aroused Himself from His holy dwelling.

—ZECHARIAH 2:15-17

This United Nations, differing from the one the world has established, is *for Israel*. Our goal is to educate the world about the Biblical politics that will bring about salvation and blessing to the nations that are now enslaved to the Egypt of UN-biblical politics (which is hateful to Israel and hateful to the God of Israel).

My desire is to bless those who bless you, but whoever curses you I will curse, and in you all the families of the earth will be blessed.

—GENESIS 12:3

Just like during the original Passover in Egypt, He has raised UNIFY under our leadership as a deliverer of nations bound by UN-Biblical politics. The UN politics now within the nations is UN-Biblical in every way: of all the condemnations declared against countries from 2005 through 2017, nearly 50% were against Israel; the other 50% was shared by the rest of the 192 nations represented in the UN. The word *bias* is written all over the UN. But this anti-Israel bias has caused all those nations in agreement with her to be enslaved to the New World Order through their UN-Biblical Politics.

Just like at the time of Moses, YHVH is using us to say, "Let My People GO!"

It is time for those who belong to the God of Israel through the Jewish Messiah Yeshua to have an Exodus from UN-Biblical politics and replacement theology. It is time for them to go out of this ungodly system in order to form the sheep nations that have been prophesied. The nation of Israel was formed as a nation only after it was separated from Egypt: the people who obeyed Moses and left Egypt after the last plague became this new nation.

They were saved by the blood of the lamb upon their doorposts, and their first-born sons did not die, but that was not enough! They also had to *flee* Egypt in a hurry, plundering the nation that enslaved them for so long, in order to form a covenant nation in the desert.

> Then I shall grant these people favor in the eyes of the Egyptians. So it will happen that when you go, you will not leave empty-handed. Every woman is to ask her neighbor and the woman who lives in her house for silver and gold jewelry and clothing. You will put them on your sons and your daughters. So you will plunder the Egyptians.
>
> —Exodus 3:21-22

Sheep nations are being formed as I write, simply using people like you and me who are willing to obey Yah—to flee from UN-Biblical politics and from enslavement to this world's system. By joining with the prophetic divinely appointed United Nations, this UNIFY (the United Nations for Israel) is fighting for His kingdom to come and His will to be done on earth as it is in heaven, in every arena of society!

> I am not asking that You take them out of the world, but that You keep them from the evil one. They are not of the world, just as I am not of the world.
>
> —John 17:15-16

We are standing on sure ground because it was prophesied thousands of years ago and is happening now. It is already a fact, and, beloved ones, this is a sure sign that the Messiah is about to return to His own land, to His own people, and to establish His kingdom on the Temple Mount in Yerushalayim, Jerusalem.

Everything that has been prophesied is coming to pass and will come to pass: the God of Israel is only looking for obedient vessels of glory through whom He will implement His awesome plan.

> **For the eyes of ADONAI range throughout the earth to strengthen those whose hearts are wholly His.**
>
> —2 CHRONICLES 16:9A

Every member of UNIFY (the United Nations for Israel)* is such a vessel of glory and a potential founder of their own sheep nation. That is the reason why the flags of our delegate and members are displayed at the Embassy on the Jerusalem Hills: their nations now have the option of coming out of the valley of judgment, out of the slavery to the New World Order and through embracing Biblical politics will become a sheep nation.

The exodus of nations from the "Egypt" of the UN and the New World Order has begun. A new Passover for the people of Israel is on the horizon, made possible by the blood of the sinless Lamb, our Messiah, and boldly demonstrated by the staunch stand and support shown to Israel by the future sheep nations, represented in the United Nations for Israel.

---

* Become a member of the United Nations for Israel at www.UnitedNationsForIsreal.org

CHAPTER 32

WITHIN YOUR GATES, O JERUSALEM

Our feet are standing within your gates, O Jerusalem.
— PSALM 122:2 NASB '95

So many believers read, pray, and sing this Scripture, but now it is a reality!

During the holy Feast of Sukkot, we shall dedicate the Embassy of the United Nations for Israel at the Gates of Yerushalayim. This will be the highlight of our Sukkot Tour this year. We shall be accompanied by about 70 members and delegates from the nations celebrating the 70th Anniversary of the miracle-reborn State of Israel, with numerous more guests and Israelis.

This is right at the West Gate, in the area where the Arab Legion blocked the way to Yerushalayim during the Independence War of 1948 for two years, causing a terrible famine to the Jewish population of the Holy City, among them my own family members.

They were led by Abdel-Kadr Al Husseini, a family member of the ex-grand mufti of Jerusalem, Haj Amin al-Husseini, the greatest friend of Hitler who (though already dead) has been implementing the Final Solution against the Jewish people till this day through the PLO and its derivatives. Haj Amin had his summer house, now in ruins, right around the corner from where my blood family lives to this day.

My Family at the Western Gate

> As the mountains surround Jerusalem, so ADONAI surrounds His people from this time forth and forever. For the scepter of wickedness shall not rest upon the land of the righteous.
>
> —PSALM 125:2.3A NASB '95

My family has been holding the most strategic Western Gate to Jerusalem open since 1927 when Meir Mizrachi, the courageous father of my cousin Eli, settled in Motsa. He suffered under this wicked mufti that unleashed a massacre against the Jews of Motsa in 1929. My cousin Eli was born in Motsa in 1932, and his ID says his parents were Palestinian. His mother, Esther, was the sister of my maternal grandfather, Mois Camhi.

All those born in the Land of Israel or that naturalized in it until 1917 during the Turkish rule were Palestinians. However, though Eli was born during the British Mandate, he was still called Palestinian, as they called the Holy Land Palestine, until 1948, when the reborn State of Israel was established.

The True Biblical "Palestinian Cause"

> I will rejoice over them to do them good and will faithfully plant them in this land with all My heart and with all My soul.
>
> —JEREMIAH 32:41 NASB '95

This is the true "Palestinian cause:" the return of the Jews to Zion and the restoration of the land that has recovered its original Biblical covenant name, Israel.

The Romans called it Palestine in memory of the Philistines, the archenemies of Israel. The Turks and the Brits called it Palestine, but from May 14th of 1948, it has been officially called Israel again!

> Who has heard such a thing? Who has seen such things? Can a land be born in one day? Can a nation be brought forth all at once? As soon as Zion travailed, she also brought forth her sons.
>
> —Isaiah 66:8 NASB '95

The Bible mentions the name of Israel about 2500 times! My cousin and great uncle Eli, along with his family and my children, Adi and Yuval, are the sons of Zion who were born in the Land of Promise.

United Nations for Israel at the West Gate of Jerusalem

> Get yourself up to a high mountain, Zion, (female) bringer of good news! Lift up your voice with strength, Jerusalem, bringer of good news! Lift it up; you must not fear! Say to the cities of Judah, "Here is your God!"
>
> —Isaiah 40:9

"Proclaimer of good news" in Hebrew is *Mevaseret Zion* (female).

The first and most difficult front of the War of Independence from the British in 1948 was the West Gate of Jerusalem, where our Embassy of UNIFY is being established.*

---

* During the Covid pandemic, the Embassy was closed, but we are located in another strategic areas in Israel and Jerusalem.

My family has fought physically with their own blood to open this gate, and now we come as reinforcements, watchmen at the gate from the United Nations for Israel to keep it open, so King Messiah can return to the land and His people can be safe and saved from spiritual and physical enemies.

> In that day ADONAI will defend the inhabitants of Jerusalem so that the weakest among them that day will be like David and the house of David will be like God—like the angel of ADONAI before them.
>
> —ZECHARIAH 12:8

During the 1948 war, the Brits left in the hands of the Arab enemies of Israel all of the key positions, including the Castel Military Outpost, where we planted the flag of the United Nations for Israel last year on Sukkot 2017, proclaiming that next year in Sukkot we shall dedicate the Embassy in these Mountains of Yerushalayim! The proclamation has come to pass, and this year, during Sukkot 2018, just like I declared, we are opening The Embassy of the Nations.

> Lift up your heads, O gates, and be lifted up, you everlasting doors: that the King of glory may come in." Who is this King of glory?" ADONAI strong and mighty, ADONAI mighty in battle!
>
> —PSALM 24:7-8 NASB '95

The Cost of Prophetic Fulfillment

It will come about in that day that I will make Jerusalem a heavy stone for all the peoples; all who lift it will be severely injured. And all the nations of the earth will be gathered against it.

—Zechariah 12:3 NASB '95

These tremendous prophetic happenings do not come without a cost, and the restoration of Israel, which is ushering in the Messiah's return, does not come without a cost.

My family, together with many more Israelis, have paid the price with their own sweat and blood. Members of my family who were living in the Jewish Quarter of the Old City of Jerusalem were taken prisoners to Jordan in 1948 when the Jordanian Legion killed, looted, and destroyed all the Jews in the Old City. Jews were banished from entering these ancient walls, including the Kotel (the Western Wall), until the miraculous Six-Day War of 1967. The Jews of the rest of Jerusalem had nothing to eat and no ammunition for two years during the blockade of 1948.

My family in Motsa fought to open the gates to the Holy City and has kept them open with their hard work and presence, often at great risk of life and possessions.

Now It's Our Turn

And in that day, I will set about to destroy all the nations that come against Jerusalem.

—Zechariah 12:9 NASB '95

It is time for *you* to represent your nation at the gates of Jerusalem with your giving, practical help, and prayers! This is an act of restitution from you, your family, and your nation to Israel.

> For behold, in those days and at that time, when I restore the fortunes of Judah and Jerusalem, I will gather all the nations and bring them down to the valley of Jehoshaphat. Then I will enter into judgment with them there on behalf of My people and My inheritance, Israel, whom they have scattered among the nations; and they have divided up My land.
>
> —Joel 3:1-2 NASB '95

Seeds that are Soldiers at the Gate of Jerusalem

> And I will bless those who bless you, and the one who curses you I will curse. and in you all the families of the earth will be blessed.
>
> —Genesis 12:3

Your faithful partnership will be helping to overturn the wicked results of the policies of the United Nations against Israel in general and against Jerusalem being recognized as the eternal capital of Israel forever! The enemies are too many to count, but the Almighty can do wonders through even a few willing vessels that pray and give.*

Our feet, our seed, our heart, and our prayers are standing within your gates, O Jerusalem!

> "Our feet are standing in your gates, Jerusalem—"
>
> —Psalms 122:2

Those who love her in action, will prosper! (Psalm 122:6)

---

* To support the United Nations for Israel, visit www.unitednationsforisrael.org

2018

CHAPTER 33

REASONING WITH SCORPIONS

> But if you do not drive out the inhabitants of the land from before you, then it shall come about that those whom you let remain of them will become as pricks in your eyes and as thorns in your sides, and they will trouble you in the land in which you live. And as I plan to do to them, so I will do to you.'"
>
> — NUMBERS 33:55-56 NASB '95

The Holy Scriptures give very clear instructions concerning war and often admonishes Israel to drive out their enemies, not reason with them. To the humanistic and politically correct, this sounds like a drastic and cruel measure. Shouldn't we have compassion for our fellow humans? The question is not whether we should have compassion or not; the question is: "Who is really fighting us?" Would you have compassion for a cobra or scorpion trying to bite you? Would you "psychologize" and try to speak with a cobra? Would you try to "convince" the scorpion not to bite you? "Come on, dear scorpion, let us reason together." We know what reasoning with the snake caused Adam in the Garden (Genesis 3).

Yeshua instructs us to *trample* on snakes and scorpions, not to "reason" with them!

> Behold, I have given you authority to trample upon serpents and scorpions, and over all the power of the enemy; nothing will harm you.
>
> —LUKE 10:19

Terrorism is a snake and a scorpion not to reason with but to trample, to squelch, and to destroy. Infrastructures of terror in Israel and in every nation like the USA, Nigeria, France, the UK, and others must be totally, radically, and purposefully destroyed. Sometimes, a hard choice must be made, especially for all of us peace-loving people.

Will I protect my baby from the terrorist or will I protect the terrorists "human rights" to express his violence? Do I protect the anger of Hamas that leads to murdering my baby, destroying my fields, shell shocking my children, and sacrificing their babies on the evil altar of Jihad?

The Holy Scriptures are very clear when it comes to what we believers should permit and what we should forbid. It calls it *binding* and *loosing*.

> "I will give you the keys of the kingdom of heaven; and whatever you bind on earth shall have been bound in heaven, and whatever you loose on earth shall have been loosed in heaven."
>
> —MATTHEW 16:19 NASB '95

Whatever we *forbid* on earth is forbidden in heaven! Humans must make the decision to *forbid* Islamic terror. We, as believers in the God and Messiah of Israel, should be the first ones to stand up on behalf of our nations and say "No" to anti-Israel, anti-Jewish, anti-Zionist, anti-Messiah terror. If we are *silent*, then YHVH will be silent! We *must* speak up, pray up, broadcast, and do all in our power to bring forth the Spirit of Truth into international politics. We must espouse

Biblical politics and forbid the evil agenda of Hamas, Haman, Amalek, and Satan himself. Whatever we bind and forbid on earth will be bound and forbidden in Heaven. To bind and loose includes prayer, speech, and action.

We must globally *reeducate* all nations with the truth about Israel and the Jewish Messiah.

> **For Zion's sake I will not keep silent, and for Jerusalem's sake I will not keep quiet, until her righteousness goes forth like brightness, and her salvation like a torch that is burning.**
>
> —Isaiah 62:1 nasb '95

Hamas is harming their own people.

> **When the righteous increase, the people rejoice, but when a wicked man rules, people groan.**
>
> —Proverbs 29:2 nasb '95

The people of Gaza are groaning under a terrible, demonic regime that is causing them misery, death, and poverty. They are groaning under a regime that is using their own people as human shields and sending their youth to fly incendiary kites and destructive balloons over innocent Israeli farmers who are making the desert of Israel bloom.

These sacrificial and precious, hard-working Israeli people, husbands, wives, pregnant women, children, babies, and the disabled, are living under the constant threat of another deadly kite, balloon, or rocket from Gaza, running to the bomb shelter, sometimes as much as 20 times a day! And the hypocritically "politically correct" UN wants Israel to "forbear" and to let Hamas have the freedom to continue ruling with terror against Israel and over their own people!

The UN is a politically and hypocritically obsolete organization that is the root of most evil that is happening in the world today. Supposedly being the policeman of the nations, it only polices what is convenient to their pockets and to their thwarted anti-Jew/anti-Israeli/anti-Zionist hateful agenda.

Do not be fooled for a moment! The UN could have stopped Hamas long agoin the same way that the world could have stopped Hitler, but they chose not to. It is high time for nations to UNEXIT and start making up their own minds as to what is right and what is evil in the eyes of an all-seeing God. It is time for the governments of nations to line up with the Creator of humankind, who is, not mistakenly, also called the God of Israel!

And He said to leave no survivors among the Amalekites!

> **Thus says the LORD of hosts, 'I will punish Amalek for what he did to Israel, how he set himself against him on the way while he was coming up from Egypt. Now go and strike Amalek and utterly destroy all that he has, and do not spare him; but put to death both man and woman, child and infant, ox and sheep, camel and donkey.'**
>
> —1 SAMUEL 15:2-3 NASB '95

To Moses He said:

> Therefore, it shall come about when the LORD your God has given you rest from all your surrounding enemies, in the land which the LORD your God gives you as an inheritance to possess, you shall blot out the memory of Amalek from under heaven; you must not forget.
>
> —DEUTERONOMY 25:19 NASB '95

I pray for all the enemies of Israel to *repent* and to come to salvation and to eternal life, for He wishes no one to perish. But what happens if they do not repent, if they do not choose *life*, Yeshua, and Salvation? What needs to be done to prevent evil from running rampant through terror? Would you let murderers roam in your neighborhood freely? Would you let them enter your houses and murder your families? Why, then, would anyone agree with the rulership of Hamas in Gaza and its constant harassment of Israel on top of their cruelty and murder of their own people? Isn't that hypocritically insane?

> Woe to those who call evil good, and good evil; Who substitute darkness for light and light for darkness; who substitute bitter for sweet and sweet for bitter!
>
> —Isaiah 5:20 nasb '95

Woe Means Judgment

> Thus says Adonai, "As for all My evil neighbors who strike at the inheritance that I bequeathed to My people Israel—I am about to uproot them from their land and pluck the house of Judah from them. Yet it will come to pass, after I have uprooted them, that I will again have compassion on them and I will bring them back, each one to his inheritance and each one to his land. "So it will come to pass, if they will diligently learn the ways of My people—to swear by My Name, 'As Adonai lives,' just as they taught My people to swear by Baal—then they will be built up in the midst of My people. But if they will not obey, then I will uproot that nation, plucking it up and destroying it." It is a declaration of Adonai.
>
> —Jeremiah 12:14-17

Why would baby murderers and terrorists be allowed to live, roam freely, and even rule Gaza, which is part of the promised land to Israel? On top of it, Israel is the promised land, not to Muslims or Arabs but to the natural descendants of Abraham, Isaac, and Yaakov. The Bible never calls it Palestine or Philistine land, but rather the Land of Israel, and the name of *Israel* is mentioned 2500 times in the Bible.

> "Remember Abraham, Isaac and Israel, Your servants, to whom You swore by Your own self, and said to them, 'I will multiply your seed as the stars of heaven, and all this land that I have spoken of I will give to your offspring, and they will inherit it forever.'"
>
> —Exodus 32:13

Those (Arabs) who are not promised the land from the River of Egypt to the Euphrates can be blessed in it *only* if they choose to live in shalom and peace with Israel. There are plenty of examples of Arab villages inside of Israel that live in peace with their Jewish neighbors and honor the Israeli government, and because of that they have thriving prosperity! This can be the situation also for the inhabitants of Gaza, but not while the cobra snake and poisonous scorpion of Hamas is ruling.

The Spirit of Samson and David

> When it was told to the Gazites, saying, "Samson has come here," they surrounded the place and lay in wait for him all night at the gate of the city. And they kept silent all night, saying, "Let us wait until the morning light, then we will kill him." Now Samson lay until midnight, and at midnight he

arose and took hold of the doors of the city gate and the two posts and pulled them up along with the bars; then he put them on his shoulders and carried them up to the top of the mountain which is opposite Hebron.

—Judges 16:2-3 nasb '95

We must pray for the Israeli government and the IDF to be endowed with the spirit of Samson and David to do what is right in Yah's eyes and to do it swiftly with confidence so that loss of life on both sides can be spared and many can come to salvation. It is time to pull out the evil gates of Gaza!

The people groan when evil rules, and the UN and a "compliant" Israel have allowed evil to proliferate in Gaza since the infamous Gaza Disengagement. Also, evil has ruled through Hezbollah at the border with Lebanon since the ridiculous pullout from there.

As the mountains are around Jerusalem, so Adonai is all around His people, both now and forever. For a scepter of wickedness will not rest over the land of the righteouslest the righteous set their hands to evil. Do good, Adonai, to the good, and to those upright in their hearts. But as for those who turn aside to their crooked ways, Adonai will lead them away with evildoers. Shalom be upon Israel.

—Psalm 125:2-5

You Can Make a Difference—Be Salt & Join UNIFY

You are the salt of the earth; but if the salt has become tasteless, how can it be made salty again? It is no longer good for anything, except to be thrown out and trampled underfoot by men.

—Matthew 5:13 NASB '95

We invite you to make a Biblical difference in Israel and your nation—join the United Nations for Israel and fight with us in prayer and global reeducation for Biblical politics to be implemented, the Name of the God of Israel to be exalted, and sheep nations to come forth! Everyone who is a believer should make a difference in this world and should seek to instruct the nations in the ways of the kingdom covenant. The God of Israel will not keep silent—will you?

For Zion's sake I will not keep silent, and for Jerusalem's sake I will not keep quiet, until her righteousness goes forth like brightness, and her salvation like a torch that is burning.

—Isaiah 62:1 NASB '95

Even if you are a-political or even if you are against any kind of political involvement because it is "unspiritual," just know this: You are involved in politics through the government of your nation, whether you like it or not. And if your nation is a member of the UN, you are involved in unbiblical, ungodly politics concerning Israel. Furthermore, you are involved in a passive way with your government's stand with the New World Order prophesied in the Holy Scriptures!

I am inviting you to come out of this ungodly, unbiblical politics cycle by joining the United Nations for Israel, making a Biblical stand and a difference. Even if your government is anti-Israel or has been in the past, you are the spiritual government of your nation. By being an active member and partnering with the United Nations for Israel's

Knesset of the Nations, you are agreeing for His kingdom to come and His will to be done on earth as it is in Heaven, in Israel as it is in Heaven, and in your nation as it is in heaven.

Do not "play dead," and do not "play passive," but make a difference for eternity with UNIFY! Our battle is a spiritual battle, and we must fight it with spiritual weapons; so while the IDF and the government of Israel do what they need to do with physical weapons, let us back them up with the power of the Word, prayer, presence, and global reeducation and broadcasting.

> **For the weapons of our warfare are not of the flesh, but divinely powerful for the destruction of fortresses. We are destroying speculations and every lofty thing raised up against the knowledge of God, and we are taking every thought captive to the obedience of Messiah.**
>
> **—2 Corinthians 10:4-5 nasb '95**

The United Nations for Israel was envisioned in Israel, launched in America, dedicated on the mountains of Jerusalem with the delegates of many nations, and now established at the gates of Yerushalayim-Jerusalem through the Embassy of the Nations.* This is a divinely ordained movement that will usher the return of the Messiah to Jerusalem, Israel.

UNIFY is standing with Israel against all odds and saying *never again* to the plan of Haman to annihilate her one more time. Together, we are turning nations into sheep nations, one person at a time.

You are that *one person* who can turn your nation into a sheep nation with the United Nations for Israel!

I will bless those who bless you Israel. (Genesis 12:3)

---

* Now we are located in another strategic areas in Israel and Jerusalem.

CHAPTER 34

SEVENTY YEARS AND COUNTING

Israel is 70—Historical Edition
5708-5778 / 1948-2018

> The word came to Jeremiah from ADONAI, saying: thus says ADONAI, the God of Israel: "Write all the words that I have spoken to you in a scroll. For behold, the days are coming," declares ADONAI, "when I will return My people Israel and Judah from exile," declares ADONAI. "I will bring them back to the land that I gave to their fathers, and they will possess it."
>
> — JEREMIAH 30:1-3

WE HAVE COME TO a turning point in history, and it is a point of no return! The reborn nation called Israel has made it to age 70. She has survived despite all international opposition from the United Nations, seven wars with her neighboring Arab countries, two intifadas, and numerous battles with Muslim terror! A country that was formed by the Jewish survivors of the most hideous happening in history, namely the Shoah (or called by many the Nazi Holocaust), is now one of the happiest and most thriving countries in the world!

A Few Enlightening Facts about Our Beloved Israel

The Jewish Boston weekly magazine tells us that:

- Relative to its population, Israel has absorbed more immigrants than any other country, with newcomers from more than 100 countries.
- Israeli humanitarian aid workers are often the first to respond to disasters around the world.
- Israel's Save a Child's Heart organization performs life-saving heart operations for children worldwide, including many Palestinians, free of charge.
- Israel is the only country in the Middle East where the number of Christians is increasing.
- Life expectancy in Israel is among the highest in the world, at 82 years.
- Israel has won more Nobel Prizes than all other Middle East countries combined.
- Israel is the 11th happiest country in the world (the U.S. is 14th) of more than 150 ranked.
- Jerusalem has over 1,500 public parks and gardens.
- People of the book: Israel publishes more books per capita than any other country.

This is in addition to Israel being one of the most important start-up and innovative nations in the world! Without Israel, you could not eat cherry tomatoes (engineered in Israel), use cell phones, Google, Waze (a traffic and navigation app), or voice mail.

What Google says about Israel:

Google now employs more than 600 engineers in the country, and they work on several of Google's core products, including Search, Maps, and Live Results. About half of Google's engineers in Israel are graduates of Tel Aviv University, Don Dodge (a Google executive) said. "There's an amazing source of talent here."

Dodge said cheaper engineers in places like Russia, India, and China were often not as good: "It's about innovation, creativity, taking tremendous risks, understanding how to get to market. That's what Israel does. It's not about the cost."

What Facebook says about Israel:

Adi Soffer Teeni (Facebook Israel CEO) also stressed that the mentality and culture at Facebook's Research and Development Center in Israel were comparable to Facebook's R&D facilities in Silicon Valley, where engineers "move fast and break things" while wearing "shorts and flip-flops."

"Something is happening here in Israel," she said. "There's a magic and it's not easy to explain what it is, but Israel's a playground where it feels like home for the multinational."**

Prophetic Fulfillment

Out of the roughly 9 million inhabitants in Israel, about 6.5 million of them are Jewish, which is 43% of all the known Jews in the world. This is a growth of 700% since 1948, when only 6% of the world's Jews lived in Israel! The Jewish people have come back to Israel from over 100 nations after about 2000 years of exile! This supports the fulfillment of many ancient prophecies, such as the one below:

** www.businessinsider.com/facebook-google-microsoft-israel-rd-2016-10

> So now, do not fear, Jacob My servant," says ADONAI, "nor be dismayed, O Israel, for behold, I will save you from afar, your seed from the land of their exile. Jacob will again be quiet and at ease, and no one will make him afraid.
>
> —JEREMIAH 30:10

Israel and the USA

About the same number of Jewish people (6.5 million) also live in the USA, which makes it a "second Israel" for many Jews. Thus, the USA is very important for Israel's sake, and Israel is very important for the wellbeing of the USA. YHVH promised Abraham that He will bless those who bless Israel—this was the *key* to the wellbeing of every nation on the earth. (Genesis 12:3)

In fact, He promised that though He would punish His people, Israel, for their misgivings, yet He would have compassion on them and bring them back to their land. However, He would destroy all the other nations where the Jews had been scattered; thus, the life of *every* nation is now hanging in the balance.

> "For I am with you," declares ADONAI, "to save you, for I will make a full end of all the nations where I scatter you. But I will not make a full end of you. For I will discipline you justly, but will not leave you unpunished."
>
> —JEREMIAH 30:11

The most important question:

How have the nations behaved with the Jewish people while in exile? And how are they behaving with Israel while back home in her land? This will determine the destiny of all nations, starting with the

USA. Therefore, it is so important and life-saving that President Donald Trump is officially inaugurating the USA Embassy in the Holy City of Jerusalem this year in May. Any delays on this could cause a serious judgment—like we saw during Hurricane Irma in the State of Florida, when the governor, Mr. Rick Scott, issued a historic order to evacuate the entire state of 9 million people (just equal to Israel's population).

There was no hope for the State of Florida then, but the Almighty answered our desperate prayers and had mercy. Right after this, the presidential administration of the US chose to follow through with the recognition of Jerusalem as the eternal capital of Israel and initiated the long-awaited and long-postponed Embassy move from Tel Aviv to the Holy City of Jerusalem.

Even Google recognized Jerusalem as the Capital of Israel!

The global search engine Google and Google Maps have even now changed the capital of Israel from Tel Aviv to Jerusalem. This came just as the US President Donald Trump was due to recognize Jerusalem as the capital of the State of Israel and would announce the US embassy move from Tel Aviv to Jerusalem.

This internet giant has come under immense criticism after making the change as it was completed before Trump's decision was made public. Also, it is stated that the US recognition does not change the status quo, as per UN resolutions, which have included that the status of Jerusalem will be decided during future UN negotiations.[*]

---

[*] www.middleeastmonitor.com/20171208-google-declares-jerusalem-the-capital-of-israel

70 Years: The Line has Been Drawn

> I lifted up my eyes—and behold, I saw a man with a measuring line in his hand. I asked, 'Where are you going?' He answered me, 'To measure Jerusalem to see how wide and how long it is.' Then behold, the angel speaking with me left and another angel went out to meet him, saying to him, 'Run, speak to this young man saying: "Jerusalem will be inhabited as a village without walls because of the great number of men and livestock in it. For I"—it is a declaration of Adonai "will be a wall of fire around it and I will be the glory inside it.
>
> —Zechariah 2:5-9

From this year, the historical 70th of Israel, the Almighty is watching every nation. Which ones will honor Israel and Jerusalem as its eternal, undivided capital, and which ones will not? Which ones will stand with Israel and Yah's Biblical plans to restore her to the *fullness* of her land promised to Abraham, Isaac, and Jacob, and which will not? Those that will oppose His plans will now be judged very swiftly without any more periods of grace. Seventy years are now up!

> For thus says Adonai-Tzva'ot, He has sent me after glory to the nations that plundered you—because whoever touches you touches the apple of His eye—'For behold, I will shake My hand against them and they will be plunder to their servants.' Then you will know that Adonai-Tzva'ot has sent me.
>
> —Zechariah 2:12-13

Yet all who devour you will be devoured, and all your foes—all of them—will go into captivity. Those plundering you will be plundered, and all preying on you I give as prey.

—Jeremiah 30:16

For Adonai has a day of vengeance, a year of recompense for the hostility against Zion.

—Isaiah 34:8

About Israel, the Almighty says:

"For I will restore health to you and will heal you of your wounds." It is a declaration of Adonai. "For they called you an outcast: 'Zion—no one cares about her.'" Thus says Adonai, "Indeed, I will return Jacob's tents from exile, and have compassion on his dwellings. The city will be rebuilt on her mound. The citadel will stand in its rightful place. Out of them will come thanksgiving and the sound of celebration. I will multiply them, so they will not decrease. I will also honor them, so they will not be insignificant. His children also will be as formerly—his community set up before Me—and I will punish all his oppressors.

—Jeremiah 30:17-20

We encourage all nations to follow the president of the USA in moving their embassies. May all follow Google in declaring the eternal and undivided capital of Israel: The Holy City of Yerushalayim-Jerusalem! Yeshua, the Jewish Messiah, will soon return to rule and reign over the nations with a "rod of iron" from the Temple Mount. The future of Israel is brilliant—what is the future of your nation?

'In that day many nations will join themselves to Adonai and they will be My people and I will dwell among you.' Then you will know that Adonai-Tzva'ot has sent me to you. Adonai will inherit Judah as His portion in the holy land and will once again choose Jerusalem. Be silent before Adonai, all flesh, for He has aroused Himself from His holy dwelling.

—Zechariah 2:15-17

CHAPTER 35

WHO ARE THE HEIRS OF THE LAND OF ISRAEL?

> Yes, I will establish My covenant between Me and you and your seed after you throughout their generations for an everlasting covenant, in order to be your God and your seed's God after you.
>
> — GENESIS 17:7

THE BATTLE OF THE ages, which is the culmination of all prophecies, is in the ancient land of Canaan. It is that strip of land between the River of Egypt and the River Euphrates in Syria. Today, only a small part of what was known as Canaan—the land between the Taba border with Egypt in Eilat and the Golan Heights—is called the country of Israel. The rest of the original land of Canaan has been divided among other countries. A large portion of the East bank of the Jordan River—the area of ancient Gilead, Bashan, and Moab towards Edom—is the British artificially created country of Jordan. North of the Golan Heights are the two countries of Syria and Iraq, and to the South is the Sinai Desert all the way to the River of Egypt.

> On that day, ADONAI cut a covenant with Abram, saying, "I give this land to your seed, from the river of Egypt to the great river, the Euphrates River."
>
> —GENESIS 15:18

According to numerous prophecies in the Holy Scriptures, this land that comprises about 60,000 square miles is the God-given inheritance to Abraham and his descendants forever. The present-day Land of Israel is only 1/3 of the Biblical Promised Land!

The question is this: Who are Abraham's descendants to whom the land is promised?

> **Indeed, I will greatly bless you, and I will greatly multiply your seed as the stars of the heavens and as the sand which is on the seashore; and your seed shall possess the gate of their enemies.**
>
> —GENESIS 22:17 NASB '95

According to the above Scripture, Abraham's descendants would be as numerous as the stars in heaven and the sand on the seashore. If that is so, then how can this vast number of people fit in the Promised Land between the River of Egypt and the Euphrates? How many people can live within a 60,000 square miles (155,000 square kilometers) strip of land?

As an example, I will take one of the most densely populated cities in the world, Hong Kong, and her territories, consisting of 1,064 square miles (2,755 square kilometers). 7.43 million people live in a bit over 1,000 square miles. If we could do the same in the Land of Promise, taking into consideration unlivable terrain and desert sand where no high risers can be built (over 2/3 of the Land—40,000 square miles—is desert), we could fit up to 150 million people, packed like sardines, in the livable remaining 1/3 of the land. A few more people could be added as Israel has built apartment buildings in the desert, but because it is not safe to build high risers on the sand, this cannot compare to the way Hong Kong has used its land.

- In Israel, the present-day population is about 9 million.
- In Syria (which may be part of the Promised Land), there are about 18 million people.
- In the Sinai Peninsula (60,000 kilometers area) less than one million live because of the desert terrain.

At this point in time, about 20 million people live in the area defined as the Promised Land. If Abraham's descendants were so numerous, they would have to occupy the entire globe!

Is there a direct correlation between the quantity of descendants and the Land of Promise? Or is it that only *some* of his descendants are the heirs of this land and not *all* of the uncountable?

Let us see who Abraham's descendants are:

1. All those born of Abram and Hagar, the Egyptian maid of Sarai through Ishmael (Yishmael); those are many of the Arabs of today. (Genesis 17:20)
2. All those born of Abraham and Sarah through Isaac (Yitschak). (Genesis 17:19)
3. Yitschak bears Jacob (Yaakov) and Esau (Esav), who is Edom. (Genesis 25:22-23)
4. All of the descendants of Yaakov, namely the 12 Tribes of Israel. (Isaiah 41:8, 1 Kings 18:31)
5. All the descendants of Esav with his different Canaanite wives, all the Edomites and his descendants, mostly Arabs today. (Genesis 36)

6. The descendants of Abraham through Keturah, probably in the area of the Silk Road and the Far East, an uncountable number of people and nations! (Genesis 25)

7. The descendants of King Solomon with the Queen of Sheba in Africa, which is another staggering number of people who claim to be the children of Abraham. Though there is absolutely no biblical proof that the Queen of Sheba left the presence of King Solomon pregnant, there are substantial reasons to suspect that she took Solomon's seed in her womb. (2 Chronicles 9)

8. All the descendants of the Northern Kingdom of Israel that was cut off from Israel forever and exiled due to idolatry: the Word calls them "Ephraimites" or "the fullness of the Gentiles," in Hebrew *Melo HaGoyim*. They alone are as numerous as the stars of heaven and the sand on the seashore. (Genesis 48:19, Hosea 1:6, Hosea 7:8, Hosea 9:3)

9. All the descendants of the Southern Kingdom—the House of Judah, the Jewish people of today, which is a "countable number" thanks to so much genocide (especially by the Christian nations in Europe). (Hosea 1:6,7, Book of Esther, Nehemiah, Ezra, the 4 Gospels)

10. All the descendants of the Spanish (Sephardic) Jews that converted to Catholicism throughout the Spanish Inquisition, many of them by force.

11. All those who claim to be the children of Abraham *by faith* in the Jewish Messiah Yeshua, again an uncountable number! (Galatians 3:7-8)

Relating to all the above, we can see that the prophecy about the children of Abraham becoming as numerous as the stars in heaven and as the sand on the seashore has already come to pass. Some are children of Abraham by faith, and some are natural children of Abraham. The question is, who is the heir of the Land of Promise?

Obviously, all the uncountable millions above cannot be the heirs because of a logistic and demographic problem. Let me elaborate on this further,

1. All the descendants of Yishmael and Esau combined are now about 423 million!
2. The descendants of those claiming to be Palestinians alone are about 12 million.
3. The descendants of Abraham through Ketura, probably in the area of the Silk Road and the Far East, are an uncountable number of people and nations! They would not fit in the Land of Canaan.
4. The descendants of King Solomon with the Queen of Sheba in Africa are uncountable. Although there is absolutely no biblical proof that the Queen of Sheba left the presence of King Solomon pregnant, there are substantial reasons to suspect that she took Solomon's seed in her womb. This happened about 3,000 years ago, and there is no way to prove descendancy. In any case, there would be too many for them all to live in Israel!
5. The descendants of the cut-off Ephraimites, the Northern Kingdom, are impossible to assess as there was no identity mark left on them; they totally mixed with the nations. There are some tribes here and there who bear some marks, like the Bnei Menashe in India, but all in all, there is no way to know 2,800 years later who is of Ephraim and who is not. In any case, it could be into the hundreds of millions! Definitely, there is not enough space in the Land of Canaan for them.

6. The descendants of the Sephardic Jews who converted to Catholicism and lost their identity due to the Spanish Inquisition run into 60 million and above, according to the research of Professor Benzion Netanyahu, the late father of Israeli PM Benjamin Netanyahu.
7. All of those among the Christians or Messianic Gentiles who call themselves children of Abraham by faith are about 2.2 billion people. It is impossible to fit them in the strip of land between the River of Egypt to the Euphrates.
8. The Jewish people of today are about 15 million in total, and they can easily fit in the Promised Land.

The Land of Israel, from the River of Egypt to the Euphrates, is promised to a special group among Abraham's descendants. These are the Jewish people of today who have survived untold persecutions and humiliations, including pogroms and genocides in the nations of their exile. Yet, they did not forsake their Jewish identity. Among them, there is a representative remnant of all the 12 Tribes, as many from the Northern Kingdom joined Judah and the Southern Kingdom prior to the Assyrian Exile in the 8th Century BC. They all became Jews (grafted into Judah).

They are provable and recognizable Jews!

They will be joined by a remnant of Jews who were forcibly converted to Catholicism or Islam and who have been raised as Catholics or Muslims. These will return in measured numbers and join the Jewish people of today, who are the people of Israel. These are the legal heirs of the land promised to Abraham, Isaac, and Jacob as an inheritance for 1,000 generations.

> He remembers His covenant forever—the word He commanded for a thousand generations—which He made with Abraham, and swore to Isaac, and confirmed to Jacob as a decree, to Israel as an everlasting covenant, saying, "To you I give the land of Canaan, the portion of your inheritance."
>
> —Psalm 105:8-11

The land covenant given to Abraham and his descendants runs through a particular line of descendants and not through all of them. It does not run through Yishmael:

> And Abraham said to God, "Oh that Ishmael might live before You!" But God said, "No, but Sarah your wife will bear you a son, and you shall call his name Isaac; and I will establish My covenant with him for an everlasting covenant for his descendants after him."
>
> —Genesis 17:18-19 NASB '95

It does not run through Esau:

> Yet before the sons were even born and had not done anything good or bad—so that God's purpose and choice might stand not because of works but because of Him who calls it was said to her, "The older shall serve the younger."As it is written, "Jacob I loved, but Esau I hated."
>
> —Romans 9:11-13

It does not run through Ephraim—the House of Israel:

> Then she conceived again and bore a daughter. And He said to him: "Name her Lo-ruhamah for no longer will I have compassion on the house of Israel that I should ever pardon them.

> But on the house of Judah I will have compassion and deliver them by ADONAI, their God, yet not by bow, sword or battle, nor by horses and horsemen."
>
> —HOSEA 1:6-7

Ephraim becomes as an uncircumcised Gentile and as such can inherit salvation like all the other Gentiles, which is why the promise to Ephraim is to become "the fullness of the nations" or *Melo HaGoyim* and *not* "the fullness of Israel."

> But his father refused and said, "I know, my son, I know. He also will become a people, and he also will become great. But his younger brother (Ephraim) will become greater than he and his seed will be the fullness of the nations." Then he blessed them that day saying, "In you shall Israel bless by saying: 'May God make you like Ephraim and like Manasseh.'"
>
> —GENESIS 48:19-20

It does not run through the children of Abraham by faith:

The only promise for the Gentile believers in Messiah is salvation when they are grafted into the olive tree representing the Jewish people and the Jewish Messiah. There is no land promise to the Gentiles.

> But if some of the branches were broken off and you—being a wild olive—were grafted in among them and became a partaker of the root of the olive tree with its richness, do not boast against the branches. But if you do boast, it is not you who support the root but the root supports you.
>
> —ROMANS 11:17-18

It *does* run through Jacob:

> The land that I gave to Abraham and to Isaac I give it to you, and to your seed after you I will give the land." Then God went up from him at the place where He had spoken with him. Jacob set up a memorial stone in the place where He had spoken with him—a stone pillar—and he poured a drink offering on it and poured oil on it. Jacob named the place where God spoke with him Beth-El.
>
> —GENESIS 35:12-15

It does run through Judah. It does run through the Southern Kingdom that included the tribes of Judah, Benjamin, and Levi and were joined by a *small* remnant from the Northern Kingdom, called Ephraim (or the House of Israel), prior to the Assyrian exile in the 8th century BC. After the Babylonian exile of the House of Judah, all those who returned to the land were Jews (see the books of Ezra and Nehemiah). Yet, they were also called the House of Israel, or Israel, although the Northern Kingdom of the 10 Tribes was exiled to Assyria 200 years earlier, and they were no longer in the land. Those Jews who returned from the Babylonian exile were the Jews of the Second Temple Period (the Israel of Yeshua's time), from whom the Jewish people of today come. These were the Jews who were exiled by Rome in the year 70 AD for nearly 2,000 years until the official establishment of the State of Israel in 1948!

> Yet ADONAI, the God of Israel, has chosen me out of all my ancestral house to be king over Israel forever. For He chose Judah as ruler, and of the house of Judah, my father's house, and of my father's sons, He took pleasure in me to make me king over all Israel.
>
> —1 CHRONICLES 28:4

> Thus says ADONAI, "As for all My evil neighbors who strike at the inheritance that I bequeathed to My people Israel—I am about to uproot them from their land and pluck the house of Judah from them. Yet it will come to pass, after I have uprooted them, that I will again have compassion on them and I will bring them back, each one to his inheritance and each one to his land.
>
> —JEREMIAH 12:14-15

> Yes, I will restore the captivity of My people Israel. They will rebuild desolated cities and dwell in them. They will plant vineyards and drink their wine. They will also make gardens and eat their fruit. Yes, I will plant them on their land, and they will never again be plucked up out of their land that I have given to them." ADONAI, your God, has said it.
>
> —AMOS 9:14-15

Since we have proven that the land covenant runs through Judah, the Jewish people of today, what remains to be seen is what will happen to those who oppose it or claim the land as theirs because "they are also children of Abraham."

> Thus says ADONAI, "As for all My evil neighbors who strike at the inheritance that I bequeathed to My people Israel—I am about to uproot them from their land and pluck the house of Judah from them. Yet it will come to pass, after I have uprooted them, that I will again have compassion on them and I will bring them back, each one to his inheritance and each one to his land. So it will come to pass, if they will diligently learn the ways of My people—to swear by My Name, 'As ADONAI lives,' just as they taught My people to swear by Baal—then

they will be built up in the midst of My people. But if they will not obey, then I will uproot that nation, plucking it up and destroying it. It is a declaration of ADONAI.

—JEREMIAH 12:14-17

This applies to all those *within* Israel who call themselves Palestinians. (The way the Romans and the British called the Land of Israel Palestine, which means "Philistines.") The only hope for those who currently live in the land to inherit the land with the Jewish people is to become *Gerim* or grafted into Israel, becoming as Jews, forsaking Islam and Allah altogether.

Among those who claim to be descendants of Ephraim, this is a non-sustainable claim because Ephraim is totally mixed with the Gentiles and cannot claim identity for the purpose of land possession. Their promise is to become "the fullness of the nations" and not the fullness of Israel.

Many of the Ephraimite descendants are mixed with the Jewish people of today already since they joined Judah right before the Assyrian exile in the 8th century BC. The modern people of Israel are a mix of all the 12 Tribes, but predominantly they are from the tribe of Judah, Benjamin, and Levi. These were the Jewish people of the Second Temple Period; the time Yeshua walked the Land of Israel.

Among the lost Sephardic Jews who are among the Catholics in the nations, there can be a remnant who will return to their Jewish identity and also to the land. The promise is in the Book of Obadiah,

The exiles of this army of Bnei-Yisrael will possess what belonged to the Canaanites as far as Zarephath, while the exiles

of Jerusalem, who are in Sepharad, will possess the cities of the Negev.

—OBADIAH 1:20

Among the Sephardic (Spanish and Portuguese) Jews who became Catholics about 500 years ago, there is the possibility of tracing their roots. Although it can be a complex process, more and more information about their family names and traditions has recently been and continues to be discovered, so this movement is on the rise. Nevertheless, not all of their descendants will want to claim Jewish identity and come to live in the Land of Israel, and not all the Spanish Jews were forcibly converted; some did it willingly.

There is yet another group of Jews who lost their identity in Islam because of Muslim persecution while in exile in Arab countries. Some are waking up to their roots and wanting to return, which is, again, a complex process. Some of them are already living within the confines of the Promised Land. Some are in the River of Egypt area of Egypt, or in Syria or Iraq of today towards the river Euphrates, and others are within the so-called "Palestinian territories."

There is a terrible judgment promised to anyone who touches the land promised to the Jewish people as the heirs of theILand promised to Abraham.

> For look, Your enemies make an uproar. Those who hate You lift up their head. They make a shrewd plot against Your people, conspiring against Your treasured ones. "Come," they say, "let's wipe them out as a nation! Let Israel's name be remembered no more!"
>
> —PSALM 83:3-5

Who said, "Let us take possession of the pasturelands of God."

—Psalm 83:13

My God, make them like tumbleweed, like chaff before the wind. As a fire burns a forest, and as a flame sets mountains ablaze, so pursue them with Your tempest, and terrify them with Your storm. Cover their faces with shame, so they may seek Your Name—Adonai. Let them be ashamed and dismayed forever. Let them be humiliated and perish. Let them know that You alone whose Name is Adonai are El Elyon over all the earth.

—Psalm 83:14-19

Conclusion

The Land of Israel, from the River of Egypt to the Euphrates, is promised to a special group among Abraham's descendants. These are the Jewish people of today who have survived untold persecutions and humiliations, including pogroms and genocides in the nations of their exile. Yet, they did not forsake their Jewish identity. Among them, there is a representative remnant of all the 12 Tribes, as many from the Northern Kingdom joined Judah and the Southern Kingdom before the Assyrian exile in the 8th Century BC. They all became Jews (grafted into Judah).

They are provable and recognizable Jews! They will be joined by a remnant of Jews who were forcibly converted to Catholicism or Islam and who have been raised as Catholics or Muslims. These will return in measured numbers and join the Jewish people of today, who are the people of Israel. These are the legal heirs of the land promised to Abraham, Isaac, and Jacob as an inheritance for 1,000 generations.

> **He remembers His covenant forever—the word He commanded for a thousand generations—which He made with Abraham, and swore to Isaac, and confirmed to Jacob as a decree, to Israel as an everlasting covenant, saying, "To you I give the land of Canaan, the portion of your inheritance."**
>
> **—Psalm 105:8-11**

As for all the other children of Abraham by faith, the possible descendants of Solomon in Africa or of Ephraim and the like, you are most welcome to visit the land, to support the modern-day State of Israel and to fight alongside us with your prayers, your finances, in the media, in politics, and against BDS (boycott, divestment, sanctions) for the fullness of the promise to Abraham to come to pass from the River of Egypt to the Euphrates! This will incur the blessing for you and for the nations that you represent.

Genesis 12:3 Paraphrased

I will bless those who bless you (Abraham, Isaac, and Jacob through the Jewish people of our day). I will annihilate those who take you (Jews) lightly. And in you (the Jewish people, all the way to the Jewish Messiah Yeshua from the House of Judah!) all the nations of the earth will be blessed.

We invite you to enter into the above-promised blessing by joining the *United Nations for Israel** and help us to globally reeducate all nations as we fight for the national restoration of the Jewish people in the Land of Israel and for your nation to become a sheep nation.

---

* Join the *United Nations for Israel* at www.UnitedNationsforIsrael.org

'In that day many nations will join themselves to ADONAI and they will be My people and I will dwell among you.' Then you will know that ADONAI-Tzva'ot has sent me to you.

—Zechariah 2:15

CHAPTER 36

EXPEL THE DARKNESS

Hanukkah Edition 2017/5778

For behold, darkness covers the earth, and deep darkness the peoples. But ADONAI will arise upon you, and His glory will appear over you. Nations will come to your light, kings to the brilliance of your rising.

— ISAIAH 60:2-3

WHAT A TIME WE are living in! These are times of prophetic fulfillment just like in 1947 when the UN voted to partition the area then called Palestine, which is the Biblical Land of Israel, into two nations—one Arab and one Jewish. The Arabs *rejected* the resolution of the UN and thus lost the opportunity forever to become a nation in the Land of Israel.

Then, in 1967 in a political attempt to gain sympathy and support for their goal of taking over all of the Land of Israel to create an Arab-only state, they changed their designation from Arabs living in Palestine (just like there were Brits or Jews living in Palestine) to the name of "Palestinians." They have made the world believe that a people called "Palestinians" actually exist and have existed forever!*

This is a big, fat lie that has had all the nations in darkness and deep deception.

Now, the 151 nations that sided with the UN resolution of November 30, 2017 (100 years after the Balfour Declaration on November 2, 1917) to disavow Jerusalem from the Jewish people, plus the nine nations that abstained, thereby failing to stand with the Jewish people, are deep in the valley of judgment of the Almighty God of Israel and have nothing to expect but trouble and catastrophes!

> **And in that day I will set about to destroy all the nations that come against Jerusalem.**
>
> —Zechariah 12:9 nasb '95

All that because *one* man, the Grand Muslim Mufti of Jerusalem by the name of Haj Amin al-Husseini, who was the most important Islamic figure during the Nazi Shoah (Holocaust) and the Second World War, concocted a hideous plan: The Palestinian cause = The Final Solution.

Haj Amin Al Husseini visited Hitler in 1942 and asked the Fuhrer to raise him an army in the Land of Israel that had been renamed "Palestine" by the Roman occupiers in the 1st century (meaning Philistine). What kind of army? He requested the evilest man that ever lived to raise him an army like the Nazi army, an army with one purpose and only one purpose: to implement the Final Solution that Hitler so loved, in order to annihilate *all* the Jews in Palestine once and for all! Hitler gladly complied and trained this Arab army as he trained

---

* *For a brief history of where this name came from, see* www.eretzyisroel.org/~jkatz/meaning.html

his own Nazi army! Out of this plan, the whole "Palestinian cause" developed! That's right, the Palestinian cause, which includes the PLO, Fatah, Hamas, Hezbollah, and all the way to ISIS, is the love child of Hitler. Now think about this: all these 151+9 UN nations that have disavowed Jerusalem from the Jewish people have officially and publicly sided with Hitler for the annihilation of Israel.

> **O God, do not remain quiet; do not be silent and, O God, do not be still. For behold, Your enemies make an uproar, and those who hate You have exalted themselves. They make shrewd plans against Your people, and conspire together against Your treasured ones. They have said, "Come, and let us wipe them out as a nation, that the name of Israel be remembered no more." For they have conspired together with one mind; against You they make a covenant.**
>
> —PSALM 83:1-5 NASB '95

Expel the Darkness of Neutrality and Passivity

> **Deliver those who are being taken away to death, and those who are staggering to slaughter, Oh hold them back. If you say, "See, we did not know this," does He not consider it who weighs the hearts? And does He not know it who keeps your soul? And will He not render to man according to his work?**
>
> —PROVERBS 24:11-12 NASB '95

Are you a citizen of one of those nations that are included in the UN's anti-Israel, anti-Jerusalem, anti-God resolution? If so, please be warned—even if you are a believer in the Messiah, and you are doing nothing about this predicament, then you will be in the "same boat" as your nation, and I assure you that this "boat" is going to sink rapidly! YHVH does not have any time to waste until He restores *all* of Israel, as He has promised in numerous scriptures in the Bible. He is in a hurry to restore Zion, His dwelling place, and that means Israel with Jerusalem as its capital. The Messiah will soon return and set His rulership on the earth in Yerushalayim, on the Temple Mount. He will not rule from a mosque, neither shall His Holy City be called Al Quds. And I promise you that the chants all over the city will not be "Allah Akbar," Allah is the greatest—but rather, HaleluYah or Praise to YAH, YHVH, the God of Israel!

> **On your walls, O Jerusalem, I have appointed watchmen; all day and all night they will never keep silent. You who remind the LORD, take no rest for yourselves; and give Him no rest until He establishes and makes Jerusalem a praise in the earth.**
>
> **—ISAIAH 62:6-7 NASB '95**

So, back to you, beloved believer in Messiah! The God of Israel is not one to sanction neutrality, passivity, or inactivity. If you are in one of those nations that have come against Israel and Jerusalem, then you and your family and your Christian friends are in danger! You see, the same Arabs that are now called "Palestinians" have been sanctioned by the UN to annihilate Israel. One of the nations that voted to sanction this annihilation is Germany. Others include all the European countries and Africa, most of the Pacific, South America, Asia, and the Middle East.

Over seven and a half billion people on planet earth are in danger of total destruction.

If you think that I am a sensationalist or exaggerating, please read below what the King of the Jews, the Creator of heaven and earth Himself, says about it.

> **Draw near, O nations, to hear; and listen, O peoples! Let the earth and all it contains hear, and the world and all that springs from it. For the LORD's indignation is against all the nations, and His wrath against all their armies; He has utterly destroyed them, He has given them over to slaughter. So their slain will be thrown out, and their corpses will give off their stench, and the mountains will be drenched with their blood.**
>
> —Isaiah 34:1-3 nasb '95

Why is He bent on destroying *all* the nations? He continues in the same chapter:

> **For ADONAI has a day of vengeance, a year of recompense for the hostility against Zion.**
>
> —Isaiah 34:8

He is about to take *revenge* for all the blood of His Jewish people that has been spilled on the earth. This includes not only the recent UN resolutions but also all the blood spilled in the name of Jesus Christ and Christianity through the Crusades, the Spanish and Portuguese inquisitions, the pogroms, the untold expulsions, humiliations, the Nazi Shoah (Holocaust), to all the anti-Zionism in the UN, and all the Christian NGOs that have sided with the "Palestinian cause" with their money and their voices. The entire United Nations has sided with Hitler's plan through Haj Amin al-Husseini, the PLO, the Fatah, and the Palestinian cause—a Trojan horse to destroy Israel.

Passivity is the Same as Siding with the Enemy

Yeshua will separate the nations according to how they have treated the Jewish people—not only if they did something against them, but also if they did nothing to help them when needed.

> Then He will also say to those on His left, 'Depart from Me, accursed ones, into the eternal fire which has been prepared for the devil and his angels; for I was hungry, and you gave Me nothing to eat; I was thirsty, and you gave Me nothing to drink; I was a stranger, and you did not invite Me in; naked, and you did not clothe Me; sick, and in prison, and you did not visit Me.' Then they themselves also will answer, 'Lord, when did we see You hungry, or thirsty, or a stranger, or naked, or sick, or in prison, and did not take care of You?' Then He will answer them, 'Truly I say to you, to the extent that you did not do it to one of the least of these, you did not do it to Me.' These will go away into eternal punishment, but the righteous into eternal life."
>
> —Matthew 25:41-46 nasb '95

Who are the "least of these" that Yeshua is referring to? They are the least of the Jewish people He was speaking to.

You Are Your Nation

> I searched for a man among them who would build up the wall and stand in the gap before Me for the land, so that I would not destroy it; but I found no one.
>
> —Ezekiel 22:30 nasb '95

You will not be able to stand before Yeshua, the King of the Jews, and say, "I could do nothing about it; it just happened," because He will hold each one of us accountable! Did we raise our voices to rebuke and dispel this darkness? Did we act for Israel's sake? Did we spend some effort seeking Him as to what to do? Did we support financially, and in serious prayer, the cause of Zion? Or were we just like the German and Polish Christians who smelled the Jews being burned in the crematorium of the death camps and continued singing from their hymnals in the churches? They were too busy protecting themselves by pretending to ignore the terrible slaughter the Jews were going through. They were too steeped in the hateful Christian replacement theology to care. There were only a very few who rose against the Nazi regime or who acted to rescue Jews, and we salute them! But they were too few, and not *one* Christian organization stood up to Hitler, not one.

And what about now, in the 21st century, with this modern-day plan to use the UN to exterminate Israel officially? Do you really think that you can escape because you are a Christian or even Messianic? Beloved ones, the same radical Muslims that want to exterminate every Jew, want to exterminate you, too! They are bent on Islam ruling the world, not Judaism or Christianity, only Islam. We are not out of harm's way, beloved!

But really, the One we should fear the most is the God of Israel Himself, not radical Islam. He promised to destroy the nations that have come against Jerusalem, and that includes your nation—unless *you* rise up like the ancient Maccabees to expel the darkness and light up your nation's Hanukkah menorah!*

---

* A Hanukkah menorah, or hanukkiah, is a nine-branched candelabrum lit during the eight-day Jewish feast of Hanukkah.

> Arise, shine; for your light has come, and the glory of YHVH has risen upon you.
>
> —Isaiah 60:1 NASB '95

The Maccabees were Jewish priests who stood up against the mighty Greek empire that was bent on conquering all of Israel and forcing the Jewish people into idolatry. They had overtaken the Holy Temple on the Temple Mount and were burning pigs on the altar. Then, this small band of Jewish priests arose and defied them all! They took the Temple back and cleansed it from all idolatry. By faith in the miracles of YHVH, the God of Israel, they reinstituted Divine worship and relit the seven-branch Menorah. Thus, they expelled the darkness of their time!

They did this at great cost, against all odds, risking their lives at every turn. But doing what was right in the eyes of YHVH was much more dear to them than preserving their lives.

> But I have this against you, that you have left your first love. Therefore remember from where you have fallen, and repent and do the deeds you did at first; or else I am coming to you and will remove your lampstand (Menorah) out of its place—unless you repent.
>
> — Revelation 2:4-5 NASB '95

Are You Like Noah or Like the Rest that Drowned?

And just as it happened in the days of Noah, so it will be also in the days of the Son of Man: they were eating, they were drinking, they were marrying, they were being given in marriage, until the day that Noah entered the ark, and the flood came and destroyed them all.

—Luke 17:26-27 nasb '95

Noah was building an ark because Elohim-God (God of Israel) was about to destroy the world because of their wickedness and rebellion. But He had given instructions to *one* man on how to build a boat big enough to rescue as many people and as many animals as possible. However, besides his own family, no one else wanted to help him with the project. They mocked him and did not believe that it would rain, as it had never rained before. They did not believe in the warnings of righteous Noah that Elohim, the Creator, was about to annihilate *all* of mankind. When the flood came, they all perished because of unbelief in the judgment of God. I am sure there were some religious people among them, but they had no fear of Yah, fear of God.

According to a false gospel preached in the 21st century, God is too good to judge or to destroy. Do not believe it for a moment! The God of the New Testament is exactly the same one as in the "Old" Testament (The Holy Scriptures), and the same principles apply today as they did in the days of Noah.

All the Maccabees are Called to Come on Board

During this fateful historical time of all the world (minus five countries) turning against Israel, Jerusalem, and the Jewish people, we are building Noah's ark again! It is called the United Nations for Israel. We invite you to board the ark and act with us during these dangerous times to support Israel actively, to stand with her like Ruth with Naomi, and to turn your nation from an obvious goat nation into a sheep nation, *one person at a time!*

Are You a Son of Zion or a Son of Greece?

> I will bend Judah as my bow and fill it with Ephraim. I will rouse your sons, O Zion against your sons, O Greece. I will wield you like a warrior's sword. Then ADONAI will be seen over them as His arrow flashes like lightning. ADONAI Elohim will blow the shofar and march in whirlwinds of the south.
>
> —ZECHARIAH 9:13-14

Either you are a modern-day Maccabee, a son or daughter of Zion and stand up against unrighteousness, or you are a son or daughter of Greece, a "Greek idolater" (steeped in replacement theology, Romanized Christianity, pagan feasts, and lukewarm or prideful towards Israel). Either you board the United Nations for Israel, or you stand with the present-day UN against Israel—neutrality is not acceptable in the eyes of YHVH.

This is not a church, nor just a ministry; this is a movement just like the Maccabees of old and like the building of Noah's Ark. Let us work while it is still day, as the night is coming! Expel the darkness of deception, replacement theology, and anti-Messiah, anti-Israel, anti-Torah, anti-Jewish, anti-Zionist now from your life, your family, church, ministry, and as many people as possible. Tomorrow may be too late!

We welcome the modern-day Maccabees and Noah-like people to help us build the ark called the United Nations for Israel, transforming your nation into a sheep nation, one person at a time.

Is everyone on board? The doors are about to close! YHVH Himself shut the doors of Noah's ark, and He will do it again. How long do we have until the time is up?

We must work the works of Him who sent Me as long as it is day; night is coming when no one can work.

—John 9:4 nasb '95

CHAPTER 37

STORMY WEATHER—HURRICANE IRMA

*Praise the L*ORD *from the earth, sea monsters and all deeps; fire and hail, snow and clouds; stormy wind, fulfilling His word.*

— PSALMS 148:7-8 NASB '95

THE RECENT HURRICANE IRMA failed to destroy the State of Florida by sheer prayer and mercy. However, it left millions of people displaced and half of the state without electricity.

This chapter contains revealing excerpts from my book *Stormy Weather** and a concise report written by our team member, Rev. Debra Barnes, from Alabama. She explains how a much greater catastrophe was averted by Archbishop Dominiquae calling for prayers of repentance and a Midnight Watch on-site in St. Augustine, Florida, where theministry is currently based, through the internet on Facebook Live.

---

* For a full understanding of these storms and catastrophes and how to prevent them altogether, please get my book *Stormy Weather* from www.ZionsGospel.com

Excerpts from the book *Stormy Weather*:

(Stormy Weather, page 19)

On Christmas Day of 2001 in Santiago, Chile, the Almighty visited me and told me that He will judge the nations according to these two principles:

1. His righteous laws and commandments.

> For the wrath of God is revealed from heaven against all ungodliness and unrighteousness of men, who hinder the truth in unrighteousness, because that which is known of God is manifest in them; for God manifested it unto them. For the invisible things of Him since the creation of the world are clearly seen, being perceived through the things that are made, [even] His everlasting power and divinity; that they may be without excuse: because that, knowing God, they glorified Him not as God, neither gave thanks; but became vain in their reasoning, and their senseless heart was darkened. Professing themselves to be wise, they became fools, and changed the glory of the incorruptible God for the likeness of an image of corruptible man, and of birds, and four-footed beasts, and creeping things. Wherefore God gave them up in the lusts of their hearts unto uncleanness, that their bodies should be dishonored among themselves: for that they exchanged the truth of God for a lie, and worshiped and served the creature rather than the Creator, who is blessed forever. Amen.
>
> —Romans 1:18-25 ASV

(*Stormy Weather*, page 20)

> For this cause, God gave them up unto vile passions: for their women changed the natural use into that which is against nature: And likewise, also the men, leaving the natural use of the woman, burned in their lust one toward another, men with men working unseemliness, and receiving in themselves that recompense of their error which was due. And even as they refused to have God in [their] knowledge, God gave them up unto a reprobate mind, to do those things which are not fitting; being filled with all unrighteousness, wickedness, covetousness, maliciousness; full of envy, murder, strife, deceit, malignity; whisperers, backbiters, hateful to God, insolent, haughty, boastful, inventors of evil things, disobedient to parents.
>
> —Romans 1:26-30 ASV

The moral condition of the nations demands a serious response from the Holy God who sent His Son to die for us so that we might repent from our own ways of wickedness. The world needs to wake up to the fact that it is running out of time, that these are the last minutes of grace from heaven before His wrath will be poured out—just like He did in ancient times when He destroyed Sodom and Gomorrah because of the idolatry, homosexuality, witchcraft, and wickedness. The Most High has given us His best, His Holy Son, that whoever calls on His name, Yeshua the Messiah, can be saved from the wrath to come.

(*Stormy Weather*, page 21)

2. How the nations have treated Israel, the apple of His eye.

For 2000 years, the nations and, most particularly, the Christians since the 4th century have hated Israel and persecuted it in the Greek name - Jesus Christ. This kind of hatred culminated in the Spanish Inquisition and the Nazi Holocaust; both events have taken place in predominantly Christian nations - Catholic Spain and Protestant Germany. Nowadays, hatred of Jews is predominant all over the world, especially among Muslims who would like the tiny nation of Israel destroyed and wiped off the map altogether. However, the last word remains with the Most High God, who created Israel for His Glory and who promised to destroy those who harm His people.

> "Oy, Zion! Escape, you who are living with the daughter of Babylon." "For thus says ADONAI-Tzva'ot, He has sent me after glory to the nations that plundered you—because whoever touches you touches the apple of His eye."
>
> —ZECHARIAH 2:11-12

> "I will bless those who bless you, and I will curse him who curses you. In you will all of the families of the earth be blessed."
>
> —GENESIS 12:3 NKJV

After 2000 years of hatred against the Jews, there are many nations that are about to incur God's judgment. These are the last minutes in the hourglass for the world to repent! He said that the *key* to the blessing of all nations was to bless and do good to His Jewish people, the natural offspring of Abraham. This key, which I call the "Key of

Abraham", can open the blessing or the curse on the nations depending on their behavior toward the Jews.

(*Stormy Weather*, page 22)

I wrote a book called "*Sheep Nations*" as a fruit of this visitation and I encourage you to order it and to read it.*

> "As the days of Noah, so will be the coming of the Son of Man. For as in those days which were before the flood, they were eating and drinking, marrying and giving in marriage, until the day that Noah entered into the ark. And they didn't know until the flood came, and took them all away, so will be the coming of the Son of Man."
>
> —Matthew 24:37-39

Hurricane Irma: Act of repentance & midnight watch by Rev. D. Barnes

This week, the Holy Spirit led our ministry team to go before His throne on behalf of the USA during this critical time, as Hurricane Irma was threatening devastation to much of the state of Florida.

> ...*if* My people who are called by My name will humble themselves, and pray and seek My face, and turn from their wicked ways, *then* I will hear from heaven, and will forgive their sin and heal their land.
>
> —2 Chronicles 7:14

This Scripture is very clear—there is the word "if," and there is the word "then." When we fulfill the "if," YHVH will perform the promises after "then." So, our act of repentance began just as Shabbat was

---

* Order *Sheep Nations* at www.ZionsGospel.com

ending on the evening of September 9 at precisely 7:14 p.m. EST. It was strategically led by Archbishop Dominiquae Bierman from her home in St. Augustine, FL. Hurricane Irma was about to saturate the state with ferocious wind and rain, unleashing a devastating storm surge from the seas. In His wrath, we were crying out for mercy!

The issues we were led to repent for were numerous: abortion, mammon worship, and the failure of the Trump administration to keep their promise to move the US Embassy to Jerusalem.* Our international group gathered, by phone and Facebook, in one accord (*Hebr. echad*), asking for the imminent disastrous judgment of Florida to be reversed.

There were immediate answers to our sincerely repentant hearts' cry: the monster storm was expected to be a possible Category 5, which brings "catastrophic damage" from winds over 150 mph. The next day, when Irma made landfall at Marco Island, FL, she was actually downgraded considerably to Category 3 with 115 mph winds. We rejoiced at His mercy and goodness to those affected, especially those in the direct path! But it was not over yet.

Shortly thereafter, Archbishop Dominiquae was led to call a special Midnight Watch on 9/11/17—as Category 2 Irma's eye was still raging along the western coast of Florida. Her effects were being felt for hundreds of miles in diameter across the state (affecting our connection during the Watch). In His mercy, we were led to declare peace to the storm:

Then as they were sailing, He fell asleep. A violent windstorm came down on the lake, and they were swamped with water

---

* You can listen to the recording of this powerful intercessory Act of Repentance on Facebook at m.facebook.com/story.php?story_fbid=10212914293149564 &id=1157414214 (Note: there were power disruptions caused by the storm, but we continued to tap into His Almighty Power!)

and in danger. They came to Yeshua and woke Him, saying, "Master, Master, we're perishing!" He got up and rebuked the wind and the surging wave of water. Then they stopped, and it became calm. Then Yeshua said to them, "Where is your faith?" But they were afraid and marveled, saying to one another, "Who then is this? He commands even the winds and the water, and they obey Him!"

—Luke 8:23-25

One of the other major factors brought to us as we faced this wicked storm's damage was to repent for the seniors of America. This was strategic as Florida is known as a retirement destination for millions from all over the country. The prayers and declarations made were to call forth the destiny of those over age 60—it is not time to sit and retire, but it is time to "refire" and come forth in your calling. It is time for them to arise as the Joshua and Caleb to this next generation who desperately need to be mentored and discipled in His ways. The harvest is ripe. The eternal destiny of many is at stake. This is no time to rest.

Additional areas of focus included the Spanish and Jewish populations. The sinfulness of the Spanish population here in America, especially in Florida, founded by the Spanish, was repented for by intercessors of Spanish descent as they interceded powerfully before Yah. Many Jewish people from Florida also need to make aliyah—this may be their wake-up call!

> Adonai, I have heard the report about You and I have come to fear. Adonai, revive Your work throughout the years, throughout the years make it known, in wrath remember compassion (mercy).
>
> —Habakkuk 3:2

Thank you, YHVH, for your abundant mercy in Florida! The damages were so much less severe than anticipated in many areas. May Your compassion fail not throughout all of America as we continue to awaken to our greatest need: to embrace the Torah and become obedient, even unto death. Yeshua is our example. May we all follow Him—before it is too late.

Immediately after the midnight watch, the news flashed that Hurricane Irma had been downgraded to Category 1. A few hours later, it became a tropical storm and was diffused altogether. According to the prognosis, it should have raged across four states from Florida to Alabama, but it could not because of our intercession before the throne of YHVH. Praise be to Him who sits on the throne, who has had mercy!

Just as a comparison, the same Hurricane Irma killed 70% of the Island of Barbuda and destroyed 90% of its property, according to news sources.* This is what would have happened in Florida, but Abba heard our prayers, and we are eternally grateful! We are also grateful to all who prayed with us, and now we must preach repentance all over this nation. Please stand with us in prayer and financial partnership to continue broadcasting the truth far and wide so many can come to repentance!

Sadly, large portions of the Caribbean have been left practically uninhabitable! This should have happened in Florida, too, but His mercy has spared us this time.

---

* www.weather.com/amp/storms/hurricane/news/hurricane-irma-before-after-images-barbuda-virgin-islands.html

CHAPTER 38

THE OVERTURNING HAS BEGUN

When Hanukkah and Purim Kiss Each Other

Haman recounted to his wife Zeresh and all his friends everything that had happened to him. His advisers and his wife Zeresh said to him, "Since Mordecai, before whom you have begun your downfall, is of Jewish descent, you won't be able to stand against him. In fact, you will certainly fall before him!"

— ESTHER 6:13

THE LONG-AWAITED OVERTURNING HAS begun. The Haman of this world, in the guise of the UN's anti-Israel policies, "political correctness," and "the Palestinian cause," together with all the false and unbiblical "peace initiatives" that have led to more and more terror, has begun to fall!

This Haman has used the UN as its vessel to cause 151+6 nations to turn their backs on Israel and Jerusalem, its eternal capital. This wicked scheme of Satan is now being overturned in the same way King Ahasuerus recognized and honored Mordecai.

The king said to Haman, "Go quickly! Take the robe and the horse, just as you suggested, for Mordecai the Jew, who sits at the king's gate! Do not neglect anything that you recommended." So, Haman took the robe and the horse, robed Mordecai, and paraded him through the city streets, proclaiming: "This is what is done for the man whom the king desires to honor."

—Esther 6:10-11

On December 6, 2017, President Donald Trump acted like King Ahasuerus of our time by recognizing Jerusalem as the capital of Israel and thus honoring the people of Israel! In the same way that the King forced Haman to honor the Jew that he hated, now President Trump's righteous move is forcing the Haman governments of the nations to bless and honor Israel. Yes, even nations that have disavowed the Jewish people from Jerusalem, and even those that abstained, will be forced to follow the example of the USA and recognize Jerusalem as Israel's capital.

This overturning started right before Hanukkah of 2017, and we will see an upsurge in Purim this year as Israel prepares to celebrate its 70th anniversary in May.

The plan of Haj Amin al-Husseini, Hitler, and the PLO to annihilate the Jewish people from within the Land of Israel is being hanged on the gallows!

Harbonah, one of the eunuchs attending the king, said, "Look, a gallows fifty cubits high is standing next to Haman's house. Haman himself made it for Mordecai, who spoke good on behalf of the king!" The king said, "Hang him on it!"

—Esther 7:9

Haman and all his wicked sons and terror groups thereof get hanged on the gallows—and yet, his plan to annihilate the Jews continues.

> So, they hanged Haman on the gallows that he had prepared for Mordecai. Then the king's rage subsided.
>
> —Esther 7:10

But the good news is, now Israel can defend itself without apologetics and push the enemy back without any obstruction from America,* as in the past. Donald Trump, the King Ahasuerus of our time, has now granted Israel the validity of self-defense without apologetics.

> The king granted the right for Jews in every city to assemble themselves and to protect themselves—to destroy, kill and annihilate any army of any people or province that might attack them and their women and children, and to plunder their possessions.
>
> —Esther 8:11

And many will become Jews! Yes, even among the enemies of Israel of today, even many Muslims! Many will be saved by the 3rd Day Revival,** not by a replacement theology gospel divorced from Israel, but by the gospel made in Zion with Jewish roots and foundations, Biblical feasts, and the name of Yeshua. Many Catholics and others from different Christian denominations will embrace the Jewish Messiah, the Torah, and the Holy Spirit. Therefore, they will "become Jews" just like the believers of the first century, when Gentiles joined the Jewish believers and were grafted into the olive tree.***

> Throughout every province and throughout every city, wherever the king's edict and his law went, the Jews had gladness

---

* Unfortunately, this was not the case under the Biden administration after the massacre by Hamas on October 7, 2023.
** Download the free book at www.ZionsGospel.com
*** Read all of Romans 11

and joy, banquets and holidays. Many peoples of the land became Jews, because the fear of the Jews had overcome them.

—Esther 8:17

So why a Purim story on Hanukkah? Because the season of miracles is here, and the Light is overturning the darkness. An unprecedented, all-encompassing awakening and revival is on the way!

CHAPTER 39

TIME TO UNEXIT

> Therefore it was named Babel, because there the LORD confused the language of all the earth; and from there the LORD scattered them abroad over the face of all the earth.
>
> — GENESIS 11:9 NASB '95

A FEW YEARS AGO, YHVH gave me a word: United Nations for Israel. I began to declare that a United Nations for Israel was about to be birthed. We created flags, banners, and T-shirts projecting the heavenly vision in the USA and Israel and throughout the nations through the participants of our Israel tours. I knew in 2014 that the Almighty is *done* with the United Nations! I know this may sound a bit radical to some people, but the UN has "tipped over" into the judgment of God, and my prayer is that as many nations as possible will do a UNEXIT before it is too late.

Anti-Israel Resolutions in the UN Between 2015-2016

UN Watch - unwatch.org:*

---

* www.unwatch.org/un-to-adopt-20-resolutions-against-israel-3-on-rest-of-the-world

The U.N. General Assembly's 2015 session is adopting 20 resolutions singling out Israel for criticism and only 3 resolutions on the rest of the world combined.

All but one of the texts have already been adopted by the plenary yesterday, or have been approved at the initial committee vote.

The three that do not concern Israel are: one on Syria, a regime that has murdered more than 200,000 of its own people, one on Iran, and one on North Korea.

Not a single UNGA resolution this year (70th session) is expected to be adopted on gross and systematic abuses committed by China, Cuba, Egypt, Pakistan, Russia, Saudi Arabia, Sri Lanka, Sudan, Yemen, Zimbabwe, or on dozens of other perpetrators of gross and systematic human rights violations.

Why are the nations in an uproar and the peoples devising a vain thing? The kings of the earth take their stand and the rulers take counsel together against the LORD and against His Anointed, saying, "Let us tear their fetters apart and cast away their cords from us!" He who sits in the heavens laughs, The LORD scoffs at them. Then He will speak to them in His anger and terrify them in His fury, saying, "But as for Me, I have installed My King Upon Zion, My holy mountain.

—PSALM 2:1-6 NASB '95

The UN has touched Israel, the apple of Yah's (God's) eye. Most of the UN resolutions are anti-Israeli, anti-Zionist, and anti-Jewish State. This is not speculation or interpretation; these are cold, hard facts, and it is time to wake up before the resulting plagues reach your nation.

I will bless those who bless you (Israel) and I will curse those who curse you!

—Genesis 12:3

We applied healing to Babylon (UN), but she was not healed; forsake her and let us each go to his own country, for her judgment has reached to heaven and towers up to the very skies.

—Jeremiah 51:9 nasb '95

Sheep Nations and UNEXIT

"Ho, Zion! Escape, you who are living with the daughter of Babylon." For thus says the Lord of hosts, "After glory He has sent me against the nations which plunder you (Israel-the Jews!), for he who touches you, touches the apple of His eye.

—Zechariah 2:7-8 nasb '95

I have been dreaming for many years of the sheep nations, and the vehicle to achieve this is a body of nations called the United Nations for Israel. This is a body of nations that will decide to do a UNEXIT. Am I dreaming? Maybe! But Joseph dreamt too, and his dreams came to pass, though they seemed far-fetched at the time. So, let me dream on. My spirit has been clearly hearing the word UNEXIT, which appears to be the only solution for nations to escape the coming judgment that is now falling on the UN.

For all the nations have drunk of the wine of the passion of her immorality, and the kings of the earth have committed acts of immorality with her, and the merchants of the earth have become rich by the wealth of her sensuality." I heard another voice from heaven, saying, "Come out of her, my people, so that you will not participate in her sins and receive of her plagues; for her sins have piled up as high as heaven, and God has remembered her iniquities.

—Revelation 18:3-5 nasb '95

There are two issues by which YHVH will judge every nation:

1. Obedience to His righteous commandments, which are the foundation for any Godly society.
2. Supporting/blessing Israel.

For the Lord has a day of vengeance, a year of recompense for the cause of Zion.

—Isaiah 34:8 nasb '95

Time and again, the UN has shown itself to be an enemy of the Jewish State. Time and again, the UN has called Zionism racism, given the right hand of fellowship to those who want to annihilate Israel, and denounced Israel unjustly with great imbalance and partiality. The hypocrisy of the UN has reached the heavens in the same way that the rebellion of the tower of Babel reached the heavens.

Adonai said, "Look, the people are one and all of them have the same language. So this is what they have begun to do. Now, nothing they plan to do will be impossible. Come! Let Us go down and confuse their language there, so that they will not understand each other's language." So Adonai scattered

them from there over the face of the entire land, and they stopped building the city.

—Genesis 11: 6-8

YHVH allowed the tower of Babel to be built up to a point that was the point of *no return*. The UN is at the point of no return. YHVH will come down to dismantle it and confuse its languages. That is why a UNEXIT is the only sound thing for any nation that wants to escape the chaos, the confusion, the curse, and the judgment to come.

> **Flee from within Babylon! Each one, escape with his soul! Be not silenced in her iniquity!**
> **For it is a time of vengeance for Adonai. He will repay her recompense. Babylon has been a golden cup in Adonai's hand, intoxicating the whole earth. The nations drunk her wineso the nations are going crazy. Suddenly Babylon is fallen! Shattered!**
>
> **—Jeremiah 51:6-8a**

Do not be fooled by what seems to be "all as usual." In the days of Noah, they were also functioning as usual and doing business as usual when the flood came. During the building of the tower of Babel, they were also building as usual and following their wicked blueprint and construction plans as usual—and suddenly, YHVH came down and stopped the work. A sudden intervention is on its way, and my prayer is that many nations will hear this word and do a UNEXIT and join the United Nations for Israel, which is about to be birthed!*

May YHVH have mercy on the nations caught up in the UN's web of iniquity, lies, and hypocrisy. May He help them exit this ungodly

---

* United Nations for Israel was birthed in 2018. For more information, visit www.unitednationsforisrael.org

institution at the speed of light! May righteous governments arise in many nations so this dream of sheep nations can be fulfilled.

> "But when the Son of Man comes in His glory, and all the angels with Him, then He will sit on His glorious throne. All the nations will be gathered before Him; and He will separate them from one another, as the shepherd separates the sheep from the goats; and He will put the sheep on His right, and the goats on the left.
>
> —Matthew 25:31-33 nasb '95

A Word to the USA

America, stop funding the United Nations and your economy will recover!

Farewell, Ban Ki-moon! Why did you not speak earlier during your ten years of service at the UN? Better late than never?

> United Nations Secretary-General Ban Ki-moon, who is stepping down at the end of the year (December 2016), acknowledged in a departing speech that there is "disproportionate" bias against Israel at the world body. "We must never accept bias against Israel within U.N. bodies," Ban said Friday.
>
> Ban went on to admit that the U.N. has a "disproportionate volume of resolutions, reports and conferences criticizing Israel," and that "in many cases, rather than helping the Palestinian cause, this reality has hampered the ability of the U.N. to fulfill its role effectively."

Israeli Ambassador to the U.N. Danny Danon commended Ban's statement and noted the disproportionate number of anti-Israel resolutions passed at the U.N. in recent years.*

It will come about in that day that I will make Jerusalem a heavy stone for all the peoples; all who lift it will be severely injured. And all the nations of the earth will be gathered against it.

—Zechariah 12:3 NASB '95

As for me, I will keep on dreaming, singing, and prophesying about UNEXIT, United Nations for Israel, and sheep nations until it happens, simply because dreaming the dreams of YHVH/Yeshua, prophesying them, and singing them works! It does so in the face of all adversity and against all odds. I will not tire of proclaiming UNEXIT, United Nations for Israel, and sheep nations. Would you, beloved reader, proclaim it with me?

---

* Read more at www.breakingisraelnews.com/80352/un-head-ban-ki-moon-admits-anti-israel-bias-departing-speech/#dfmkjefekcmDx8ih.99

CHAPTER 40

BLOW THE TRUMPET, SOUND THE ALARM

Mona Allen & Rev. Debra Barnes

This is urgent: we are down to the final hours and days concerning the fate of Jerusalem and the Land of Israel. The United Nations, led by President Obama and leaders in Paris, is planning by the end of 2016 to bring a resolution before the UN Security Council (UNSC). This resolution is calling for a vote to divide Jerusalem and take Israel back to the 1967 borders.*

Is this UNSC vote placing the United Nations literally into the Valley of Jehoshaphat prophesied in Joel Chapters 1 through 3? If we look at this portion of Scripture, it clearly speaks about the days concerning the times we are *now* in.

The Valley of Jehoshaphat (also called the Kidron Valley) is geographically located between the base of Jerusalem and the Mount of Olives. God says He will gather all nations (UN), and bring them down into the Valley of Jehoshaphat, and will plead with them there for "My people and for My heritage Israel, whom they have scattered among the nations, and parted My land." (Joel 3:2). "Multitudes, multitudes are in the valley of decision" (according to Joel 3:14). The UN *is a* multitude,

---

* www.conservativepapers.com/news/2016/06/03/obamas-plan-to-give-jerusalem-to-the-arabs-in-the-unsc-phase-i-the-paris-conference/

and *they are* planning to make a decision in 2016 to divide Jerusalem, which is literally attached to this actual Valley of Jehoshaphat.

This vote could be one of the most important decisions to affect Jerusalem and Israel since they became a State in 1948. It seems like our news media are silent, and even our Christian leaders appear to be unaware.

I was in Israel during the 1st UN Vote in November 2012, which attempted to give the Palestinians a state by dividing the land, going back to the 1967 borders. I will never forget that day. I believed I was to go to the Knesset, Israel's parliament, on the day of the vote and stand in the gap for them. I felt like I was to pray and declare and decree the Biblical boundary lines given by God in Joshua chapter 1 over the nations voting that day. I remember praying and saying, "LORD, I am standing with Israel today like Ruth did Naomi." The LORD of Hosts even sent a lady named Ruth to go with me.

We caught a bus and walked up to the guards guarding the Knesset. We told them we wanted to stand up and pray for them regarding the UN vote. They gave us a little gap of time, and we cried out for the nation of Israel and the vote, declaring God's words in Scripture for the land and people.

The vote did not pass, but only by a small margin. I am from the USA, and President Obama voted *not* to divide the land at that time. As I listened to the report, I knew this was not the end of this issue; they spoke of bringing it up again later. So, I have been waiting and watching for this to return, as I felt like they would try to vote again in a moment of time that people would least expect it.

Here we are in 2016, and just as I thought, nobody is talking about this upcoming plan to divide Jerusalem at the UN. I personally believe it is because there are so many issues concerning the presidential election in the USA that have deliberately dominated the news media to cover up this UN vote story.

Several other recent or current events also align with the prophecy in Joel chapters 1-3 for 2015-2016. Four blood moons (a tetrad) occurred on the Feast Days of the LORD: Passover and Feast of Tabernacles in 2014, and then Passover and Feast of Tabernacles in 2015. We read in the book of Joel:

> **And I will shew wonders in the heavens and in the earth, blood, and fire and pillars of smoke. The Sun shall be turned into darkness and the Moon to blood before the great and terrible day of the LORD come!**
>
> **—JOEL 2:30-31 ASV**

I was on tour with Archbishop Dominiquae Bierman, and we were on the Mount of Olives during this last blood moon of September 28, 2015. Archbishop Dominiquae was speaking of the Valley of Jehoshaphat below us, and as I looked at the moon, I saw that there was only a little white light left before the total eclipse. This Scripture came to mind from Isaiah 55:6, *"Seek the LORD while he may be found; call on Him while He is near."* Right there, I prayed for the USA: "LORD, do not let us be found in this valley of judgment." Immediately, I saw a picture flashing before me of many different nations in military uniforms gathering there. (Now I am beginning to realize this could be the UN that represents almost every nation.)

I believe that the LORD gives us warnings and physical signs that represent what is going on in the spiritual realm. I began to research Scripture and found that when a city is being seized, you will usually see fire. Joel 2:3 mentions a *fire burning*: *"A fire devoureth before them; and behind them a flame burneth."* On May 27, 2016, Israel AM news reported several fires were burning on the outskirts of Jerusalem and approaching inhabited areas. The Haftarah Portion Bible reading for that day was called *Behar*, which means *on the mountain*. This included Jeremiah 32:6-27. Just two verses later in Jeremiah 32:29, it speaks of the Chaldeans coming to set *fire* to the city. This reading was on the exact same day Jerusalem was literally on fire!

I am reminded of the Twin Towers in New York on 9/11 that were on fire; it took a fire to wake America up. I am sure there were warning signs that would have prevented this disaster, but they were ignored, as in Jeremiah's day of warning.

In Joel 3:4 it mentions the name *Palestine*. This is the name the UN wants to give this new state by 2016. In Joel 3:9 it warns to prepare for war! If The God of Israel allows this vote to take place as He did with Gaza, this could possibly be the beginning of WWIII. This will put the Jewish people past indefensible lines. That is one of the biggest reasons they had this battle in 1967.

Joel 3:5 says, *"Because ye have taken my silver and my gold and have carried into your temples my goodly and pleasant things."* This story is similar to what happened with King Belshazzar (in Daniel 5), who ordered the gold and silver vessels to be brought in that were taken from the Temple in Jerusalem. They began to drink and give praise to their gods of gold and silver, bronze and iron, wood and stone. That same hour came forth a man's hand and wrote on the wall, over against the candlestick of the king's palace. Then, the king's countenance changed when he read of God's judgment.

If this vote takes place, they will literally bring the Holy City, Jerusalem, into the UN building, mocking God as Belshazzar did. All this will take place by signing with their hands. But I know the God of Israel's hand will have the last say so!

I feel like a line in the sand is being drawn with this vote, requiring a choice between the God of Israel or their gods. Elijah, in I Kings 18:21-39, stood on the mountain in Israel against the gods of Baal. He said, *"How long halt ye between two opinions?"* Then he asked if the LORD (God of Israel) be God, follow him, but if Baal (be your god), then follow him. He also drew a line in the sand. We must now choose.

But when the Son of man shall come in His glory, and all the holy angels with him, then shall He sit upon the throne of His glory. And before Him shall be gathered ALL NATIONS (UN); and He shall separate them one from another, as a shepherd divideth his sheep from the goats: And He shall set the sheep on his right hand, but the goats on the left.

—MATTHEW 25:31-33 ASV

(I want to make sure that I am standing on the sheep's side with Israel as the line is drawn.)

Each nation will have to cast their vote in this Valley of Jehoshaphat concerning Jerusalem and Israel. May the USA be on the right side. I hope this alert sends out a warning to all leaders, Israel supporters, and believers to awaken and begin to take action to stop this vote immediately!

Many people begin to say what the UN and the enemy are going to do, and they repeat what the media is saying as truth and fact. It is important to only magnify God's Name, Words, and will concerning the land. I have placed the Words of our God before you to fight this battle. Because the Word of God divides the truth from a lie, it is sharper than any two-edged sword; His Word sets the captives free. Proverbs 18:21 says, "Death and life are in the power of the tongue…" choose life. Speak only what God's Word says!

Here are declarations, decrees, and prayers for Jerusalem and Israel to be spoken daily.

First: Lift up and exalt His Name: The God of Israel. (scriptures from various translations)

1. **I Kings 18:36**: ... LORD God of Abraham, Isaac, and of Israel, let it be known this day that thou art God in Israel, and that I am thy servant, and that I have done all these things at Thy Word. KJV

2. **Psalm 86:9-10**: All the nations you have made will come and bow before You, ADONAI; they will honor Your Name (The God of Israel).For you are great, and you do wonders; you alone are God. CJB

3. **Isaiah 45:22-23**: Look unto me, and be ye saved, all the ends of the earth: For I AM God, and there is none else. I have sworn by My own Name; I have spoken the truth, and I will never go back on my word: Every knee will bend to me, and every tongue will declare allegiance to me."

4. **Psalm 91:14**: Because He loves me, I will rescue him; because he knows My Name (The God of Israel), I will protect him. CJB

5. **Psalm 96:2, 3, 10**: Sing to ADONAI, bless His Name(The God of Israel)! Proclaim His victory day after day! (3) Declare His glory among the nations, his wonders among all peoples! (10) Say among the nations, "ADONAI is king!"... CJB

Second: Declare the Biblical boundary lines given to Israel in Joshua 1 and Numbers 34: 1-18.

1. The God of Israel has drawn a line in the sand.
   Psalms 78:55: He cast out the heathen also before them, and divided them an inheritance by line, and made the tribes of Israel to dwell in their tents. KJV
2. **Joshua 1:2-6**: ... now therefore arise, go over this Jordan, thou, and all this people, unto the land which I do give to them, even to the children of Israel.
   Every place that the sole of your foot shall tread upon, that have I given unto you, as I said unto Moses. From the wilderness and this Lebanon even unto the great river, the river Euphrates, all the land of the Hittites, and unto the great sea toward the going down of the sun, shall be your coast. There shall not any man be able to stand before thee all the days of thy life: as I was with Moses, so I will be with thee: I will not fail thee, nor forsake thee. Be strong and of a good courage: for unto this people shalt thou divide for an inheritance the land, which I swore unto their fathers to give them. KJV
3. Declare no vote; their plans will come to naught:
   Isaiah 8:9-10—Raise the war cry, you (UN) nations, and be shattered! Listen, all you distant lands. Prepare for battle, and be shattered! Prepare for battle, and be shattered! Devise your strategy, but it will be thwarted; propose your plan {UN}, but it will not stand, for God is with us (Israel). NIV
4. Speak and declare to the mountains (Jerusalem) the Word of God:

- **Ezekiel 36:1-11**: Also, thou son of man, prophesy unto the mountains of Israel, and say, Ye mountains of Israel, hear the word of the Lord: thus saith the Lord God; because the enemy hath said against you, aha, even the ancient high places are ours in possession: therefore prophesy and say, thus saith the Lord God; because they have made you desolate, and swallowed you up on every side, that ye might be a possession unto the residue of the heathen, and ye are taken up in the lips of talkers, and are an infamy of the people:

Therefore, ye mountains of Israel, hear the word of the Lord God; thus saith the Lord God to the mountains, and to the hills, to the rivers, and to the valleys, to the desolate wastes, and to the cities that are forsaken, which became a prey and derision to the residue of the heathen that are round about; therefore thus saith the Lord God;

Surely in the fire of my jealousy have I spoken against the residue of the heathen, and against all Idumea, which have appointed my land into their possession with the joy of all their heart, with despiteful minds, to cast it out for a prey. Prophesy therefore concerning the land of Israel, and say unto the mountains (Jerusalem), and to the hills, to the rivers, and to the valleys.

Thus saith the Lord God; Behold, I have spoken in my jealousy and in my fury, because ye have borne the shame of the heathen: Therefore thus saith the Lord God; I have lifted up mine hand, Surely the heathen that are about you, they shall bear their shame. But ye, O mountains of Israel, ye shall shoot forth your branches, and yield your fruit to my people of Israel; for they are at hand to come.

For, behold, I am for you, and I will turn unto you, and ye shall be tilled and sown: And I will multiply men upon you, all the house of Israel, even all of it: and the cities shall be inhabited, and the wastes shall be builded: and I will multiply upon you man and beast; and they shall increase and bring fruit: and I will settle you after your old estates, and will do better unto you than at your beginnings: and ye shall know that I am the LORD. KJV

- **Isaiah 40:1-5**: "Comfort, O comfort My people," says your God. "Speak kindly to Jerusalem; And call out to her, that her warfare has ended, that her iniquity has been removed, that she has received of the LORD'S hand double for all her sins." A voice is calling, "Clear the way for the LORD in the wilderness; make smooth in the desert a highway for our God. "Let every valley be lifted up, and every mountain and hill be made low; and let the rough ground become a plain, and the rugged terrain a broad valley; then the glory of the LORD will be revealed, and all flesh will see it together; for the mouth of the LORD has spoken." NASB '95

5. Pray that the land will never be divided into two nations again.
   Ezekiel 37:22: I will make them one nation in the land, on the mountains of Israel. There will be one king over all of them and they will never again be two nations or be divided into two kingdoms. NIV

6. Alert other watchmen and warriors to take action: begin to pray and fast!
   In **Ezekiel 22:30**: And I sought for a man among them, that should make up the hedge, and stand in the gap before me For The Land, that I should not destroy it: but I found none. KJV

I will stand in the gap. Will you?

In 2 Chronicles 20, King Jehoshaphat finds himself surrounded by kings who are going to destroy Jerusalem and the people in this same valley. He calls an assembly and declares a fast. As the praises go up, the God of Israel fights the battle and wins. He will win again.

> **I have set watchmen (and that includes us women) upon thy walls, O Jerusalem, which shall never hold their peace day nor night: ye that make mention of the LORD, keep not silence…**
>
> —Isaiah 62:6 KJV

We, as believers, have received much from Israel and Jerusalem. My prayer and hope is that we will take 10 minutes a day to pray, declare, and decree these scriptures or, at least once a week, to build up a hedge for the land.

If you are planning a trip or if you know of any tours that will be traveling in this Valley of Jehoshaphat, between Jerusalem and the Mount of Olives, please have them stop and pray for their own nations while they are in the land. A tour that is going into this valley can represent up to 50 nations or more. This Biblical Holy Land was given to Abraham and his seed Israel forever as a covenant from the God of Israel. (Genesis 13:14-17)

> **Pray for the peace of Jerusalem: those that love thee shall be brought into rest.**
>
> —Psalm 122:6

May the LORD bless each one of you as you stand on God's Word for His land. Selah.

X
2016

CHAPTER 41

THE RULE OF MESSIAH ON EARTH

> This power He exercised in Messiah when He raised Him from the dead and seated Him at His right hand in heaven. He is far above any ruler, authority, power, leader, and every name that is named— not only in the olam ha-zeh but also in the olam ha-ba. God placed all things under Messiah's feet and appointed Him as head over all things for His communitywhich is His body, the fullness of Him who fills all in all.
>
> — EPHESIANS 1:20-23

Three major events are converging in 2017 Biblical 5777/5778:

1. The Jubilee of the Unification of Jerusalem after the Miracle Six-Day War in June 1967.
2. The 120th year of the establishing of the First Zionist Congress in Basel in August of 1897.
3. The 500th year since Luther's Reformation in 1517 Halloween (or All Saints Day - October 31st).

YHVH spoke to me, as we start this new Yovel (Jubilee) cycle, the following:

I am the ruler of the nations, and I am looking for vessels of glory that will implement my absolute sovereignty and rulership on planet earth. The nations are My inheritance, and all the ends of the earth My possession! I am knocking on the gates of nations to come in as the King of Glory and to overthrow wicked, unrighteous governments and establish righteous governments. I am looking to see sheep nations come forth! What seems impossible with humans is possible with YHVH. My bride will implement this, My will for the nations.

My Book *Sheep Nations*

In 2001, I was visited by Yeshua on Christmas Day while visiting my native land, Chile (from which I made aliyah or returned to my ancient homeland, Israel, as promised in the Holy Scriptures). That day, most churches were in services celebrating the pagan date that was established in the 4th century as the birth date of Messiah. I was in prayer, and Yeshua showed up and asked me a question:

"How many nations will be sheep nations if I return today?"

He then proceeded to tell me that He will judge the nations according to these two principles:

How have the nations behaved with His people, Israel (the Jewish people)?

How are the nations honoring His Ten Commandments or His Torah?

I knew in 2001 that no nation qualified as a sheep nation, so I begged Yeshua for more time to run with the message of sheep nations and repentance towards YHVH. It was to the Church we needed to run, and we definitely have run into 50 nations and counting. Our books, eBooks, music CDs, Shabbat letters, teachings, TV programs, Bible School, and tours of Israel have run together with us, multiplying the seed of His Word and of this calling to the *global repentance for global awakening!*

By His grace and faithfulness to carry us through, and by the faithfulness of our precious partners and disciples, we have broken through impossible territory. Now, it is time to take possession of land and nations with the gospel made in Zion!

The Arising of His Bride Will Position New Governments

We are destined to be a catalyst for the establishment of righteous governments on the earth. While most Christians are passively waiting for a takeover by the New World Order and the Antichrist, His true bride is actively working for a takeover of righteous presidents and governments.

> So now, O kings, be wise, take warning, O judges of the earth! Serve ADONAI with fear, and rejoice with trembling.
>
> —PSALM 2:10-11

The nations belong to Yeshua and not to the devil. The nations are His inheritance, but a lukewarm, immoral, idolatrous, deceived church—full of replacement theology and pagan Christmas and Easter traditions, fed with a sugar-coated gospel—has not had the strength, glory, power, or authority to implement His will on earth. It is through His Body, composed of Jew and Gentile, grafted into the olive tree (not the Christmas tree), that He works His will on earth. Since the divorce of the Church from its Jewish roots and foundations by Constantine and the Council of Nicaea in the 4th century, the nations have been further and further away from becoming sheep nations. The bride of Messiah has been undone or in hiding. But, in this new Jubilee cycle, it is time for the anointed and holy Messianic-apostolic-prophetic bride in combat boots to arise!

He is knocking on the gates of nations to position righteous governments, and He can implement that only as His bride goes into both prayer and actions in every arena, including financial and "political," which I will call *governmental*.

At the center of all this, Messiah rules the ecclesia. The ecclesia, you see, is not peripheral to the world; the world is peripheral to the ecclesia. The ecclesia is Messiah's body, in which he speaks and acts, by which he fills everything with his presence.

—Ephesians 1:20-23
(the message with updated names)

Prepared to Rule and Reign

To the intent that now the manifold wisdom of God might be made known by the church to the principalities and powers in the heavenly places.

—Ephesians 3:10 nkjv

A radical change of mind is happening in His true bride in combat boots. The bride is being cleansed from the ravages of religion, most particularly Babylonian Christianity, pagan feasts, and alienation from Israel and the Torah. This is preparing us to marry the Jewish King, but it is also preparing us to rule and reign with Him and to implement His reign on earth.

What Religion Has Masked

> Elohim raised him from death and set him on a throne in deep heaven, in charge of running the universe, everything from galaxies to governments, no name and no power exempt from his rule.
>
> —EPHESIANS 1:21
> (THE MESSAGE WITH UPDATED NAMES)

Religion has masked the fact that the Messiah rules in *this world* and not only in the world to come. The very mistaken and cruel crusaders knew it and were trying to implement His rule on the earth by conquering Jerusalem in the 11th Century, burning alive the Jewish population there while singing praise hymns! They were sorely mistaken as His kingdom must be implemented by His Spirit and in His order, which is, as usual, to the Jew first.

By getting rid of the Jews, they were getting further away from creating sheep nations or bringing His rule on earth and further into the curse. Through the crusaders, Christianity was bringing on the New World Order, with Jerusalem at its center, in the 11th Century AD. They were fulfilling the desire of the builders of the tower of Babel in Genesis 11.

> Then they said, "Come! Let's build ourselves a city, with a tower whose top reaches into heaven. So let's make a name for ourselves, or else we will be scattered over the face of the whole land."
>
> —GENESIS 11:4

The Christian crusaders were defeated by the Muslims, and Christians are again being defeated by the Muslims in the 21st Century! ISIS is advancing in what used to be Christian nations all over Europe, America, and South America. History is repeating itself ten centuries later.

Ten Jubilees Since Luther's Reformation

This year of 2017 commemorates and completes 10 Jubilees, namely 500 years since the start of Martin Luther's reformation. It is quite revealing that this reformation started officially on Halloween, which Christianity adopted as All Saints Day. However, Halloween is All Witches Day, and it is far from being a holy day or holy celebration. That was the imperfection of Luther's reformation—even though it touched on the important issue of salvation by grace through faith, it failed to reconnect to the Jewish roots and the original Gospel made in Zion, leaving the Church hanging in the balance.

Ten is the number of completion, order, and judgment. YHVH is judging *all* religions and religious systems and establishing His kingdom through His bride, wanting to get His inheritance, the nations, back. He wants sheep nations! He wants righteous governments; He wants a takeover of righteousness. At the darkest time, He wants His Glory to shine. Nothing is impossible with Him!

> "Rise up and shine, for your light has come. The shining-greatness of the Lord has risen upon you. For see, darkness will cover the earth. Much darkness will cover the people. But the Lord will rise upon you, and His shining-greatness will be

seen upon you. Nations will come to your light. And kings will see the shining-greatness of the LORD on you.

—ISAIAH 60:1-3 NLV

This is about Israel being the chief sheep nation, but is also true for His bride that has repented from replacement theology, going past Luther's reformation, and has returned home to the original Gospel made in Zion, joining Israel rather than Rome.

Israel, the Chief Sheep Nation, and The Jubilee of Yerushalayim

The real name of Jerusalem is Yerushalayim, which includes the Hebrew words *Yerusha* and *shalom*. *Yerusha* means *inheritance*. *Shalayim* means *a double portion* of *shalom* or *completeness* and well-being.

2017 marks 50 years since the miraculous Six-Day War, when the Holy City was finally unified. It will be good to understand, once and for all, that the territory that Israel gained in this miraculous war is a covenant issue and was given to her by YHVH Himself. Any nation that is trying to make her go back to the borders before 1967 or 1948 will find itself in serious trouble.

> On that day I will make Jerusalem a heavy stone for all the people. All who lift it will be hurt. And all the nations of the earth will be gathered against it.
>
> —ZECHARIAH 12:3 NLV

All the end-time Scriptures indicate that Israel is the most important nation in the world and Yerushalayim (Jerusalem) is the center of the world. A failure to understand this will cause untold woes. She is not the most important because of her decision, but because of Yah's (God's) choice. She is YHVH's inheritance and, thus, *all* the nations are called to come up to Zion in these end-times. Rain and blessing in the nations will depend on the world governments honoring Israel and the King of Israel, Yeshua.

> Then it will come about that any who are left of all the nations that went against Jerusalem will go up from year to year to worship the King, The LORD of Hosts and to celebrate the Feast of Booths. And it will be that whichever of the families of the earth does not go up to Jerusalem to worship the King, the LORD of hosts, there will be no rain on them.
>
> —ZECHARIAH 14:16-17 NASB '95

Israel is Being Prepared

An awakening is taking place in Israel; there is a miraculous turning towards a restoration of identity, and we will see more of this in the days to come as two particular groups begin to gain momentum: the Messianic Jews and the religious Orthodox Zionists. They will seem to run parallel for a while, but it will culminate in an all-encompassing revival in Israel!

> I will pour out on the house of David and on the inhabitants of Jerusalem, the Spirit of grace and of supplication, so that they will look on Me whom they have pierced; and they will mourn for Him, as one mourns for an only son, and they will weep bitterly over Him like the bitter weeping over a firstborn.
>
> —ZECHARIAH 12:10 NASB '95

A United Nations for Israel is Being Prepared

This is the new thrust of all our Israel tours and many of our actions in the nations. Theodor Herzl, the Jewish Prophet who believed for Israel to become a nation again and established the First Zionist Congress in 1897, said:

Im tirzu ein zo hagadah!
If you will it, this will not be a fable!

Can nations unite for Israel as much as the obsolete, irrelevant New World Order-United Nations today is staunchly against Israel? Yes, they can, but there will be a new prophetic platform for this to happen with authority from heaven.

> **In that day many nations will join themselves to ADONAI and they will be My people and I will dwell among you.' Then you will know that ADONAI-Tzva'ot has sent me to you. ADONAI will inherit Judah as His portion in the holy land and will once again choose Jerusalem.**
>
> **—ZECHARIAH 2:15-16**

And to the opinionated "politically, or humanistically 'correct,'" He says: "Shut up!"

> **Be silent before ADONAI, all flesh, for He has aroused Himself from His holy dwelling.**
>
> **—ZECHARIAH 2:17**

Bride of Messiah, put your combat boots on and take ground in the ministry, in the harvest field, in the financial arena, in the marketplace, and in the governmental (political) arena. Do not put any limitations on how the King desires to use us to implement His sovereign rule on the earth. It is the Messiah, not the anti-Messiah, that is ruling!

2015

CHAPTER 42

A TICKING BOMB

A fire consumes before them and behind them a flame burns. The land is like the garden of Eden before them but a desolate wilderness behind them, and nothing at all escapes them.

— JOEL 2:3

In the wake of terrible catastrophes like the one that just happened in Paris, the French Capital, leaving at least 128 people dead in various coordinated attacks by ISIS, I cannot think of a better scripture to describe Islamic terror, especially ISIS. Wherever Islam goes, it leaves terrible desolation behind, creating a physical desert, death, and destruction. Islam is an *abomination that causes desolation.* In Hebrew: *Shikuts Meshomem*

> **From the time that the daily burnt offering is taken away, and abomination of desolation is set up, there will be 1,290 days.**
>
> —Daniel 12:11

It means an *idol* that causes desolation and destruction. Islam is an idolatrous religion serving a demon by the name of "Allah" and a false prophet by the name of Muhammed, whose only cause is the destruction of the chosen people of Israel and world domination. That is ISIS's agenda, and they are fiercely going after it. ISIS is Islam gone back to its roots, to the original teachings of Muhammed. Wherever this idolatrous and bloodthirsty religion goes, it leaves desolation and destruction behind. Just look at what is happening in Syria and Iraq, South Sudan and Eritrea, and look at the outspoken agenda of Iran— all in the name of Allah! There is no difference between the agenda of ISIS, Hamas, Hezbollah, or the Palestinian cause. They are one and the same: Islam! It is an abomination (idolatry) that causes desolation (destruction).

The Palestinian Cause is the Idol of the Nations

> I will gather all the nations and bring them down to the valley of Jehoshaphat. Then I will enter into judgment with them there on behalf of My people and My inheritance, Israel, whom they have scattered among the nations; and they have divided up My land. "They have also cast lots for My people, traded a boy for a harlot and sold a girl for wine that they may drink.
>
> —Joel 3:2-3 nkjv

The international media is constantly twisting the truth and manipulating information so that the whole world would believe their lies about "the poor Palestinians." Ninety-nine-point nine percent of this news are lies. Mostly European journalists roam Judea and Samaria and all the Palestinian areas looking for evidence against Israel. When Palestinian children armed with knives stab Jewish people, including children, the news shows the child terrorists as victims instead of who they are: Muslim terrorists! Hitler said, "Tell a big lie often enough and loud enough, and everyone will believe it!" Much of the international media has heeded the instruction of "the great führer," the murderer of over 6 million Jews.

A Trojan Horse in Europe

On top of supporting the enemies of Israel, Europe has also opened its doors to an influx of about 30 million (!) Arab Muslim immigrants who will never let go of their agenda of world conquest in the name of Allah, who is *not* the Creator God or the God of Israel, but rather the moon god from Muhammed's pantheon of family gods chosen to represent Islam.

The Muslim population in Sweden and Denmark doubled in the last 14 years. The total percentage of Muslims in Europe is nearly 8% of the population, numbering over 50 million Muslims.*

In countries like Norway, which is waking up to the fact that Islam is a Trojan horse in the nation, the Prime Minister of Norway is doing something sane:

The new Norwegian Prime Minister, Erna Solberg, began a program that deports Muslims who have ties to radical groups. And something stunning occurred: the country's violent crimes are down more than 31% in less than a year since Muslim deportations began!**

I wish that Israel would do the same thing without fear of public opinion, like the wise Norwegian Prime Minister.

France's Muslim population is over 6 million, which is 10% of the population of the nation. France has been under the terror of its Muslim citizens for many years now, and so has every other nation in Europe that has hosted them and allowed them in, having much "pity" for them—a pity they never showed towards the Jewish refugees

---

* In google says 44 million or 5 % of the total population wikipedia
** toprightnews.com

during the Nazi era. "Good-hearted" Europe has great mercy over the enemies of Israel but not over Israel, whom it constantly bashes in the media for not making peace with terrorists that try to annihilate her. Europe has been extremely hypocritical, harboring the same feelings prior to the Nazi Shoah (Holocaust) concerning the Jews but masking it as "anti-occupation" and "anti-Zionist." Really, it is the same hatred, and it is magnified today because of high tech and media.

The Modern-Day Yellow Star: BDS Labels

What has ignited the wick of the bomb is the latest "Boycott, Divestment, and Sanctions" campaign from the European Parliament to label all Israeli products manufactured by Israeli citizens in Judea and Samaria, which they call "The West Bank of Jordan" instead of by its Biblical name, Israel. The spokesman for the European Union Parliament said: "We are not anti-Israel; we are just labeling the products that are in occupied territories that we do not consider to be Israel." Well, sir, maybe you do not consider it as Israel, but YHVH, the God of the Bible, who dwells in Zion, does! Moreover, this "labeling" of the products reminds us of the infamous yellow star by which the Jews were forced to be labeled in Nazi Europe!

These words were spoken in the same week that the terrible Islamic terror attacks in the theater of Paris and other places happened, leaving over 128 people murdered, as I write this letter on the day of the attack, on Shabbat, the 14th of November 2015.

All of Europe is like a ticking bomb because they have set themselves against Israel, Israeli products, and the right of Israel for the land promised to Abraham, Isaac, and Jacob for 1000 generations, siding with her Arab and Muslim enemies and funding them.

> For the day of the LORD draws near on all the nations. As you have done, it will be done to you. Your dealings will return on your own head.
>
> —OBADIAH 15 NASB '95

Europe is Like a Ticking Bomb

> For ADONAI has a day of vengeance, a year of recompense for the hostility against Zion.
>
> —ISAIAH 34:8

All of Europe at this point is like a "ticking bomb," and it is only a matter of time before more terrible catastrophes take place. The reasons for this distressful state of affairs is as old as the Bible: "Good" old-fashioned hatred against Israel and the Jewish ppeople has put Europe in direct collision with Almighty God, who happens to call Himself, "The God of Israel."

> O LORD of hosts, the God of Israel, who is enthroned above the cherubim, You are the God, You alone, of all the kingdoms of the earth. You have made heaven and earth.
>
> —ISAIAH 37:16 NASB '95

Europe has been funding and hosting Muslim terror since the PLO and Palestinian cause was launched in order to destroy the newborn State of Israel. In fact, even before Israel was officially a State, the Grand Mufti of Jerusalem, the highest Muslim personality of the time, visited Hitler in 1942 and asked for help. The help he needed was to establish

---

* Haj Amin al-Husseini

an Arab army in then-called Palestine in order to implement the Final Solution from within the Holy Land against those Jews that were already peacefully living there and farming and planting even before Israel officially became a state recognized among the nations.

Where are the European Christians?

> Then the LORD said to Cain, "Where is Abel your brother?" And he said, "I do not know. Am I my brother's keeper?" He said, "What have you done? The voice of your brother's blood is crying to Me from the ground.
>
> — GENESIS 4:9-10 NASB '95

It would be almost "comforting" to say that this is limited to Hitler's support of the Palestinian cause, as everyone knows that Hitler was the most wicked man in modern-day history. But the truth is that Europe is the biggest sponsor of the Palestinian cause, whose agenda has been proclaimed openly by its leaders and on TV: namely, removing all Jews from Israel and establishing all Israel as Arab Muslim Palestine. That is also the agenda of ISIS.

Many European countries, through various humanitarian organizations, have funneled billions into the West Bank (real name is Judea and Samaria) and East Jerusalem. The Europeans and Scandinavians are enamored with the "Palestinian cause" for the simple reason that Jew-hatred now in the name of "Anti-Zionism" has never ceased in post-Christian Europe, just like it was in Christian Europe at the time.

Christianity, through replacement theology and ancient hatred against the Jews for "killing Christ," established Anti-Jewish policies that were fertile ground for the Christian Jewish hatred that led to the Shoah (Holocaust) and to countless murderous events such as the Spanish Inquisition, the Crusades, and countless pogroms and expulsions of Jews all over Europe. This history is amply proven and well-known.

It is also well-known that not one church organization opposed Hitler. Where is the Church right now in post-Christian Europe? A few precious believers are making their voices heard, but what about the vast majority of European Christians? Sadly, the vast majority of European Christians have become the enemies of the God of Israel by siding with the Palestinian cause, funding it, or being silent despite the injustice of the nations against Israel.

> **Because of violence to your brother Jacob, you will be covered with shame, and you will be cut off forever. "On the day that you stood aloof, on the day that strangers carried off his wealth, and foreigners entered his gate and cast lots for Jerusalem—You too were as one of them.**
>
> **—Obadiah 1:10-11 nasb '95**

Churches all over Europe need to wake up and repent for Replacement Theology* and for forsaking Israel. That is the only hope for any country in Europe!

> **And I will bless those who bless you, and the one who curses you I will curse. And in you all the families of the earth will be blessed.**
>
> **—Genesis 12:3 nasb '95**

---

* To learn more, read my book *The Identity Theft*; available at www.ZionsGospel.com

CHAPTER 43

HIGHWAY 60

*For they said,
"Let us seize for our own use these pasturelands of God!"*

— PSALM 83:12 NLT

Highway 60, or Route 60, is a south-north intercity road in Israel that stretches from Beersheba to Nazareth. It is 235 kilometers (146 miles) long and reaches six major cities: Jerusalem, Hebron, Gush Etzion, Beersheba, Nazareth, and Afula.

Highway 60 is deemed to be the most dangerous highway in Israel. There have been many attacks by Arab terrorists on this highway. A very well-known reporter from the leftist news channel, Arutz 2* decided to do an experiment. He took a bullet-proof van and his TV news crew and traveled on this threatened highway. He saw people hitchhiking and gave them a ride while interviewing them. He did this at random with whoever he found. The people he picked up were all Jewish settlers in Judea and Samaria (politically called the West Bank).

All of them, without exception, reiterated their commitment to the Land of Israel and to be victorious over terror and fear by on purpose

---

* Renamed Aruz 12 today

traveling on the said highway and even hitchhiking on it! Their age group varied from a young woman in her twenties to seniors in their seventies! They were all religious Jews in some way, though none of them were ultra-orthodox. They were mostly traditional/conservative and full of faith. None of them was a secular Jew.

And without faith it is impossible to please Him, for he who comes to God must believe that He is and that He is a rewarder of those who seek Him.

—Hebrews 11:6 nasb '95

This experiment was very revealing, especially since it was broadcasted by a leftist news channel such as Arutz 2, which is also the most-watched channel in Israel. It gave powerful insights into the true spirit of faith that has made Israel a reality after 2000 years of exile. It is the only attitude that will help Israel overcome all future conflicts and attacks.

The spirit of faith is contested by the wicked spirit of secular humanism, which is always trying to undermine the importance of the Bible and the promises of Yah (God). Most of the media functions under this spirit of *secular humanism*. Secular humanism puts man and his will in the center rather than the will of God. It is the most detrimental spiritual problem of Israel, and it is rooted in unbelief, ignorance, and rebellion. Israel is rapidly being divided between those who will continue to "sell Israel cheap" by giving up Biblical land to "peace partners" that do not exist and want to annihilate her, and those who believe in the Biblical promises against all odds!

Highway 60 connects many prophetic Biblical sites and crosses most of the Land of Israel from Beersheba to Nazareth in the Galilee.

Psalm 83 tells us what is the purpose of the enemies of Israel that are attacking this Biblical area:

> For they said, "Let us seize for our own use these pasturelands of God!"
>
> —Psalm 83:12 NLT

Highway 60 connects Yerushalayim (Jerusalem) with Hebron.

Hebron

The Cave of Machpelah in Hebron, where Abraham, Isaac, Yaakov, Sarah, Rivka, and Leah are buried, is the *first* piece of property purchased with money by Abraham to bury his dead.

Jerusalem

The Temple Mount, or Zion, Jerusalem, is the recognized site of Mount Moriah, where Abraham went to sacrifice Isaac. It is also the threshing floor of Araunah the Jebusite, which was purchased with money by King David to sacrifice to YHVH in order to stop the plague in Israel. Eventually, the Temple of YHVH was built here by King Solomon and rebuilt by Ezra the Priest after the Babylonian Exile. It was expanded and refurbished under King Herod. Jerusalem is the city that the God of Israel calls His dwelling place forever!

> Blessed be ADONAI out of Zion, who dwells in Jerusalem. Halleluyah!
>
> —Psalm 135:21

Gush Etzion

Gush Etzion is known as the Southern Gate of Jerusalem, protecting the holy city from the south from invading armies. This area became very strategic during the 1948 War of Independence when more than 10 Arab armies attacked young Israel! It is packed full of Biblical history. Abraham passed through here on his way to Mount Moriah to sacrifice Isaac, and Ruth gathered sheaves in its fields, the fields of Bethlehem, and David shepherded his father's sheep here.

Beersheba

Beersheba is also known as the City of Abraham, and it means the Well of the Seven or the Oath, as Abraham purchased the well from Abimelech, the king, for seven ewe lambs. Just like Jerusalem and Hebron, this is land purchased by our forefathers! Today, Beersheba is the capital of the Negev, the South Desert of Israel.

Nazareth

Nazareth was an insignificant Jewish agricultural community in Galilee at the time of Yeshua; it is the place where the Jewish Messiah was raised. Today, lower Nazareth is mostly inhabited by Arabs, both Christian and Muslim, and the upper city is inhabited by the Jews. In Nazareth, there are many churches of various persuasions, and there is a constant tension between Christianity and Islam. It is located in the Galilee of the present-day State of Israel and is unofficially regarded as the "Arab Capital" of Israel because of its predominant Arab population.

Afula

Afula is regarded as the capital city in the Biblical Jezreel Valley, which saw many of the wars and events mentioned in the Book of Judges. In 1925, the American Zionist Commonwealth completed a purchase of the Afula Valley from the Sursuk family of Beirut.[*]

An Attacked Biblical Highway

Some of the most recent attacks on innocent Jewish civilians passing through Highway 60 have been especially in the Gush Etzion and Hebron areas:

A Palestinian stabbed a mother of eight in the back at the Gush Etzion junction late Wednesday afternoon. Nirit Zimora, of the Beit Hagai settlement in the South Hebron Hills, was rushed to Shaare Zedek Medical Center in Jerusalem with the knife still in her back. She underwent surgery and was listed in satisfactory condition.[**]

Let us pray for the deliverance of Highway 60 from danger and terror as we stand in agreement with the faith-filled and brave citizens of Jerusalem, Judea, and Samaria. They will not escape or pull back, knowing that they trust in the One that promised:

> He has remembered His covenant forever, the word which He commanded to a thousand generations, the covenant which He made with Abraham and His oath to Isaac. Then He confirmed it to Jacob for a statute, to Israel as an everlasting cov-

---

[*] The American Zion Commonwealth Company was founded in the United States in 1914 by American Zionists with the purpose of acquiring lands for Jewish settlement in the Land of Israel.

[**] Accessed 4/1/2024. www.jpost.com/arab-israeli-conflict/palestinian-terrorist-shot-while-attempting-to-stab-soldier-in-hebron-430310

enant, saying, "To you I will give the land of Canaan as the portion of your inheritance."

—Psalm 105:8-11 nasb '95

CHAPTER 44

ISRAEL RED ALERT

O God, do not be silent! Do not be deaf. Do not be quiet, O God. Don't you hear the uproar of your enemies? Don't you see that your arrogant enemies are rising up?

— PSALM 83:1-2 NLT

Since Sukkot (Tabernacles) 2015, when the 4th Blood Moon Tetrad occurred, we have entered another dispensation of time. The moon is the symbol of Islam, and that it was *red* speaks of bloodshed coming from the Muslim world. This is exactly what started happening in Israel right after it appeared in the sky on the 28th of September 2015. Jerusalem and then the rest of Israel started suffering a terrible onslaught of stabbing attacks, instilling terror throughout the land. The tension has been almost unbearable, as it could come from every direction. Also, the lies of the press have been extreme, especially since Palestinian Chairman Mahmoud Abbas has, as usual, twisted the truth and spun farfetched lies, making the Palestinian Arabs the victim and Israel the aggressor. The naked truth is that the enemy is seeking to destroy Israel. This is not new, but the question is what do we do at such a time like this?

Before I answer this poignant question, let me expose another important truth: As much as what is happening to Israel right now is very distressful, it is important to understand that the signs in the heavens, such as the 4th Blood Moon Tetrad, are also a sign of judgment over the nations that have either attacked Israel or forsaken Israel.

Let us consider the following scriptures:

> "At the time of those events," says the LORD, "when I restore the prosperity of Judah and Jerusalem, I will gather the armies of the world into the valley of Jehoshaphat. There I will judge them for harming My people, My special possession, for scattering My people among the nations, and for dividing up My land."
>
> —JOEL 3:1-2 NLT

> "Come here and listen, O nations of the earth. Let the world and everything in it hear my words. For the LORD is enraged against the nations. His fury is against all their armies. He will completely destroy them, dooming them to slaughter. Their dead will be left unburied, and the stench of rotting bodies will fill the land. The mountains will flow with their blood. The heavens above will melt away and disappear like a rolled-up scroll. The stars will fall from the sky like withered leaves from a grapevine, or shriveled figs from a fig tree.
> And when My sword has finished its work in the heavens, it will fall upon Edom, the nation I have marked for destruction. The sword of the LORD is drenched with blood and covered with fat –with the blood of lambs and goats, with the fat of rams prepared for sacrifice. Yes, the LORD will offer a sacrifice in the city of Bozrah. He will make a mighty slaughter in Edom. Even men as strong as wild oxen will die- the young

men alongside the veterans. The land will be soaked with blood and the soil enriched with fat. For it is the day of the Lord's revenge, the year when Edom will be paid back for all it did to Israel."

—Isaiah 34:1-8 nlt

"Because of the violence you did to your close relatives in Israel, you will be filled with shame and destroyed forever. When they were invaded, you stood aloof, refusing to help them. Foreign invaders carried off their wealth and cast lots to divide up Jerusalem, but you acted like one of Israel's enemies."

—Obadiah 1:10-11 nlt

"After a period of glory, the Lord of Heaven's Armies sent me against the nations who plundered you. For he said, 'Anyone who harms you, harms my most precious possession. I will raise my fist to crush them, and their own slaves will plunder them.' Then you will know that the Lord of Heaven's Armies has sent me."

—Zechariah 2:8-9 nlt

"And I will bless those who bless you and curse those who treat you with contempt. All the families on the earth will be blessed through you."

—Genesis 12:3 nlt

Israel is suffering "as usual" at the hands of the nations that contest her validity as a nation with a promised land. In the following

Scripture, we will see that the Almighty calls those nations "My wicked neighbors."

> "Now this is what the LORD says: 'I will uproot from their land all the evil nations reaching out for possession I gave my people Israel. And I will uproot Judah from among them. But afterward I will return and have compassion on all of them. I will bring them home to their own lands again, each nation to its own possession. And if these nations truly learn the ways of My people, and if they learn to swear by My name, saying, -as surely as the LORD lives- (just as they taught My people to swear by the name of Baal, then they will be given a place among My people. But any nation who refuses to obey me will be uprooted and destroyed. I, the LORD, have spoken!'"
>
> —JEREMIAH 12:14-17 NLT

Why does He call them "My wicked neighbors" and promises complete destruction to them unless they stop attacking Israel, forsake Islam and Allah, and put their trust in YHVH, the God of Israel? Because the physical address of YHVH on earth is Zion-Israel-Yerushalayim (Jerusalem).

> "The LORD be praised from Zion, for He lives here in Jerusalem. Praise the LORD!"
>
> —PSALM 135:21 NLT

> "Then you will know that I, the LORD your God, live in Zion, my holy mountain. Jerusalem will be holy forever, and foreign armies will never conquer her again."
>
> —JOEL 3:17 NLT

He also calls the enemies of Israel His enemies:

> "O God, do not be silent; do not be deaf. Do not be quiet, O God. Don't you hear the uproar of your enemies? Don't you see that your arrogant enemies are rising up?"
>
> —Psalm 83:1-2 NLT

The Arab nations are using the Israeli Arabs and the so-called Palestinians within the land of Israel as their emissaries to attack Israel. Thus, the God of Israel calls them "My enemies" because they have come against "My dwelling place" or "My land." However, it is not only the Arabs and the so-called Palestinians that are His enemies, but everyone and every nation that has supported their cause of attacking, terrorizing, and obliterating Israel altogether.

So many organizations, churches, individuals, and nations have been funneling billions into their wicked cause, hypocritically "espousing human rights" but rather venting their ancient hatred for the Jews. Among those nations that have funneled enormous amounts of funds to the enemies of God, who are the enemies of Israel, we find "surprisingly": Germany, Switzerland (neutral?), and Norway as one of the first ones, and German Christians most particularly. Those are "nice Christians" who are really concerned with the wellbeing of the murderers of Jews and the enemies of Israel but do not give a dime for the wellbeing of the Jewish people and their state, Israel. Only Arab causes are on their agenda. They go around in Judea and Samaria with their cameras, trying to report every incident of what the "terrible" IDF soldiers are doing to these "innocent civilian Arabs" that throw stones, run babies over with their cars, blow themselves up in buses and malls, and stab people right and left. The hypocrisy of the nations and among those who profess to be nice humanistic Christians has come up to heaven!

Surprising? Not really, since the Palestinian cause is "Hitler's Child." The Grand Mufti of Jerusalem, Haj Amin El Husseini, went to visit Hitler in 1942, before the establishment of the State of Israel in 1948. He asked Hitler to build him an army of "Palestinian Arabs." This wicked Muslim person asked Hitler to build him an army to implement the Final Solution in the Land of Israel among the Jews that had been living there since time immemorial and the new settlers that were coming to improve the barren, rocky, sandy, swampy, and malaria-infested land with the sweat of their brows to establish agriculture.

Hitler complied happily, and the PLO was born. Its representative today is the well-loved "political figure" by all the nations and the UN, the "peace partner" as labeled by America: Mahmoud Abbas. Mahmoud Abbas, with his smooth-snaky tactics, is actually the representative of Haj Amin al-Husseini's plan to implement the Final Solution among the Jews in Israel.

Therefore, Abbas and all the PLO (not only the recognized terrorists such as Hamas or Hezbollah) are the direct arm of Hitler's Final solution from within Israel! Any country that is siding with them is siding directly with Hitler; though dead and in the grave, his wicked plan goes on through the PLO and all its derivatives. Thus, it is no surprise that the primary nations that have been funding the PLO and the "Palestinian cause" are Germany, Switzerland, and Norway. Of course, there are many others as well, and unfortunately, our former best friend, the USA, has just released billions into Iran. LORD, have mercy!

---

* At that time, everyone was called a "Palestinian," Jews included, since this was the name the Romans gave to Israel, replacing the Biblical name for an enemy name of the Philistines.

My beloved people and nations, this is the time for definition! Are you a friend or an enemy of the God of Israel? If you are siding with Israel's enemies, if you are funding Israel's enemies, if you are championing their hideous cause to remove Israel off the map or to divide any part of the Promised Land or Jerusalem, then you and your nation are YHVH's enemies. There are no two ways about it.

This is a red alert for definition! You had better define what side you are on, as "neutral" people like the Swiss and the Norwegians end up in the camp of the enemy.

> "Let the nations be called to arms. Let them march to the valley of Jehoshaphat. There I, the LORD, will sit to pronounce judgment on them all. Swing the sickle, for the harvest is ripe. Come, tread the grapes, for the winepress is full. The storage vats are overflowing with the wickedness of these people. Thousands upon thousands are waiting in the valley of decision. There the day of the LORD will soon arrive. The sun and moon will grow dark, and the stars will no longer shine. The LORD's voice will roar from Zion and thunder from Jerusalem, and the heavens and the earth will shake. But the LORD will be a refuge for His people, a strong fortress for the people of Israel."
>
> —JOEL 3:12-16 NLT

This is what you can do:

1. Repent on your behalf and on behalf of your nation. (2 Chronicles 7:14)
2. Talk, write, and shout the truth to your Church leaders and government representatives. Direct them to our books or eBooks.* Buy the books in bulk and give them away. We have

---
* Visit our online shop at www.ZionsGospel.com

no time for "political correctness" now; people, and especially government and church leaders, must know the truth rapidly. (Isaiah 62:1)

3. Pray for Israel's strength against her enemies, protection, and salvation. Pray against the enemies of Israel and that every wicked plan against her gets exposed. Do not pray "nice," but pray seriously with authority. YHVH promised me that He will cover Israel from north to south and east to west with a mantle of mercy if our brothers and sisters in the nations will but pray!*

Extreme times require extreme means. Let us not miss the opportunity to make a difference while we still can!**

> "Thousands upon thousands are waiting in the valley of decision. There the day of the LORD will soon arrive."
>
> —JOEL 3:14 NLT

---

* Psalm 122:6; Psalm 137:5-6; Psalm 121; Zechariah 12
** To support our mission, visit at www.UnitedNationsForIsrael.org

CHAPTER 45

THE ABOMINATION OF DESOLATION

Shikutz Meshomem

His forces will rise up and profane the fortified Temple; they will stop the daily offering and set up the abomination of desolation.

— DANIEL 11:31

No other subject can engage the imagination more than the study of the end times, especially all connected with the Antichrist. But what is the *abomination of desolation*?

In Hebrew, the word is, *shikutz meshomem.*

Shikutz is the word for an idol or any idolatry or paganism. Since Daniel tells us that the *shikutz* is standing in the Holy Temple, and so does Yeshua, it gathers that *shikutz* or the *abomination* is idolatry in the temple of Yah (God). *Meshomem* means that which causes a "desert" (from the word *shmama)* or that which causes desolation, devastation, or destruction. In rabbinical literature, we find that the word *Shomem* is given to *Baal*, who is also Jupiter, Zeus, Tammuz, or the "sun god." It is called *baal shamem*, and it is a perversion of *baal shamayim*, which means the LORD *of heaven*. Jupiter or Zeus used to be called "the LORD of heaven." Thus, to demote his power and not to mention his expressed name (names have power), it was distorted to *baal shamem* or *the LORD of desolation* or the desert or destruction.

Both according to Daniel's description and Yeshua's description, the Abomination of Desolation is some sort of idol or idolatry in the Holy Temple in Jerusalem, and because of it, Jerusalem would be destroyed. These particular prophecies of the *shikutz meshomem* are mentioned throughout Daniel 9, 11, and 12 and in the Apocrypha in the book of 1 Maccabees, chapter one, as well as the synoptic gospels, especially in Matthew 24 and Mark 13, though Luke also mentions the desolation in Chapter 21.

What Do Jewish and Christian Scholars Believe?

The rabbinical consensus is that the expression refers to Antiochus IV Epiphanes's desecration of the Second Temple by erecting a Zeus statue in its sacred precincts. Some rabbis, however, see in it an allusion to Manasseh, who is reported to have set up "a carved image ... in the house of God."

Church Fathers

Church Father John Chrysostom understood this to refer to the armies that surrounded Jerusalem and the factions fighting within it, which preceded the destruction of the city in the year 70 AD by the Romans[*] Scholars have different views about Shikutz Meshomem. (Some believe that the prophecy of Daniel was fulfilled in the second century BC during the time that the Greeks desecrated the Holy Temple in Jerusalem. They set up a *shikutz* in the form of an image of Jupiter. This stirred up the Levitical family of the Maccabees to challenge the mighty

---

[*] Wikipedia; Siege of Jerusalem (70 CE). (2024, March 12). In Wikipedia. en.wikipedia.org/wiki/Siege_of_Jerusalem_(70_CE)

Greek Empire, and at great risk and sacrifice to get the Temple back and rededicate it to YHVH removing all idolatry and desecration from it. Out of this event comes the Feast of Hanukkah, normally celebrated during the month of December. Yeshua celebrated this feast, too, as mentioned in John, Chapter 10.

But What About Yeshua's words?

"So, when you see the abomination of desolation spoken of by the prophet Daniel, standing in the holy place (let the reader understand), then let those who are in Judea flee to the mountains."

—Matthew 24:15-16 NASB '95

Surely the prophecy would be for a future time after Yeshua's death, burial and resurrection! Indeed, it was fulfilled by the year 70 AD, when Jerusalem was surrounded by the Roman armies and the Jewish people were exiled for 2000 years. Jerusalem was then leveled to the ground by Emperor Hadrian, and its name was changed to Helia Capitolina, establishing the worship of Jupiter Capitolinus. Also, the Romans permanently changed the name of Israel to "Palestina," commemorating the wicked enemies of Israel, the Philistines. The name was restored to Israel with the establishment of the State of Israel on May 14th of 1948, fulfilling numerous Biblical prophecies!*

Islam, The Shikutz Meshomem

However, I believe that this prophecy is also in action right now, since 632 AD, through Islam. From the 7th century and on, after the death of Muhammad, the Muslims have sought to expand and conquer.

---

* For example, see Ezekiel 36, 37, Jeremiah 30, 31, 32, and Amos 9.

Though Jerusalem is not mentioned in the Quran, not even one time by name, they interpreted some of the verses talking about a "remote sanctuary", where Muhammad took his journey to heaven, to be Jerusalem, or more specifically, the ancient site of the Holy Hebrew Temple. According to their interpretation, their prophet Muhammad went on a night journey to heaven mounted on a mythological winged horse named *al buraq*. The horse wastied to what is the Kotel or the Western Wall today. On the said journey, he met with Angel Gabriel, who entrusted him with the Quran, the foundation for Islam. *Islam* means *submission* and, most particularly, submission to a demon god by the name of "*Allah*." Interestingly, the name *Allah* in Hebrew means a "decreed curse that causes desolation or destruction."

The Temple Mount, where the Jewish Holy Temple used to be, until its destruction by the Romans in 70 AD, is also the original site of Mount Moriah, where Abraham sacrificed the son of promise, Isaac (Genesis 22). Isaac is a type and a shadow of the Son of God, Yeshua, who, through His sacrifice on the Roman execution cross in Golgotha, paid for the sins of us all. According to Muslim tradition, it was not Isaac who was sacrificed on Mount Moriah but rather Ishmael, the son of Abraham with Sarah's Egyptian maid Hagar. Islam completely rejects the fact that Israel is the chosen people with a promised land. They believe they are the chosen people, and they have usurped the title to the land that Yah calls "Mine" and to Jerusalem that He calls "My dwelling place."

> **Blessed be ADONAI out of Zion, who dwells in Jerusalem. Halleluyah!**
>
> —PSALM 135:21

So how does Islam through the Dome of the Rock and the Mosque of Al Aqsa on the Temple Mount fit the bill of The Abomination that causes Desolation, or *shikutz meshomem?*

It is very simple: Those Muslim shrines on the Holy Hill of Zion or the Temple Mount are idolatry, pure and simple. It is elevating the name of a foreign god named "Allah" that is not the God of Israel, who is the God of Abraham, Isaac, and Jacob. So, these shrines are a *shikutz* or an idol in the holiest place in the world, the Temple Mount or Zion. Here, King Solomon built the first temple, and Ezra built the second temple after the Babylonian exile. King Herod elevated and expanded the second temple, whose only remains is a retaining wall called the Kotel or Western Wall, the holiest site of prayer for the Jewish people yearning for the rebuilding of the temple. From the Temple Mount, Yeshua the Messiah will also rule the nations with a rod of iron, sitting on His holy throne on what will become the third temple.

> **He who sits in heaven laughs! ADONAI mocks them. So He will speak to them in His anger, and terrify them in His fury: "I have set up My king upon Zion, My holy mountain."**
>
> **—PSALM 2:4-6**

Islam is a murderous religion. It is a religion of conquest, and it will stop at nothing until the whole world is Muslim or YHVH destroys it altogether. The demon Allah that rules Islam knows full well that while they have the Temple Mount, they will rule. It is a proven fact that any people group that holds the Temple Mount becomes the world empire of their time. This happened with Israel after King Solomon built the temple, then with Babylon when it was destroyed and possessed, then with Greece and Rome, and now Islam. Have you ever wondered why the Muslims are growing so fast? It is because Israel gave autonomy to the *Wakf* under Jordanian supervision to the Muslim authorities after the miraculous Six-Day War of 1967. This terrible tactical mistake of the Israeli government then has cost us untold suffering, as the center of the conflict is the Temple Mount and the Holy City of Jerusalem.

> **On that day I will make Jerusalem an immovable rock. All the nations will gather against it to try to move it, but they will only hurt themselves.**
>
> —Zechariah 12:3 nlt

The Status Quo Over the Temple Mount

> **He (Menashe) even built altars in Adonai's House, where Adonai had said, "In Jerusalem I will put My Name."**
>
> —2 Kings 21:4

The famous "status quo" over the Temple Mount has been that only Muslims can pray. No Jews or Christians are allowed to pray or even have a Bible with them when they visit the Temple Mount. As long as this "status quo" is kept, there will be bloodshed, because it gives Islam and the *Shikutz* or *Idol* of the Dome of the Rock and the Mosque of Al Aqsa the spiritual power to rule. They rule by *prayer* to the demon god Allah as they exalt his name over loudspeakers five times a day.

Additionally, their imams or spiritual leaders incite the Muslim masses every Friday to "defend Al Aqsa from the Zionists" and

---

* The Jordanian-appointed organization responsible for controlling and managing the current Islamic edifices on the Temple Mount in the Old City of Jerusalem, known to Muslims as Al-Aqsa, which includes the Dome of the Rock. *Jerusalem Waqf. (2024, April 6). In Wikipedia. en.wikipedia.org/wiki/Jerusalem_Waqf*

to murder the Jews. This "status quo" of prayers to a demon god and incitement has been allowed by the Israeli government since 1967, thinking that this will "appease" the Arabs. But instead of "appeasing" them, it has strengthened and emboldened them. It has caused desolation and destruction. The abomination that causes desolation in this present time is Islam, as manifested by the Al Aqsa Mosque and the Dome of the Rock on the Temple Mount. Islam causes desolation, and even green lands turn into deserts wherever it goes.

Just pay attention to what is happening in all the Muslim countries, and now with ISIS, which is Islam at its "best" or worst! Desolation, murder, rape, cruelty, and destruction happen wherever Islam goes. The fact is that 99% of all terror attacks worldwide are done by Muslims. I praise China and Angola that restricted Islam altogether in their countries; this is wisdom from above.

Right after Prime Minister Netanyahu promised the UN and Germany that Israel is "committed to keep the status quo," the most terrible storm was unleashed in Israel. My daughter called me from the Tel Aviv area, saying it was the most terrible storm she had ever seen. Her phone is cut off as I am writing these lines. The storm has now reached Eilat, and driving is a hazard; the sky is dark. Is this a coincidence or judgment from YHVH for wanting to keep a "status quo" that He does not want to keep? And could it be that the keeping of this "status quo" will lead to the UN taking over and eventually the Anti-Messiah sitting on the Temple Mount as the ultimate abomination of desolation?

One thing I can tell you is that YHVH is not happy with the "status quo." He is not happy with Israel appeasing Islam and all the nations of the world by allowing a demon god by the name of "curse" (Allah) to be exalted above all other names in Israel. We must cry out for the

Spirit of grace and supplication to fall upon Israel! A true awakening is urgently needed in Israel. Pray for it fervently!

> For I have known that ADONAI is great, and that our LORD is above all gods. Whatever ADONAI pleases, He does, in heaven and in earth, in the seas and in all deeps. He makes clouds rise from the ends of the earth. He makes lightning for the rain. He brings wind out of His storehouses.
>
> —PSALMS 135:5-7

Most probably, the abomination that causes desolation through the Muslim shrines on the Temple Mount will be appeased by the politicians of the nations, promising more "status quo" until the next time that the Arabs decide to break the said status quo by launching more desolation and destruction throughout Israel. As long as Israel keeps the infamous "status quo," this will be the cycle. This will be so until a generation like Joshua and Caleb arise in Israel, full of faith in YHVH, and with His power dethrone the *Shikutz Meshomem* of Islam from the Temple Mount.

For sure, when Yeshua returns, He will not sit to rule and reign from within a mosque! So, keep your eyes and prayers on the Temple Mount, and agree with the God of Israel that this is His dwelling place forever, and the anti-Christ Islam that is sitting there must be dethroned!

Keep up your prayers for Israel's deliverance from Islam and terror and, of course, from unbelief and sin.

> "Then you will know that I, the LORD your God, live in Zion, my holy mountain. Jerusalem will be holy forever."
>
> —JOEL 3:17 NLT

CHAPTER 46

SHEEP AND GOAT NATIONS

The King will answer and say to them, 'Truly I say to you, to the extent that you did it to one of these brothers of Mine, even the least of them, you did it to Me.'

— MATTHEW 25:40 NASB '95

How have the nations behaved with Israel when she is in need? This is one of the determining factors that will separate the sheep from the goats, both people and nations.

During this last month, Israel was mightily rescued by the Almighty and the IDF. The Hamas terror organization that has been ruling in Gaza has dug over 31 terror tunnels with many "heads" or exits into urban areas of Israel. They even had motorbikes hidden in there in order to strike quickly once hundreds or thousands of terrorists would exit the tunnels. Terrorists would be dressed in Israeli soldier uniforms and would kidnap as many Israelis as possible, then drag them through the tunnels. Other terrorists had planned to wear explosive vests and to detonate themselves in city centers, schools, hospitals, malls, and wherever they would find. The plan was to be operated by Rosh Hashanah, the Feast of Trumpets and the Jewish New Year, in September 2014.

> God, do not keep silent. Do not hold Your peace, O God. Do not be still. For look, Your enemies make an uproar. Those who hate You lift up their head. They make a shrewd plot against Your people, conspiring against Your treasured ones. "Come," they say, "let's wipe them out as a nation! Let Israel's name be remembered no more!"
>
> —Psalm 83:2-5

Lately, a very enlightening video from the son of a major Hamas leader by the name of Mosab Hassan Yousef has been broadcast through CNN and YouTube. The young man turned his back on Islam and terrorism and became a Christian. He warned the Western world that Hamas worships death and does not care about the lives of anyone, not even their own people or their own lives, as long as they achieve their goal of world conquest! That is the reason they use their babies and all civilians as human shields!

Our precious IDF soldiers, mostly young men from 18-21 years old, have risked their lives courageously to give us this year a Happy New Year and Feast of Trumpets! May the memory of all those killed in battle be blessed, their families greatly comforted, and the wounded quickly restored to health and salvation!

Keep Lifting Your Hands

> So it came about when Moses held his hand up, that Israel prevailed, and when he let his hand down, Amalek prevailed.
>
> —Exodus 17:11 NASB '95

We thank all of you who have been praying, especially those following the strategy we sent from Exodus 17 by lifting up your hands in prayer one hour a day for Israel. Please keep it up! The battle for the salvation and redemption of Israel has only started. Millions of Jews in the world are in great danger as antisemitic waves of hatred have been unleashed on them throughout Europe. The Jews are once again in fear in Germany, UK, and France. Many are on their way to make aliyah; pray for them as aliyah is the answer to terror!

> "Therefore, the days are quickly coming," declares ADONAI, "when it will no longer be said. 'As ADONAI lives, who brought up the children of Israel out of the land of Egypt.' Rather, 'As ADONAI lives, who brought up the children of Israel from the land of the north and from all the lands where He had banished them.' So I will bring them back into their land that I gave to their fathers. "Behold, I will send for many fishers," says ADONAI, "and they will fish for them. After that, I will send for many hunters, and they will hunt them down from every mountain and from every hill, and out of the clefts of the rocks.
>
> —JEREMIAH 16:14-16

Below is a special testimony of our team member, Hadassah Danielsbacka, who visited the wounded IDF soldiers in the Beersheba Hospital in 2014 during Operation Protective Edge.

Kol a Kavod! A Way to Go!

"Kol a kavod, kol a kavod!" She was repeating these words over and over again and crying! This young woman next to me was the sister of a soldier who had just been seriously wounded in Gaza. She was sitting in a waiting room at the Beersheba hospital, the place where most of the wounded soldiers from Gaza are brought. At any moment, her brother would be brought in, and seeing our team present there, supporting her and her people, brought her comfort.

I am a young woman from Finland, and I am visiting Israel to be a blessing here. I received the privilege of visiting the hospital in Beersheba with other intercessors and two people who work in an organization that helps terror victims. When I got this opportunity to go with them, I did not really know what was awaiting me since there had never been a war in Finland during my lifetime or any rockets falling on our country. But I wanted to go and show that Finland and I are supporting and blessing them. I felt Yeshua saying: "As my soldiers here have been brought into the hospital by their comrades and my people, I want you to carry them into the Father's presence with your prayers."

Yeshua gives us a very serious teaching in Matthew 25. He tells us that when nations are brought before Him for judgment, He separates the sheep from the goats. Who are the sheep nations, and who are the goat nations? Sheep nations are those who blessed Yeshua in action:

> 'For I was hungry, and you gave Me something to eat; I was thirsty, and you gave Me something to drink; I was a stranger, and you invited Me in; naked, and you clothed Me; I was sick, and you visited Me; I was in prison, and you came to Me.'
>
> —MATTHEW 25:40 NASB '95

And when those righteous ask when they saw Yeshua in those conditions, He simply says:

'Truly I say to you, to the extent that you did it to one of these brothers of Mine, even the least of them, you did it to Me.' (Matthew 25:40 NASB '95) By His brothers he means Jewish people, Israel!

I saw many of His brothers and sisters, mothers, and fathers in Beersheba hospital. And yes, they were hurting! Most of the soldiers are young boys, around 18-24. They are very courageous, but they need our prayers from the nations to put a mantle of grace and protection upon them. Their families need prayer, too, urgently! There is no better time to be present in this land to show that we care. This is the last moment for the nations to become sheep nations!

There was a woman who had waited for almost two weeks for her son, a soldier, to wake up from a coma. Very soon, it would be her birthday, and she said that the best present she could ever imagine would be for her son to come back alive and wake up! We encouraged her and promised to stay in prayer for that miracle. Shortly after our visit, we read from the newspaper about a miracle awakening: that very soldier had awakened after weeks in a coma! We are filled with joy!

Israeli families need our prayers now and also our presence. When we told them that we were from Finland and other nations far away who had come here to bless and support them, the people were so thankful and touched. There were special people Yah wanted us to especially bless. If we had not gone, we would have missed the opportunity and rejected Yeshua himself.

After witnessing the pain of Yeshua's family in the hospital: seriously injured soldiers brought in and their families waiting, praying, and hurting, I now have a better understanding of how to bless Israel. I lay my hands on them in the Spirit daily and declare life and comfort!

You are called to come to Israel for such a time as this. Your prayers and your presence can mean life to someone here. Never be afraid for your own life and miss the place Yah is calling you! There is no safer place than where He wants you to be. Lose your life to gain it! Our Israel tours are waiting for you.

In Finland, it is peaceful now, but I certainly know that if I had not been obedient to come here but stayed in Finland to enjoy that peace, then I would be in danger as I would be opposing the Most High. The safest place to be is where He calls us, even in the midst of a storm, or if he would allow us to be thrown into a fiery furnace, like the three Hebrew boys, Hananiah, Mishael, and Azariah.* But that was the safest place for them because Yeshua Himself was there with them! Right now, many, many Hebrew boys have been and are going through their fiery furnace, and we need to represent Yeshua for them and be with them both in prayer and action.

If we are out of Yah's will because of our fear or pursuit of convenience, we lose His presence and, with that, everything! Let us be like our beloved Archbishop Dominiquae and Rabbi Baruch, who decided to lose their lives many times with great risks to bring the presence of Yeshua to us in the nations. Now, we can pay back as we bring the presence of Yeshua back to Israel.

A beautiful Jewish woman sat at her son's bedside at Beersheba Hospital. Her son, a young soldier, was very weak with an IV drip. We had the opportunity to bless them. Abba showed me a picture of a flourishing tree and gave me Psalm 1:1-3 to give them. Let us declare it over every soldier and Israel as we go throughout all the Land:

> Happy is the one who has not walked in the advice of the wicked, nor stood in the way of sinners, nor sat in the seat of scoffers. But his delight is in the Torah of ADONAI, and on His Torah he meditates day and night. He will be like a planted tree over streams of water, producing its fruit during its season. Its leaf never droopsbut in all he does, he succeeds.
>
> —Psalm 1:1-3

Welcome to be a blessing and to inherit a blessing!**

---

* See Daniel 3

** Join our Israel tours: www.kad-esh.org/tours-and-events

2013

CHAPTER 47

WATCHMEN ON THE WALLS

> I have posted watchmen on your walls, Yerushalayim;
> they will never fall silent, neither by day nor by night.
> You who call on ADONAI, give yourselves no rest;
>
> — ISAIAH 62:6-7 CJB

US PRESIDENT OBAMA HAS decided to back Israel to the wall, and rumors say that he is bent on earning himself a Nobel prize as this is his last chance to become "famous." According to the Holy Scriptures, the type of fame that he could earn for himself would win him a place with the friends of the Anti-Messiah himself. However, Israel is between "a rock and a hard place" and the pressure on PM Benjamin Netanyahu is beyond bearing.

What is the solution to this hideous plan? Can we stop it? Will there be peace? Will the peace last? Are we now in the 70th week of Daniel? There are many questions that arise as we watch in disbelief and horror the plan of removing 100,000 Jewish citizens from the Biblical heartland of Judea and Samaria advancing before our eyes. On top of it, many Arab terrorists with much blood on their hands have been freed (to the dismay of the families of the victims) in order to "bribe"

Abu Mazen to continue the "peace talks". Will this horror movie end, or are we getting ready for the final show of the Antichrist?

I do not intend to give all the answers and speculations. I believe in prophetic ministry, and the Bible does tell us enough about the happenings prior to the return of the Messiah. All the prophets of old prophesied the restoration of Israel and the return of the people to the land at the time of greatest distress, judgment, and exile. They warned the people from the impending judgment but prophesied hope for the future!

The call to be watchmen on the walls is to protect Israel and Yerushalayim. We are to pray day and night until all of Yah's promises are fulfilled and the Holy City is a praise in the earth. So, despite all of the abominable plans to divide Yerushalayim and to remove precious cities in Samaria, we are assigned to pray and declare Yerushalayim's wellbeing and restoration!

> **Pray for shalom in Yerushalayim; may those who love you prosper. May shalom be within your ramparts, prosperity in your palaces.**
>
> —Psalm 122:6-7

Why would YHVH give us the instruction to pray for the shalom of Yerushalayim? Because that shalom will be endangered! Shalom is not peace but rather wholeness, completeness, and total well-being.

We are to pray for Yerushalayim to be *one* and not divided and for all the Land of Promise to be *one* and not divided, to be whole. We are to pray for Israel to succeed against the enemies opposing the covenant promises of possessing the land. There are many opponents to the covenant, and we are to stand with Israel as watchmen praying day and night for the covenant promises to be fulfilled! Even if we see the enemy advancing, we are assigned to declare "the end of the book"; even if the enemy seems to be succeeding, we are to believe that YHVH is faithful, and He will accomplish what He promised, and no one will stop Him. When all seems lost, that is the time to keep believing! The Prophet Habakkuk, a mighty watchman, gave us a powerful example of this when Israel had gone into exile. He lived through such a period of darkness, yet His trust was in the God of His salvation, in Yeshua.

> **Though the fig tree does not blossom, and there is no yield on the vines, Though the olive crop fail, and the fields produce no food, the flock is cut off from the fold, and there is no cattle in the stalls. Yet will I triumph in ADONAI, I will rejoice in the God of my salvation!**
>
> **—HABAKKUK 3:17-18**

He also declared in the midst of judgment that when YHVH acts, it's best to be *silent* before Him. This theme of *silence* when YHVH acts is repeated a few times in the Holy Scriptures.

> **But ADONAI is in His holy Temple. Let all the land be silent before Him.**
>
> **—HABAKKUK 2:20**

But how can we be silent and yet pray day and night as watchmen on the walls of Yerushalayim? I believe that the call is to silence the flesh and the opinions of men about Yah's will.

> **ADONAI will inherit Judah as His portion in the holy land and will once again choose Jerusalem. Be silent before ADONAI, all flesh, for He has aroused Himself from His holy dwelling.**
>
> **—ZECHARIAH 2:16-17**

People are very opinionated, and they think they know better, especially when it is about Israel. Political views and opinions run across the spectrum. There are many "experts" on the Israel subject, but this is a time when we cannot just "babble" prayers or pray our wish list; we must pray according to the Spirit and according to the promises of Yah alone, without allowing the circumstances to block our view. We are watchmen, so we need our view open and our eyes clear. The only way to bring about Elohim's salvation on the earth is from a place of quietness and confidence, not from a place of anxiety and fear. Our hearts as watchmen on the walls for Yerushalayim and for anything else must be in shalom.

> For thus says ADONAI Elohim, the Holy One of Israel: "By repentance and rest you are saved, in quietness and trust is your strength."
>
> —Isaiah 30:15a

From the place of intimacy that only teshuva, repentance, can bring, we can proceed to pray God's heart rather than our own. Each one of us has to take the time to get quiet and ask Him to bring us to repentance so that we can stand in the gap for Israel and for others and even pray for ourselves.

> Search me, God, and know my heart; test me and know my anxious thoughts. See if there is any offensive way in me, and lead me in the way everlasting.
>
> —Psalm 139:23-24

Repentance brings about great cleansing and then confidence, for when we have repented and we know we are forgiven, there is no guilt inside and no inner lies that can block our "hearing" and our "seeing."

> **Beloved, if our heart does not condemn us, we have confidence before God.**
>
> —1 John 3:21 nasb '95

When we have true confidence, we have boldness; we are not moved by circumstances or by fear, and we are deaf to the cry of our enemies.

> **"Adonai will fight for you, while you hold your peace."**
>
> —Exodus 14:14

As watchmen on the walls, we are going to get a first view of all the enemies that are coming against Israel. But do not get discouraged; remember to prophesy the Word of truth even when all seems lost. Ezekiel prophesied during the time of the Babylonian exile about the restoration of Israel and that prophetic Word of Ezekiel 37 was found under the ground of the archeological dig of the Fortress of Masada in the Judean Desert. The true prophetic Word comes to pass even if it needs to be resurrected from the ground! Our job as watchmen is to pray according to Yah's will, Word, and heart, and the outcome we leave with Him!

> **So I prophesied as He commanded me, and the breath came into them, and they came to life and stood on their feet, an exceedingly great army.**
>
> —Ezekiel 37:10 nasb '95

We are living in that mighty promise today in Israel, but when it was prophesied, there was no indication that it would ever come to pass—rather, the opposite. Watchmen are not directed by the natural realm but only by what the Holy Spirit reveals to them, and they pray and prophesy from there.

The call to be watchmen on the walls is to all who call upon His name!

> "You who remind Adonai, take no rest for yourselves, and give Him no rest until He establishes and makes Jerusalem a praise in the earth.
>
> —Isaiah 62:6b-7

CHAPTER 48

ISRAEL AND THE NATIONS—A DIVINE ALIGNMENT

How the Establishing of the State of Israel Affects the Nations
Celebrating Israel's 66th Anniversary

> Before she travailed, she brought forth; before her pain came,
> she gave birth to a boy. "Who has heard such a thing?
> Who has seen such things? Can a land be born in one day?
> Can a nation be brought forth all at once?
>
> — ISAIAH 66:7, 8A NASB '95

The establishment of the State of Israel is the biggest miracle in history since the coming of the Messiah, and it affects the whole world! No wonder that the Holy City of Yerushalayim (Jerusalem) has more news reporters than any other city in the world. While important things are happening in other nations, good or bad, and no one pays attention, not so with Israel. We "sneeze" in Israel, and the whole world knows it! The nations are affected by what happens in Israel, and those who love her and actively work for her well-being will be in great shalom and prosperity.

> Pray for the peace (shalom) of Jerusalem: "May they prosper who love you."
>
> —Psalm 122:6 NASB '95

What is it about Israel that affects the whole world? YHVH promised Abraham a holy reciprocity between Israel and the nations. Israel would be the greatest blessing to the nations *if* the nations honor and respect her as the mother nation of all nations (Genesis 12:3). When Israel is favored and blessed, all the nations can be favored and blessed. It restores Elohim-God's order and focus of worship to the nations and brings back the correct knowledge of who YHVH is and who Yeshua is as a Jewish Messiah and the Lion from the tribe of Judah. Yerushalayim is the center of the world! (Jeremiah 3:17) The Word admonishes us not to forget her, and those who do can lose their authority and their speech ability:

> If I forget you, O Jerusalem, may my right hand forget her skill. May my tongue cling to the roof of my mouth if I do not remember you, if I do not exalt Jerusalem above my chief joy.
>
> —Psalm 137:5-6 NASB '95

Jerusalem is Again the Center of Holy Worship for all Nations

The restoration of the chosen nation of Israel in its own land is bringing order and focus to the worship of the nations. Just like before the exile of 2000 long and painful years, the nations that love the God of Israel are coming now to worship in Jerusalem and bring their gifts there.

Israel and the Nations—A Divine Alignment

> The word which Isaiah, son of Amoz saw concerning Judah and Jerusalem: It will come to pass in the last days that the mountain of ADONAI's House will stand firm as head of the mountains and will be exalted above the hills. So all nations will flow to it.
>
> —ISAIAH 2:1-2

Nations are commanded to worship the King in Yerushalayim, celebrating the Biblical feasts as established in the Hebrew Holy Scriptures (wrongly called the Old Testament).

> Then all the survivors from all the nations that attacked Jerusalem will go up from year to year to worship the King, ADONAI-Tzva'ot, and to celebrate Sukkot. Furthermore, if any of the nations on earth do not go up to Jerusalem to worship the King, ADONAI-Tzva'ot, they will have no rain.
>
> —ZECHARIAH 14:16

This is already happening as thousands of believers from many nations arrive at Yerushalayim every year to celebrate Sukkot, the Feast of Booths/Tabernacles. Nations are commanded to celebrate all of Yah's Shabbats, that is both the seventh day of rest and all the other major feast days or *Moadim*.*

> "And it will come to pass, that from one New Moon to another, and from one Shabbat to another, all flesh will come to bow down before Me," says ADONAI.
>
> —ISAIAH 66:23

---

* See Leviticus 23 for God's *Moadim*, the *appointed times*.

But it is not the center of worship for all religions or, as the politicians call it, the three monotheistic religions: Judaism, Christianity, and Islam. No! It is the center of worship of the Creator of the Universe, YHVH, the God of Israel, and not of any other god, idol, or religious system. Jerusalem is not an interfaith city, but it is the city of *one* faith, *one* Elohim, and *one* Messiah!

> *Shema Israel,* A{DONAI} *Eloheinu,* A{DONAI} *Echad*
> Hear O Israel, the L{ORD} our God, the L{ORD} is one. Love A{DONAI} your God with all your heart and with all your soul and with all your strength.
>
> —D{EUTERONOMY} 6:4-5

> We all like sheep have gone astray. Each of us turned to his own way. So A{DONAI} has laid on Him (Yeshua the Jewish Messiah and Savior) the iniquity of us all.
>
> —I{SAIAH} 53:6

> But as for Me, I have installed My King upon Zion, My holy mountain.
>
> —P{SALM} 2:6 {NASB} '95

Jerusalem is the place where the nations are commanded to bring their wealth. The Apostle Paul reminds the Gentiles that they are indebted to the Jewish people. The Gentiles have received all their spiritual riches from the people of Israel and are commanded to reciprocate by bringing their material riches.

Yes, they were pleased to do so, and they are indebted to them. For if the Gentiles have shared in their spiritual things, they are indebted to minister to them also in material things.

—Romans 15:27 nasb '95

Even all of Africa will bring their gifts and offerings to Israel, just like at the time of the Queen of Sheba.

For then I will restore to the people (Gentile nations) pure speech, so that all of them may call upon the Name of Adonai and serve Him shoulder to shoulder. From beyond the rivers of Ethiopia, My worshipers, the daughter of My scattered ones will bring My offering.

—Zephaniah 3:9-10

They come to honor Israel at the time of her restoration. All nations bring their wealth and the good news, and all kings of the earth will honor Israel, including Arab and African nations.

Arise, shine, for your light has come! The glory of Adonai has risen on you. For behold, darkness covers the earth, and deep darkness the peoples. But Adonai will arise upon you, and His glory will appear over you. Nations will come to your light, kings to the brilliance of your rising. Lift up your eyes and look all around: they all gather—they come to youyour sons will come from far away, your daughters carried on the hip. Then you will see and be radiant, and your heart will throb and swell with joy. For the abundance of the sea will be turned over to you. The wealth of nations will come to you. A multitude of camels will cover you, young camels of Midian and Ephah, all those from Sheba will come. They will bring gold and frankincense, and proclaim the praises of ADONAI.

—Isaiah 60:1-6

An Open Door of Salvation and Instruction for All Nations

When Israel is restored, the Word of YHVH comes out of Zion again, bringing light unto the nations, and in Zion Salvation-Yeshua can be found!

> Then all who call on ADONAI's Name will escape, for on Mount Zion and in Jerusalem there will be rescue, as ADONAI has said, among the survivors whom ADONAI is calling.
>
> —Joel 2:32

Not long ago, a Polish brother arrived to worship with us in the Eilat Prayer Tower. A few months before, he had come to Israel for the first time. He was touring the Negev Desert of Israel, "looking for God." He met a Messianic Israeli believer who introduced him to Yeshua and he got saved! Then he connected with us. Salvation is found in Zion again, so nations are coming to "look for God!"

> Then many peoples will go and say: "Come, let us go up to the mountain of ADONAI, to the House of the God of Jacob! Then He will teach us His ways, and we will walk in His paths." For Torah will go forth from Zion and the word of ADONAI from Jerusalem.
>
> —Isaiah 2:3

An Open Door of Salvation for Israel's Wicked Neighbors

The United Nations is raging against Israel, and President Obama has done everything in his power to establish a Palestinian terror state in the Land of Israel.

> It will come about in that day that I will make Jerusalem a heavy stone for all the peoples; all who lift it will be severely injured. And all the nations of the earth will be gathered against it.
>
> —Zechariah 12:3 NASB '95

Fatah and PLO have had and still have, through "the Palestinian Authority or PA," a sworn agenda to annihilate Israel all the way from the days of Hitler and the Grand Mufti of Jerusalem, Haj Amin El Husseini. That is why they have refused to recognize Israel as a Jewish state, and that is why they have now made an alliance with Hamas in Gaza. The world agrees that Hamas is a terror organization but is espousing the PA as people who really want "peace" with Israel. Now that they have come out of the closet and shown the world their alliance with sworn terrorists, they have shown their true face without political masks! What is the Biblical predicament for the Palestinians and all the hostile Arab nations around Israel?

> Thus says ADONAI, "As for all My evil neighbors who strike at the inheritance that I bequeathed to My people Israel—I am about to uproot them from their land and pluck the house of Judah from them. Yet it will come to pass, after I have uprooted them, that I will again have compassion on them and I will bring them back, each one to his inheritance and each one to his land. "So it will come to pass, if they will diligently learn

the ways of My people—to swear by My Name, 'As ADONAI lives,' just as they taught My people to swear by Baal—then they will be built up in the midst of My people. But if they will not obey, then I will uproot that nation, plucking it up and destroying it." It is a declaration of ADONAI.

—JEREMIAH 12:14-17

Now is the time to preach the Gospel to the Muslims and to all those wicked neighbors of Israel who try to strike at her Yah (God)-given inheritance! Those who accept Yeshua as a Jewish Messiah who died for them and through Him make allegiance with the God of Israel, YHVH, and not Allah, will receive an inheritance in the midst of the Land of Israel—not as a separate Palestinian state but as part or grafted into Israel through faith in Messiah Yeshua and Torah. If they do not forsake Islam and the Palestinian agenda, including the name Palestine derived from the Philistines and the archenemy of Israel in the Bible, they will be completely destroyed. The Muslims must get to know Yeshua as a Jewish Messiah and not through Christianity. They must receive the true Gospel of the kingdom "made in Zion," not Western Christianity! Those who realize that a Jew died for them will repent and will dwell in the midst of Israel forever.

That is Yah's plan, *not* the establishment of a separate Palestinian State.

Answered Prayer to the Nations That Come to Honor YHVH's Name

One of the most important things people do when they come to Israel is to go pray at the *Kotel* or Western (Wailing) Wall. They bring their prayers written on little pieces of paper and leave them in the creases of the stone wall. Why do they do that? And why does Yah (God) answer those prayers, and why do many miracles happen to people who pray there? When King Solomon dedicated the first temple, he prayed:

> **Also concerning the foreigner who is not from Your people Israel, when he comes from a far country for Your great name's sake and Your mighty hand and Your outstretched arm, when they come and pray toward this house, then hear from heaven, from Your dwelling place, and do according to all for which the foreigner calls to You, in order that all the peoples of the earth may know Your name, and fear You as do Your people Israel, and that they may know that this house which I have built is called by Your name.**
>
> —2 CHRONICLES 6:32-33 NASB '95

Before the establishment of the modern-day State of Israel on May 14th of 1948, the Kotel was in Turkish hands, and then Arabs showed their true face without political masks. The place had become a dumpster as the Muslims sought to desecrate that Holy Place, the retaining wall of what used to be YHVH's Holy Temple. They named the gate that leads to the Kotel "The Dung Gate." Can you imagine? Only when, after the miraculous Six Day War in 1967, we took back the Old City of Yerushalayim, we cleansed the Kotel precinct and rededicated it to prayer. Since then, people of all nations have come to pour their hearts out before YHVH and entreat the God of Israel for breakthroughs and miracles in their lives. It is now a place of open heavens, and prayer goes up there 24/7.

Now you can understand why the Muslims want Yerushalayim and the Temple Mount. It is the place where the Messiah will sit on His throne and rule the nations with a rod of iron during the millennial reign of Messiah.

> At that time they will call Jerusalem the throne of ADONAI and all the nations will gather into it, to Jerusalem, in the Name of ADONAI. No longer will they walk according to the stubbornness of their evil heart.
>
> —JEREMIAH 3:17

The restoration of the nation of Israel in its own Biblical Land of Promise is preparing the land and the nations for the return of the Messiah.

> "Look, your house is left to you desolate! For I tell you, you will never see Me again until you say, 'Baruch ha-ba b'shem ADONAI. Blessed is He who comes in the name of the LORD!'"
>
> —MATTHEW 23:38-39

Today there are many thousands of Messianic Jewish believers in Messiah Yeshua welcoming the Messiah back in the Land of Israel.

> Repent, therefore, and return—so your sins might be blotted out, so times of relief might come from the presence of ADONAI and He might send Yeshua, the Messiah appointed for you. Heaven must receive Him, until the time of the restoration of all the things that God spoke about long ago through the mouth of His holy prophets.
>
> —ACTS 3:19-21

The restoration of all things that the prophets (*neviim*) spoke about is the restoration of Israel—both the physical return to the land and the spiritual restoration through salvation, faith in Messiah and the Torah written in their hearts.

> For I will take you from the nations, gather you from all the lands and bring you into your own land. Then I will sprinkle clean water on you, and you will be clean; I will cleanse you from all your filthiness and from all your idols. Moreover, I will give you a new heart and put a new spirit within you; and I will remove the heart of stone from your flesh and give you a heart of flesh. I will put My Spirit within you and cause you to walk in My statutes, and you will be careful to observe My ordinances. You will live in the land that I gave to your forefathers; so you will be My people, and I will be your God.
>
> —Ezekiel 36:24-28 nasb '95

The restoration of all things is the restoration of Israel, without which the Messiah will not return, and this world will self-destruct because of sin, just like at the time of Sodom and Gomorrah. Actively working and supporting the restoration of Israel, which includes the restoration of the true Gospel made in Zion to the nations, is accelerating the return of Messiah Yeshua to establish His millennial reign in the only city that is His throne, Yerushalayim, the eternal capital of Israel!

> But Judah will be inhabited forever Jerusalem from generation to generation. I will acquit their bloodguilt that I had not acquitted, for Adonai dwells in Zion.
>
> —Joel 4:20-21

Judgment to Those That Oppose Israel's Restoration

Jerusalem is also the place of judgment for all the nations that have opposed Israel's restoration and well-being. The judgment will take place in the Valley of Jehoshaphat (Hebr. *meaning Yah's judgment*) right below the Mount of Olives, in the same place where the tomb of Absalom is located. Absalom was King David's son who rebelled against him and tried to usurp his position as the king. In the same way, nations that will not honor Israel and have rebelled against her position as the chosen nation of YHVH will be judged just like Absalom, who usurped the place of his father, King David.

> "For behold, in those days and at that time, when I restore Judah and Jerusalem from exile, I will gather all nations and bring them down to the valley of Jehoshaphat. I will plead with them there on behalf of My people, even My inheritance, Israel, whom they scattered among the nations and they divided up My land."
>
> —Joel 4:1-2

The same One that has restored His people back to their land is the same one that will bring them deliverance.

> "For as soon as Zion was in labor, she gave birth to her children. "Will I bring the moment of birth, and not give delivery?" says Adonai. "Will I who cause delivery shut up the womb?" says your God.
>
> —Isaiah 66:8b-9

The nations can choose to be on His "right side" and be blessed as they bless Israel or on His "wrong side" and be cursed as they oppose the Biblical restoration of Israel. Both nations and individuals from the nations are affected by their stand.

> **And I will bless those who bless you, and the one who curses you I will curse. And in you all the families of the earth will be blessed.**
>
> —Genesis 12:3 NASB '95

In the midst of the controversy of the nations about Israel, let us choose life as we stand by Israel's right to be established in *all* of its covenant land, and we cry out for her salvation in Yeshua's Mighty Name!

> **For Zion's sake I will not keep silent, and for Jerusalem's sake I will not keep quiet, until her righteousness goes forth like brightness, and her salvation like a torch that is burning. The nations will see your righteousness, and all kings your glory.**
>
> —Isaiah 62:1-2a NASB '95

CHAPTER 49

JERUSALEM, SUCH A BIG DEAL

The Freezing Storm

> It will come about in that day that I will make Jerusalem a heavy stone for all the peoples; all who lift it will be severely injured. And all the nations of the earth will be gathered against it.
>
> — ZECHARIAH 12:3 NASB '95

WHY IS JERUSALEM SUCH a big deal? So many people have so many opinions, so many nations have coveted her, and so many passions are provoked by this one city! What makes Yerushalayim the center of the world? I will endeavor to bring you a thorough answer. For now, it is enough to know that Yerushalayim is the city of the Great King, the throne of YHVH, the headquarters of the kingdom of YHVH on earth, and the eternal capital of Israel!

> At that time they will call Jerusalem the throne of ADONAI and all the nations will gather into it, to Jerusalem, in the Name of ADONAI. No longer will they walk according to the stubbornness of their evil heart.
>
> —JEREMIAH 3:17

All nations that attempt to divide the Holy City will be seriously judged and destroyed (Joel 3).

It is YHVH'S personal address in the midst of His Jewish people,

> **But Judah will be inhabited forever Jerusalem from generation to generation. I will acquit their bloodguilt that I had not acquitted, for ADONAI dwells in Zion.**
>
> —JOEL 4:20-21

Since US President Barack Obama came to Israel in July of 2013, Israel has been under heavy pressure from the USA to finalize a peace agreement with the so-called "Palestinians" and establish a Palestinian free state. This includes the division of the Land of Israel to the 1967 borders prior to the miraculous Six-Day War and the division of Yerushalayim into two capitals: the capital of Israel and the capital of Palestine. Please remember that Yerushalayim (the true name of Jerusalem) is YHVH'S personal address on earth, and He does not like His hto be divided!

> **I will gather all the nations and bring them down to the valley of Jehoshaphat. Then I will enter into judgment with them there on behalf of My people and My inheritance, Israel, whom they have scattered among the nations; and they have divided up My land.**
>
> —JOEL 3:2 NASB '95

So how is He demonstrating His displeasure with this plan? He does it through snowstorms and terrible freezing. The worst snowstorm in 20 years happened in the USA in January, the exact time that US Secretary of State Kerry arrived in Israel on his 10th visit in less than a year!

"Yet all who devour you will be devoured, and all your foes— all of themwill go into captivity. Those plundering you will be plundered, and all preying on you I give as prey. For I will restore health to you and will heal you of your wounds." It is a declaration of ADONAI. "For they called you an outcast: 'Zion—no one cares about her.'"
Look! A storm of ADONAI! Fury has burst out as a churning storm, whirling about the head of the wicked. ADONAI i's fierce anger will not turn back until He has done it, until He fulfills the purposes of His heart. in the last days you will understand it.

—JEREMIAH 30:16-17, 23-24

Kerry Arrives in Israel

Jerusalem Post, January 2, 2014 by Herb Keinon, Khaled Abu Toameh

US Secretary of State John Kerry arrived in Israel on Thursday afternoon in a bid to further push the peace process forward.

Kerry is scheduled to meet separately with Prime Minister Binyamin Netanyahu and Palestinian Authority President Mahmoud Abbas this evening to discuss his ideas for a framework agreement that would serve as an outline for a final agreement.

A senior State Department official said Kerry was not expecting any breakthrough during this trip, his 10th to the region since taking office in February. Rather, he said, Kerry was pushing for the sides to agree on guidelines for what the final deal would look like. Then the job would be to fill in the details.*

---

* www.jpost.com/diplomacy-and-politics/kerry-arrives-in-israel-set-to-meet-netanyahu-to-talk-peace-33690702 Jan 2014 by Herb Keinon, Khaled Abu Toameh, accessed 4/1/2024

As Secretary of State Kerry was in Israel for five days, the most terrible freeze came upon the USA. This was the coldest weather in 20 years. 17,000 flights were canceled. The freezing weather wave began on the same day that Kerry landed in Israel (2nd of January) and began to break one day after Kerry left Israel (7th of January), and within three days, it passed completely! This was Kerry's 10th visit since he took office in February of 2013, and 10 days of freeze happened in the USA. Number 10 is very revealing as it reminds us of the ten plagues that hit Egypt for keeping the children of Israel in captivity.

Right before Kerry arrived in Israel, there was terrible freezing weather in Jerusalem and all over the country. It was the coldest weather in over twenty years, and the center of it was the Holy City of Yerushalayim.

As usual, when America makes a move towards unbiblical politics concerning Israel, it is hit with terrible weather and especially storms. In this case, it was a snow and freeze storm.

Winter Blizzard Blankets Northeast

21 in. of snow in Boston, 18 in parts of upstate New York, January 2, 2014.

A blistering winter blizzard covered large swaths of the Northeast U.S. in snow Thursday, (On the day that Kerry lands in Israel—D.B.) canceling flights, shutting down highways closing schools Friday and causing at least eleven deaths.

More than 100 million people almost one-third of the U.S. population were in the path of a storm that started battering the Midwest and the East Coast with snow early Thursday. By late Thursday night, the National Weather Service said 21 in. snow had fallen in a town just north of Boston. About 18 in. fell on parts of upstate New York, and New York City was bracing for heavy snowfall overnight and into Friday morning. Schools in Boston and state government offices in Massachusetts will remain closed on Friday as Gov. Deval Patrick advised residents to remain indoors and avoid "very, very dangerous" temperatures. New York Gov. Andrew Cuomo declared a state of emergency and ordered three major highways across the state shut, the Associated Press reports.

There were sub-zero windchill temperatures in New York City overnight and into Friday morning, and John F. Kennedy International Airport was closed.*

20 Years Ago: the Oslo Accords and the Storm of the Century

What happened 20 years ago since this was the most terrible snowstorm and freeze in 20 years, both in Yerushalayim and in the USA?

20 years ago, throughout the year of 1993, the Oslo Accords were being finalized!

> The Oslo I Accord or Oslo I, officially called the Declaration of Principles on Interim Self-Government Arrangements or Declaration of Principles (DOP), was an attempt in 1993 to set up a framework that would lead to the resolution of the ongoing Israeli–Palestinian conflict. It was the first face-to-face agreement between the government of Israel and the Palestine Liberation Organization (PLO).**

---

* www.nation.time.com/2014/01/02/weather-forecast-winter-storm-buries-us-snow/
** en.wikipedia.org/wiki/Oslo_I_Accord

The Storm of The Century

The Storm of the Century, also known as the '93 Superstorm, or the (Great) Blizzard of 1993, was a large cyclonic storm that formed over the Gulf of Mexico on March 12, 1993, and dissipated in the North Atlantic Ocean on March 15. It is unique for its intensity, massive size and wide-reaching effect. At its height, the storm stretched from Canada towards Central America, but its main impact was on the Eastern United States and Cuba.

Oslo Accords were signed in August that year and on the 13th of September 1993, Rabin shook hands with infamous terrorist and PLO leader Arafat.*

20 years later, as Kerry is coming to finalize the ungodly plan that was put in effect in 1993, the biggest snowstorm and freeze in 20 years starts on the 2nd of January as Kerry lands in Israel. Coincidence?

Weather Speaks Yah's Word of Judgment Over All Nations for the Cause of Zion

> He made the earth by His power, established the world by His wisdom, and stretched out heaven by His understanding. When His voice thunders, waters in heaven roar. He makes clouds rise from the ends of the earth. He makes lightning for the rain and brings forth wind from His storehouses.
>
> —Jeremiah 10:12-13

For thus says ADONAI, the God of Israel, to me: "Take this cup of the wine of fury from My hand, and make all the na-

---

* en.wikipedia.org/wiki/1993_Storm_of_the_Century

tions to whom I am sending you drink it. They will drink, and reel to and fro, and be like madmen, because of the sword that I will send among them.

A noise has come to the end of the earth, for ADONAI has a dispute with the nations. He is passing judgment on all flesh. As for the wicked, He has given them over to the sword." It is a declaration of ADONAI. Thus says ADONAI -Tzva'ot: "Evil will soon go forth from nation to nation. A great storm is being stirred up from the uttermost parts of the earth."

—JEREMIAH 25:15-16, 31-32

"Yet all who devour you will be devoured, and all your foes—all of themwill go into captivity. Those plundering you will be plundered, and all preying on you I give as prey. For I will restore health to you and will heal you of your wounds." It is a declaration of ADONAI. "For they called you an outcast: 'Zion—no one cares about her.'"

Look! A storm of ADONAI! Fury has burst out as a churning storm, whirling about the head of the wicked. ADONAI's fierce anger will not turn back until He has done it, until He fulfills the purposes of His heart. In the last days you will understand it.

—JEREMIAH 30:16-17, 23-24

So pursue them with Your tempest, and terrify them with Your storm. Cover their faces with shame, so they may seek Your NameADONAI. Let them be ashamed and dismayed forever. Let them be humiliated and perish. Let them know that You alonewhose Name is ADONAI are El Elyon over all the earth..

—PSALM 83:16-19

CHAPTER 50

BREAKING THROUGH THE PASSIVITY TOWARDS ISRAEL

The King will answer and say to them, 'Truly I say to you, to the extent that you did it to one of these brothers of Mine, even the least of them, you did it to Me.'

— MATTHEW 25:40 NASB '95

In the midst of the stormy weather accompanying the 2012 elections in the USA, we pray for the safety of all of our partners there in the path of Hurricane Sandy.

A few people asked me if there is a connection between some anti-Israel political events and hurricanes. I have written an entire book called *Stormy Weather** to answer that question. From it, you will understand more about all these "natural disasters" and will also be able to stay safe amid the stormy judgment by applying the principles in this book. Suffice it to say that the center of the hurricane is New York, the seat of the United Nations that is constantly sanctioning Israel and that has hosted the modern-day Hitler, Iranian President Ahmadinejad.

We pray for a mighty awakening in America and serious repentance before these coming elections that will manifest in the polls. May Yah's mercy be poured out one more time so that all passivity concerning

---

* Order the *Stormy Weather* book at www.ZionsGospel.com

Israel in the American churches may break before it is too late. Many American saints have been pressing on this issue, but there are many more that are still steeped in replacement theology and passive enough to allow their nation to veer towards Islam.

Breaking the passivity concerning Israel is the key to the salvation of any nation in the end times! (Genesis 12:3)

Many years ago, a dear Jewish partner and disciple from California shared with me an amazing story. She had died clinically, and when she was dead, she had an encounter with Yeshua. She also saw a Christian minister who was arriving at the Pearly Gates of Heaven, and Yeshua asked him the following:

"What did you do to comfort My people?"

His answer was: "Lord, I have spent all my life comforting the hurting in the church, praying for the sick, and doing good to all my Christian brethren and to the lost."

Yeshua said to him, "Depart from me, I never knew you," and threw this Christian minister out of His presence!

He continued, "I called you to comfort My Jewish people. What did you do for them?"

This goes right alongside the words of Yeshua in the book of Matthew:

> Then He will also say to those on His left, 'Depart from Me, accursed ones, into the eternal fire which has been prepared for the devil and his angels; for I was hungry, and you gave Me nothing to eat; I was thirsty, and you gave Me nothing to drink; I was a stranger, and you did not invite Me in; naked, and you did not clothe Me; sick, and in prison, and you did not visit Me.' Then they themselves also will answer, 'Lord, when did we see You hungry, or thirsty, or a stranger, or na-

ked, or sick, or in prison, and did not take care of You?' Then He will answer them, 'Truly I say to you, to the extent that you did not do it to one of the least of these, you did not do it to Me.' These will go away into eternal punishment, but the righteous into eternal life.

—Matthew 25:41-46 nasb '95

Who are the least of His brethren? Who was He talking about? This whole passage is about the judgment on the nations for the way they have treated the Jewish people, His brethren.

But when the Son of Man comes in His glory, and all the angels with Him, then He will sit on His glorious throne. All the nations will be gathered before Him; and He will separate them from one another, as the shepherd separates the sheep from the goats; and He will put the sheep on His right, and the goats on the left.

—Matthew 25:31-33 nasb '95

Restitution Time

For it is time for judgment to begin with the household of God; and if it begins with us first, what will be the outcome for those who do not obey the gospel of God?

—1 Peter 4:17 nasb '95

We must understand that judgment always starts in the house of God. In other words, He wants His own to be accountable to Him first. What can the majority of the church say at this point in time if they were asked the same question: What did you do to comfort and practically bless My Jewish people? How many would be going to the left (the side of the goats) instead of to the right (sheep)? This is an urgent question that demands an urgent answer and *action*.

Ask yourself, ask your pastor, ask your family, ministry, and friends: What have we done for Israel? How are we actively involved in making restitution for so many sins committed against the Jewish people through Christianity? Is this a message we don't want to hear any more? Have we really considered the seriousness of rejecting it?

King David's Wisdom

> Now there was a famine in the days of David for three years, year after year, so David sought the face of ADONAI. ADONAI replied, "It is because of Saul and his bloody house, for he put the Gibeonites to death.
>
> —2 SAMUEL 21:1

If King David had not made restitution to the Gibeonites for the bloodshed during Saul's reign, all of Israel would have starved to death. He was wise enough to understand that the sins of the ancestors affect us to this day.

> Thus, David said to the Gibeonites, "What should I do for you? And how can I make atonement so that you may bless the inheritance of the LORD?"
>
> —2 SAMUEL 21:3 NASB '95

But it is not only the ancestors, for large portions of the present-day church are totally divorced from Israel and will do nothing to comfort or bless God's chosen nation. Just like in the times of King David, as long as we are passive about Israel, a spiritual drought shall remain in the body. But as soon as *restitution* happens, we can expect revival!

> **For if their rejection is the reconciliation of the world, what will their acceptance be but life from the dead?**
>
> **—Romans 11:15 nasb '95**

Restitution must provoke the wronged party to *bless* the aggressor! Remember that the blood is crying vengeance from the ground, but when we make restitution, the cry of vengeance turns into a cry of forgiveness and blessing. That is the power of restitution! It is high time for all members of the body of Yeshua who profess to be children of God to act like David and make restitution through prayer, finances, and all other means to Israel and the Jewish people. Restitution is the order of the hour!

We have to proclaim this truth until this urgent message sounds loud and clear from every congregation, church, and Christian TV program and until every child of God is completely involved in an active manner in the restoration of Israel. This will turn the cry of the Jewish blood in the ground of Europe from vengeance to blessing and in any nation that has been influenced by European Christianity (most nations).

Passivity is Deathly

> **Because of violence to your brother Jacob, you will be covered with shame, and you will be cut off forever. "On the day that you stood aloof, on the day that strangers carried off his**

wealth, and foreigners entered his gate and cast lots for Jerusalem—You too were as one of them.

—Obadiah 1:10-11 nasb '95

This is the history of most Christians: They stood "aloof" (passive and separate) during all pogroms and the Nazi Shoah (Holocaust), and they stand "aloof" today when terror threatens Israel within and without, but YHVH is not "aloof." God's word says that those who "stood aloof" and are still standing aloof and passive shall be covered with shame. He says to give Him no rest on this issue:

On your walls, O Jerusalem, I have appointed watchmen; all day and all night they will never keep silent. You who remind the Lord, take no rest for yourselves; and give Him no rest until He establishes and makes Jerusalem a praise in the earth.

—Isaiah 62:6-7 nasb '95

Many Christian leaders get upset with this message, call it "radical" or "extreme," and continue leading their sheep to the slaughter of passivity. YHVH will judge the passive with the guilty, and there will be no distinction. Entire Christian churches are in danger of being covered with shame on this one issue. The call is to repent! It is better to be Biblically correct than "politically correct."

A Radical Ruth-Church is the Answer

This is the time for every Christian and Christian leader to find a way to bless in action the work of the Lord in the Land of Israel and among the Jewish people. The only way that this impending judgment can be overturned on your behalf and behalf of your nation is by displaying the love of Ruth towards Israel. Was Ruth a radical? Let us review her eternal words to her Jewish mother-in-law:

> But Ruth said, "Do not urge me to leave you or turn back from following you; for where you go, I will go, and where you lodge, I will lodge. Your people shall be my people, and your God, my God. Where you die, I will die, and there I will be buried. Thus, may the LORD do to me, and worse, if anything but death parts you and me."
>
> —RUTH 1:16-17 NASB '95

She literally laid down her life for Naomi and got grafted into Israel. But when she did that, the curse that YHVH Himself had uttered against the Moabites for refusing to help Israel in the desert was overturned!

> No Ammonite or Moabite is to enter the community of ADONAI—even to the tenth generation none belonging to them is to enter the community of ADONAI foreverbecause they did not meet you with bread and water on the way when you came out from Egypt, and because they hired against you Balaam son of Beor from Petor of Aram-naharaim to curse you. But ADONAI your God refused to listen to Balaam, and ADONAI your God turned the curse into a blessing for you because He loves you. You are never to seek their shalom or welfare all your days.
>
> —DEUTERONOMY 23:4-7

Ruth became the queen of Bethlehem and joined the royal line of King David and Messiah Yeshua. A cursed Moabite had the highest honor because she was making restitution for her people who did not help Israel in the desert.

> **Salmon was the father of Boaz by Rahab, Boaz was the father of Obed by Ruth, and Obed the father of Jesse. Jesse was the father of David the king.**
>
> —Matthew 1:5-6 nasb '95

Ask yourself: Who is your Naomi in Israel? Is there someone, some ministry in the land, to whom you have become their Ruth? If not, then you are still too passive, and it is time to seek YHVH to show you your Naomi, your contact point among the Jewish people, to make restitution on behalf of you and your Christian ancestors and your nation. I am certain that every Christian and every congregation and ministry should "adopt" one Israeli ministry to bless sacrificially, making restitution so that the cry of the blood for vengeance will be overturned by the blessings and thanksgiving of Yah's (God's) people in His land!

CHAPTER 51

THE AMALEK FACTOR IN THE WAR WITH HAMAS

Special Pillar of Cloud War Report

After 12 years and 12,000 rockets launched against innocent Israeli civilians around Gaza and the Negev, Israel started Operation Pillar of Cloud to bring some sort of quiet to this terribly battered area. The voices that are heard throughout the south of Israel, all the way from Ashdod to Eilat, are: Make sure that this time we truly destroy the terror infrastructures, for if we don't, the rockets will continue, and life will be unbearable again! The question is, what is the source of this seemingly never-ending conflict between Israel and the Arab nations? The source is what I would call "The Amalek Factor."

Who is Amalek?

> But the children struggled with one another inside her, and she said, "If it's like this, why is this happening to me?" So she went to inquire of ADONAI.
>
> —Genesis 25:22

Amalek is the grandson of Esau, who is the brother of Jacob and became his archenemy due to an ancient offense.

> Timna was a concubine of Esau's son Eliphaz and she bore Amalek to Eliphaz. These are the sons of Esau's wife Adah.
>
> —Genesis 36:12 NASB '95

This offense and anger are rooted in the fact that from the start, when the twins Jacob and Esau were in Rebecca's womb, YHVH said that the older would serve the younger.

> **Adonai said to her: "Two nations are in your womb, and two peoples from your body will be separated. One people will be stronger than the other people, but the older will serve the younger."**
>
> —Genesis 25:23

Later, we see that Jacob purchases the primacy from Esau and becomes the firstborn by election, since YHVH already told Rebecca that the oldest (Esau) will serve the younger (Jacob). Contrary to what most theologians have interpreted, Jacob is not a manipulative individual who stole the inheritance from his poor "abused" older brother, but rather Jacob is responding to a prophetic word given to his mother when he was still in the womb! His response was to be willing to obtain that inheritance, which he did by denying himself the pleasure of food and selling his food to his brother to obtain it. This is a legal purchase and transaction; this is an exchange. Esau couldn't have cared less about his rights as a firstborn, which included preeminence and the wealth of his father and, more than anything, the blessing of YHVH. Esau was a very carnal and even brutal man who cared only about his flesh, lust, and earthly desires. He was totally "earthly-minded" or "carnally-minded." Now, we can understand why YHVH loved Jacob and hated Esau from the start.

> Just as it is written, "Jacob I loved, but Esau I hated."
>
> —ROMANS 9:13 NASB '95

It is very revealing that in most Christian theologies and interpretations of the events that take place in Genesis 25, Jacob is always described as an "usurper" and Esau as the "underdog" or the wrongly abused party. Until today, that keeps happening when it comes to Israel and the Palestinians. In many Christian circles and also, of course, non-Christian international media, Israel is described as the usurper of "Palestinian land" and the "poor Palestinians" as victims when the reality is totally opposite to that perverted picture. The mindset of Jacob as a "usurper" must be eradicated by truth so we can see the real picture. Jacob was *obedient* to the prophetic Word and cherished it! Esau despised his inheritance.

> Esau said, "Behold, I am about to die; so, of what use then is the birthright to me?" And Jacob said, "First swear to me"; so he swore to him, and sold his birthright to Jacob. Then Jacob gave Esau bread and lentil stew; and he ate and drank and rose and went on his way. Thus, Esau despised his birthright.
>
> —GENESIS 25:32-34 NASB '95

Later, we see that Rebecca feels a personal responsibility concerning the prophetic Word that she received when the sons were in her womb, and she gives an instruction to Jacob. Jacob obeys his mother's instruction (who is actually willing to die for that prophetic word to come to pass). Therefore, he disguises himself as Esau and "tricks" his father, Jacob, into giving him the blessing of the firstborn.

> Now Rebekah was listening when Isaac was speaking to Esau his son. So while Esau went to the field to hunt game to bring in, Rebekah said to Jacob her son, "Look, I heard your father speaking to your brother Esau saying, ⁷ 'Bring me some game and prepare me a delicious meal that I may eat and bless you in ADONAI's presence before my death.' So now, my son, listen to my voice, to what I am commanding you. Go now to the flock and bring me two good young goats from there, so that I may prepare them as a delicious meal for your father—that he'll love. Then you'll bring it to your father to eat, so that he may bless you before his death. But Jacob said to Rebekah his mother, "Look, my brother Esau is a hairy man, but I'm a smooth man. Perhaps my father will touch me, and he'll take me for a mocker, and I'll bring upon myself a curse and not a blessing." Then his mother said to him, "Let your curse fall on me, my son. Just listen to me, and go, get them for me."
>
> —GENESIS 27:5-13

Many religious people would say that he lied, tricked, or manipulated and that he is a usurper! This is because they see the God of Israel with their "religious glasses" obtained from replacement theology and the Tree of Knowledge of Good and Evil. In the same way, we could say that Rahab, the prostitute that hid the Israeli spies, lied to her authorities in Jericho so the spies could escape or that Catholic nuns who hid Jews in Germany, Austria, and Poland to rescue them from the Nazis lied when asked by the authorities if they had any Jews in there. The truth of the matter is that this was the *only* way for Yah's prophetic word to come to pass since Isaac would not have agreed to the plan of YHVH because his "eyes were dim." He could not see very well physically, but actually, his problem was spiritual: he had lost his spiritual sight. For if not, why would he have called Esau to give him the blessing of the firstborn if Elohim had already spoken His sovereign will when the sons were in the womb?

> **Now it came about, when Isaac was old and his eyes were too dim to see, that he called his older son Esau and said to him, "My son." And he said to him, "Here I am."**
>
> —**Genesis 27:1 nasb '95**

Therefore, Rebecca had to act in great wisdom despite the carnality of her husband! We can see this type of situation also at the time of David, when Abigail, the wife of Nabal, had to act behind the back of her own husband to prevent a catastrophe from happening (1 Samuel 25).

It would definitely have been a catastrophe if Esau had received the blessing of the firstborn and thus had the Word of YHVH fall to the ground. That, of course, could not happen, and therefore, the way that Rebecca and her son Jacob acted was not in "usurpation" but in obedience to the prophetic Word and taking into consideration that Jacob had already purchased the inheritance for a "lentil stew" and that Esau had willingly relinquished it. So, both spiritual protocol (the prophetic word of promise) and earthly protocol (the actual purchase) had already come to pass.

Having established the fact that Jacob is not a usurper, now we connect with the true meaning of his name Yaakov, which means "to follow closely," and indeed, he followed closely after the instructions of YHVH, and like his mother, he was a follower of the Almighty all his life!

Esau's Murder Vow

> So, Esau bore a grudge against Jacob because of the blessing with which his father had blessed him; and Esau said to himself, "The days of mourning for my father are near; then I will kill my brother Jacob.
>
> —Genesis 27:41 NASB '95

Esau was so angry with Jacob for supposedly "stealing" his inheritance and firstborn rights that, like every carnal victim, he became a murderer and vowed to kill Jacob. From then on, Jacob would have to protect himself from Esau's murderous attitude. We can see that this vow of Esau to kill the promised seed (Jacob, Israel) is haunting Israel until this day, and it kept on manifesting through the offspring of Esau, namely Amalek, who attacked the Israelites fiercely in the desert upon their exodus from Egyptian slavery.

> Then the Amalekites came and fought with Israel at Rephidim.
> ADONAI said to Moses, "Write this for a memorial in the book, and rehearse it in the hearing of Joshua, for I will utterly blot out the memory of the Amalekites from under heaven." Then Moses built an altar, and called the name of it ADONAI-Nissi. Then he said, "By the hand upon the throne of ADONAI, ADONAI will have war with Amalek from generation to generation."
>
> —Exodus 17:8, 14-16

YHVH promised that He (not Israel) will have a battle with Amalek from generation to generation, completely blotting out the very memory of Amalek! King Saul lost the crown and received a generational curse because he refused to obey this instruction to completely annihilate all Amalekites.

> Since you did not obey the voice of ADONAI and did not execute His fierce wrath on Amalek, so ADONAI has done this to you today. Moreover, ADONAI will also give the Israelites who are with you into the hand of the Philistines. Tomorrow you and your sons will be with me! Yes, ADONAI will give the army of Israel into the hand of the Philistines.
>
> —1 SAMUEL 28:18-19

The name Palestinian is derived from the name Philistine. The only way to get rid of the conflict between Israel and the nations is to defeat Amalek, which tries to annihilate Israel through the PLO and all its derivatives like the Fatah, Hamas, Hezbollah, Al Qaeda, and others.

Important Fact

The PLO is Hitler's Child! The Grand Mufti of Jerusalem, Haj Amin al-Husseini, visited Adolf Hitler in 1942 and asked him to build the Arabs in the then-called Palestine a "Nazi Army" to implement the Final Solution against the Jews in the Land of Israel. Hitler gladly agreed, and he trained this army to become the Palestinian Liberation Organization, the PLO, as a "trojan horse" in the land. The PLO will use politics, world opinion, and terror to reach its goal, which from the start was the annihilation of Israel, the fulfillment of Esau's murder vow.

Because Saul did not do his job right, Amalek is still attacking Israel from the rear, especially the weak, the children, and the women. That is exactly the tactic of "Palestinian terror."

> Remember what Amalek did to you along the way when you came out from Egypt, how he met you along the way and attacked among you all the stragglers at your rear when you were faint and weary; and he did not fear God.
>
> —Deuteronomy 25:17-19 nasb '95

That is the tactic of Islam, and it is called *hudna*. "When your enemy is strong, make peace with him, but when he is weak, attack and conquer." That has always been Amalek's tactic. Do not be fooled by any political move to achieve peace with Hitler's Child!

During Queen Esther's time, Haman the Agagite was an Amalekite who tried to annihilate Israel again, but he was stopped by Mordechai's keen perception and the intervention of Queen Hadassah (Esther) (See the Book of Esther). So, we can see that all the descendants of Esau and Amalek carry within them the seed of hatred and murder against Jacob-Israel and all her descendants.

Another name for Esau is *Edom* (meaning red because of the red lentil stew by which he sold his primacy to Jacob) and *Seir* (*hairy*) because he had lots of hair. Both the book of Obadiah and Ezekiel 35 tell us that the end of Esau, Edom or Seir, is total destruction because of his hatred against Jacob-Israel.

> "Son of man, set your face against Mount Seir and prophesy against it."
> "therefore, as I live"—it is a declaration of Adonai—"I will deal with you with the same anger and envy that you had because of your hatred against them. I will make Myself known among them, when I judge you."
>
> —Ezekiel 35:2, 11

The Dwelling Place of Amalek

> Amalek is living in the land of the Negev and the Hittites and the Jebusites and the Amorites are living in the hill country, and the Canaanites are living by the sea and by the side of the Jordan.
>
> —Numbers 13:29 NASB '95

Esau was born in the Negev, in the area of Beersheba, and later established himself in the land of Edom right across the city of Eilat and the Red Sea, which is the south gate of the Negev. From the windows of the Eilat Prayer Tower, we overlook the Mountains of Edom. Edom or *adom* means *red*. Esau inherited this name because he sold his inheritance for a stew of *red* lentils. His grandson Amalek dwells in the Negev (south desert of Israel). The Negev starts from Ashdod and Ashkelon in the north, all the way to Eilat. Therefore, we can see why Hamas in Gaza has been targeting the Negev and trying their best to murder the Israeli citizens there and to discourage them so they leave the Negev! The battle with Amalek is the battle for the Negev, which is the inheritance of the Sephardic (Spanish) Jews.

> And the exiles of Jerusalem who are in Sepharad will possess the cities of the Negev.
>
> —Obadiah 1:20b NASB '95

The Negev is the future of Israel according to our historical (after 2000 years of exile) first Prime Minister David Ben Gurion, and it is 55% of the land within the modern-day State of Israel. The battle with Amalek will be decided in the Negev! To strengthen the Negev with

Jewish presence and more and more new immigrants is the mandate of the hour. The proper response to this threat from Hamas is to let the *anusim* (descendants of the Spanish Jews who lost their identity due to the Spanish Inquisition) settle the Negev at the speed of light!

> The ransomed of ADONA will return and come to Zion with singing, with everlasting joy upon their heads. They will obtain gladness and joy, and sorrow and sighing will flee away.
>
> —ISAIAH 35:10

The Birth of Islam-Amalek Unmasked

> Because of violence to your brother Jacob, you will be covered with shame, and you will be cut off forever.
>
> —OBADIAH 1:10

This seed of hatred and murder became a world-conquering religion called Islam, born of hatred, jealousy, and murder through a very violent man called Muhammed, who became the prophet of Islam. Because the seed of hatred is so strong in the descendants of Esau (and others like Ishmael and Egypt), Islam took root, especially among the Arabs, and thus, *all* Arab nations have Muslim rule. In every country where Islam takes root, there is great violence, hatred, and terror. Islam sees Jews and Christians as their target. It calls Israel "the little Satan" and the USA "the big Satan." There is no such thing as "mild Islam." Mild Islam is not Islam but another hybrid religion, since the foundation of Islam is *Jihad*, which is a "holy Muslim war," to conquer until the whole world is Muslim and all other non-Muslims live under "the boot" of Islam as second-class citizens.

Please notice that Islam's god, Allah, is not YHVH, the God of Israel, but an idol that Mohamed and his family worshiped. It is a type of "moon god" represented by the symbol of Islam, the moon crescent. Since the Koran (Muslim book) and Islam is a replacement for Torah and Judaism, then everything in it tries to be "better than" the Jews. If the Jews pray three times a day, the Muslims pray five times! If the Jews fast one day a year (Yom Kippur), the Muslims will fast 30 days (Ramadan); if the Jews celebrate Shabbat, the Muslims will "one-up" them by one day and will take Friday as the day of worship. If the Jews do not eat pork and shellfish, the Muslims will not eat pork but will feast on shellfish, and so on. As the promised son is Isaac, the Muslims based their entire religion on Ishmael being the son of promise and, therefore, will never stop trying to annihilate Israel and to conquer the land promised to Abraham, Isaac, and Jacob until 1000 generations!

> **He has remembered His covenant forever, the word which He commanded to a thousand generations, the covenant which He made with Abraham and His oath to Isaac. Then He confirmed it to Jacob for a statute, to Israel as an everlasting covenant, saying, "To you I will give the land of Canaan as the portion of your inheritance,"**
>
> **—Psalm 105:8-11 nasb '95**

As long as the Arab world remains Muslim, the Israeli-Arab conflict shall continue. The only hope is repentance from Islam and the ancient murder vow of Esau. Remember that Amalek and all of Edom (Esau) are promised total destruction by YHVH Himself:

And he looked at Amalek and took up his discourse and said, "Amalek was the first of the nations, but his end shall be destruction."*

—Numbers 24:20 nasb '95

---

* Listen to the Purim 2024 teaching *Exposing Haman, Amalek and Hamas*. Order at www.zionsgospel.com/product-category/teaching-series

CHAPTER 52

THE RISE AND FALL OF THE MOSQUITO KILLER

After glory He has sent me against the nations which plunder you, for he who touches you, touches the apple of His eye.

— ZECHARIAH 2:8 NASB '95

Almost everyone is talking about the danger that Israel is in because of the nuclear bomb in Iran and, of course, the pressure from all the Arab nations around her. But not many realize that Iran and all the other anti-Zionist nations are in a much more dangerous predicament than Israel! Poking the Almighty in the "apple of His eye" is bound to cause a terrible reaction.

From Arutz 7, 5/2012

This past week President Ahmadinejad of Iran likened Israel to a mosquito that there is no need to be afraid of and of course (implied) it is easy to smash.

Iranian President Mahmoud Ahmadinejad compared Israel to an annoying insect on Saturday, maintaining that the Jewish state poses no threat to Tehran's nuclear program.

"Israel is nothing more than a mosquito which cannot see the broad horizon of the Iranian nation," he said in northeastern

Iran's Khorasan province, according to the semi-official Fars news agency.

After reading this fascinating description of Israel's insignificance, I remembered that all the past empires that have likened Israel to vermin, insects, rats, cockroaches, and the like are simply no more! Therefore, it is obvious to me that very soon, we will be telling the story of the rise and fall of Ahmadinejad and the Iranian "empire."

> For ADONAI is enraged at all the nations, and furious at all their armies. He will utterly destroy them. He will give them over to slaughter.
> For ADONAI has a day of vengeance, a year of recompense for the hostility against Zion.
>
> —ISAIAH 34:2, 8

I would like to mention here that this "insignificant mosquito" called Israel is mentioned more than 2000 times in the Holy Book. So, even if the world thinks of Israel as "insignificant" because of its size and past history of great suffering and persecution, YHVH, the Almighty, thinks the world of her. You really must be in love with someone to mention her over 2000 times in your book!

> Thus says ADONAI: "The people surviving the sword found grace in the wildernesswhere I gave Israel rest." "From afar ADONAI appeared to me." "Yes, I have loved you with an everlasting love. Therefore I have drawn you with lovingkindness. Again I will build you, so you will be rebuilt, virgin Israel! Again you will take up your tambourines as ornaments, and go out to dances of merrymakers."
>
> —JEREMIAH 31:1-3

Egypt to Follow the Mosquito Killer

They have said, "Come, and let us wipe them out as a nation, that the name of Israel be remembered no more." for they have conspired together with one mind; against You they make a covenant.

—Psalm 83:4-5 nasb '95

Tzvi Ben Gedalyahu writes on Arutz 7* about Egypt and the Northern "Axis of Evil:"

> Israel may face a new Iranian-Egyptian threat if presidential candidate Hisham El-Bastawisi wins his bid to succeed Egyptian President Hosni Mubarak, whose ousting he encouraged.
>
> Backed by the left-wing Tagammu party, El-Bastawisi said on Saturday that building good relations with Iran would be one of his highest priorities. Israel already faces a northern "axis of evil" by the alliance between Iran, Syria, and Lebanon.
>
> El-Bastawisi also promised to revise the Camp David Accords to allow the army to increase an armed presence in the Sinai Peninsula, the Egyptian website Ahram reported.

Increasing an armed presence in the Sinai Peninsula is a direct threat to the City of Eilat and the whole Negev. We must pray that YHVH will smash these evil plans like mosquitos!

In Isaiah 19, we learn that the Almighty will smash Egypt, and only after it is thoroughly humbled will He heal it. Egypt will then be at peace with Israel and become a blessing.

---

* "Egyptian Presidential Hopeful Backs Ties with Iran" Israel National News Arutz Sheva, Tzvi Ben Gedalyahu, May 13, 2012, 3:51 PM Accessed 4/1/2024

> So ADONAI will strike Egypt—striking yet healing—so they will return to ADONAI, and He will respond to them and heal them.
>
> —ISAIAH 19:22

Is this the time for this prophecy to come to pass in Egypt? It certainly looks that way! In fact, the removal of President Mubarak has made way for a much more hostile regime against Israel to arise in Egypt. This, of course, is a well-known ticket for disaster as YHVH promised to curse those who curse Israel.

> The burden of Egypt: Behold, ADONAI rides upon a swift cloud and comes to Egypt. Egypt's idols tremble before Him and Egypt's heart melts within them. I will stir up Egyptian against Egyptian. Everyone will fight against his brother, and everyone against his neighborcity against city, kingdom against kingdom. The spirit of Egypt will drain within it, and I will confuse its counsel. So they will resort to idols, charmers, mediums and familiar spirits. I will give the Egyptians into the hand of a cruel mastera fierce king will rule over them. It is a declaration of ADONAI-Tzva'ot.
>
> —ISAIAH 19:1-4

Will Israel Attack Iran?

> So now, O kings, be wise, take warning, O judges of the earth! Serve ADONAI with fear, and rejoice with trembling. Kiss the Son, lest He become angry, and you perish along your way.
>
> —PSALM 2:10-12A

The most important move of Prime Minister Netanyahu has been to form a unity government with Shaul Mofaz from Kadima Party, the past Chief of Staff of the IDF, the army of Israel. Though there is a political agenda here, this is a very wise move as it gets the right person, with the right experience at the right time, on the right Hand of Benjamin Netanyahu. *Benjamin* means "the son of the right hand."

I have no doubt that Prime Minister Netanyahu is seriously considering the possibility, but as usual, the US may want to stop it to protect itself, especially before the elections. Barack Obama may not want to have his name involved in a dangerous war at this moment, as he is running with all his might and with slim chances to be reelected. So, Israel may have to decide all alone!

Come what may, we need to realize that no empire ever survived a direct affront against God's holy people, Israel—and Iran is no exception! Our prayer is that in the midst of judgment, YHVH will remember to be merciful to the Farsi people (the original Persians) who hate their own Islamic regime and who yearn for freedom. In the face of all these threats, let us continue praying for revival in Israel and for courage to stand in faith because of the Word of the covenant.

> **The wicked flee when no one pursues, but the righteous are bold as a lion.**
>
> —Proverbs 28:1 nasb '95

May Israel arise as a lion in the face of all mosquito killers!

> **"Be silent before Adonai, all flesh, for He has aroused Himself from His holy dwelling."**
>
> —Zechariah 2:17

CHAPTER 53

TYCOONS OF RIGHTEOUSNESS

A Tribute to the 64th Anniversary
of the Re-Born State of Israel

That they might be called oaks of righteousness, the planting of ADONAI, that He may be glorified.

— ISAIAH 61:3B

This week (from Wednesday night), we are celebrating the 64th "Yom Haatsmaut," the anniversary of establishing the State of Israel. The biggest miracle of the 20th Century was the rebirth of the people of Israel in their own land as promised to Abraham, Isaac, and Jacob.

> He has remembered His covenant forever, the word which He commanded to a thousand generations, the covenant which He made with Abraham, and His oath to Isaac. Then He confirmed it to Jacob for a statute, to Israel as an everlasting covenant, saying, "To you I will give the land of Canaan as the portion of your inheritance.
> Psalms 105:8-11 nasb '95

The biggest miracle of the 21st Century is that Israel is still standing and thriving! Despite being surrounded by hateful Muslim nations, despite being the "punching bag" of the international media and being infiltrated with suicide bombers from within, Kassam rockets from Gaza and Katyusha rockets from Lebanon, and despite having to accommodate large quantities of Jews making aliyah (new immigrants) and needing a huge military budget because of the situation and the needs of self-defense, Israel is still prospering and actually is in much better financial shape than the nearby nations of Europe that are struggling with a possible collapse of the Euro.

The celebrations of the 64th anniversary of Israel this year come under the mark of a great awakening and awesome occurrences, as prophesied by Isaiah in chapter 64.

> Oh, that You would rend the heavens and come down, that the mountains might quake at Your presenceAs fire kindles the brushwood, as fire causes water to boilTo make Your name known to Your adversaries, that the nations may tremble at Your presence!
>
> —Isaiah 64:1-2 nasb '95

Israel a Blessing to the Nations

> And I will make you a great nation, and I will bless you, and make your name great; and so, you shall be a blessing.
>
> —Genesis 12:2

We recently came back from the Island of Rhodes, one of the 12 Greek Islands called "Dodecanese Islands." As you well know, Greece has been on the verge of a terrible financial collapse and is being held through "artificial financial respiration" from the international community. Rhodes totally depends on incoming tourism; without tourism, it cannot survive. So, who is keeping Rhodes alive financially? Mostly Israelis. The largest incoming tourism group in Rhodes is Israelis. It is good to know that the modern-day State of Israel is blessing Greece financially. In fact, Israel has been a blessing to many, many nations financially and through her expertise in agriculture, science, education, and technology. Israel has constantly championed the cause of the "underdogs" and has absorbed many Muslim refugees from war-torn Sudan, and in the past also from Vietnam and others. Whenever there is a catastrophe, a tsunami, or an earthquake in the world (even in enemy countries like Turkey), Israel is the first to send rescue teams and field hospitals with highly qualified medical teams.

Little Israel or Superpower?

Little Israel functions as a superpower when it comes to helping and blessing the nations. Despite all of her internal and external struggles, despite this being a nation built by Shoah (Holocaust) survivors, Israel is always willing to super extend and expend herself in blessing the nations. She is not perfect in any way, but please show me another nation the size of Israel that is influencing the world for good as Israel is! This is the divine call of Israel: to be a light unto the nations and a source of blessing for all nations.

Look at these examples:

Earthquake in China, May 2008:

In a gesture of support, one of the world's smallest countries is sending aid to the world's most populous nation in the form of $1.5 million worth of equipment for earthquake relief. The first three tons of Israeli supplies to earthquake-ravaged China included sleeping bags, blankets, and personal water purification units. The supplies arrived in China May 22 on an El Al flight to Beijing. Israel will send the remaining 70-90 tons of equipment on a cargo plane directly to the city of Chengdu in the coming days. The Israeli government is working from a list of needs drawn up by the Chinese government. Israelis and Jews in China are also helping with the relief effort in Sichuan province. Dini's kosher restaurant in Beijing is donating 10 percent of this month's sales toward the earthquake relief effort.[*]

Earthquake in Haiti, January 2010:

The Israeli Foreign Ministry has prepared a 220-member rescue team for departure to the disaster-stricken country, including elite army corps engineers and a field hospital. The military has leased two Boeing 747s from El Al airlines to transport the team and equipment.

Earthquake in Turkey, August 1999:

Immediately after news of the earthquake disaster in Turkey, the Israeli government made preparations to extend emergency assistance. On August 17, Israel Air Force planes airlifted the Israeli team, comprising 250 persons, as well as sophisticated rescue equipment and rescue dogs. The Israeli team began almost immediately to work at several locations, in coordination with the Turkish government.

On August 18, an additional IAF plane was sent to Turkey, carrying the staff and equipment for a field hospital, which will comprise two hospital wards for adults and children, an isolation room, an operating room, an X-ray laboratory, two clinics, and medical equipment.

---

[*] www.greenpagan.newsvine.com/_news/2008/05/27/1514692-

The Search and Rescue Team of the IDF Home Front Command, established in its present form in 1984, performs search and rescue operations in Israel and abroad, in both routine and emergency situations. (In the earthquake of October 2011, Turkey refused to receive any help from Israel though the Israeli government offered it immediately!)

Israelis are Called to be Tycoons of Righteousness

> So they will be called oaks of righteousness, the planting of YHVH, that He may be glorified.
>
> —Isaiah 61:3b

The word translated to *trees of righteousness* here is *eilei tsedek,* which also means magnates, chiefs, and Lords; its synonyms are: baron, captain, czar king, lion, Lord, mogul, monarch, Napoleon, prince, tycoon.[*]

In other words, they will be very wealthy, influential, and righteous! That is the call of Israel as a nation and the call of everyone in the nations who are grafted into the Olive tree with Israel through the blood of Yeshua.

> But if some of the branches were broken off, and you, being a wild olive, were grafted in among them and became partaker with them of the rich root of the olive tree.
>
> —Romans 11:17 nasb '95

The true Gospel "made in Zion" always called us to greatness, but all kinds of religious traditions and replacement theology have

---

[*] www.merriam-webster.com

"impoverished" the Gospel, and instead of good news, we have mainly received mixed news at best and mostly bad news! But the true "Jewish Gospel" that Yeshua the Messiah preached is a Gospel of greatness; it is a Gospel that makes magnates out of us, that makes us into tycoons of righteousness, that makes us great!

> "Do not think that I came to abolish the Law or the Prophets; I did not come to abolish but to fulfill. For truly I say to you, until heaven and earth pass away, not the smallest letter or stroke shall pass from the Law until all is accomplished. Whoever then annuls one of the least of these commandments, and teaches others to do the same, shall be called least in the kingdom of heaven; but whoever keeps and teaches them, he shall be called great in the kingdom of heaven.
>
> —Matthew 5:17-19 nasb '95

The Word of Elohim (God) in the Hebrew Holy Scriptures (wrongly called "Old Testament") is very clear about the terms of the covenant with the Living God. Righteousness is always rewarded, holiness is always a blessing, and obedience always releases the blessing. The outcome of the true Gospel made in Zion that brings salvation, healing, and deliverance is the glory!

> To console those who mourn in Zion, to give them beauty for ashes, the oil of joy for mourning, the garment of praise for the spirit of heaviness, that they might be called oaks of righteousness, the planting of Adonai, that He may be glorified.
>
> —Isaiah 61:3

When we are saved, healed, and set free from bondage through the Spirit and power of Elohim, the blood, and the name of Yeshua, we move from the abject poverty of spirit and in the natural to being glorious tycoons of righteousness! We become builders and restorers; we become landowners and vineyard planters. We become priests of the Most High and enjoy the wealth of the nations. Everything in our lives becomes royal and blessed!

> They will rebuild the ancient ruins. They will restore former desolations. They will repair the ruined cities, the desolations of many generations. Strangers will stand and shepherd your flocks, children of foreigners will be your plowmen and vinedressers. But you will be called the kohanim of ADONAI, they will speak of you as the ministers of our God. You will eat the wealth of nations and boast in their abundance.
>
> —ISAIAH 61:4-6

Since Israel has been restored as a nation in its own promised and covenant land, the nations have greatly profited. Israel is already showing signs of fulfilling its mandate of being tycoons of righteousness even in her unredeemed state. Can you imagine what it will be like when all of Israel is saved? It will be life from the dead to all the nations of the world!

> For if their rejection is the reconciliation of the world, what will their acceptance be but life from the dead?
>
> —ROMANS 11:15 NASB '95

Israel is a nation of builders and restorers; the very spirit and anointing of restoration rests in the entire nation of Israel. So, when Israel is restored, her anointing of restoration is released for the sake of all the nations of the world. That is why the Word tells us that the Messiah will only return when all of Israel is restored.

> Repent, therefore, and return—so your sins might be blotted out, so times of relief might come from the presence of ADONAI and He might send Yeshua, the Messiah appointed for you. Heaven must receive Him, until the time of the restoration of all the things that God spoke about long ago through the mouth of His holy prophets.
>
> —ACTS 3:19-21

The restoration of Israel brings about the return of the Messiah, and Messiah ruling from Jerusalem with His Israeli tycoons of righteousness will bring about the restoration of all the surviving nations after the great tribulation or the great judgment of the nations that have come against Israel. All the nations of the world will come up to Zion to pay homage to the King of kings, the King of the Jews, the King of all tycoons of righteousness!

> "Indeed, many peoples and powerful nations will come to seek ADONAI-Tzva'ot in Jerusalem, and to entreat the favor of ADONAI." Thus says ADONAI-Tzva'ot, "In those days it will come to pass that ten men from every language of the nations will grasp the corner of the garment of a Jew saying, 'Let us go with you, for we have heard that God is with you.'"
>
> —ZECHARIAH 8:22-23

We invite you to pray and bless this nation that is raised from the dead to be a blessing to all nations! Come and visit her and partake of her great calling to be a restorer and a blesser of all nations of the earth.*

---

* To join our Israel tours, visit at www.Kad-Esh.org, press on Tours

And I will bless those who bless you, and the one who curses you I will curse and in you all the families of the earth will be blessed.

—Genesis 12:3 nasb '95

CHAPTER 54

SPIDERS OVER AN OPEN FLAME

> And the Lord will cause His voice of authority to be heard, and the descending of His arm to be seen in fierce anger, and in the flame of a consuming fire in cloudburst, downpour and hailstones.
>
> — ISAIAH 30:30 NASB '95

The pressure on Israel to relinquish the Promised Land is in all flanks. The latest in this year, 2012, is that the Vatican has negotiated with Israel a hideous agreement to have sovereignty over the Upper Room in Mount Zion. The problem is that the Tomb of King David is also on Mount Zion, adjacent to the Upper Room or the Last Supper Room. However, the hunger of the Vatican does not stop there, as it is also negotiating portions of the Mount of Olives and the Temple Mount. The purpose is to actually remove the Jewish presence from the holy sites that are connected with the return of the Messiah. What is most distressing is that the Israeli government, in its desperation for acceptance from the nations, has been yielding to these dangerous requests. Jerusalem is going towards a takeover of the three monotheistic religions!

The Holy City is becoming increasingly religious in every aspect. Extreme Haredi (Orthodox Jews) have been moving into Jerusalem by thousands in the last few years. Extreme Muslims flood Jerusalem every Friday to pray Jihad ("holy war") against Israel at the Al Aqsa Mosque on the Temple Mount (the site of Mount Moriah and where the Holy Temple and the Ark rested), and now staunch Catholics are flooding the Holy City more than ever before. Most of these groups are dressed in black garments. Jerusalem has always been called the City of the Three Faiths but under Jewish sovereignty. This Jewish sovereignty is now being seriously threatened as Jerusalem is being divided and dished out to Islam and Catholicism. This is hastening the day of judgment in many nations. And just like the garments of the different religious groups are mostly black, so there are black clouds over many nations with the threat of much more stormy weather ahead.

> For behold, in those days and at that time, when I restore the fortunes of Judah and Jerusalem, I will gather all the nations and bring them down to the valley of Jehoshaphat. Then I will enter into judgment with them there on behalf of My people and My inheritance, Israel, whom they have scattered among the nations; and they have divided up My land.
>
> —Joel 3:1-2 nasb '95

Sinners in the Hands of an Angry God

The famous revivalist of the Great Awakening, Jonathan Edwards, preached in Connecticut in 1741 a sermon that unleashed the fear of Yah (God) in religious Christian America in an unprecedented manner. This long, poignant, and scary sermon caused the repentance of thousands! He likened humans as "spiders over an open flame." The condition of the unrepentant and unredeemed is so flimsy that they are like these spiders at the mercy of the whims of the Creator. If He chooses, He can let them fall into the flames in a flicker of a second! Edwards describes very graphically how serious it is to resist the Living God. His famous sermon is based on the Word only. As serious as it is to resist salvation through Messiah Yeshua, it is also very serious to resist His plan for the restoration of Israel (Read Psalms 83).

Jonathan Edwards was preaching to the "church goers" of his time:

The God that holds you over the pit of hell, much as one holds a spider, or some loathsome insect over the fire, abhors you, and is dreadfully provoked: His wrath towards you burns like fire; He looks upon you as worthy of nothing else, but to be cast into the fire; He is of purer eyes than to bear to have you in His sight; you are ten thousand times more abominable in His eyes, than the most hateful venomous serpent is in ours. You have offended Him infinitely more than ever a stubborn rebel did his prince, and yet it is nothing but His hand that holds you from falling into the fire every moment. It is to be ascribed to nothing else that you did not go to hell the last night; that you were suffered to awake again in this world after you closed your eyes to sleep. And there is no other reason to be given, why you have not dropped into hell since you arose in the morning, but that God's hand has held you up. There is no other reason to be given why you have not gone to hell, since you have sat here in the house of God, provoking His pure eyes by your sinful wicked manner of attending His solemn worship. Yea, there is nothing else that is to be given as a reason why you do not this very moment drop down into hell.*

---

* Sinners in the Hands of an Angry God. (2024, January 5). In Wikipedia. en.wikipedia.org/wiki/Sinners_in_the_Hands_of_an_Angry_God; www.minio.la.utexas.edu/webeditor-files/coretexts/pdf/174120sinners20angry20god.pdf

Nations Like a Spider Over an Open Flame

> For ADONAI is enraged at all the nations, and furious at all their armies. He will utterly destroy them...
> For ADONAI has a day of vengeance, a year of recompense for the hostility against Zion.
>
> —Isaiah 34:2, 8

There are many nations that are hanging like a "spider over an open flame" because of their ungodly "political behavior" towards Israel, the people, and the land. Consider that unless true and poignant repentance-*teshuva* falls on many nations, they could be destroyed in a flicker of a second, just like New Orleans during Hurricane Katrina or large portions of Thailand during the Great Tsunami in 20001. It can happen as fast and dramatic as the Twin Towers that fell on 9/11! What I find most astounding is that the world goes on as if nothing has happened or nothing is happening. And what I find even more disturbing is that large portions of the church are totally asleep, unaware the nation they are in is under heavy judgment and actually has been promised total destruction because of the "cause of Zion." (Isaiah 34:8)

YHVH has already pre-judged and pre-destroyed all the nations that oppose the restoration of Israel in its own land. This is a done deal, and the fact that He has not fully implemented it *yet* is because some true saints and believers are standing in the gap and holding His hand from striking! It is only because of those who are actively praying and working towards the restoration of Israel that He is still waiting, but not for long, beloved, not for long.*

---

* Read Isaiah 34

A Matter of Life and Death

The repentance of the church in the nations concerning replacement theology is a matter of life and death. Unfortunately, many hear with uncircumcised ears as if it is just a nice cliché: "a matter of life and death." But remember that when people say, "peace and safety," sudden destruction comes! Do you know how many people have lost their homes in the USA and all over the world because of storms, floods, and recession?

CBC News, Mon, June 6, 2011, 01:28 CDT

About 42 million people were forced to flee their homes because of natural disasters around the world in 2010, more than double the number during the previous year, experts said Monday. One reason for the increase in the figure could be climate change, and the international community should be doing more to contain it, the experts said.

The Internal Displacement Monitoring Centre said the increase from 17 million displaced people in 2009 was mainly due to the impact of "mega-disasters" such as the massive floods in China and Pakistan and the earthquakes in Chile and Haiti.

It said more than 90 per cent of the disaster displacements were caused by weather-related hazards such as floods and storms that were probably impacted by global warming, but it couldn't say to what extent.*

"The intensity and frequency of extreme weather events is increasing, and this trend is only set to continue. With all probability, the number of those affected and displaced will rise as

---

* CBC News, Mon, June 6, 2011, 01:28 CDT, *Associated Press*

human-induced climate change comes into full force," said Elisabeth Rasmusson, the secretary general of the Norwegian Refugee Council.*

Stormy Weather

So pursue them with Your tempest and terrify them with Your storm.

—Psalms 83:15 nasb '95

In 2004, as we were landing in South Korea, the Almighty spoke to me and said: "You will be writing another book. It shall be called *Stormy Weather*.** We spent a week in Prayer Mountain, and while rabbi and another intercessor were praying, I wrote *Stormy Weather* in five days! We launched it in Japan about a month later. This book should be distributed in the thousands and millions and should be in the hands of all governments of the earth. It contains the *key* to get rescued from the stormy weather ahead! It is time for a *great awakening* all over the nations to the fact that if entire nations do not repent for pressurizing Israel to relinquish land, they are already like "spiders over an open flame!" We have no time to waste! Indeed, we have an angry God that is ready to judge. The Judge is at the door of many nations as I write.

Urgency

This is so urgent that even as we think or we linger, terrible floods and "natural disasters" are being prepared, not to mention terror waves, recession, bankruptcies, and foreclosures. I do not like to "sour the

---

* www.preventionweb.net/news/42-million-displaced-sudden-natural-hazards-2010-study
** Order the *Stormy Weather* book at www.ZionsGospel.com

party," but I do not want the blood of the nations on my hands. We must preach this message everywhere, through every channel, harnessing every technology possible. Each one of us is called urgently to the greatest army of all times to preach the Gospel made in Zion towards Yeshua and to preach the love of Israel. Spiders cannot remain for too long over an open flame without being completely scorched.

> ADONAI will inherit Judah as His portion in the holy land and will once again choose Jerusalem. Be silent before ADONAI, all flesh, for He has aroused Himself from His holy dwelling.
>
> —ZECHARIAH 2:16-17

The Land of Goshen

Just like YHVH separated the children of Israel from the Egyptians when He plagued Egypt, He is making a distinction between Israel and the nations and between those in the church who are His and those who are not. The new covenant tells us clearly about the separation of individuals (sheep and goats) and nations (sheep and goat nations).

> All the nations will be gathered before Him; and He will separate them from one another, as the shepherd separates the sheep from the goats.
>
> —MATTHEW 25:32 NASB '95

The Messiah of Israel

Are there not many here who have lived long in the world, and are not to this day born again? And so are aliens from the commonwealth of Israel, and have done nothing ever since they have lived, but treasure up wrath against the day of wrath?*

The division line between Goshen and Egypt—whether people have put their trust in the Messiah of Israel, Yeshua, or not—is not between Christians or non-Christians. Yeshua did not bring Christianity into the world; Constantine** did! There are multitudes of so-called "Christians" who do not believe in the Jewish Messiah.

> **Loved ones, do not believe every spirit, but test the spirits to see if they are from God. For many false prophets have gone out into the world. You know the Ruach Elohim by this—every spirit that acknowledges that Messiah Yeshua has come in human flesh is from God, but every spirit that does not acknowledge Yeshua is not from God. This is the spirit of the anti-messiah, which you have heard is coming and now is already in the world.**
>
> **—1 John 4:1-3**

Whoever rejects His Jewishness rejects Him; there is no other Messiah. There is no Christian Messiah; there is only a Jewish Messiah. Think about this: if you reject the Jewishness of the Messiah (the way He came in the flesh is as a Jew), you are actually worshiping another god, a god of your own making, a "cultural god." Paul said that it is the Spirit of anti-Messiah or anti-Christ.

Large portions of the "church" are actually worshiping "another god," and they have not even noticed that they are also like "spiders over an open flame". It is very scary as we are coming to the end of the times of the Gentiles, and repentance needs to be swift. All those

---

* From "Sinners in the Hands of an Angry God" by Jonathan Edwards on July 8, 1741.
** The Emeror of Eastern Rome who through the Council of Nicaea in 325 established Christianity as an official religion of the Byzant

Christians who are arrogant against Israel and the Jewish roots of the Gospel are in danger of being cut off the olive tree! They can be Protestants, Catholics, Evangelicals, Pentecostals, and Charismatics; it does not matter—any arrogance against the Jewish branches and the Hebrew foundations of faith will be swiftly punished. This is a covenant issue! Gentiles do not *replace* Israel on the olive tree but rather *join* Israel.

> **Do not be arrogant toward the branches; but if you are arrogant, remember that it is not you who supports the root, but the root supports you. For if God did not spare the natural branches, He will not spare you, either. Behold then the kindness and severity of God; to those who fell, severity, but to you, God's kindness, if you continue in His kindness; otherwise you also will be cut off.**
>
> —Romans 11:21-22 nasb '95

We are preaching this message with great urgency and out of great love for all who would listen. I know the time is short, much shorter than most know. The news agrees with me more than most pastors and preachers. It seems to me that the world knows better than most of the church!

> **Multitudes, multitudes, in the valley of decision! For the day of Adonai is near in the valley of decision. The sun and the moon become dark, the stars withdraw their brightness. Adonai will roar from Zion and give His voice from Jerusalem. Heaven and earth will shudder, but Adonai will be a refuge for His people, and a safe place for the children of Israel.**
>
> —Joel 3:14-16

When He judges the nations because of their sins towards Israel, He makes a distinction, and He protects Israel in the day of wrath.

> **Egypt will become a desolation and Edom a desert wasteland, because of the violence against the children of Judah, because they shed innocent blood in their land. But Judah will be inhabited forever Jerusalem from generation to generation. I will acquit their bloodguilt that I had not acquitted, for ADONAI dwells in Zion.**
>
> —JOEL 3:19-21

The Separation

He makes a separation between those who love Him and love His people, Israel, just like the blessing comes upon the lovers of Israel in action and the curse over those who take Israel lightly.

> "And I will bless those who bless you, and the one who curses you I will curse"
>
> —GENESIS 12:3A NASB '95

CHAPTER 55

CAN A NATION BE BORN IN ONE DAY?

> Who has heard such a thing?
> Who has seen such things?
> Can a land be born in one day?
> Can a nation be brought forth all at once?
>
> — ISAIAH 66:8 NASB '95

On the 14th of May of 1948, Israeli Prime Minister David Ben Gurion declared in a building in Tel Aviv: "Today, the State of Israel has been born." This was an indescribable miracle after 2000 years of long, painful exile for the ancient people of Israel, the Jews. The excitement and joy ran high on that day not only among the Jewish people but also among many nations. When YHVH brought back the captive ones of Zion, we were like those who dream.

> Then our mouth was filled with laughter, and our tongue with a song of joy. Then they said among the nations, "ADONAI has done great things for them." ADONAI has done great things for us—we are joyful!
>
> —PSALMS 126:2-3

Indeed, we were like those who dream, and many nations said, "Great things has YHVH done with them, we are glad!" Until that awesome day, most people of the world were affected by Christianity, and the common belief among Christians was, "God is done away with Israel." Most of the more prominent theologians had come to the conclusion that Israel sinned by rejecting Messiah as a nation (the religious government) and that they would always be under a curse because, at the time of Yeshua's crucifixion, the mob hired by the High Priest of the time was shouting, *"Let His blood be on us and our children."* (Matthew 27:25 NASB '95)

Christian doctrine went as far as to concoct the lie that "Jews killed God/Christ," and for that, they deserve to pay with their own blood. Every Easter, when reenacting the Passion, many Jewish villages in Poland and other European countries were sacked and the people murdered to "avenge the blood of Jesus Christ." This belief ran its course during the Nazi Shoah (Holocaust), where Hitler, quoting Martin Luther's infamous book "On the Jews and Their Lies," expelled all the Jews of Germany for "killing Christ" and eventually exterminated six million of them in horrible gas chambers and other terrible means.

With that kind of atmosphere in the nations towards the Jews for nearly 2000 years, it was unheard of that all of a sudden "in one day," the Jews experienced so much favor as to "be born in one day" back in their ancient and Biblical promised land after 2000 years of such exile. This kind of miracle had never occurred before in the world! The same ancient people, back to their same ancient homeland, with the same ancient language of the Holy Scriptures—Hebrew!

Slowly, slowly, Bible-believing Christians began to catch up with the immensity of this event, and they began to call Israel "The Time Clock of the Nations." Many began to realize that this single miracle of Israel, "born in one day," fulfilling countless prophecies in the Holy Bible, was the biggest and most prominent sign of the soon return of the Messiah to Jerusalem! Indeed, from the 14th of May 1948, we can boldly say we are living in the last days, and Yeshua is about to return. He said 2000 years ago to the people of Israel,

> For I tell you, you will never see Me again until you say, 'Baruch ha-ba b'shem ADONAI. Blessed is He who comes in the name of the LORD!'
>
> —MATTHEW 23:39

The people of Israel, in their own Land with Jerusalem as its capital, would be the only people that can usher the Messiah back and welcome Him officially back to earth to establish His one-thousand-year reign!

The Judgment of the Nations

> For behold, in those days and at that time, when I restore the fortunes of Judah and Jerusalem, I will gather all the nations and bring them down to the valley of Jehoshaphat then I will enter into judgment with them there on behalf of My people and My inheritance, Israel, whom they have scattered among the nations; and they have divided up My land.
>
> —JOEL 3:1-2 NASB '95

At the same time that the Almighty returned the fortunes of Judah and Jerusalem by restoring the Jewish people back to their ancient promised land, He also began to judge the nations for the way they had treated the Jewish people for the last 2000 years. He began to fill the Valley of Jehoshaphat (Judgment of Yah-God) with "candidates" for destruction. Indeed, the Word of God says that He has already given them over to the slaughter (past tense). Spiritually, the Judge of the universe has already pre-judged the nations that had misbehaved with Israel, and now the manifestation of that judgment is being felt in the form of earthquakes, tsunamis, terror attacks, and "global warming warning."

> Draw near, O nations, to hear, and listen, O peoples! Let the earth hear, and all it contains, the world, and all its offspring! For ADONAI is enraged at all the nations, and furious at all their armies. He will utterly destroy them. He will give them over to slaughter.
> For ADONAI has a day of vengeance, a year of recompense for the hostility against Zion.
>
> —ISAIAH 34:1-2, 8

Now, that does not sound like good news, especially since He said that He will plunder those who have plundered the Jews, and that touching Israel is a serious thing that incurs His divine wrath.

> For thus says ADONAI-Tzva'ot, He has sent me after glory to the nations that plundered you—because whoever touches you touches the apple of His eye.
>
> —ZECHARIAH 2:8

Jewish Blood Crying from the Ground

> He said, "What have you done? The voice of your brother's blood is crying to Me from the ground.
>
> —GENESIS 4:10 NASB '95

Too much Jewish blood is crying from the ground of the nations, and He must avenge that blood. There is a time, and it is now when He has to judge all that has happened in past generations concerning Israel. Israel has already suffered double for all her sins, and it is time to comfort her.

> "Comfort, comfort My people," says your God. Speak kindly to the heart of Jerusalem and proclaim to her that her warfare has ended, that her iniquity has been removed. For she has received from ADONAI's hand double for all her sins.
>
> —Isaiah 40:1-2

But the nations will now suffer double for all their sins concerning Israel and concerning rejecting the Jewish Messiah Yeshua that has been presented to the Gentiles under the name of Jesus Christ for 2000 years. The Word of God says that *first* the Jew suffers and then the Greek (or Gentile non-Jew).

> There will be tribulation and distress for every soul of man who does evil, of the Jew first and also of the Greek, but glory and honor and peace to everyone who does good, to the Jew first and also to the Greek.
>
> —Romans 2:9-10 NASB '95

The Jew has already suffered untold pain, and *now* the Gentiles are in the valley of judgment.

The Mercy Seat

> For judgment will be merciless to one who has shown no mercy; mercy triumphs over judgment.
>
> —Yaakov (James) 2:13

Many years ago, the Almighty told me that He was sending me as the mercy seat to Switzerland. The mercy seat is the "lid" of the ark of the covenant that used to be in the tabernacle of Moses and in the Holy Temple in Jerusalem. The blood of a perfect animal was spilled over the mercy seat, symbolizing the throne of God on earth. Once the High Priest presented the blood during the Day of Atonement, Yom HaKippurim (Leviticus 16), then on behalf of that blood Sacrifice the people of Israel would be forgiven of their sins for one more year.

When Yah (God) sent me as the mercy seat to Switzerland and to other nations, He was saying to me: "I want to extend *mercy* to the nations though they deserve judgment, and I want to use you (me) as the contact point for the release of that mercy. You are a *Jew*, and your ancestors suffered at the hands of the nations and, most particularly, Christians. If the nations that I send you to receive you, honor you, and repent of their sins towards the Jews, then instead of judgment, I will bring revival, and entire nations will become sheep nations and will be born again in one day!"

It took me a while until I understood the magnitude of my task (I am still in the process of understanding), but I have already seen signs of the magnitude of this. When I am well received in a nation by the hosting pastors/bishops and/or government, great grace is released quite instantly. If the priests (church) of that nation follow through with blessing Israel, an overturning of the judgment begins to happen.

> And I will bless those who bless you, and the one who curses you I will curse and in you all the families of the earth will be blessed.
>
> —GENESIS 12:3 NASB '95

Remission of Sins

> But so that you may know that the Son of Man has authority on earth to forgive sins—then He said to the paralytic, "Get up, pick up your bed and go home."
>
> —MATTHEW 9:6 NASB '95

When Yeshua was in Capernaum, some people brought Him a paralytic man on a stretcher and lowered him through the roof of Peter's house, where He was preaching. This paralytic man could not bring himself to the LORD; he needed the *friends* to bring him. Yeshua said to him, "Your sins are forgiven," and the invalid man was instantly healed and stood to his feet!

In the same manner, the nations of the earth are like that invalid man; they are unable to bring themselves before Elohim-God. They are paralyzed by their own sin and especially those committed against Israel, most of them by the historical church in the name of Jesus Christ! The nations need some "friends" to bring them to the LORD for healing. Those friends are the priest of the nations, the saints of God in any given nation.

> But you are a chosen race, a royal priesthood, a holy nation, a people for God's own possession, so that you may proclaim the excellencies of him who has called you out of darkness into his marvelous light;
>
> —1 Peter 2:9 NASB '95

Only lately have I begun to understand the magnitude of this mercy seat anointing. The Lord has spoken to me two times in the last year: "Acceleration". He wants entire nations to be born in one day, just like Israel; entire nations to be *restored* and to be born again! Israel is a reborn nation in the natural.

The strategy that He has given me is the remission or forgiveness of sins.

> "If you forgive the sins of any, their sins have been forgiven them; if you retain the sins of any, they have been retained."
>
> —John 20:23 NASB '95

I have exercised the authority of remission of sins over helpless people that we could not reach through conventional methods, such as people in a coma (my dad), clinically dead (my own son), the elderly (when they are not responsive and their mind is gone), mentally sick, and the like. The Holy Spirit has given me the revelation of the enormous weight of authority that we carry as end-time Jewish apostles, and that includes the remission of sins, an amazing divine weapon that has been neglected. But we need the "friends of the paralytic nations" to bring the nations before God in repentance so we can release forgiveness of sin as Jewish apostles-prophets to that nation.

For judgment will be merciless to one who has shown no mercy; mercy triumphs over judgment.

—Yaakov (James) 2:13 nasb '95

CHAPTER 56

TIME TO DEFEAT AMALEK

Adonai said to Moses, "Write this for a memorial in the book, and rehearse it in the hearing of Joshua, for I will utterly blot out the memory of the Amalekites from under heaven."
Then he said, "By the hand upon the throne of Adonai, Adonai will have war with Amalek from generation to generation."

— EXODUS 17:14, 16

But who is Amalek, and why Amalek? Why would YHVH want to fight him from generation to generation and destroy the very memory of Amalek? Amalek is the son of Eliphaz, the grandson of Esau.

> Timna was a concubine of Esau's son Eliphaz and she bore Amalek to Eliphaz. These are the sons of Esau's wife Adah.
>
> —Genesis 36:12

Esau sold his inheritance to Jacob for some lentil stew (a bit of fleshly satisfaction) and later regretted it and became bitter and hateful against Jacob, desiring to murder him just like Cain murdered Abel.

> So Esau bore a grudge against Jacob because of the blessing with which his father had blessed him; and Esau said to himself, "The days of mourning for my father are near; then I will kill my brother Jacob."
>
> —**Genesis 27:41**

YHVH said that He loved Jacob and hated Esau! In the Book of Obadiah, He promises to destroy Edom (Esau) altogether.

> Then your mighty men will be dismayed, O Teman, So that everyone may be cut off from the mountain of Esau by slaughter. Because of violence to your brother Jacob, you will be covered with shame, and you will be cut off forever.
>
> — **Obadiah 1:9-10**

This kind of jealous and murderous spirit has been manifesting against the Jewish people since ancient times. Wicked Haman in the Book of Esther, who plots to annihilate the Jews altogether, was from the family of Amalek.

> For Haman the son of Hammedatha, the Agagite, the adversary of all the Jews, had schemed against the Jews to destroy them and had cast Pur, that is the lot, to disturb them and destroy them.
>
> —**Esther 9:24**

Haman was a grandson of Agag, King of the Amalekites, whom King Saul did not utterly destroy, disobeying the commandment of YHVH and, thus, losing the kingdom and the crown for all his generations.

> He captured Agag the king of the Amalekites alive, and utterly destroyed all the people with the edge of the sword.
>
> —1 Samuel 15:8

King Saul let Agag, the king of the Amalekites, live, and though Samuel the prophet killed him, some of his children were left to live. His grandson, Haman, plotted and almost succeeded to exterminate all the Jews had it not been for Jewish Mordechai and Queen Esther.

Ephraim's Amalekite Roots

Part of the tribe of Ephraim representing Northern Israel, who was cut off from the land because of idolatry and later became the fullness of the Gentiles (Genesis 48:19, Romans 11:25), has its roots in Amalek, mixed and intermarried with Amalek against Yah's will.

> From Ephraim those whose root is in Amalek came down, following you, Benjamin, with your peoples; From Machir commanders came down, and from Zebulun those who wield the staff of office.
>
> —Judges 5:14

According to Romans 11:25, the fullness of the Gentiles are Gentile believers in Messiah, Christians or commonly called "the church."

> For I do not want you, brethren, to be uninformed of this mystery—so that you will not be wise in your own estimation—that a partial hardening has happened to Israel until the fullness of the Gentiles has come in; and –so all Israel will be saved; just as it is written,
>
> —Romans 11:25

Every persecution and extermination of Jews by Christianity in the name of Jesus Christ and by Muslims in the name of Allah, such as pogroms, crusades, the Spanish inquisition, Peruvian inquisition, Nazi Shoah (Holocaust), anti-Zionism, terror attacks, and the like, have been inspired and directed by the principality of Amalek.

How Does Amalek Operate?

Since Satan is a coward, Amalek functions as a coward: it always attacks the weak ones, the stragglers, the women, and the children.

> **Remember what Amalek did to you along the way when you came out from Egypt, how he met you along the way and attacked among you all the stragglers at your rear when you were faint and weary; and he did not fear God.**
>
> — DEUTERONOMY 25:17-18

You can expect Amalek to attack all those who love Israel and are true believers in Messiah, grafted into the olive tree. He is the dragon from the book of Revelation that first persecutes the woman (Israel) and then her offspring, all Messianic believers, Jews, and Gentiles.

> **So the dragon was enraged with the woman, and went off to make war with the rest of her children, who keep the commandments of God and hold to the testimony of Yeshua.**
>
> — REVELATION 12:17

Since this hideous principality attacks like a coward, it attacks Israel when it is weak. In the Koran (Muslim book), it is written that "when your enemy is strong, make peace (*hudna* or temporarily pretending peace) with him; when he is weak, attack and conquer." That is how

Islam operates. Therefore, every time that Israel gives away land, it is interpreted as weakness, and the Muslim Arabs get stronger and have more demands. The only "peace" (*hudna*, pretend peace) possible is when Israel is totally strong and gives up nothing! As long as Amalek is ruling through Islam, no peace is possible. When Arabs repent and leave Islam for the Jewish Messiah, then there is true peace and hope.

Amalek Works Within the Church

I already explained that the spirit of Amalek is working in the church through replacement theology and the Council of Nicaea. Since YHVH Himself has a war against Amalek from generation to generation, and He will blot the very memory of Amalek from under heaven (Exodus 17:8-16), then He is judging this demonic principality in the church and will leave no traces of it! He warns us against it through Apostle Shaul-Paul in Romans 11:

> But if some of the (Jewish) branches were broken off, and you, being a wild olive, were grafted in among them and became partaker with them of the rich root of the olive tree, do not be arrogant toward the branches; but if you are arrogant, remember that it is not you who supports the root, but the root supports you. You will say then, "Branches were broken off so that I might be grafted in." Quite right, they were broken off for their unbelief, but you stand by your faith. Do not be conceited, but fear; for if God did not spare the natural branches, He will not spare you, either. Behold then the kindness and severity of God; to those who fell, severity, but to you, God's kindness, if you continue in His kindness; otherwise you also will be cut off.
>
> — Romans 17:22

Many gentile branches (Christians) have been cut off from the olive tree because of harboring the spirit of Amalek or antisemitism. In these end-times, the Almighty is calling all Christians to forsake replacement theology in all its aspects. He told me that it is a matter of life and death!*

Just like King Saul, who disobeyed the commandment of YHVH to totally exterminate all Amalekites and left some "good stuff" alive for his pleasure, those who will not totally reject replacement theology and the spirit of Amalek will be in danger of losing the crown and the kingdom.

> For it is time for judgment to begin with the household of God; and if it begins with us first, what will be the outcome for those who do not obey the gospel of God?
>
> —1 Peter 4:17

It is High Time to Defeat Amalek

We are calling all of you to join us in this corporate fast to defeat the demonic principality of Amalek in the church, in Israel, among the Arabs, in the United Nations, and in *every* nation. Remember that this dragon comes against all the Jews and those who are grafted into the olive tree with Israel. It attacks when we are weak and when we struggle and causes death before its time. It attacks our children and families, and now it is attempting to annihilate Israel from within through the establishment of a sovereign, armed, terror Palestinian State.

> Thus says ADONAI-Tzva'ot: 'I remember what Amalek did to Israel, how he set himself against him on the way while he was

---

* To learn more, order my book *The Healing Power of the Roots* at www.ZionsGospel.com

coming up from Egypt. Now go and strike down Amalek and put all he has under the ban of destruction—so have no pity on him; but kill both men and women, children and nursing infants, oxen and sheep, camels and donkeys.'

—1 Samuel 15:2-3

Since our battle is not against flesh and blood, we shall fight with spiritual weapons by corporately fasting and praying (Ephesians 6:10-12). We do not want to lose our crown like King Saul, who disobeyed the command of YHVH (1 Samuel 15), but rather like King David, who struck the Amalekites and took back spoils!

Then it happened when David and his men came to Ziklag on the third day, that the Amalekites had made a raid on the Negev and on Ziklag, and had overthrown Ziklag and burned it with fire; and they took captive the women and all who were in it, both small and great, without killing anyone, and carried them off and went their way.

—1 Samuel 30:1-2

King David was in dire straits because of Amalek, and many of us reading this have been spoiled by Amalek as well. When David was battling YHVH's battles, Amalek attacked the defenseless in his city and family.

Important: It is when you do Yah's (God's) will that you can expect Amalek to attack!

David encouraged Himself in ADONAI, who told him to *go* and recover all that had been stolen:

So David recovered all that the Amalekites had taken, and rescued his two wives. But nothing of theirs was missing, whether small or great, sons or daughters, spoil or anything that they had taken for themselves; David brought it all back. So David had captured all the sheep and the cattle which the people drove ahead of the other livestock, and they said, "This is David's spoil."

—1 Samuel 30:18-20

Through this corporate 40-d fast, we will take *all* that Amalek has stolen *back* and, on top of it, *spoil*. This includes many sheep of Messiah released from replacement theology along with the wealth, HaleluYah!

Fight for Israel, fight for your families, fight for those trapped in replacement theology, and fight for us and Kad-Esh MAP Ministries, like Aaron and Hur stood with Moses when Joshua fought and defeated the Amalekites in the desert.

So it came about when Moses held his hand up, that Israel prevailed, and when he let his hand down, Amalek prevailed. But Moses' hands were heavy. Then they took a stone and put it under him, and he sat on it; and Aaron and Hur supported his hands, one on one side and one on the other. Thus his hands were steady until the sun set. So Joshua overwhelmed Amalek and his people with the edge of the sword.

—Exodus 17:11-13

Let us defeat and overwhelm Amalek with the edge of the sword of the Spirit!

CHAPTER 57

UNDER THE SHADOW OF HIS WINGS

Under His wings you may seek refuge.

— **PSALMS 91:4B NASB '95**

Between the 18th and the 23rd of March of 2011, the enemy hit Israel from many sides. Wicked Haman always tries to strike Israel when Purim comes in order to foul the commemoration of the great victory against the spirit of hatred without cause against the Jews during the time of Mordechai and Queen Esther. This is not the first Purim season that we suffered from his taunting. On the 18th, the 62nd anniversary of Eilat, our navy seals caught the ship Victoria loaded with lethal weapons of destruction, possibly from Iran, headed for Gaza! Then, on the 22nd, a rocket fell in Ashdod. On the 23rd, a rocket from Gaza fell in Beer Sheba, the capital of the Negev Desert, and a bomb exploded near the central bus station in Jerusalem, killing one lady and injuring 25.

This was the first of such bombings in Jerusalem since 2004 when there were dozens of suicide bombings. Fifty mortar shells were fired from Gaza after this Shabbat, causing damage and injuring many. On Shabbat, the IDF executed an operation against terror cells in Gaza.

This escalation of events happened after the horrendous massacre of the Fogel family in the Samaritan settlement of Itamar on the 11th of March when Palestinian terrorists entered their peaceful habitation after the Shabbat dinner and murdered the father, the mother, and three children, one of them a baby, in cold blood, in their beds. After this massacre, for the first time, Israel decided to publish photos of the massacre for all the world to see.

Abba's Miracle Protection

For it is He who delivers you from the snare of the trapper...

—Psalms 91:3

On the 23rd of March, when the bombing happened in Jerusalem, my daughter called me and said, "Mum, my cousin passed through the bus station area a few minutes before the explosion!" We sighed in relief and praised the Living God! Then, one of our volunteers and his mum, a pastor, were supposed to be traveling from the bus station back to the Eilat Prayer Tower on that day. We sighed in great relief when they reached us in Eilat and praised the Almighty for protecting our own!

But inside, we mourned for the dead lady and the wounded, some of them with serious injuries. Anne, another one of our volunteers, had asked my permission to travel to Jerusalem that day, and I asked her not to travel but to postpone her journey, not knowing that had she gone, she would have been in the surroundings of the explosion in Jerusalem around that time. How important it is to obey the instructions of your leaders!

However, the story of Hanna, which you will find below, is so moving that we decided to publish it. Hanna is like a daughter to us, and she was in her bed at 5 AM on the 23rd, right before the scud missile from Gaza fell on Beer Sheba.

I received an SMS from her that day: n*es gadol*, which means a Big Miracle! Being very busy as we taped our testimonies of salvation for outreach on that day, I did not immediately call her. When I did, I was awed by the faithfulness of the Living God as we pray for all our children, disciples, students, and ministry partners every night, declaring Psalms 91.

Nes Gadol—Hanna's Miracle Story

> He who dwells in the shelter of the Most High will abide in the shadow of the Almighty.
>
> —Psalms 91:1 NASB '95

I want to share with you what happened on the 23rd of March, 2011. For me, this will be a memorable date as I see again the hand of Adonai in my life, fulfilling His promises. He said, "No weapon formed against you shall prosper," and that I am covered under His wings. It was 5.05 AM when the terror alarm sounded, alerting us that a rocket was on its way to fall in Beer Sheba. I knew that this was the alarm preparing us for yet another terror attack. I instantly sprang out of my bed and went to the little room in my apartment and covered myself with a thin mattress. About 10 seconds later, I left the shelter of this room because I heard the voice of my neighbor's children at my doorstep, and they were crying and screaming in terror. When I opened the door of my apartment, there was an explosion that shocked me. It was a rocket or a "Kassam" that hit about half a block from my home. The building shook so much that it looked like it would collapse.

I entered my neighbor's house to help her calm the children down. They were crying from the cold and fear as they were yanked out of their beds abruptly to protect them from the coming blast. They had taken shelter in a corner of the apartment that had no glass windows. I returned to my apartment about 10 minutes later and saw that my home had suffered damages from the explosion; the living room, my bedroom, and my balcony were covered in broken glass—it was chaos! I literally lost all the shutters and the windows of my house that were lying all over, broken into pieces. *So, what do I do now?* I asked myself. A short while later, the police, the ambulances, and the press came to the scene to see if there were any wounded.

I can say *nes gadol* (a big miracle) because if I had not left my bed *instantly* when the terror alarm sounded, I would not be writing this email. All the glass windows in my bedroom were shattered into pieces and fell on my bed! I praise ADONAI, for yet again, He has protected me from the hand of the enemy!

I got to know that my neighbors suffered damages and injuries in their bodies and faces because of the shattered glass and the metal that collapsed. In fact, two of them had to be taken to the emergency room. In my building, there are elderly ladies and small children who had suffered terrible shock and trauma due to the blast of the rocket. I do not know how to explain it, but I felt a very ugly internal feeling that I had never felt in my life before; this was a shock and a trauma. I began to shake and shiver without control as I imagined the sound of the terror alarm sounding again. Today is the 27th, and I still do not have windows in my house. The government told me they would help me but that I needed *savlanut* (patience or long-suffering) as I am not the only one affected, and citizens in many buildings throughout Beer Sheba were affected by this rocket attack from Gaza. So, I am waiting for my turn until they install my new windows. Savlanut, savlanut, patience, patience...

Please pray Psalms 91 over us, our team, and families, and over all of Israel every day.

CHAPTER 58

PROPHETIC ACCELERATION

> It will come about in that day that I will make Jerusalem a heavy stone for all the peoples; all who lift it will be severely injured and all the nations of the earth will be gathered against it.
>
> — ZECHARIAH 12:3 NASB '95

WE HAVE SEEN AN acceleration in the end time scenario described in Zechariah 12 as many South American nations have moved too quickly to recognize a Palestinian State. At the same time, the Arab countries around Israel are boiling with internal unrest and political upheavals, Egypt leading in this, having ousted her long-lasting dictator, President Mubarak.

> The burden of Egypt: Behold, ADONAI rides upon a swift cloud and comes to Egypt. Egypt's idols tremble before Him and Egypt's heart melts within them. I will stir up Egyptian against Egyptian. Everyone will fight against his brother, and everyone against his neighbor—city against city, kingdom against kingdom.
>
> —ISAIAH 19:1-2

Though Israel has had a peace treaty with Egypt for many years now, the relationship has always been tense. However, the relationship may become much more tense if the change of government becomes more radical Islamist. This political unrest is also in Syria and Iran. Ultimately, Egypt will bow down the knee before Yeshua and will be in covenant with Israel!

> So ADONAI will strike Egypt—striking yet healing—so they will return to ADONAI, and He will respond to them and heal them. In that day there will be a highway from Egypt to Assyria, and the Assyrians will come to Egypt, and the Egyptians to Assyria, and the Egyptians will worship with the Assyrians. In that day Israel will be the third, along with Egypt and Assyria—a blessing in the midst of the earth.
>
> —ISAIAH 19:22-24

Acceleration in the Restoration of Israel

I woke up the other day with the word "acceleration". This was the second time since November of 2010 that I heard the word acceleration in a very clear manner. It reminds me of when Yeshua was celebrating the Passover Seder ("Last Supper") with His *talmidim* (disciples) prior to His crucifixion. He spoke to Judas Iscariot and told him to hurry:

> And with that bit, satan entered into him. Then Yeshua tells him, "What you're about to do, do quickly!"
>
> —JOHN 13:27

It looks like all the nations of the earth are at this point in the valley of decision concerning betraying Israel's security and her rights to the

Prophetic Acceleration

land of the Bible. The fact that South America has been leading in recognizing a Palestinian State is very meaningful. South America is full of millions of descendants from the Jewish *Anusim*, the Conversos from the Spanish Inquisition, and YHVH is calling them back to return home to Israel and to their identity as Jews. The Word of God speaks about them in Obadiah 20,

> **And the exiles of Jerusalem who are in Sepharad will possess the cities of the Negev (South).**
>
> **—Obadiah 1:20 nasb '95**

Sepharad is the ancient biblical name for Spain. Many of those "Sephardic Jews" lost their identity due to the forced conversions at the time of the Spanish Inquisition that spread to Portugal and to all Latin America. Millions of these "Converso Jews" or their descendants are all over Latin America! The mere fact that their governments are turning "pro-Palestinian" and are practicing unbiblical politics concerning Israel will provoke acceleration in their return to their Jewish roots. There will be an accelerated awakening among them! They will cry,

> **Restore us from captivity, Adonai, like streams in the Negev.**
>
> **—Psalms 126:4**

The Government of Israel will find itself in need of quick answers to an ever-growing number of those returning Jews who were lost to Catholicism and will need to have an accelerated program for their restoration. They will settle in the Negev (south desert of Israel) and will be a deterring force against the quick spreading of Islam in 55% of the Land of Israel.

Aliyah is the Answer

The answer for the terrible pressure that Israel is in from within and from all around is *aliyah*, which is the term used for Jews to come up or to return to Zion. The accelerated growth of antisemitism all over the world will help *accelerate* the aliyah of many Jews who would have never come otherwise.

> Rather, 'As ADONAI lives, who brought up the children of Israel from the land of the north and from all the lands where He had banished them.' So I will bring them back into their land that I gave to their fathers. "Behold, I will send for many fishers," says ADONAI, "and they will fish for them. After that, I will send for many hunters, and they will hunt them down from every mountain and from every hill, and out of the clefts of the rocks.
>
> —JEREMIAH 16:15-16

The time of the "fishermen" is coming to an end, and the time of the "hunters" is at hand. Today, the situation in the world, especially in the financial arena, is much like before World War 2. Antisemitism or Anti-Zionism is on the rise as Muslims have managed to infiltrate most countries all over the world. Many Jews will find out very quickly that Israel is still safer and will return. All this will be very challenging for the Israeli government, which will need all the help it can get to accommodate a growing number of immigrants in the midst of great pressure; Israel will have to build lots of housing in a hurry.

> "Your children will come quickly. Your destroyers and devastators will go away from you. Lift up your eyes around and see: all of them will gather and come to you." "As I live"—it

is ADONAI's declaration—"you will wear them all as jewelry and bind them on like a bride." For your waste and desolate places and your destroyed land will now be surely too small for the inhabitants, and those who swallowed you up will be far away. The children of your bereavement will yet say in your ears, "The place is too cramped for me! Make room for me to settle in."

—Isaiah 49:17-20

Church Divided Over Israel

And I will bless those who bless you, and the one who curses you I will curse and in you all the families of the earth will be blessed.

—Genesis 12:3 NASB '95

In the days to come, people in the church will be divided over Israel. Jerusalem will become a very heavy stone, not only for the secular governments but for church leaders as well. This division and redefinition are also taking place at an accelerated pace. There will be entire church camps that will quickly fall into great deception for refusing to stand with God's plan for the restoration of Israel. There will be great apostasy and growing immorality in many organizations for rejecting the call to bless Israel in her time of need and for rejecting the Jewish roots of the faith.

On the other hand, many unknown ministers and preachers will arise suddenly with much glory and anointing to preach a radical end-time message of holiness, repentance, and identification with Israel.

These things have begun to happen already, but as of this year, 2011, it will move much, much faster.

> **I declared the former things long ago and they went forth from My mouth, and I proclaimed them. Suddenly I acted, and they came to pass.**
>
> —Isaiah 48:3 nasb '95

Israel is being re-gathered and restored at an accelerated pace despite all the pressure and opposition from the nations. In the same manner, the nations that are turning against Israel and are opposing its restoration will be swiftly and sternly judged. YHVH's quick reaction will be seriously felt as He is very "sensitive" when someone pokes Him in the eye!

> **For thus says Adonai-Tzva'ot, He has sent me after glory to the nations that plundered you—because whoever touches you touches the apple of His eye.**
>
> —Zechariah 2:8

There is an acceleration in the spiritual realm concerning revival. Those who will be swift to answer the call to repentance will be mightily visited with many angelic visitations and will be given powerful weapons.

> **Adonai has opened His armory and brought out the weapons of His indignation.**
>
> —Jeremiah 50:25a

There will be swift judgment over all unrepented sin in the church as YHVH will have a holy people!

> "Then I will draw near to you in judgment, and I will be a swift witness against sorcerers, adulterers, perjurers those who extort a worker's wage, or oppress the widow or an orphan, those who mislead a stranger. They do not fear Me," says ADONAI-Tzva'ot.
>
> —MALACHI 3:5

ADONAI (the LORD) is calling us to quick repentance and quick obedience. The time clock of the nations is ticking its last seconds, and then all of Israel will be saved just as it is written.

> For I do not want you, brethren, to be uninformed of this mystery—so that you will not be wise in your own estimation—that a partial hardening has happened to Israel until the fullness of the Gentiles has come in; and so all Israel will be saved; just as it is written, "THE DELIVERER WILL COME FROM ZION, HE WILL REMOVE UNGODLINESS FROM JACOB."
>
> —ROMANS 11:25-26 NASB '95

CHAPTER 59

FOCUS ON ISRAEL

The Defeat of Leviathan

Elohim blesses us, that all the ends of the earth may fear Him.

— PSALMS 67:7

So they motioned to their partners in the other boat to come and help them; and they came and filled both boats to the point of sinking.

—LUKE 5:7 CJB

WE ARE IN THE midst of earth-shaking world event. On the one hand, because of the global warming warning, the world is experiencing tremendous financial shakings. Many people are losing their homes and properties, some because of natural earthquakes and tsunamis and others because of financial earthquakes. Overall, and especially in the satisfied West, the pocket is starting to seriously hurt.

For thus says ADONAI-Tzva'ot: "In just a little while I will shake the heavens and the earth, the sea and the dry land,

—HAGGAI 2:6

On the other hand, Israel, which has been under the "financial gun" of nations such as the USA, EU, UN, and most all the nations, is now beginning to prosper in a real sense. Many years ago, I prophesied that the new Israeli shekel would be the strongest currency in the world, and it is coming to pass. At a time when the US dollar is at an all-time low, when Israel has been pressured to divide Jerusalem and dismantle 100,000 citizens from Judea and Samaria, YHVH is showing up mightily!

> "And I will shake all the nations. The treasures of all the nations will come, and I will fill this House with glory," says ADONAI-Tzva'ot.
>
> —HAGGAI 2:7

Israel has found oil and gas in the same place just off the cost of Haifa. This is called the Leviathan Oil Field; what a name! Truly, Leviathan has been defeated. Leviathan is the principality of *pride*. That principality has been pushing Israel to the limits and has mocked the God of Israel, who gave the Jewish people His land.

Leviathan Oil Field Could Sustain Israel for Decades[*]
By Christopher Helman

All big oil and gas fields have geopolitical significance, but we haven't seen a big oil find in recent years that could matter more than the Leviathan Field in the Mediterranean Sea off of Israel. In recent days, Houston-based Noble Energy and its Israeli partner Delek (controlled by Israeli billionaire Yitzhak Tshuva) announced that Leviathan could hold upwards of 4.3 billion barrels of oil.

---

[*] www.forbes.com

This is hugely important for Israel, which doesn't exactly see eye-to-eye with its oil-rich Arab neighbors. Israel is almost completely reliant on imported oil, producing less than 4,000 barrels per day of its 250,000-bpd demand. If Leviathan pans out, it could have enough oil to satisfy Israel for more than two decades.

> "Can you drag out Leviathan with a fishhook, and press down his tongue with a rope?
> He looks on everything that is high; He is king over all the sons of pride."
>
> — Job 41:1, 34 NASB '95

All those nations that have proudly boycotted Israel, pressing her to halt building in Jerusalem and Samaria and to give away precious Biblical land using their "petrol power," have been ruled by King Leviathan. This demonic principality is the king over all sons of pride that contend with the inheritance that Elohim gave to His Jewish people. This oil find called the "Leviathan Energy Field" is a sign that the principality of Leviathan in the nations is being defeated. Israel has always been used to instruct the nations in the ways of Yah (God), and He does it best when the nations come to His land!

> Then many peoples will go and say: "Come, let us go up to the mountain of ADONAI, to the House of the God of Jacob! Then He will teach us His ways, and we will walk in His paths." For Torah will go forth from Zion and the word of ADONAI from Jerusalem.
>
> —Isaiah 2:3

Until recently, all eyes were on Israel because of the troubles and wars that we experienced; but this is changing, and all eyes are on us because of the oil that we have found. We have prayed so much for Yah to bless us, as when we are truly blessed, the nations fear His Name and are saved! It is the blessing of Israel that will bring about revival.

May God be gracious to us and bless us. May He cause His face to shine upon us—Selah. So that Your way may be known on earth, and Your salvation among all nations.

—Psalm 67:2-3

There is no doubt that wars will be unto the end; however, there is a time when Yah shows Himself mightily on behalf of His covenant people because He is righteous and keeps His Word.

If we are faithless, He remains faithful, for He cannot deny Himself.

—2 Timothy 2:13 nasb '95

The Importance of Your Prayers

Many years ago, Abba spoke to me clearly, and He said: "I am covering Israel with a mantle (tallit) of mercy from north (where the Leviathan Oil Field is near Haifa) to south (where the second oil deposit was found in the Negev) and from east to west. It is the prayers of your brothers and sisters in the nations that are causing Me to do this!"

The reciprocity between Israel and the nations is vital for the well-being of mankind. When the nations bless Israel, and Israel is blessed, then the blessing falls.

The Negev is the Focus

Oil has been found not only near the coast of Haifa in the north but also in the south, in our beloved Negev Desert of Israel. We do not know how big the field in the Negev is, but the Leviathan Field near Haifa is about 6 billion barrels of oil big; that is a Leviathan of a field! At the same time, finding oil in the Negev is very meaningful as the Negev is now drawing attention for its development and, with it, the restoration of the Spanish/Sephardic Jews to it as prophesied.

> **And the exiles of Jerusalem who are in Sepharad will possess the cities of the Negev.**
>
> —Obadiah 1:20b NASB '95

All prophecies are starting to be fulfilled, and as usual, "when it rains, it pours"! Once the fulfillment starts, it is "far exceedingly, abundantly above all that we may ask or think" (Ephesians 3:20 NASB '95). This does not mean that there are no troubles ahead; challenges will always be, but it is so exciting to see Yah's eternal Word come to pass!

Record Number of Tourists

This year, 2010, Israel recorded the largest number of tourists ever on record. We had 2 million tourists! In a country of 7.5 million inhabitants, 2 million tourists are a lot of tourists. The hotels were so full that the prices shot up incredibly. It was hard to find space in decent hotels, not only during feast times but before and after, as well. If you want to make it to visit Israel, you'd better hurry. The prognosis of our Ministry of Tourism is 3 million tourists for 2011; O Lord, help us with hotels!

But this is the prophecies of Isaiah and Zechariah coming to pass. All nations will indeed flock to Jerusalem and Zion.

> Indeed, many peoples and powerful nations will come to seek Adonai-Tzva'ot in Jerusalem, and to entreat the favor of Adonai.
>
> —Zechariah 8:22

In fact, for the believer in Messiah, grafted into the olive tree, it is a mandate to come; it is part of "blessing Israel" in action.

> Nations will come to your light, and kings to the brightness of your rising.
>
> —Isaiah 60:3

From Israel to The Kehila (Church)

He is visiting His covenanted people, grafted in the olive tree, with prophetic fulfillment, just like He visited Abraham after a long wait for His son of promise to come to pass. This visitation brings life from the dead to the womb of Sarah, and laughter (Yitzhak-Isaac) and joy break out in their tents. Sarah laughed to herself, saying,

> "After I have become old, shall I have pleasure, my Lord being old also?"
>
> —Genesis 18:12 nasb '95

On the other hand, Lot is going to experience the loss of all in the judgment of Sodom and Gomorrah. All that he loved and cherished was going to be lost in the flames of that judgment. He chose that area as his dwelling place because of its *wealth,* being willing to overlook the wickedness of its inhabitants. He was willing to compromise with the world system in order to enjoy life. Abraham, on the other hand, only took the "leftovers" of whatever Lot did not want. His humble attitude paid off in the end when he was visited with life and Lot with death, though he escaped by the skin of his teeth because of Abraham's covenant walk.

> **Thus it came about, when God destroyed the cities of the valley, that God remembered Abraham, and sent Lot out of the midst of the overthrow, when He overthrew the cities in which Lot lived.**
>
> **—Genesis 19:29 nasb '95**

So, it is with all of us in these end times that are so peculiar as we walk the very "tightrope" between judgment and revival. Will we stay faithful to the end? Are we willing to pour our lives, represented by what we own, into kingdom purpose, or will we lose them all in these financial shakings?

> **For where your treasure is, there your heart will be also.**
>
> **—Matthew 6:21 nasb '95**

At the same time that Israel is finding oil, the nations are financially shaking. It is quite reasonable to believe that Israel will be blamed for the woes of the nations as it has always been, which causes outbursts of hate against the Jewish people and the Nation of Israel. In a sense, the nations are right, for Yah judges the nations according to how they treated or mistreated Israel.

> For ADONAI is enraged at all the nations, and furious at all their armies. He will utterly destroy them. He will give them over to slaughter.
> For ADONAI has a day of vengeance, a year of recompense for the hostility against Zion.
>
> —Isaiah 34:2, 8 NASB '95

However, turning against Israel will prove once again to be the wrong move as the Almighty has a very sensitive eye.

> "For thus says ADONAI-Tzva'ot, He has sent me after glory to the nations that plundered you—because whoever touches you touches the apple of His eye—"
>
> —Zechariah 2:12

But to those who fear His name, the sun of righteousness shall rise with healing in His wings. And to those who go ahead to sow financially and to pray for the restoration of Israel, there shall be unprecedented favor like the favor of Ruth, Cornelius, and Rahab. Although from heathen origin and from nations doomed to destruction such as Moab, Rome, and Jericho, they obtained mercy, blessing, prosperity, and honor, to them and to those under their roof!

> "I will bless those who bless you, curse those who curse you and in you all the families of the earth shall be blessed."
>
> —Genesis 12:3 NASB '95

CHAPTER 60

THE RAGING DRACONIC FIRES

When the dragon saw that he had been hurled to the earth, he persecuted the woman who had given birth to the male child.

— REVELATION 12:13 NASB '95

This past week, Israel has been living through an end-time war scenario straightaway from horror pictures or the Book of Revelations. Raging fires devoured ancient forests in the "Little Switzerland" area of the famous Carmel Mountains. For more than four days, the fires could not be put out. Israel received help even from her enemies as planes from all over the world, including countries such as Turkey, Jordan, and Saudi Arabia, came to the rescue—not to attack Israel but to actually help Israel to put out the raging fires! About 18,000 people have lost their homes to the fires and have been evacuated; 41 young people from the age of 16 to 40, mostly police cadets, have lost their lives and have been already buried. This is a national catastrophe like no other and the worst fire Israel has ever experienced, made worse by the fact that the country has been suffering from a terrible drought. So, what is happening, and who is to blame for this tragedy?

Another Kind of Terror

Looking at this terrifying scenario, I believe that we are standing in front of another kind of terror. Though some reports say that two young men from a Druze village "unintentionally" lit the fire, there are other reports that point to a "Palestinian" Arab and an Israeli Arab as the culprits for the fire or at least for feeding it. Some Arabs even shot firecrackers into it while the firefighters were trying to put it out: a fact that made it a thousand times harder to overcome! At the same time, some other hostile Arab citizens from the south of Israel lit some fires in the South, taking advantage of the fact that we were totally concentrated in the north of Israel, thus trying to break down the country. Those southern fires were put out fairly quickly; praise the Living God! We are outside of the country at the moment in the USA and Peru, but prayers keep on going in the South Gate of Israel, our Living Worship Prayer Tower, thanks to the volunteers from the nations that come and go from there!

From One Fire to Another Fire

> Then you will call on the name of your god, and then, I will call on the Name of ADONAI. The God who answers with fire, He is God.
>
> —1 KINGS 18:24

Mount Carmel is the site of another kind of fire, the fire of Elohim, when Elijah confronted the prophets of Baal and Asherah thousands of years ago! I believe that very soon the fire of Elohim will again fall upon

Israel to devour all idolatry and bring in the most powerful revival that Israel has even seen prior to the return of the Messiah.

> I will pour out on the house of David and on the inhabitants of Jerusalem, the Spirit of grace and of supplication, so that they will look on Me whom they have pierced; and they will mourn for Him, as one mourns for an only son, and they will weep bitterly over Him like the bitter weeping over a firstborn.
>
> —Zechariah 12:10 NASB '95

The Mantle of Mercy

> "Comfort, O comfort My people," says your God.
>
> —Isaiah 40:1 NASB '95

How can we pray for Israel at this time? Many years ago, YHVH spoke to me that He was covering Israel with a mantle of mercy from north (Carmel is in the north) to south (Eilat is in the south) and from east to west. He said to me, "It is the prayers of your brothers and sisters in the nations that are causing me to do this." A "mantle" is a "tallit" or prayer shawl. In other words, He is covering Israel with a tallit of mercy when *you*, our brothers and sisters in the nations, pray for Israel!

But *how* to pray? It is very important to pray according to Yah's (God's) promises about its *restoration*. His purpose is not to destroy Israel but to restore it. In fact, Yeshua will not return until all things (especially Israel) are restored.

> Repent, therefore, and return—so your sins might be blotted out, so times of relief might come from the presence of

ADONAI and He might send Yeshua, the Messiah appointed for you. Heaven must receive Him, until the time of the restoration of all the things that God spoke about long ago through the mouth of His holy prophets.

—ACTS 3:19-21

Restoration is always a by-product of *repentance*:

And My people who are called by My name humble themselves and pray and seek My face and turn from their wicked ways, then I will hear from heaven, will forgive their sin, and will heal their land.

— 2 CHRONICLES 7:14 NASB '95

God's Word says that His *goodness* leads to *repentance,* and indeed, His goodness has been manifesting since the rebirthing of the State of Israel in 1948 after 2000 years of painful exile. Jews from all over the world have returned to the homeland of their forefathers, fulfilling Biblical prophecy.

Israel Restored

For I will take you from the nations, gather you from all the lands and bring you into your own land. "Then I will sprinkle clean water on you, and you will be clean; I will cleanse you from all your filthiness and from all your idols. "Moreover, I will give you a new heart and put a new spirit within you; and I will remove the heart of stone from your flesh and give you a heart of flesh.

—EZEKIEL 36:24-26 NASB '95

The purpose of bringing us back to the land is to bring us back to the God of the land, the God of Israel. Until Israel wakes up to the fact that we can be like no other nation and that the Land of Israel is truly God's Holy Land, difficult fires will be raging over her. Her enemies have wanted to devour her since her inception thousands of years ago, but the One that is an all-consuming fire is YHVH Himself, who will purify His people through the refiner's fire until we bow down our knees before Him. Does that mean that "God sent this fire over Israel?" No, but it does mean that He will be with us through the fires of affliction until Messiah returns to establish His millennial reign in Jerusalem. He is totally committed to the restoration (not the destruction) of His Holy people, Israel.

> But now, thus says ADONAI—the One who created you, O Jacob, the One who formed you, O Israel: "Fear not, for I have redeemed you, I have called you by name, you are Mine. When you pass through the waters, I will be with you, or through the rivers, they will not overflow you. When you walk through the fire, you will not be burned, nor will the flame burn you.
>
> —ISAIAH 43:1-2

He will have a holy nation that He will rule and reign from over all the other nations of the earth. The reign of the antichrist is about to start, and the last week of Daniel is about to begin. All the artifacts of the Temple are ready to be used, and sacrifices could start any moment on the Temple Mount, if we were allowed to put a holy altar there. This will surely happen as the Word also says,

> "And he will make a firm covenant with the many for one week, but in the middle of the week he will put a stop to sacri-

fice and grain offering; and on the wing of abominations will come one who makes desolate, even until a complete destruction, one that is decreed, is poured out on the one who makes desolate."

—Daniel 9:27 nasb '95

Time is very late. The Word is "acceleration"; Yeshua is pressing to *return*. We must watch and pray over Israel like never before that she will be strengthened and that, in Yah's mercy, she will open her eyes to the *only* One who can be a refuge in times of trouble. She cannot trust the USA, the UN, or the EU, but only our Abba Shebashamayim (Father in Heaven).

Please pray like never before for Israel's protection from within ("Palestinian Arab terror") and from without (Iran, Syria, Lebanon, and so forth). Also pray regarding threats from all around (hostile international media) and from underneath, Satan and the anti-Messiah himself!

What About Us, the Believers in Messiah?

So the dragon became enraged at the woman and went off to make war with the rest of her offspring—those who keep the commandments of God and hold to the testimony of Yeshua.

—Revelation 12:17

The same dragon that wants to destroy Israel desires to destroy the believers in Messiah worldwide, especially the Messianic. Please pray for the Messianic Body all over Israel and the nations to be purified and restored to holy worship. Pray that the fire of the Holy Spirit will burn bright and clear through the bride of Messiah, that she be rescued and restored through the fires of affliction that are raging all over, for her to be *relevant* and to take her royal position on behalf of Israel and the salvation of the nations "for such a time as this".

Remember that dragons spew fire, so pray that the dragon's (Satan's) fire will be put out quickly and that Yah's holy fire will replace it. Please pray for the thousands that have been left homeless in the North and for the families of the bereaved to be comforted.

> **Speak kindly to the heart of Jerusalem and proclaim to her that her warfare has ended, that her iniquity has been removed. For she has received from ADONAI's hand double for all her sins.**
>
> **—ISAIAH 40:2 NASB '95**

Maranatha, Baruch Haba Beshem ADONAI!* Come quickly, Yeshua!

---

* Blessed is he who comes in the name of the LORD

CHAPTER 61

TWENTY-FOUR HOURS LATER

For thus says ADONAI-Tzva'ot, He has sent me after glory to the nations that plundered you—because whoever touches you touches the apple of His eye.

— ZECHARIAH 2:8

Quoting the Biblical prophecies of Carl Gallups, a talk-radio host and Baptist pastor in Florida, WND reports:

April the 19th, Israel celebrates its independence in 2010," Gallups says in narration on the video. "On April the 19th, Fox News reports that the U.S. will no longer automatically support Israel in the United Nations. The next day, on April the 20th, the Deepwater Horizon oil rig explodes (known as the BP Gulf Oil Spill). Coincidence? Or the hand and judgment of God?"

In a surprising manner and after only a few days of landing in Israel after our very meaningful Florida and Peru apostolic journey, Yah made it abundantly clear that we had to leave Israel yet again to go to Florida and Peru. We landed in Miami on July 21st after about 35 hours of flying and waiting in airports. I truly suggest that unless the Spirit of Elohim sends you out not to travel in July or August—everyone seems to be flying at the same time! But we were not going on holidays; rather, we were being sent urgently by the Holy Spirit to Florida again.

A few years ago, YHVH told me clearly, "Target Florida." My book *Grafted In** (that has by now become our most important manual of instruction as we read the Bible in the Hebrew context) was written as Hurricane Charlie was landing in Orlando, Florida. I will never forget the feeling: It was the sunset of Friday, the start of Shabbat, and I was writing about the importance of restoring the 4th Commandment, the Shabbat. Then the Hurricane fell, and it landed with a fury!

We taped it on video, and the following morning saw the terrible devastation of cars and houses damaged, and trees fell everywhere. What was most amazing is that our van was parked in the same place we left it and trees fell all around it, but our van was intact, not even a leaf on it, while other cars were damaged all around! Our God is a Mighty God and knows how to keep His faithful servant protected during difficult times; praise His Holy Name! However, Hurricane Charlie has come and gone, and Hurricane Katrina has come and gone. Now, the BP Gulf Oil Spill has been in the news for nearly three months. What do these hurricanes and terrible disasters have in common? They all happened exactly 24 hours after the USA made an anti-Israel move or a pro-Palestinian State move!

On April 19th, Fox News reported that the US will no longer automatically support Israel in the United Nations. The next day, on April 20th, the Deepwater Horizon oil rig exploded (known as the BP Gulf Oil Spill). For those who are wary of mixing politics with church doctrine, I have one thing to say, and the word is Biblical politics. World politics should be out of the church, but Biblical politics should be in

---

* Order the *Grafted In* book at www.ZionsGospel.com

the church! The Almighty Himself is the author of this one. He has written countless warnings about this issue:

> For thus says ADONAI-Tzva'ot, He has sent me after glory to the nations that plundered you—because whoever touches you touches the apple of His eye.
>
> —ZECHARIAH 2:8

> And I will bless those who bless you, and the one who curses you I will curse and in you all the families of the earth will be blessed.
>
> —GENESIS 12:3 NASB '95

> For behold, in those days and at that time, when I restore the fortunes of Judah and Jerusalem, I will gather all the nations and bring them down to the valley of Jehoshaphat then I will enter into judgment with them there On behalf of My people and My inheritance, Israel, whom they have scattered among the nations; and they have divided up My land.
>
> —JOEL 3:1-2 NASB '95

We are after the glory of God in the midst of this terrible disaster in the USA that is described as the worst oil spill in American history. The media tells us that until April 28th, the Exxon Valdez oil spill of 1989 was the largest of its kind. However, that was until the BP Deepwater Horizon sank and began leaking oil, taking the reigning title of the largest oil spill in American history. The residents of Prince William Sound, Alaska, can very much sympathize with those of the Gulf of Mexico as they helplessly watched millions of gallons leaking into the waters, which many used as a source of income. From fishery to tourism, the BP oil spill has been a disaster many will never fully understand. At the same time that the Almighty is *again* choosing Jerusalem and restoring Judah, He is judging the nations that have come against her in one way or another.

> **Adonai will inherit Judah as His portion in the holy land and will once again choose Jerusalem.**
>
> **—Zechariah 2:16**

He is commanding all flesh to be silent before this plan. He wants no "commentaries" or "manmade political opinions" on it. He only cares about His own Biblical politics regarding this!

> **"Be silent before Adonai, all flesh, for He has aroused Himself from His holy dwelling."**
>
> **—Zechariah 2:17**

He has sent us now to the USA and especially to the State of Florida, which has been plagued with storms and disasters and now with the oil spill. He has sent us "after glory," but what does this mean? In the same chapter of Zechariah 2, we learn that those nations and people who *repent* will be joined to the Lord at the same time that YHVH is judging the nations for Israel's sake.

> **In that day many nations will join themselves to Adonai and they will be My people and I will dwell among you.' Then you will know that Adonai-Tzva'ot has sent me to you.**
>
> **—Zechariah 2:15**

In the midst of judgment, He is using us to preach *repentance* so that there can be revival, and many can be saved before it is too late!

Our mission in Florida also impacts all of Latin America since Miami is the *gateway* from North to South America. Among the Spanish, there are millions (about 60 million) Jewish descendants from the Jews who converted to Catholicism during the Spanish Inquisition.

Revival has been prophesied to start from the Spanish in the USA and in Israel! In fact, the hunger that we see among the Hispanics in Miami is absolutely heartwarming. We feel that there is a volcano ready to explode in Miami and that we are sent as the detonator. The MAP message of repentance and restoration to the love of Israel and to the apostolic Hebrew foundations of faith is the *key* to the end time revival and the salvation of the nations.

O, Zion! Escape, you who are living with the daughter of Babylon.

—Zechariah 2:7 NASB '95

The acceptance of the Jews and the Jewish roots of the faith brings life from the dead; it brings revival!

For if their rejection is the reconciliation of the world, what will their acceptance be but life from the dead?

—Romans 11:15 NASB '95

Now is the time for the entire world to repent from replacement theology, from hatred towards Israel, and for rejecting the Jewish Messiah Yeshua. The true gospel that was preached by Jewish Apostles 2000 years ago is again coming out of Zion. Praise His Holy Name!

> For Torah will go forth from Zion and the word of ADONAI from Jerusalem.
>
> —ISAIAH 2:3B

The time limit of the "knee-jerk" reaction of YHVH against the USA or any nation that "touches Israel as the apple of His" eye is only 24 hours! (Not even 40 days as when Jonah preached to Nineveh). That is why we must run with His gospel and the truth about this so that many can repent and be saved.[*]

We thank all those praying for us and supporting us as we go forth, sent from Zion, to bring the Gospel "made in Zion," followed by signs, wonders, and miracles.

Many years ago, the LORD took me to heaven in a vision and had me looking down. I saw the fields totally white! He said to me:

> "The fields are white unto the harvest, and I have called you to Go and pick up the Harvest of the Nations!"

---

[*] Order my book *Stormy Weather* at www.ZionsGospel.com to lean more on this subject.

CHAPTER 62

WHY REMEMBER THE SHOAH?

Special Memorial and Israel's 62nd Independence Day Edition

ADONAI said to Moses, "Write this for a memorial in the book, and rehearse it in the hearing of Joshua, for I will utterly blot out the memory of the Amalekites from under heaven."

— EXODUS 17:14

THIS NEXT SUNDAY-TUESDAY IS Memorial Day for the Israel fallen soldiers and Israel's 62-year anniversary, the year where Isaiah 62 is the main issue in the agenda of the Father in heaven.

> For Zion's sake I will not keep silent, and for Jerusalem's sake I will not keep quiet, until her righteousness goes forth like brightness, and her salvation like a torch that is burning. The nations will see your righteousness, and all kings your glory.
>
> —ISAIAH 62:1-2A NASB '95

This past week we commemorated "Shoah (Holocaust) Memorial Day" in Israel in memory of the over 6 million Jews that were exterminated during the Nazi Regime between the years of 1938-1945. I took our international team here in Eilat to participate in the yearly

The Israel Factor

ceremony in this city, and though they do not understand Hebrew for the most part, they could feel the spirit, and they were mightily touched! One of the most meaningful parts of the ceremony was when a man who is a Shoah survivor stood on the stage together with his son and grandson born in Israel. This man, Alberto, was born in Hungary and managed to survive the extermination of all Hungarian Jews. After the liberation, he traveled to Chile trying to find his father, who had escaped to Chile. In Chile, Alberto got married and bore his son Oliver. Oliver says that his father never told him anything about the Shoah. Most survivors did not share the truth with their children, and yet the children could feel that something had happened but did not know what!

Later, Alberto brought his family to Israel, fulfilling the commandment to make aliyah (come up and return to Zion). They naturalized in the miraculously reborn State of Israel! Here, Oliver learned about the Shoah and began to ask questions, which his father painfully answered about all the horrors. It was very important for Oliver to know. Oliver got married and bore a son by the name of Yonatan. Yonatan is a Sabra (native-born Israeli). Yonatan also wanted to know the truth about what happened to his grandfather, and he joined the yearly delegation of high school students who traveled to Poland to visit the death camps such as Auschwitz, Treblinka, Majdanek, Sobibor, and the like. Of course, this trip impacted him tremendously, and now he has made it his business to make sure that other young people do not forget the Shoah and its aftermath.

Why would Yonatan, a young teenage Israeli boy, care about remembering such a horrific past in his family? Humanly speaking, we could say that it is so that it will *never* happen again! If humanity learns from history, then maybe it can correct its ways and does not repeat the same horrors. However, besides all these important and humane good intentions, there is the will of God, YHVH, the Creator. He commanded us to *remember*:

> "Remember what Amalek did to you along the way when you came out from Egypt"
>
> —Deuteronomy 25:17 nasb '95

The Nazi spirit, the same spirit of Haman during the reign of Queen Esther, is also called Amalek. This spirit has always tried to destroy the Jewish people so that the name of Israel will be remembered no more.

> **O God do not remain quiet; do not be silent and, O God, do not be still. For behold, Your enemies make an uproar, and those who hate You have exalted themselves. They make shrewd plans against Your people and conspire together against Your treasured ones. They have said, "Come, and let us wipe them out as a nation, that the name of Israel be remembered no more."**
>
> —Psalms 83:1-4 nasb '95

So how does Amalek operate and what are the promises of YHVH concerning Amalek?

Amalek attacks when we are weak; he attacks the feeble.

> "Remember what Amalek did to you along the way when you came out from Egypt, how he met you along the way and attacked among you all the stragglers at your rear when you were faint and weary; and he did not fear God."
>
> —Deuteronomy 25:17-18 nasb '95

Elohim is always the protector of the weak, and He hates those who "play dirty" by attacking those in distress. The same spirit of Amalek rose up to destroy the Shoah survivors after the Second World War. Living skeletons arrived in Israel after 2000 years of exile, and they were attacked from all flanks by all the Arab armies in 1948. After the time that small and feeble Israel won the Independence War, not by might, not by power but by the Spirit of ADONAI, the Arabs kept on attacking with many, many more wars: The Sinai War, the Yom HaKippurim War, the First and Second Lebanon wars, and the Palestinian Intifadas.

The qassam rockets fall from Gaza on defenseless Sderot, the Katyusha rockets from Hezbollah fall on the babies of Maalot and Kiryat Shmone in the north, and the suicide bombers blow themselves up in coffee shops, malls, schools, public buses, and youth gathering places. The snipers attack families and children that travel to and from the roads of Judea and Samaria. The crazy Palestinian terrorist ran over innocent pedestrians and passers-by in the city of Jerusalem with a tractor! The wickedly misled Palestinian boys and girls throw rocks from the Temple Mount on those who are praying and crying before God and are vulnerable in their neediness. The Arab armies attacked us during the Day of Atonement in 1973 when we were all fasting and praying in the synagogues and were weak physically! The evildoers attack Jews who go to synagogues in France and in many other places in the world. All these are the spirit of Amalek in operation!

YHVH said to *remember* what Amalek did to us. Why? Isn't it better to actually forget these horror memories? I think we Jews would all like to forget! Except Amalek does not let us forget, for as we are recovering from one of his attacks trying to forget the pain, he attacks again from the rear! Islam is possessed of the spirit of Amalek, for the Koran instructs all Muslims to "make peace" with your enemy when he is strong. But when your enemy is weak, attack him and overpower him. That's Amalek! And that is how Islam operates! Therefore, all those nations, presidents, and governments that are pressuring Israel to "make peace" with our Islamic neighbors and to give away precious promised land for "peace" are actually cooperating with Amalek for the destruction of Israel.

Do not be fooled by any peace process! Muslims are commanded to make peace with the enemy when the enemy is strong. That is called "hudna," and it is not real peace but rather a "cease-fire" until the enemy weakens, and then they attack to murder! There can be no peace with Amalek! That is the reason why YHVH said to *remember* and not to forget. He will totally destroy Amalek, just like the Israelites were commanded to destroy all Canaanites when they conquered the land thousands of years ago. YHVH said not to make *any* covenant with them. So, we are not to make any "peace covenant" with Amalek!

> **Now when ADONAI your God grants you rest from all the enemies surrounding you in the land ADONAI your God is giving you as an inheritance to possess, you are to blot out the memory of Amalek from under the heavens. Do not forget!**
>
> **—DEUTERONOMY 25:19**

As long as Islam is the ruling spirit amongst the Arabs, there is no hope for peace with them because Elohim Himself has said to blot out the memory of Amalek, and Islam is ruled by the spirit of Amalek!

King Saul lost his crown because he did not totally blot out Amalek and kept their king alive.

> **But Saul and the people spared Agag as well as the best of the sheep, the cattle, even the fatlings and the lambs, and all that**

> was good, since they were not willing to utterly destroy them; everything that was worthless and feeble, they destroyed completely. Then the word of ADONAI came to Samuel saying: "I regret that I made Saul king, for he has turned back from following Me and has not carried out My commands." So Samuel was troubled and cried out to ADONAI all night long.
>
> —1 SAMUEL 15:9-11

That stronghold has been bothering Israel ever since. So how can we blot out the memory of Amalek from under heaven? We must remember that the same Amalek spirit operates in the Church through replacement theology and has caused the death of many Jews through antisemitism in the church, pogroms, inquisitions and finally, the Shoah (Holocaust) that was also perpetrated in the name of Jesus Christ when Hitler expelled all Jews in Germany, waving the cross!

We must repent for all replacement theology and antisemitism and then be praying for Israel to be strong against Amalek, not to give into the false peace process and the division of Jerusalem!

Also, by praying for and preaching the gospel to the Muslims so they forsake the Amalekite spirit of Islam, and they have the spirit of the Jewish Messiah Yeshua. Many Muslims will accept Yeshua in this end of times at great cost as the spirit of Amalek is a terrible murderer and he will attempt to murder all those who forsake Islam. However, many more will not accept Yeshua and YHVH will fight against them and strengthen Israel to win the war against them.

The problem is that the memory of all those people and nations that side with the "Palestinian cause" will also be "blotted out!" They are siding with the Amalekite cause of annihilating Israel. The PLO (Palestinian Liberation Organization) is the mother organization of *both* Fatah and Hamas. It was formed by Hajj Amin Al Husseini, the Mufti of Jerusalem who visited Hitler and asked Hitler to help him raise an Arab army that will finish what Hitler started in Europe by annihilating all the Jews in Palestine.

> Thus says ADONAI, "As for all My evil neighbors who strike at the inheritance that I bequeathed to My people Israel—I am about to uproot them from their land and pluck the house of Judah from them. Yet it will come to pass, after I have uprooted them, that I will again have compassion on them and I will bring them back, each one to his inheritance and each one to his land. "So it will come to pass, if they will diligently learn the ways of My people—to swear by My Name, 'As ADONAI lives,' just as they taught My people to swear by Baal—then they will be built up in the midst of My people. But if they will not obey, then I will uproot that nation, plucking it up and destroying it." It is a declaration of ADONAI.
>
> —JEREMIAH 12:14-17 NASB '95

So, why remember the Shoah? Because YHVH has commanded us to *remember* so that Israel overcomes Amalek and destroys it before Amalek destroys Israel! Amalek seeks to discredit YHVH as the covenant-keeping God of Israel.

> He has remembered His covenant forever, the word which He commanded to a thousand generations, the covenant which He made with Abraham, And His oath to Isaac. Then He confirmed it to Jacob for a statute, to Israel as an everlasting covenant, Saying, "to you I will give the land of Canaan as the portion of your inheritance.
>
> —PSALMS 105:8-1 NASB '95

My prayer is that many Muslims accept the Lord's grace and salvation and forsake Amalek and that all those misguided Christians who have sided with Amalek in the name of "peace" and "humanism" repent before it is too late. Time is short, and the Father, who is also the judge of all mankind, is about to launch His plan for the annihilation of Amalek and for the restoration of Israel.

Where will you be? On what side will your family, church, or nation be when He executes His judgment? My prayer is that you are on God's side, and He said:

> And I will bless those who bless you, and the one who curses you I will curse and in you all the families of the earth will be blessed.
>
> —Genesis 12:3 NASB '95

> For Zion's sake I will not keep silent, and for Jerusalem's sake I will not keep quiet, until her righteousness goes forth like brightness, and her salvation like a torch that is burning.
>
> —Isaiah 62:1 NASB '95

X 2009

CHAPTER 63

A CALL TO TRUE UNITY

Feast of Trumpets 2009 / Jewish New Year of 5770

> May they be brought to complete unity to let the world know that you sent me and have loved them even as you have loved me.
>
> — JOHN 17:23B NASB '95

From the eve of Friday the 18th to Saturday the 19th, we are celebrating the prophetic Feast of Trumpets and the season of repentance of the 10 Days of Awe leading to Yom Hakippurim (Day of Atonement). This is also called "Rosh Hashanah," as it marks the start of the New Year in Israel for all civil affairs.

> "Speak to Bnei-Yisrael, saying: In the seventh month, on the first day of the month, you are to have a Shabbat rest, a memorial of blowing (shofarot), a holy convocation. You are to do no regular work, and you are to present an offering made by fire to ADONAI."
>
> —LEVITICUS 23:24-25

We are entering into a season that many would describe as "tumultuous." Israel is under unbearable pressure to relinquish large portions of Judea and Samaria and to divide the Holy City of Jerusalem. The unheard-of is already happening as Prime Minister Benjamin Netanyahu has agreed to a freeze on all construction in Samaria for six months. He is still holding the position that "Jerusalem is non-negotiable;" the question is, for how long will he hold on? Experience says that not for too long, but most of the people of Israel today are awakening to the fact that "land for peace" is not a good deal. I remember that when they removed the Gush Katif settlements in Gaza, I asked Yah why He was allowing this. His answer to me was: "Because there is no *unity* in the country!»

Some Israelis were against the pullout, while many others were pushing for it; even our PM then, Ariel Sharon, a military legend and the father of all the Gush Katif settlers, betrayed them at that time. Meanwhile, the Palestinians have turned the beautiful hot houses of Gush Katif into qassam rockets, launching pads against innocent Israeli civilians. That led to the Gaza War called "Operation Cast Lead" last December. At this point, there is a hopeful sign of more UNITY in Israel about the pullout from Judea and Samaria and about the possible division of Jerusalem. Polls are showing that most of the Israelis are against it! This is indeed a hopeful sign.

Our prayers for *unity* in Israel against the «land for peace» process are urgently needed! YHVH is waiting for unity in His people in order to *act* and intervene as He promised in the Holy Scriptures.

> **In that day ADONAI will defend the inhabitants of Jerusalem so that the weakest among them that day will be like David and the house of David will be like God—like the angel of ADONAI before them.**
>
> —ZECHARIAH 12:8

Unity is the *key* for Elohim to defeat our enemies. This applies to Israel as it applies to our marriage, family, congregation, ministry, or workplace. The enemy knows that unity is the *key*, so he has been working overtime to divide and rule. He has been doing that in the church for nearly 1900 years, and especially since the Council of Nicaea 1700 years ago. The divorce from the Jews and the Jewish roots of the faith through replacement theology has wreaked havoc in the church all over the world. We are split into countless denominations, and even within denominations there are so many splits. Unity and harmony are hard to come by in Christianity! No wonder that the world at large wants nothing to do with the church.

I have been an Israeli tour guide for over 25 years now, and I remember the first time that I took tourists to visit the Holy Sepulcher Church in Jerusalem. I pointed to the unfinished ceiling of what is supposed to be the place of burial of the Messiah, and I said: "Do you know why it is unfinished?" Because Christians do not agree with each other, and the different denominations in charge have been quarreling over the budget for many years. It was a disgrace! I did not know Yeshua then, but as an Israeli tour guide, I knew about Christianity. It definitely did not inspire me for to seek salvation!

> **"Sanctify them in the truth; Your word is truth."**
>
> **—John 17:17 nasb '95**

There is only one way to come to UNITY so the world will believe: by the knowledge of the truth, not by man-made opinions and not man/demon-made doctrines. There is only one truth. Yeshua said, "I am the way, the truth, and the life." Yeshua prayed that we would be sanctified by His Word; the Word is purifying/cleansing water.

> So that He might sanctify her, having cleansed her by the washing of water with the word, that He might present to Himself the church in all her glory, having no spot or wrinkle or any such thing; but that she would be holy and blameless.
>
> —EPHESIANS 5:26-27 NASB '95

For us to really *know* the truth from the written and living Word, we must be filled with the Spirit of truth, who will lead us into all truth. No manner of figuring it out by our logic will do; we must receive revelation from the Holy Spirit!

> But when He, the Spirit of truth, comes, He will guide you into all the truth; for He will not speak on His own initiative, but whatever He hears, He will speak; and He will disclose to you what is to come.
>
> —JOHN 16:13 NASB '95

Most people are not guided by the Spirit of truth but rather by whatever they have been taught about Christianity. The problem is that the faith in Messiah departed from its Hebrew foundation through replacement theology to the point that the Hebrew Holy Scriptures were called Old Testament and were disregarded for many years. Even today, most Christians will call the New Testament a Bible. And what about the Hebrew Holy Scriptures that created the most awesome apostles and disciples for over 300 years before the new covenant portion of the Scriptures was canonized? They have been disregarded, trampled upon, allegorized (not taken literally), and spiritualized (the church is now the true Israel; God is finished with the Jews). And for sure, they have been misunderstood and misinterpreted through the eyes of replacement theologians, and this until today. No wonder that

A Call to True Unity

there is so much division in the church. If there is no truth, there is no unity!

"Sanctify them in the truth; Your word is truth."

—John 17:17 nasb '95

The Word that Yeshua spoke about is what is wrongly called the "Old Testament"; the real name is "Tanakh" or Hebrew Holy Scriptures. Yeshua only followed the Word that had been given by His Father to the people of Israel. After He left, He knew that the Torah (5 books of the law), prophets, and writings needed to be reinterpreted in the light of the new covenant sacrifice in His blood. That is why He said that the Spirit of truth would come, and He would become our "Torah teacher," our "rabbi-teacher." That was the plan!

However, since the 4th century, the Spirit of lies through Replacement Theology has been ruling in the church. Of course, when the truth leaves, *unity* also leaves, and we have endless factions and divisions. I will never forget the day that the Father told me: "Dominiquae, I did not call theologians to rule my body; I called apostles!"

"And God has set some in the Church, first Apostles, Secondarily Prophets, thirdly Teachers..."

—1 Corinthians 12:28 nasb '95

Theologians are not mentioned at all in the Holy Scriptures, so how come they have been ruling the body for so long? Because the Spirit of truth has been rejected, and theology has replaced it! It is time to receive a fresh baptism of the Spirit of truth and be restored to the Hebrew foundations of faith and the gospel made in Zion. The time is very late. Yeshua has appeared to me twice in the last few years, telling me that He is about to return. The restoration of the ride to the Hebrew foundations and to the Spirit of truth is *urgent* and is the *key* to the end time revival. Repentance from all manner of replacement theology and reconnecting to the Jewish olive tree and to Israel is a matter of life and death. Only then will we (Jew and Gentile) be one (echad) in the same tree, the olive tree and the Tree of Life.

> **For if their rejection is the reconciliation of the world, what will their acceptance be but life from the dead?**
>
> —Romans 11:15 nasb '95

When Jew and Gentile in the Messiah are one, the world believes and revival happens!

> **May they be brought to complete unity to let the world know that You sent Me and have loved them even as You have loved Me.**
>
> —John 17:23b nasb '95

Those who refuse this move of the Spirit of truth will find themselves broken off the olive tree altogether. For if God did not spare the natural branches, He will not spare you, either.

> **Behold then the kindness and severity of God; to those who fell, severity, but to you, God's kindness, if you continue in His kindness; otherwise, you also will be cut off.**
>
> —Romans 11:21-22 nasb '95

YHVH is calling the whole Church, every denomination, to turn their hearts towards Israel in solidarity and support, to renounce the Council of Nicaea, replacement theology, and pagan feasts, and to return to Yeshua as a Jewish Messiah. He is God in the flesh, yet as a man he was, he is and will always be Jewish!

> **Behold, the Lion that is from the tribe of Judah, the Root of David, has overcome so as to open the book and its seven seals.**
>
> —**Revelation 5:5 nasb '95**

A renewed, restored bride, grafted in the olive tree filled with the Spirit of truth is emerging. Its mark will be *unity* between Jew and Gentile, and its fruit *revival*.

CHAPTER 64

RESTITUTION IS JUSTICE

> "For any kind of trespass, whether it concerns an ox, a donkey, a sheep, or clothing, or for any kind of lost thing which another claims to be his, the cause of both parties shall come before the judges; and whomever the judges condemn shall pay double to his neighbor."
>
> — EXODUS 22:9 NKJV

When people order something from the ministry and for some reason it gets damaged in the mail, or there was some mistake in the sending, it is our ministry policy to send that person a new undamaged item plus an extra gift for the grievance. Restitution always repays extra for the grievance! That is why the Torah speaks much about indemnification for damages caused to our fellow humans.

Restitution:

1. Reparation made by giving an equivalent or compensation for loss, damage, or injury caused; indemnification.
2. The restoration of property or rights previously taken away, conveyed, or surrendered.
3. Restoration to the former or original state or position.

4. Physics. The return to an original physical condition, especially after elastic deformation.

Synonyms: Recompense, amends, compensation, requittal, satisfaction, repayment.

Restitution is Justice

So they buried the bones of Saul and his son Jonathan in the country of Benjamin in Zela, in the tomb of his father Kish. They did all of what the king commanded. Afterward, God was moved by prayer for the land.

—2 Samuel 21:14

During the rule of King David, there was a terrible drought in the Land of Israel that was threatening to kill the people through starvation. When King David inquired of YHVH, He answered and said:

"It is because of Saul and his bloody house, for he put the Gibeonites to death."

—2 Samuel 21:1b

When King David understood that he was suffering because of the sins of his predecessor, he immediately sought to rectify the wrong by making restitution.

David asked the Gibeonites, "What should I do for you? How may I make atonement so that you would bless the inheritance of Adonai?"

— 2 Samuel 21:3

The Gibeonites demanded holy revenge against the house of Saul; even though they could have demanded monetary remuneration and revenge against all of Israel, they just wanted justice done on their behalf.

> Then they said to the king, "The man who consumed us and plotted against us to annihilate us from remaining in any of Israel's territory, let seven men of his sons be given over to us and we will hang them up before ADONAI at Gibeah of Saul, ADONAI's chosen." "I will give them over," the king said.
>
> — 2 SAMUEL 21:5-6

After those seven men from Saul's family were executed, Elohim heard and answered the prayers for rain, the drought broke, and Israel was spared.

> So they buried the bones of Saul and his son Jonathan in the country of Benjamin in Zela, in the tomb of his father Kish. They did all of what the king commanded. Afterward, God was moved by prayer for the land.
>
> —2 SAMUEL 21:14

Had King David decided not to make the restitution that the Gibeonites demanded, YHVH would not have opened the heavens for Israel, though Israel is His covenant people. YHVH is a just God, and he is no respecter of persons. Though the Gibeonites were the slaves and Israel the master and the sons of the covenant, Israel would suffer drought until Israel would do the right thing.

We are Called to Do What is Right

> By this the children of God and the children of the devil are obvious: anyone who does not practice righteousness is not of God, nor the one who does not love his brother.
>
> —1 John 3:10 nasb '95

So often, Christian believers in the Messiah think that because they can claim salvation by the blood of Yeshua, they can get away with everything. They feel that they have more privileges and, therefore, they don't need to behave right. I have news to tell you: If we do not do the right thing, we will be under the curse and not the blessing, even if we name and claim every promise in the Bible. If we break our promises and vows, we will suffer; if we harm someone else, we shall be judged. Furthermore, Elohim looks at us in the body of Yeshua in the same way that He looked at Israel as a nation. The whole body of Messiah is a nation—in fact, a holy nation!

> But you are a chosen race, a royal priesthood, a holy nation, a people for God's own possession, so that you may proclaim the excellencies of Him who has called you out of darkness into His marvelous light;
>
> —1 Peter 2:9 nasb '95

If believers/Christians in the past generation sinned against people groups such as against the Jews (pogroms, Spanish Inquisition, Crusades, Holocaust, and many other persecutions), the judgment over this sin will be collective upon the entire church, every denomination of it. There will be a day of drought for the entire body of Messiah, just like it was at the time of King David! On that day of drought, there will be no rain (no revival), and there will be a famine (for the Word). People will be lean in their souls. We are on that day right now! I have seen the dryness and leanness all over the world!

Preachers are going through the motions, preaching the same kind of sermons, but they are hollow and empty. They behave as if there is anointing and revival, but not one drop of heavenly rain has fallen. Many people are growing desperate and leaving churches, looking for greener pastures only to go from desert to desert, from gravel to gravel.

There is only one hope for the end time church, and that is restitution. Acts of repentance and restitution need to be done by every church and denomination on behalf of the sins of our ancestors concerning the Jewish people, the people of Israel, and other people who were harmed in the name of Christianity.*

Ruth Made Restitution and Broke the Curse

> No Ammonite or Moabite is to enter the community of ADONAI—even to the tenth generation none belonging to them is to enter the community of ADONAI forever.
>
> —DEUTERONOMY 23:4

We can see in the Word that people groups that refused to help Israel or that harmed her actively fall under the curse. The Moabites and the Ammonites refused to help the children of Israel in the desert!

> ...because they did not meet you with food and water on the way when you came out of Egypt, and because they hired

---

* For more information on the subject, read my books *The MAP Revolution* (download for free) and *The Voice of These Ashes* from our shop at www.zionsgospel.com

against you Balaam the son of Beor from Pethor of Mesopotamia, to curse you.

—Deuteronomy 23:4

Ruth was a Moabite, and just like all Moabites, she could not get saved, neither her children, grandchildren, or great-grandchildren, all the way to the tenth generation! The only way to get saved at that time was to renounce paganism and join the people of Israel by circumcision and keeping God's commandments. Imagine that the heavens were tightly shut before the Moabites; they had no hope of redemption ever! And yet one woman changed all that by doing an extreme act of restitution. She gave her life on the altar for the sake of her widowed Jewish mother-in-law, Naomi. She lost her life to accompany Naomi back to the Land of Israel to serve her in life or death.

Do not urge me to leave you or turn back from following you; for where you go, I will go, and where you lodge, I will lodge. Your people shall be my people, and your God, my God. Where you die, I will die, and there I will be buried. Thus may the Lord do to me, and worse, if anything but death parts you and me.

—Ruth 1:16-17 nasb '95

Ruth was making restitution for the sin of the Moabites against Israel by serving *one* Jewish woman. It would be as if a German woman would make restitution for her German people who exterminated six million Jews by giving her life for the sake of one Jew, by serving that Jew and blessing *for life* one Jewish person! Or any Christian serving one Jew on behalf of all the sins committed by Christianity against the Jewish people.

What can one person's restitution do? It can do so much that the curse broke completely for Ruth and all her generations! Furthermore, Ruth married Boaz, a Jewish relative of Naomi, and bore a son named Obed, the father of Jesse, who was the father of King David. Yeshua was born from David's lineage, so Ruth (a Gentile, formerly accursed Moabite) became King David's grandmother in the royal line of the Messiah[*] because of *one* act of restitution. That is the power of restitution!

> Then she fell on her face, bowing to the ground and said to him, "Why have I found favor in your sight that you should take notice of me, since I am a foreigner?" Boaz replied to her, "All that you have done for your mother-in-law after the death of your husband has been fully reported to me, and how you left your father and your mother and the land of your birth, and came to a people that you did not previously know. May the LORD reward your work, and your wages be full from the LORD, the God of Israel, under whose wings you have come to seek refuge."
>
> —RUTH 2:10-12 NASB '95

Cornelius Made Restitution and Opened the Gate of Salvation

Now there was a man at Caesarea named Cornelius, a centurion of what was called the Italian cohort, a devout man and

---

[*] Matthew 1

one who feared God with all his household, and gave many alms to the Jewish people and prayed to God continually.

—Acts 10:1-2 NASB '95

Cornelius was a Roman Captain of 100 Roman soldiers, and he was doing something that was totally opposed to the Roman regime—he was blessing the Jewish people financially! The Jews were under Roman rule. They paid tribute to the Romans and not vice versa, and here we see a Roman in a position of authority giving tzedakah (alms or a righteous offering) to the Jews. Cornelius must have been the laughingstock of all other Roman soldiers! What he was doing was certainly not popular. The Romans had plundered the Jews seriously, exacted enormous taxes, and impoverished God's people. Because of that, they were incurring Yah's judgment. He had promised through Abraham that the blessing or the curse in nations depended on how the nations would treat his descendants, the Jews.

And I will bless those who bless you, And the one who curses you I will curse and in you all the families of the earth will be blessed.

—Genesis 12:3 NASB '95

As we know today, the Roman Empire indeed collapsed and does not exist as such anymore, though the Jewish people are still here and even back in their own land after 2000 years of exile! However, one Roman soldier made a name for himself and opened the door for many Romans to be rescued from eternal damnation. The way he did it was by making financial restitution to the Jewish people whom the Romans had plundered. This moved the Almighty to action on behalf of this Roman.

> **About the ninth hour of the day he clearly saw in a vision an angel of God who had just come in and said to him, "Cornelius!" And fixing his gaze on him and being much alarmed, he said, "What is it, Lord?" And he said to him, "Your prayers and alms have ascended as a memorial before God."**
>
> —Acts 10:3-4 nasb '95

Cornelius' acts of restitution towards Yah's Jewish people built him a memorial and opened the gate of salvation for all the Gentiles. The angel of YHVH told Cornelius to summon the Jewish Apostle Peter, who came and preached the gospel to his entire household and friends.

> **While Peter was still speaking these words, the Holy Spirit fell upon all those who were listening to the message. All the circumcised believers who came with Peter were amazed, because the gift of the Holy Spirit had been poured out on the Gentiles also.**
>
> —Acts 10:44-45 nasb '95

From that moment, Gentiles came into the kingdom and could be saved. That is the power of *one* act of restitution!

At this end of times, YHVH is calling His ecclesia to make restitution towards Israel by becoming a Ruth and a Cornelius. It is Ruth-like and Cornelius-like people that will propel the end-time revival by acts of restitution towards the Jewish people. They will break the many curses that have fallen because of replacement theology that unleashed hateful spirits against the Jews and everything Jewish, culminating in terrible pogroms and Shoas (Holocausts) in past generations. As every Christian/Gentile believer in Messiah applies the restitution principle towards Israel *practically* (through finances, service, and acts of justice like King David, Ruth, and Cornelius), they will experience great favor from YHVH and will become vessels of revival and blessing for all future generations!

CHAPTER 65

WHY PRAY FOR ISRAEL?

"For I"—it is a declaration of ADONAI—*"will be a wall of fire around it and I will be the glory inside it."*

— ZECHARIAH 2:9

Three months ago, Katyusha rockets were fired at Eilat, hitting the city. The Israeli news station, Arutz 7, reported that according to police, two exploded in open areas, and three fell into the sea. No injuries were reported. Residents of the city reported hearing loud blasts at approximately 8:00 a.m. Jordanian officials reported that a rocket hit the city of Aqaba as well, exploding next to a local hotel. Four people were wounded. Israel has asked Egyptian officials to help determine the source of the rocket fire. The rocket fire is suspected to have been carried out by terrorists in Sinai, though other possibilities are being examined as well."

Praise Yah for His awesome protection over His Land and people!

As most of you know, we are at present in Miami, Florida, having been sent by the Holy Spirit as part of a great revival and awakening among the Latin American and Sephardic communities in that location. Meanwhile, our sister Abigail is holding the fort in the Prayer

Tower in Eilat, and she does the fourth watch of the night from 3–6 a.m. She covers Eilat with the blood of Yeshua every morning, declaring that the mercies of YHVH are new every morning. On Monday (August 2nd) morning, as she was praying, she received from the Holy Spirit that there was a terror attempt against a city in Israel, so she started interceding seriously without knowing it was Eilat! The Holy Spirit was so kind as not to let her know that so she would not panic as it was in our own backyard.

The Word of God speaks to us clearly about praying for Israel:

Pray for the peace of Jerusalem: May those who love you be secure.

—Psalms 122:6

In Hebrew, it says, "May those who love Jerusalem (implying all of Israel) be in total well-being!" During these shaking times, it is good to know this amazing promise! As *you* pray for Israel's protection, YHVH will make sure that you are protected. As you pray for Israel's well-being, you will be well.

The Almighty is so serious about His love for His people that He says in Isaiah 62:1, *"For Zion's sake I will not keep silent."* He also continues to say:

On your walls, Jerusalem, I have set watchmen. All day and all night, they will never hold their peace. "You who remind Adonai, take no rest for yourselves, and give Him no rest until He establishes and makes Jerusalem a praise in the earth.

—Isaiah 62:6-7

The Word of the Lord for this hour is:

Do not stop praying for Israel, and give Me no rest with your intercessions and petitions concerning my chosen people.

> "Let us not become weary in doing good, for at the proper time we will reap a harvest if we do not give up."
>
> —Galatians 6:9 nivuk

Some of the most amazing promises for Israel are in Zechariah 2. YHVH says that at the same time that He restores Israel, many nations will join themselves to Him. In other words, there is a direct connection between the wellbeing of Israel and the salvation of the nations.

> "'Sing and rejoice, O daughter of Zion! For behold, I am coming and I will live among you—it is a declaration of Adonai. 'In that day many nations will join themselves to Adonai and they will be My people and I will dwell among you.' Then you will know that Adonai-Tzva'ot has sent me to you. Adonai will inherit Judah as His portion in the holy land and will once again choose Jerusalem.
>
> —Zechariah 2:14-16

We are actually affecting the salvation of many nations when we pray for Israel and actively bless her. In fact, our stand in prayer, giving, and acting concerning the Restoration of Israel can avert a time of judgment to a time of revival!

> For thus says Adonai-Tzva'ot, He has sent me after glory to the nations that plundered you—because whoever touches you touches the apple of His eye—'For behold, I will shake

My hand against them and they will be plunder to their servants.' Then you will know that ADONAI-Tzva'ot has sent me.

—ZECHARIAH 2:12-13

So, at the same time that YHVH is judging nations that have plundered Israel, He is restoring His land and people. And whoever will side with Him for this purpose, will be blessed and will be a catalyst for revival in his/her nation.

Do you have a prayer meeting for Israel going in your home and your church or congregation? If not, this is the time to start one. It is better than any insurance you can take at the time of great shakings and "global warnings," such as oil spills and the like.

I will bless those who bless you, and whoever curses you I will curse; and all peoples on earth will be blessed through you.

—GENESIS 12:3 NIVUK

X 2024

CHAPTER 66

WARNING SIGNS IN THE HEAVENS

> "The sun shall be turned to darkness and the moon to blood before the great and glorious Day of ADONAI comes."
>
> — ACTS 2:20

WILL ISRAEL EXPERIENCE 3 years of trouble against Amalek-Iran and all their proxies?

Three consecutive lunar eclipses fall on Purim from 2024 to 2026. A lunar eclipse is a prophetic sign of trouble for Israel, while a solar eclipse is a sign of warning and impending judgment to the nations, like the one that will happen on April 8 across the USA.

Since the start of the Iron Swords war following the Massacre by Hamas on October 7, 2023, the message has been: This will be a lengthy war.

> "But the earth came to the aid of the woman. The earth opened its mouth and swallowed the river that the dragon had spewed from his mouth."
>
> —THE REVELATION 12:16

Israel needs our prayers and our support more than ever. We are part of "the earth" that will help the woman in this chapter representing Israel.

Ted M. Vanlandeghem enlightens us in his description below about the coming Solar Eclipse in North America:

> This year's total solar eclipse is on April 8, which is the 1st of Nisan on the biblical calendar, or the biblical new year, coming two weeks before Passover, which takes place on the 14th of Nisan.
>
> - April 8 is also the end of Ramadan on the Islamic calendar—a prophetic convergence.
> - This eclipse comes seven years after the last total solar eclipse.
> - The two eclipses, 2017 and 2024, make an X over New Madrid, Missouri.
>
> New Madrid is the site of two major earthquakes in the United States, in 1811 and again in 1812 (about three months before the beginning of the War of 1812).
>
> - George H. W. Bush started the peace process to divide the land of Israel in Madrid, Spain. Will judgment come upon America at New Madrid, Missouri?
> - The eclipse seven years ago passed over seven United States cities named "Salem," which means "peace" (shalom) and was the name of Jerusalem during Abraham's time. (Gen. 14:18)

This year's eclipse on the 1st of Nissan passes over and will be visible from seven cities named "Nineveh" in the United States and an additional one in Nova Scotia, Canada.

In the story of Jonah, God gave the city of Nineveh 40 days to repent:

Jonah began by going a day's journey into the city, proclaiming, "Forty more days and Nineveh will be overthrown"

—Jonah 3:4 NIV

So if this is a prophetic pattern for the United States and we are being given a 40-day window to repent as a nation, then the next question is, "What day comes 40 days after the first of Nissan?" That happens to be a day called "Passover Sheni." (Courtesy Ted M. Vanlandeghem)

The Second Passover (A Second Chance to do Passover for Those Who Are Unclean)

Is this a Second Chance for America to do right by Israel? A Second Chance for Trump to be elected to do right by Israel? Can we afford to miss it?

How are the politics of your nation, your church, your family, and yourself concerning Israel? Are you siding with the genocidal chant of the pro-Palestinian Hamas, "from the river to the sea," or with the Covenant of God with the descendants of Abraham, Isaac, and Jacob, the Jewish People forever?

"He remembers His covenant forever—the word He commanded for a thousand generations—which He made with

Abraham, swore to Isaac, and confirmed to Jacob as a decree to inheritance, an everlasting covenant, saying, "To you, I give the land of Canaan, the portion of your inheritance.

—Psalms 105:8–11

"For behold, in those days and at that time, when I restore Judah and Jerusalem from exile, I will gather all nations and bring them down to the valley of Jehoshaphat. I will plead with them there on behalf of My people, even My inheritance, Israel, whom they scattered among the nations and they divided up My land."

—Joel 4:1-2

"For Adonai is enraged at all the nations and furious at all their armies. He will utterly destroy them. He will give them over to slaughter.
Adonai has a day of vengeance, a year of recompense for the hostility against Zion."

—Isaiah 34:2, 8

"Multitudes, multitudes, in the valley of decision! For the day of Adonai is near in the valley of decision. The sun and the moon become dark, and the stars withdraw their brightness."

—Joel 4:14-15

May the God of Israel make a distinction between those who actively love Israel and support her in word and deed and between those who do not.

"All the nations will be gathered before Him, and He will separate them from one another, just as the shepherd separates the sheep from the goats."

—Matthew 25:32

Standing by Israel in action is a matter of life and death.

"My desire is to bless those who bless you, but whoever curses you I will curse, and in you all the families of the earth will be blessed."

—Genesis 12:3

CLOSURE

Our IDF soldiers are motivated by the love of God, family, and country. In contrast, the Palestinians Hamas and all their sympathizers are motivated by blind hatred, the hatred like Esau and Amalek. They do not care about their own; their children are "disposable ammunition," and their women are "human shields." UNWRA, the UN organization for the welfare of the Palestinians, has funneled billions of dollars into terror and has become a terror organization itself. UNWRA schools taught the Gaza population to hate and murder Jews; their hospitals have been headquarters of Hamas, and their operatives, together with some foreign journalists, participated in the massacre. Hamas has no human conscience, and neither does UNWRA.

How can I close when my people are still bleeding, traumatized, and displaced away from their homes? Iran and his Northern Hezbollah terror army are threatening to annihilate Israel, and deathly rockets are still falling in the North and some even in the South. So many of our young, brave soldiers who have lost limbs and body parts are still in hospitals recovering, and often, we suffer the losses of our precious warriors. And the bereaved families are crying themselves to sleep at night, while our hostages have been in the hands of Hamas hands under torment, torture, and rape for days without number. The world is chanting the genocidal chant, "From the River to the sea, Palestine will be free (of Jews)". President Biden is threatening Israel to withhold military support and pushing the IDF to a ceasefire that will bring no victory against Hamas and enable this monster to regroup.

Israel is being bashed from every side as if she is the perpetrator of the Iron Swords war initiated by Hamas with an indescribable ruthless Massacre. All our people are still trying to "digest" what really happened on October 7, 2023. How can we ever grasp the monstrous Nazi-like hatred that burnt entire families in bomb shelters, that raped our women many times in terrible brutality? Will we ever understand why those supposedly "innocent Gaza civilians" invaded Israel by droves to help Hamas in its murderous orgy and to loot and plunder 22 peace-loving communities.

The worst part of all is how can the world see those Gaza civilians as "innocent" and as the victims while they celebrated the massacre of innocent Jews and passed candy around when our babies were being beheaded.

The victim of this heartless, brutal massacre stemming from the Oslo Accords and the deceptive, concocted "Palestinian cause" is Israel, only Israel.

My prayer is that this world will wake up, or at least the Church in the nations will wake up before it's too late, and entire nations will be destroyed because of their Antisemitism and hatred for Israel.

> "Draw near, O nations, to hear, and listen, O peoples! Let the earth hear, and all it contains, the world, and all its offspring! For ADONAI is enraged at all the nations and furious at all their armies. He will utterly destroy them. He will give them over to slaughter. So their slain will be thrown out, and the

stench of their corpses will rise, and the hills will be drenched with their blood.

For My sword has drunk its fill in the heavens. See, it will come down upon Edom, upon the people I have devoted to judgment.

For ADONAI has a day of vengeance, a year of recompense for the hostility against Zion."

—Isaiah 34:1-3, 5, 8

Dear reader, since you have read this far, may the God of Israel use you to communicate The Israel Factor to others. It is a matter of life and death to change the present-day narrative and rescue many from the Valley of Judgment.

"For behold, in those days and at that time, when I restore Judah and Jerusalem from exile, I will gather all nations and bring them down to the valley of Jehoshaphat. I will plead with them there on behalf of My people, even My inheritance, Israel, whom they scattered among the nations and they divided up My land. They cast lots for My people, traded a boy for a prostitute, and sold a girl for wine, which they drank."

—Joel 4:1-3

Israel and the Jewish People have an Eternal Covenant that no other nation carries.

"Egypt will become a desolation and Edom a desert wasteland, because of the violence against the children of Judah, because they shed innocent blood in their land. But Judah will be inhabited forever—Jerusalem from generation to generation."

—Joel 4:19-20

"ADONAI bless you and keep you! ADONAI make His face to shine on you and be gracious to you! ADONAI turn His face toward you and grant you shalom!"

—NUMBERS 6:24-26

Appendix

A DIVINE CALL TO RALLY AROUND THE BANNER OF TRUTH

> ADONAI said to Moses and Aaron saying, "Let each man encamp under his own standard among the banners of their ancestral house at an appropriate distance around the Tent of Meeting.
>
> — NUMBERS 2:1

IN ANCIENT ISRAEL, EVERY tribe had its own banner or flag. When the flag was lifted up somewhere, the troops knew to rally behind their flag. Not doing so would be regarded as insurrection and being absent from service without leave (like being AWOL today). It would have been even worse to have rallied behind the flag of the wrong tribe—that would have caused serious chaos and defeat in battle, for every tribe and every flag had its place and assignment.

When the people of Israel were reestablished again in our own land after 2000 years of exile, there were *three* things that were needed in order to define us as a nation:

1. A Name
2. A Flag
3. A Purpose

It was not assured that the name finally chosen for the nation would be Israel; this was debated quite a bit. Some people wanted to call it Judah, for example. Concerning the flag chosen, there were also debates as to what could best represent our people who were exiled among the nations for about 2000 years. It was decided that the tallit (prayer mantle), with its blue and white stripes centered by a Magen David (David's Shield or called by some the "Star of David"), would be the right flag.

Wherever the young IDF would go and take more territory in defense against Arab enemies, they would raise up the flag as a sign that this was Israeli territory. The area today, called the city of Eilat, was established by raising what is known as the Ink Flag over what used to be British police stations called Um Rash Rash. There was no city there then, only desert. It was so important to raise the Israeli flag right away that since they did not have one *ready*, they drew one over a white sheet with blue ink—and therefore, it's called the Ink Flag. Flags mark territory and define the Army.

Then, the purpose of establishing the State of Israel was to have a national home for the Jewish people, a place where every Jew would be free to be a Jew without fear of persecution as it had been in the nations for nearly 2000 years. Of course, the Almighty defines the purpose of our return to the land in more precise terms and maybe less "romantic."

> "Therefore say to the house of Israel, 'Thus says the LORD GOD, "It is not for your sake, O house of Israel, that I am about to act, but for My holy name, which you have profaned among the nations where you went. I will vindicate the holiness of My great name which has been profaned among the nations, which you have profaned in their midst. Then the nations will know that I am the LORD," declares the LORD GOD, "when I prove Myself holy among you in their sight. For I will take you

from the nations, gather you from all the lands and bring you into your own land.

— Ezekiel 36:22-24

The purpose of reestablishing us in His land was to vindicate His Holy Name so the nations will *know* that He is YHVH.

We cannot separate the restoration of Israel from the salvation of the nations. The God of Israel is also the king of the nations. If Israel is restored, then the nations will be saved -- but if Israel would not have returned to its land, then there would have been no hope for the nations. Nations that oppose the restoration of Israel are actually dooming themselves to eternal judgment.

> "For thus says ADONAI-Tzva'ot, He has sent me after glory to the nations that plundered you—because whoever touches you touches the apple of His eye—"
>
> —Zechariah 2:12

> For ADONAI is enraged at all the nations, and furious at all their armies. He will utterly destroy them. He will give them over to slaughter.
> For ADONAI has a day of vengeance, a year of recompense for the hostility against Zion.
>
> —Isaiah 34:2, 8

We are calling all the believers in Messiah from the nations to rally around the right name, flag, and purpose for this end-time battle for the souls of men.

The name is the United Nations for Israel. The flag is the fully lit-up menorah superimposed over the world globe with two olive branches within the flag of Israel. The purpose is to turn nations into sheep nations, one person at a time—through a global reeducation that teaches nations to espouse Biblical politics in their internal moral affairs and their foreign affairs regarding their relationship with Israel.

As I mentioned above, it is only when nations fully support the restoration of Israel to its own land (with Jerusalem as its capital) that they can then enjoy salvation and redemption. Their well-being depends on the well-being of Israel. This is both a priestly and a kingly affair. We need to learn to pray and to do the spiritual battle necessary for this to happen; we need to get re-educated concerning Israel, and the gospel made in Zion versus the one that came from Rome. We must implement it in our spiritual communities and governments. Apart from these actions, all nations will be under judgment because of "the cause of Zion."

As you wave your national flag underneath the flag of Israel, the flag of Jerusalem, and the flag of UNIFY (United Nations for Israel), we are establishing a fact in the spiritual realm and rallying the spiritual army of the end times. This vision did not originate with us: it originated with YHVH Himself when the prophet Zechariah prophesied the following,

> 'In that day many nations will join themselves to ADONAI and they will be My people and I will dwell among you.' Then you will know that ADONAI-Tzva'ot has sent me to you. ADONAI will inherit Judah as His portion in the holy land and will once again choose Jerusalem.
>
> —ZECHARIAH 15-16

The many nations that will join YHVH on the day of the restoration of Israel, the Jewish people, and Jerusalem have a *name*: they are called: The United Nations for Israel.

This is the fulfillment of the prophecy given by the prophet Zechariah, that when nations *unite* unto YHVH on the day of the restoration of the Jewish people and Jerusalem, then the people of Israel will "know that YHVH sent Me (the Messiah) to you".*

It is only the unconditional love of the Sheep Nations that unite unto the God of Israel that will cause Israel's redemption. And it is the restoration of Israel in its own land that will cause the salvation of the nations. This is the culmination of what we call "The Key of Abraham" in Genesis 12:3,

> **And I will bless those who bless you, and the one who curses you I will curse. And in you all the families of the earth will be blessed.**
>
> **—Genesis 12:3 nivuk**

When you join the United Nations for Israel, you are joining a prophetic and divinely appointed move of global restoration.

> **Get yourself up on a high mountain, O Zion, bearer of good news, lift up your voice mightily, O Jerusalem, bearer of good news; Lift it up, do not fear. Say to the cities of Judah, "Here is your Elohim!**
>
> **—Isaiah 40:9**

You are also joining the move that will display the banner of truth before the people of Israel and before all nations.

---

* To learn more, visit at www.UnitedNationsforIsrael.org

> You have given a banner to those who fear You, that it may be displayed because of the truth. Selah.
>
> —Psalm 60:4 nasb '95

This is so important to the Almighty that He will allow no one to stop this move that He originated. In fact, He is commanding all other opposing voices and political opinions to shut up! YHVH Tzevaot, the God of the Armies, is overseeing this move Himself, and He will not be denied! He will fulfill His covenant with Israel and He will have a unity of sheep nations.

> "Be silent before Adonai, all flesh, for He has aroused Himself from His holy dwelling."
>
> —Zechariah 2:17

OUR RESOURCES

Visit our websites and follow us on social media

United Nations for Israel

Take a stand for the restoration of Israel and transform your nation into a sheep nation, one person at a time. Become a member and join our monthly members' online conferences to get equipped!

www.UnitedNationsForIsrael.org

info@unitednationsforisrael.org

Israel Tours

Travel through Israel with our "Bible School on Wheels" and watch the Hebrew Holy Scriptures come alive.

www.kad-esh.org/tours-and-events

Global Revival MAP (GRM) Israeli Bible Institute

Take the most comprehensive video Bible school online that focuses on the restoration of all things.

www.GRMBibleInstitute.com

info@grmbibleinstitute.com

Global Re-Education Initiative (GRI) Against Anti-Semitism

Discover the Jewish Messiah and defeat religious anti-Semitism! Order *The Identity Theft* and GRI Online Course Package

www.Against-Antisemitism.com

info@against-antisemitism.com

From Israel to the Nations TV Programs

Watch Archbishop Dominiquae Bierman's TV programs taped in the land of Israel!

Roku Channel: **Israel Revival**

YouTube: **Dominiquae Bierman TV**

www.youtube.com/@DominiquaeBiermanTV

Rumble: Dominiquae Bierman TV

www.rumble.com/c/DominiquaeBiermanTV

Broadcasting Schedule: www.kad-esh.org/broadcasting-schedule

MAP Prison Ministry

Through our prison ministry, pioneered by Rabbi Baruch Bierman, GRM Bible School is studied in prisons all over the USA. For more information and to support:

www.zionsgospel.com/map-prison-ministry/

Outlaw public display of Swastikas, Nazi and Hamas flags

www.change.org/BanNeoNazism-Evil-Can-Be-Stopped

For more information about the founder of the ministries:

www.DominiquaeBierman.com

BOOKS & MUSIC

For more books by Dr. Dominiquae Bierman,
order online: www.ZionsGospel.com

The Voice of These Ashes
What are the Ashes of the Exterminated Jewish People Crying For?

The Identity Theft
The Return of the 1st Century Messiah

"Yes!"
The Dramatic Life Story of an Israeli Woman who Falls and Rises Again Because of one Word: "YES!"

Restoring the Glory—Volume I: The Original Way
The Ancient Paths Rediscovered

Eradicating the Cancer of Religion
Hint: All People Have It!

The Healing Power of the Roots
It's a Matter of Life and Death!

Grafted In
It's Time to Return to Greatness!

Sheep Nations
It's Time to Take the Nations!

Yeshua is the Name
The Important Restoration of the True Name of the Messiah!

The Key of Abraham
The Blessing or the Curse?

Stormy Weather
Judgment Has Begun and Revival is Knocking at the Doors!

Restoration of Holy Giving
Releasing the True 1,000-Fold Blessing

The Bible Cure for Africa and the Nations
The Key to the Restoration of all Africa

Vision Negev
The Awesome Restoration of the Sephardic Jews!

Defeating Depression
This Book is a Kiss from Heaven!

From Sickology to a Healthy Logic
The Product of 18 Years Walking Through Psychiatric Hospitals

Addicts Turning to God
The Biblical Way to Handle Addicts & Addictions

Let's Get Healthy, Saints!
The Biblical Guide to Health

The Woman Factor: Freedom from Womanophobia
by Rabbi Baruch Bierman with Dominiquae Bierman

The MAP Revolution (free E-book)
Exposing Theologies that Obstruct the Bride

The Spider That Survived Hurricane Irma (free E-book)
God's Call for America to Repent

The Revival of the Third Day (free E-book)
The Return to Yeshua the Jewish Messiah

Tribute to the Jew in You Music Book
Notes for the Tribute to the Jew in You Music Album

Music Albums

Abba Shebashamayim

Uru

Retorno

The Key of Abraham

Tribute to the Jew in You

Tribute to the Jew in You Instrumental

Teaching Series

God of Shalom

Israel in the War Series

The Powerful Women of the Bible

SUPPORT THE MISSION

Contact Us

Dr. Dominiquae Bierman

shalom@zionsgospel.com

Kad-Esh MAP Ministries

www.kad-esh.org | info@kad-esh.org

United Nations for Israel

www.unitednationsforisrael.org

info@unitednationsforisrael.org

52 Tuscan Way, Ste 202-412, St. Augustine,
Florida 32092, USA

+1-972-301-7087

Made in the USA
Columbia, SC
10 May 2024

35091954R00359